Walking Bodies

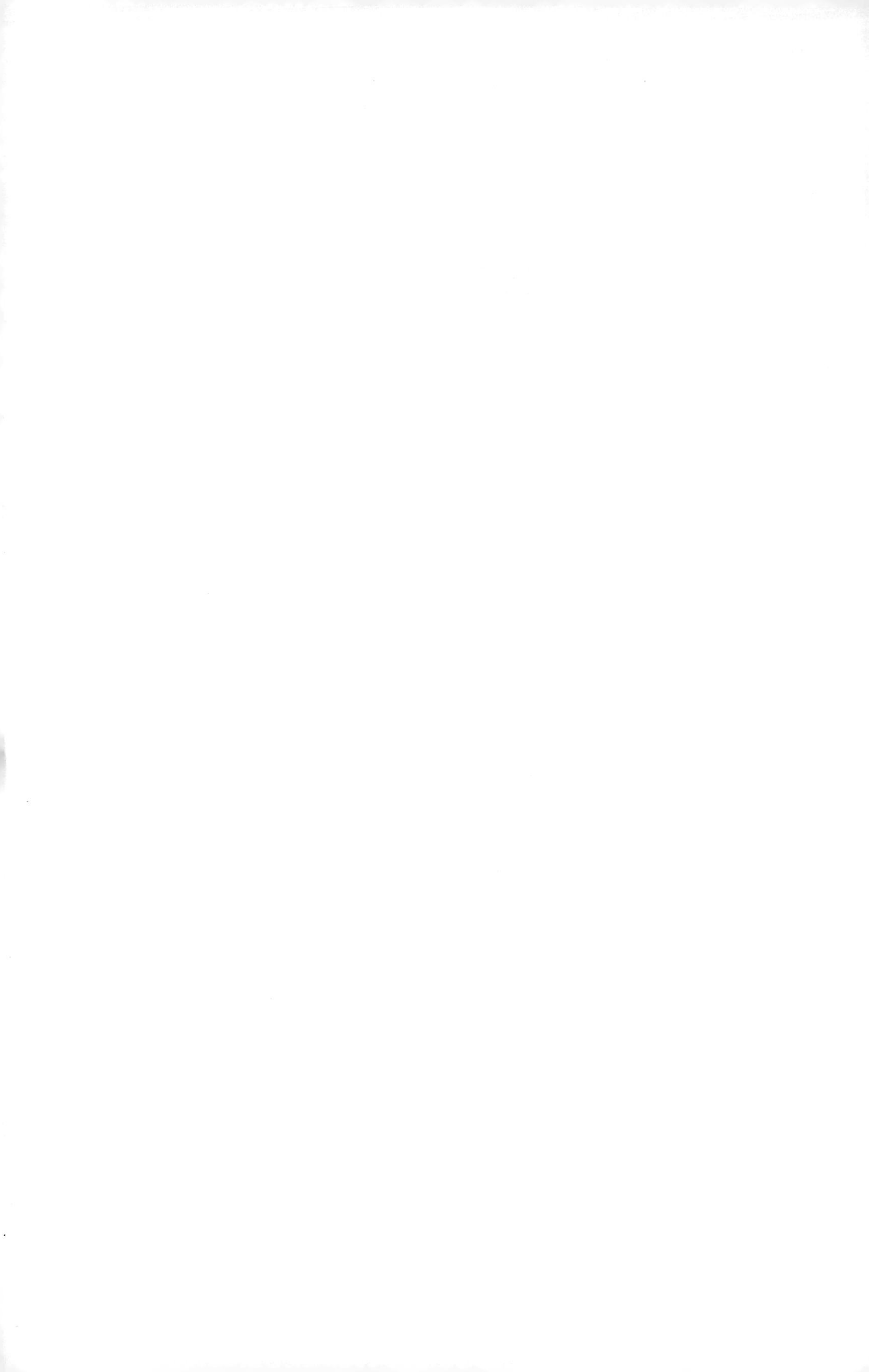

Walking Bodies

Papers, Provocations, Actions
from
Walking's New Movements, the Conference

edited by

Helen Billinghurst, Claire Hind & Phil Smith

Published in this first edition in 2020 by:

Triarchy Press
Axminster, UK

www.triarchypress.net

This collection Copyright © Triarchy Press Limited, 2020
Individual contributions Copyright © the named author(s), 2020

A catalogue record for this book is available from the British Library.

ISBNs:
Print: 978-1-913743-09-3
ePub: 978-1-913743-10-9
pdf: 978-1-913743-11-6

Front cover image: photo by Rebekah Dean.
Back cover image: drawing by Sarah Scaife.

Printed in the UK by TJ International Ltd., Padstow, Cornwall

tp

Contents

Introductions

Phil:

In our welcome to delegates at the Walking's New Movements conference in Plymouth in November 2019, introducing a programme of presentations for the following three days, we acknowledged a lack of any clear pattern to the subject matter of the various provocations, performances and papers. We wondered aloud if something more coherent might arise as a result of the events, question and answer sessions, social encounters and general interactions to come. When, a few weeks later, we came to discuss how we might invite a selection of presenters to write up their work for this book, we faced a similar confusion.

An obvious approach to selection would have been to assemble contributions around a combination of themes. Yet, for all our excitement at the multiplicity of experiences and information-exchanges that we had shared in, we retained only the vaguest sense that anything as coherent as a theme had emerged from the conference. It was only when we received the draft submissions for this book that something like the appearance of a 'movement', however partial, began to form. Not in the sense of a social movement, but rather a coalescing of quite separate ideas that seemed drawn to each other, perhaps superseding the agency of their human proposers.

This entanglement is far from an all-encompassing one. Many of the contributions to this book sit far outside its parameters and are largely untouched by its threads. However, the shift is evidenced by any reading of the chapters to follow, and may be even significant, particularly as it seems to represent something of a change of direction in walking arts. At the same time it needs to be said that the Walking's New Movements conference, as noted by some of the contributors whose chapters follow these remarks, was not fully representative of those engaged in walking arts, research and activism, let alone of the diversity of the societies from which delegates were drawn. So, this pattern, if that is what it is, is at best the product of a fraction of a fraction of a fraction. Its meaning, let alone legitimacy, has more to do with timeliness than representativeness.

So what is this pattern?

It seems to be partly constituted of a shift towards embodiment; to a walking body at the mercy of the terrain rather than one bathing in the sublime or masterfully sponging up ambiences. The relative and material nature of that 'at the mercy' is made clear in some of the chapters below; it is not something that many walkers now seek to transcend, but rather to negotiate. The dynamic pattern at play here is partly fuelled by a fracturing in psychogeography; with the unhuman geography becoming more highly prized than the human 'psycho' part. In a complex movement, the diminished 'psycho' collapses into a less introspective body; one whose senses are better defined as tentacular agents seeking out material affordances than soakers up and literary articulators of affect. Within this shift, the integrity and identity of walkers' bodies is far from sure; indeed, they are by no means necessarily human or free of hybridity. Instead, the walk is more likely shared than individual; even when walking alone, the walker is not 'lone' in the way that it was sometimes assumed they were in the recent history of walking arts.

A number of the chapters that follow attend to the unhuman others that walk with the human. In some, an account of this extended webbing of various walkings is expressed in ecological terms; in others, as a kind of animism; in a few, as both. Colour codes and fictional, even mythic, characters figure in practice and theory. This does not seem to be any kind of return to the occultism that enthused some of the situationist-influenced groups in the US and UK in the last few decades of the twentieth century; now, perhaps, there is more of an awareness of the dangers of nationalism that come with some versions of irrationalism and nostalgia. Instead, this is more of a somatic and immersed pushing back against scientism and positivism in the face of climate catastrophe. It seems to favour intuition and tacit knowledge; the value of body to body learning and transmission by repertoire as much or more than by archive; and the value of being bodily immersed and entangled with alien consciousnesses as a means to arts, research and activist practices. While familiar influences, such as Guy Debord and Rebecca Solnit, continue to be cited, stepping forward now are the more recent 'string figure' and tentacular writings of Donna Haraway, the materialist 'entanglements' of Karen Barad and the 'myth-science' of Simon O'Sullivan, while older generations of thinkers who prefigure some of their neo-vitalism, vibrant thing-power and fictioning – such as James Hillman, Henri Bergson, John Berger and even Charles Fort – make less predictable appearances.

It is far too early to say how far this fractional change will play out in walking practices more generally. A few months before the November conference, the bright red costumes of the Red Brigade were first seen on Extinction Rebellion actions; their distinctive slow-motion and enigmatic processions adding something urgent, unfathomable, extra-functional and para-theatrical to demonstrations in the face of crisis. It would be presumptuous to make too close a connection between the Red Brigade's interventions and the loose coalescing of themes in some of the chapters that follow; but if they are both responses to the same extreme circumstances by equally unusual and uneven means, then the future of the 'walking movements' looks far less predictable, far less reasonable and far less moderate now than it did before November 2019.

Claire:

The paradoxical nature of the fleeting moment is its impact. A gathering of people with a diverse range of walking practices, who meet, learn, debate, walk and socialise across a short space of time is not to be underestimated, especially if there is an opportunity to bring a variety of different disciplines into one space. Whilst we reflect upon how valuable the sharing of space and togetherness is, walking arts – what has been, what is happening now and what may come – feel like a political necessity, not just for one's own practice, but for the future of community, embodied practice and transformation.

When we feel or know something is important, even if we experience it for a brief moment, our gut instincts inform us that we need to make the most of it, not only for the experience itself, but remember it, recall it, repeat it, be inspired by it, because, it can pass us by. Many of us may understand what walking arts are, but do we know them collectively? What is happening under our feet? We asked, in our call for papers, what is happening in walking now and where are the new initiatives, changes of direction and novel terrains emerging? We wanted to think about what it is that changes when we divert walking and offer an opportunity for a diverse range of artists, academics, writers and researchers to come together to share their practices and thinking. We were curious if anyone was troubled by present trajectories, assumptions, dominant narratives, movements or complacencies within walking arts practice and as a result a series of 10-minute provocations – shared outside of the normal panel style presentation – worked as interludes between those panels. They were an exciting range of mini-manifestos and artworks for new ways of walking; some were participatory in nature, others showed how they had mapped new routes, or were short creative texts, whilst others, theatrical in nature, brought us together as audiences not simply as conference delegates. Some of those provocations are new works, tested and shared for the first time at the conference, and now realised here in this book. The event was certainly more than a gabfest; we had thought carefully and creatively about what it means to curate a conference so that 20-minute papers, walks in the city, live performances, 10-minute provocations, and short workshop experiences that purposely change our walking habits were part and parcel of the fabric of the weekend. Thinking curatorially rather than logistically seemed to create more of a festival vibe than a formal conference. Hurrah!

The social events reminded us about the importance of storytelling, not just because we find comfort in a traditional art form, but because stories come from journeys, from walking. It's not that we don't know this, it's just that never has there been a more important time than now to tell stories that relate to walking. The participatory event on the Saturday night got all in the room singing meaningful lyrics about how walking connects people, and in this moment, singing our heads off, we celebrated not only the gathering itself, but the heap of diverse ideas and practices that we had brought together in one space. It was a heartening heap. To understand the breadth of ideas and the myriad creative mediums is not to use it as a benchmark for what should be talked about or practised at a conference, but rather to host a space for all who came to set their agenda through the act of sharing, to raise an idea, provoke, challenge and importantly, have space to do this and listen. Artists don't necessarily have, and shouldn't be expected to have, all the answers; they are provocateurs and their works set acts in motion. The challenge for the conference host is to be alternative, to conjure up the gathering as an act of generosity where many moments take centre stage, where a student presents alongside an 'expert' on equal grounds, where a 10-minute workshop holds the same weight as an academic paper. The short interludes, artistic declarations, theatrical interventions sat side by side with the academic papers and they quite rightly included a nod to those who have shaped our cultural history as well as posed a challenge to them. Provocations as a form of artistic intervention aim to nudge, ignite, tease, offer something new, yet the provocations and all the art works in this book are given a space as complete things. They may be small in occupancy or they may scratch the surface of an idea but here, artists have honed their practice – essence is the quality of experience. As such, they are not simply documentations of walking arts experiences, rather they are prompts asking us to consider changing the way we engage with place and indeed space. They are instructions inviting us to respond, to act now and challenge the way we are living our lives. In their performative state, they are visual gems and, playfully, they actuate.

We have tales, and so do many other walking artists, and what gatherings do is to allow us to share stories, so that when we return to our practice, the responsibility and sense of community enriches it. This is a charged and energetic space that we have to take care of. Gatherings in some parts of the world now have restrictions attached to them, and as we write we are in the midst of a global crisis unable to comprehend the consequences of a virus outbreak and the decisions being made about large community events and gatherings.

We hope this book will be more than a document of a conference. It tells a story of walking's relationship to creative forms of writing and mark making, where texts, scripts, scores, poetry and the visual arts illuminate the diverse tapestry that is walking arts practice.

Helen:

The Walking's New Movements conference unfolded in the University of Plymouth's Roland Levinsky Building, over three wet and windy days in November 2019. A few months before this, during our earliest organisational negotiations, we (Claire Hind, Phil Smith and myself) had made a strategic decision to try to ensure that this conference would be as inclusive, accessible and affordable as possible, by keeping the conference subscriptions as low as we could.

That austerity and precarity currently loom large for many artists and academics is not news. We wanted not just to acknowledge this, but to dispose of certain conventions that can – often unintentionally – highlight hierarchies of privilege and exclusivity at such events. Through the flattening of such hierarchies, we hoped to point towards convivial and inclusive alternatives for walking, knowledge-sharing, making and doing. Such models draw from Bourriaud's 'relational aesthetics', and Haraway's 'string figuration' as a way to relay patterns and make connections in ongoing processes of sympoiesis.

To achieve our aim, contrary to what might be expected at an academic conference, we trimmed as close to the bone as we dared: there were no keynote speakers, no lunches provided, no 'optional' fancy trips or pricey conference meal. The delegates' fee was kept as low as possible (£50 for full-time academics, £25 for non-salaried artists and students). This strategy was not without risk, for the conference needed to pay for itself to go ahead. For a while, we held our breath as the small subscriptions trickled in. However, what we lacked in large delegate fees we gained by higher than expected attendance numbers and had to close registrations more than a week before the conference.

As the conference dates approached, we grew anxious that our invitation to 'bring your own flask of tea' might not be taken in the spirit it was intended by thirsty academics unused to fending for themselves in such situations.

As it unfolded, the Walking's New Movements conference evolved into a complex and perplexing body/mind assemblage: jostling, probing, playful, sensual, somatic, occasionally adversarial, sometimes subversive. A human and unhuman hybrid that walked backwards and forwards, looked to the future and leaned into the past. There was some hospitality: the 'Saturday Social', open to all, was held in the evening at the Corinthian Yacht Club on the waterfront as a storm blew through the city. We entertained each other with songs, stories, poems and performance, while in the bars new connections and exchanges were made, as wind and spray gusted through open windows to the sound of the waves breaking on the rocks below.

The gamble did seem to pay off. What this event lacked in terms of glossy brochures and goody bags, it gained through a broader variety of proposals, contributors and material than we had initially anticipated. Our advice to 'bring sandwiches' was not just begrudgingly tolerated, but enthusiastically and warm-heartedly embraced. Naturally, all conferences aim to generate social interaction and knowledge exchange: Walking's New Movements was not innovative in this respect. However, by simply levelling the playing field in economic terms, a platform was created that afforded a wider range of bodies and voices to participate and connect with each other. Not perfect, but a beginning that we hope others will embrace and build upon.

The consequence of all this was undoubtedly a more vibrant programme. Some of that rich variety and generosity is now reflected in the chapters and pages of this book.

Magical Aesthetics: walking with eight legs

Sarah Scaife

My visual art-making tunes in to the vibrations between being-in-a-body, listening and mutual space. Conversation is often an early stage of an iterative research process. I set out to both emit and receive vibrations; the work emerges through this echo-location. Behind conversations with other people lies another, more private series of dialogues with the more-than-human. These conversations take place primarily through the means of 'sign walks': walking out from a place of intention and request, walking in soft absorbency, alert to the polyphony of the cosmos. On these walks I listen and the world speaks to me.

This essay weaves together some strands of the Walking's New Movements conference 2019 (WNM, 2019) with my own presentation (Scaife, 2019). Here is another journey into not knowing. As I listened to other speakers, I made my way deeper into unexpectedly common ground of illness and recovery, joy, intersensoriality, domestic and local adventure, walking as connective practice enabling embodied dialogue with the human and the more-than-human other, phoenix growth and spiders' webs. Here is a sketch map of that journey, articulated partly in my fellow presenters' own words. I include an invitation to walk home with me from my local supermarket.

Walking took on a new significance in 2017 after I was diagnosed with breast cancer. "What happens when our bodies age and deteriorate, when pain takes over, when movement is hampered? How does a body in pain take part within a dialogue to place and movement?" asked Davina Kirkpatrick and Carol Laidler, in their performance presentation 'Walking-Not-Walking' (WNM, 2019).

More and more research shows that regular walking supports the body's immune system to deal with and recover from cancer, and I was fortunate to be able to walk almost every day during my year of treatment. I felt deep appreciation not to experience "the loss of the ability to enter a landscape due to ageing, incapacity or illness [...where] the longing to be outside remains", as spoken of by Louise Ann Wilson in her paper '"With memory I was there": The Surrogate Walker' (WNM, 2019).

However, this was a time of huge challenge and I found myself psychologically and energetically unable to draw on paper. At the same time, the world came alive with imagery and my own flesh became the porous surface of artistic enquiry. An already established practice of sign walks was one of several creative processes which flooded in from the margins to compensate for the loss of drawing. Like Kate Green, who is 'Walking the Pipe' (WNM, 2019) of the Elan Valley aqueduct and collecting oral history as she journeys, my daily walking ritual was joyfully wrapped around a bitter kernel of illness and loss.

Alistair Cunningham, a Canadian medical doctor, made a study of how people responded to the diagnosis of cancer. He found three core approaches which seem to support this unwanted journey: acceptance, authenticity and agency (Penny Brohn UK, 2017). That is acceptance of the unknown and inevitable changes which will come; authenticity in expressing thoughts, feelings and emotions; and agency, a sense of autonomy in making choices where this is possible and taking an active part in the journey as it unfolds.

I'm interested in how a magical, art-walking practice enables all three.

Described theoretically, my drawing and walking practices meet in the domain of 'Magical Aesthetics' (Dixon, 2015; Burrows and O'Sullivan, 2019). Dixon's term articulates his "desire to reclaim the importance of the poetic and non-rational in art and philosophy" (2015: 2) with the magical "as a way of being in the world" (ibid: 4) This is an aesthetic of hybridity, participation, dialogue and the making of meaning. In the face of mortality, moving through a world in soulful intuitive perception, many boundaries are blurred. Many places and things become magical. Given the opportunity to experience life in the embodied, physical world, "[w]e can proceed to build an account of the dimensions of experience that form us, that shake us up, shock us or enable us to see, feel and think differently," writes Dixon, "not just as fiction is bound up to interiority, but as proto-subjectivities located in diverse places in the world around us" (ibid: 59). Borrowing David Buuck's (2013) phrase, we can "press against the art/life divide".

For a long time now I have lived in an ongoing conversation with the inner and outer world. It's not exactly that I hear voices but the dialogue is often present. I imagine some of you experience that too. When I make a sign walk I set out to hold an explicit conversation with the more-than-human. On the day after three and a half weeks of radiotherapy I make one of my regular riverside walks, via our local supermarket. At the checkout, I caught sight of a woman older than me with a large hessian shopping bag. On the side of the bag, in large black letters, were these words: IF YOU ARE LOOKING FOR A SIGN, THIS IS IT. Who would have thought that Morrison's café could be a site of magic?

I invite you to join me in reimagining a walk I made a week or two before the Walking's New Movements conference. We will start outside the same supermarket on the edge of a small town in Devon, South West England, and walk together towards my home. This seemingly mundane route is fruitful nonetheless and we are walking in the conceptual steps of others. Gudrun Filipska and Carly Butler (WNM, 2019) present 'The S Project' which "explores the radical potential present in the circular, repetitive domestic walk set against colonial adventuring narratives." Gudrun is an initiator of The Arts Territory Exchange (aTE), "a global network of artists and art practices which respond to the geography of their territory of production" (Filipska, no date). It fascinates me that Gudrun and Carly have never met physically in person, and that to critique "the contemporary art world's jet setting travel practices", they are not present in the room (WNM, 2019).

| We just need to climb over this small wall out of the car park and onto the riverside footpath |

Philosopher Emmanuel Coccia (2019: 116) finds that all life on earth is in "an inseparable mixture". For him, "things and ideas are much less disciplined than people: they mix among themselves without worrying about taboos or etiquette". He suggests that

> we are immersed beings [in a] relationship with the world that is
> not modelled on the relationship that a subject has with an object
> but on that of the jellyfish with the sea, which allows it to be what
> it is. (ibid: 32)

The self and the world as tangled multitude. In the sign walks I step directly into this entanglement. Some days, in the rhythm of unhurried walking, it is possible even to forget that "our body, our sense of self, is something that we have extracted from the continuum of the world" (ibid: 55) and to feel instead the immersion.

Emma Bush (WNM, 2019) asks 'How do our bodies act as instruments of sensory navigation?' She makes her study through 'shared acts of sensing', a term she invented "to describe collective acts of looking, listening and more broadly sensing orientation and perception. Focusing on particular ways of framing communal observation these are performance acts aimed towards a radical permeability offering insight into embodied encounters between 'self' and 'other'." Emma describes, for example, how this can involve approaching a tree "symbiotically" rather than imposing oneself on the tree. She applies the Goethean method of observation, which allows a plant or flower to select and attract you, contrasting this conscious receptivity with the more usual pushing outwards of Western enquiry. Emma speaks of how "in the walking together we have become *the one monster*", engaging collectively in maintaining attention (although sharing, she notes, does not imply an equivalence of experience.)

| Am I walking too quickly? |

Artist and academic Simon O'Sullivan picks up Gilbert Simondon's notion that

> key points of exchange and communication between human and world can be characterised as knots in which there is an unmediated relation – a point of passage – between two realities (O'Sullivan, 2018: 6 and Fig.1, p.4).

Spiders make sense of the world through eight legs. They sit at the centre of the web with one leg on each radial thread and feel into the vibrations. Imagine… What must that be like? Emma Bush describes the spider's web as an extended biological system through which spiders sense and experience the world. Ira Livingston, director of the Poetics Lab at the Pratt Institute in New York, suggests that

> it is not *in spite of* our embeddedness in the web of forces that we study but *because* of it – because it pulls on us from various directions – that we can (like spiders) have some sense of what may be happening and where. (Livingston, 2006: 9, emphasis in original)

Spiders become a theme. I was not able to attend Helen Billinghurst and Phil Smith's (WNM, 2019) presentation of 'Web Walking', but I know of their exploration of Ariadne's threads, webs and privileged points in the tissue of the landscape. Helen too has made her own walking journey through illness and loss and brings the earth and bones of this to her exhibition, 'Walking Diagrams' (WNM, 2019). Like Emma, Helen and Phil, mine is a refractive research practice of art making as it is also life; immersed in a web of connection.

| sky wind rattle of the geese overhead, taking it in turns to lead |

Of course, these sign walks are a form of performance. In Schechner's (2006) terms they are a journey, a *'transportation'*. We are carried out of our daily world if only for a short time. This ritual takes place in what he describes as "a highly charged in-between space-time, a liminal space-time" (ibid: 72) mostly in silent or at least quiet walking.

The sign walk is often a walk within a walk. I might walk unaccompanied or with one or more human others. We usually find an existing beginning and end in the landscape which offers a rite of entry; going through a gate or over a wall, passing between two closely growing trees or stepping over a small stream. At that spot, we pause and quietly set intention: I have learned that it is important to ask. (This was one of the hardest teachings of cancer.)

From that moment we enter into heightened noticing, a changed perception. Is it an Altered State of Consciousness or simply a temporary clearing in the fog of twenty-first century market capitalism? And then, perhaps 20 minutes later at another convenient landmark, we step out of the sign walk again, with appreciation for all we have met, returning to our ordinary selves. (I have learned too that it is important to say thank you.) In this quietly alert, soft focus state, the gentle heartbeat rhythm of walking, we may lose ourselves in flow, as the Hungarian-American psychologist Csikszentmihalyi described it: "in the flow state, [...] there is little distinction between self and environment, between stimulus and response *[...]*. He suggests that this flow experience is the primary way that non-human animals move through the world, "present in the environment in relation to their bodily states" (Csikszentmihalyi, 1975, quoted in Schechner, 2006: 98).

| The tide is high just now. |

The world that we live in, as experienced through the human sensory body, seems different to the world as known through the body of a spider, or a whale, and yet it is the same world. How are we to make sense of this? Reid (2010: 57), a contemporary dance choreographer, describes this shift of perception as the point where "the body as identity is surpassed by the body as experiential landscape." In this flow state of openness, magic can happen and it is here that we might meet with the as-yet unmet. My encounter with liminality through cancer treatment took me over what academic Patricia MacCormack (2017) identifies as the queer feminist threshold, into "mucosity, viscous connectivity, art as ritual, fabulation, audaciously representing the impossible". She describes how "the self, the vulva and the world become thresholds […] The self as a crevice into which the outside slips." […] with "jubilant, productive possibilities" (ibid). As we move through spatial and temporal dimensions we might also step in and out of each other's being. Coccia (2019: 10-11) puts it this way:

> Life is a rupture in the asymmetry between container and contained. When there is life, the container is located in the contained (and is thus contained by it); and vice versa. […] To breathe means to be immersed in a medium that penetrates us with the same intensity as we penetrate it.

Magical aesthetic practices offered me the possibility of 'phoenix growth': the new growth that rises after a tree has been severely damaged and perhaps fallen, confirming my sense of a deeper dimension of what it is to be alive in the more-than-human world. Leah Lovett, Duncan Hay, Martin de Jode and Andrew Hudson-Smith spoke of this phoenix growth in relation to their work on 'Walking in Tree Time: the Listening Wood Project' (WNM, 2019). They engage with 14 veteran trees on Hampstead Heath. Here, the Internet of Things technologies are used to explore tree time/human time, temporality and subjecthood of the trees. "What then might it mean for humans to walk with trees?" they asked, finding that "traces of an animistic worldview cling to Renaissance culture. You speak with the [trees], they speak with you…" Vicky Hunter too is 'Walking / Dancing / Moving with Trees' (WNM, 2019) in the city, through a site-based body practice. She spoke of the parallels between the human body and the city space; circulatory systems, regenerative processes, water elements.

| There are so many hawthorn berries this year. Medicine for the heart. |

These papers provoke me. If the body is an experiential landscape might the landscape also be a body? I notice too my own discomfort with the mixing of the wild and the digital and question this resistance. I am more enchanted by the notion of Geraldine van Heemstra's handmade "drawing devices created from found objects that become extensions of my body" (WNM, 2019). "Walking with my devices primarily in the Hebrides, with its strong and changeable weather, I record intangibility. You only see the wind through what it touches, and my devices become the conduit for the unseen."

My own walks, understood as a magical performance process, have an aftermath. I may archive the walk in the sense that I document signs in a journal, perhaps research the implications of particular signs which I encountered and consider how they relate to the season or the phase of the moon. An object found on the walk – a stone, a berry, a found human-made object – might be added to my private collection temporarily, or for years, and perhaps be reused in a different context. There is a time of reflection, of making meaning through the signs. This may be a conversation with a friend who was or was not present.

Karen Howse (North Cornwall) and Flora McLachlan (Wales) participate in parallel Full Moon Walks. They had not met each other before the WNM 2019 conference. Together with Tiffany Robinson (West Sussex) and Melanie Rose (Winchester), they walk together but in separate locations every Full Moon. "[…] technology means we can meet afterwards in the virtual space to share our drawings, photographs, insights or experiences from each walk," writes Karen (Howse, no date) on her website: "Carving out the space of time to walk separately/together gives the walks a particular quality, like having an invisible companion. I see walking as a connective practice."

And, of course, my own walks leave memories attached to place. As I often walk similar routes again and again, these traces accumulate and have the effect of charging that route or location: Doreen Massey's notion of landscape as a 'pincushion of a million stories'. At WNM, 2019, as we participate in a street walking performance in central Plymouth, Davina Kirkpatrick and I – strangers who only met yesterday – find ourselves in rich conversation about memories of love, loss, intimacy, synchronicity and sense of place. What is it about walking alongside another which can do this? The performance is 'Dream Yards' led by Claire Hind and Gary Winters, "where the audience might [indeed] find themselves caught up in an experience of lucidity in relation to the local area."

Maybe you are wondering this: how do I recognise 'a sign'? What is it that I am experiencing, perceiving as 'signs' on these walks? It is my experience – and that of many others – that when I ask, and walk with intention, somehow the creaturely, the elemental and even the discarded shows itself and I just know! Like the classic 'duck and the rabbit' or the 'face and the vase', my perception switches and new things come to the fore. It might be a kingfisher, a seal, a robin… a rock, formations in the clouds, changes in the wind, birdsong, an old glove or a shopping bag in a supermarket café.

These signs are a version of what Guattari calls "fabulous images". Burrows & O'Sullivan (2019: 23) describe how they can "operate as experimental devices" which at once condense and open up meaning for both their maker and their viewer. Vibrations, projections, metaphors, coincidences, what Carl Jung described as synchronicity? Does it matter whether this is actual magic or human projection? I don't know. All I can tell you is that this walking in dialogue has an effect on my well-being. It is important to say that I have been walking in this way for more than 10 years now so I am not dabbling. It is a considered and developed practice. It is walking as a form of listening.

Although the signs are often visual, my sensory experience of the sign walk is closer to hearing than to seeing, a sense that we walk in a field of shared vibration. As Voeglin (2010: 1), sound artist and academic, puts it:

> such a listening does not pursue the question of meaning, as a collective, total comprehension, but as interpretation in the sense of a phantasmagoric, individual and contingent practice.

O'Sullivan writes of practices "that communicate without meaning [in the register of knowledge]". Academic, Angela Voss and others, write of re-enchanting the Academy. (Voss & Wilson, 2017: 16). Burrows & O'Sullivan (2019: 104 and Ch. 6) call up "the contemporary non-modern". This animistic experience of communication with the more-than-human is not logical or scientifically verifiable but it is a form of tacit knowing.

Both Voeglin and O'Sullivan hint that, in current times, these types of deep listening practices are socio-political acts. For O'Sullivan they "might be mobilised into a different way of being in the world (and with this foreshadow a different community yet to come)." Or, put another way, "we might say that art is that privileged point that produces a shift or gap, passage to other universes of reference (or, indeed, to the infinite whole)" (O'Sullivan, 2018: 10). For Voeglin (2010: 3):

> Listening [is] a generative and intersubjective practice [… which focuses] on the dynamic nature of things […] The spectre of sound unsettles the idea of visual stability and involves us as listeners in the production of an invisible world.

At this time of socio-political dissolving, I want to play my part in "the generation of different worlds and communities that are the potential of, and alternatives to, existing worlds" (Burrows & O'Sullivan, 2019: 6).

| Did you hear that? But we should walk on, it's getting dark |

For Burrows and O'Sullivan, "[a] fictioning practice then, involves performing, diagramming or assembling new and different modes of existence through open-ended experimentation." As they suggest, I find that "technics of *looping* and *nesting*" are inherent to this (ibid: 6, emphasis in original). This way of walking rests on the same bench as fictioning, as a means of working out, coming to terms with, making sense of the as-yet unfathomable (Kenning, 2014; Burrows & O'Sullivan, 2019).

| It's wet, so the steps might be slippery |

A particular footpath along the River Dart in Devon, England walked many times during the cancer treatment is now a highly charged pathway for me and I can return to almost any point along that route and feel immediate psychological restoration. Sometimes the walk becomes raw material in visual artworks I go on to make. Mostly these walks leave traces in my own body and allow things I no longer need or want to fall away.

| We are almost home now |

Through walking we accept the life, death, life cycle.
Through walking we express trust, participation and gratitude (Kumar, 2007).
Through walking, we perform hope.

References

Burrows, David & O'Sullivan, Simon (2019) *Fictioning. The Myth-functions of Contemporary Art and Philosophy.* Edinburgh Univ. Press

Buuck, David (2013) *How to make us flux: Scores/scripts/instructions.* Available at: bit.ly/wnm11 (Accessed: 25 June 2019)

Coccia, Emmanuel (2019) *The Life of Plants: A Metaphysics of Mixture.* Polity Press

Dixon, Tim (2015) *Magical Aesthetics: Subjectivity, Simondon, Animism, and the Aesthetic.* Available at: bit.ly/wnm12 (Accessed: 25 Nov 2019)

Filipska, Gudrun (no date) *Rural, Remote, Radical.* Available at: bit.ly/wnm15 (Accessed: 17 Dec 2019)

Howse, Karen (no date) *Full Moon Walks. Parallel Walks in Cornwall, Hampshire, Wales and Sussex. Four Women Artists.* Available at: bit.ly/wnm19 (Accessed: 12 Dec 2019)

Kenning, Dean (2014) *Thinking Through Art: The Social Body Mind Map.* Available at: bit.ly/wnm21 (Accessed 15 Jul 2019)

Kumar, Satish (2007) *Spiritual Compass: The Three Qualities of Life.* Green Books

Livingston, Ira (2006) *Between Science and Literature. An Introduction to Autopoetics.* Univ. of Illinois Press

O'Sullivan, Simon (2020) 'Myth-science as residual culture and magical thinking'. *Postmedieval* 11, 119–136. https://doi.org/10.1057/s41280-018-0086-2

Penny Brohn UK (national cancer support charity), Living Well 3-day residential course, Bristol, June 2017

Reid, Dianne (2010) 'Cutting choreography: back and forth between 12 stages and 27 seconds.' In Barrett, Estelle and Barbara Bolt (eds) *Practice as Research: Approaches to Creative Arts Enquiry.* Tauris. pp. 47-63

Scaife, Sarah (2019) 'Magical aesthetics: walking with eight legs.' [performance lecture] Walking's New Movements conference, Univ. of Plymouth, 1-3 Nov 2019

Schechner, Richard (2006) *Performance Studies. An Introduction* 2nd ed. Routledge

Voegelin, Salomé (2010) *Listening to Noise and Silence: Towards a Philosophy of Sound Art.* Continuum. Available at: bit.ly/wnm22 (Accessed: 05 May 2019)

Voss, Angela & Wilson, Simon (eds) (2017) *Re-enchanting the Academy.* Rubedo Press

Walking in Tree Time

or a walk with the woods

Duncan Hay, Leah Lovett, Martin de Jode,
Andrew Hudson-Smith

They had lived with the shadows for as long as they could remember. Shadows, barely sensed, but always present, detectable only through their symptoms. A limb amputated in a breath; a brother, a mother, a child uprooted in a single turning of the earth. New interlopers between us, strange saps and pollens. Carving their names in the heartwood. The soil broken, cut and curved with stone and iron. Grasses sprung from it, tubers buried, their sugars-bearing fruits stored in it, shadows close cropping the surface of the soil, the sapling growth, stunted. Trees to timber, sap-wet to dead-dry, the skeleton of a ship, in which the shadows ventured. Sea-changed and salt-saturated.

This chapter asks what it might mean for walking arts practices and research to recognise trees as walking subjects. How can the movements of trees over years and centuries be understood in terms of walking? What does 'walking in tree time' reveal to us about our own, human pace, perspective and interactions with the world as walking subjects? Is it possible to conceive of ways for trees and people to walk together and, if so, what techniques are available to artists for bridging the gap – practically, imaginatively – between human and arboreal walking practices and temporalities?

These are some of the questions that emerged from the multi-disciplinary research project 'The Internet of Trees', which was funded by the Engineering and Physical Sciences Research Council (EPSRC) primarily to investigate the potential for deploying Internet of Things (IoT) technologies in public spaces.

IoT, broadly defined, is a tendency whereby the increasing cheapness of networking, sensing, and artificial intelligence technologies allows more and more objects and devices to become connected to the internet. These trends enable objects not conventionally associated with connectivity – street furniture, buildings, and in our case, trees – to interact with each other and with people. The corollary of this is that we are now surrounded by objects which are communicating and acting in ways which may be invisible, out of our direct control, and beyond the perceptual limits of human experience.

The main outcome of the project was 'The Listening Wood', a digital poetic walk on Hampstead Heath created by artist Leah Lovett and technologists from the Bartlett Centre for Advanced Spatial Analysis, University College London, in partnership with the City of London Corporation. 'The Listening Wood' invited visitors to slow down and attend to the ancient and veteran trees of Golders Hill Park and the wider Heath, employing IoT technologies and SMS text message to disseminate fragments of digital poetry relating to each of the project trees and the landscape they occupy. The concept and content for this work developed over hours and days spent with the trees – observing, drawing, photographing, walking – and with the arborists, as their custodians. Stories about the veteran pear tree, the weathered sweet chestnut and the steadfast, ancient oak, told to the researchers by the Head of Trees, David Humphries, and his team profoundly challenged our preconceptions about arboreal lives, shifting the direction of the project and shaping the poetic dimension of the installation.

This text returns to 'The Listening Wood', then, not as a resolved, fixed and finalised project, but rather as an opening and a provocation to the reader to think about trees – and walking – differently. Drawing on stories shared by the arborists, archival research and reflections on the affordances of digital and IoT technologies, it sets out to discover the potential for walking *with* trees to de-centre human practices of walking and open up to indeterminate and nonhuman ways of being and relating in the world. The series of narrative interjections into the text iterate the digital installation on the Heath, interrupting and reflexively locating our discussion with imaginaries that reach beyond the limits of human temporal experience and perception. In this way, the following discussion sets out to examine how radical walking practices might be informed by and contribute to debates in the environmental posthumanities which seek to re-negotiate the concepts of nature and the human.

When David speaks of 'walking in tree time', he is referring to a phenomenon more commonly known as 'phoenix growth'. Phoenix growth can occur when a tree falls or when a storm-damaged tree loses a branch. At the cellular level, the grounded branches send out roots and re-orient themselves as trunks, becoming new trees. This motion incidentally recalls the etymological roots of the verb 'to walk' from the Germanic, *walken,* meaning to roll, toss, or turn over (Hoad, 1996). Even so, the notion of phoenix growth as a form of walking calls into question tacit assumptions about what it means to walk, what sort of entities might be able to walk, and what it might mean to take a walk in the woods. To speak of trees moving may conjure images of slow, upward growth; branches moving with the wind; the uncurling and eventual fall of a leaf. Collectively, forests grow, expand, creep, or spread. Yet to describe phoenix growth – the movement of an individual tree – as walking implies, if not necessarily purposive motion, then at least something willed. To walk is to be active, to move through the world either under one's own volition or another's compulsion. Walking implies, in short, a form of subjectivity.

As with many incidents in the lives of trees, phoenix growth takes place over seasons, years, and sometimes even centuries. Most people glimpse the falling-down walk of trees as a kind of stasis, in arrested moments. Conversely human footsteps, if they register at all, must appear as momentary flickers in arboreal lifetimes. These differing temporalities make the relationships between trees and humans oblique, the forms of subjectivity that they each might hold for themselves and for each other difficult to imagine. With human walking and tree walking appearing as incommensurate practices, how might we begin to think of walking *with* trees?

The practice of 'walking with' has been reframed and expanded in recent anthropological debates through serious engagement with Indigenous North American ontologies and methodologies, leading some theorists to propose a method of 'walking-with'. For Stephanie Springgay and Sarah E. Truman (2018: 11):

> …walking-with is accountable. Walking-with is a form of solidarity, unlearning, and critical engagement with situated knowledges. Walking-with demands that we forgo universal claims about how humans and nonhumans experience walking,

and consider more-than-human ethics and politics of the material intra-actions of walking research.

Walking-with, then, engages with marginalised and erased knowledges to bring about new forms of sociability with the other than human, the nonhuman and the inhuman. It seeks to acknowledge the alterity of human experience and nonexperienced time, to recognise the multiplicity of being and time. In the present context, the concept of walking-with allows for the recognition of nonhuman entities, including trees, as actors with their own distinct peripatetic practices and experiences of walking – as what with Donna Haraway (2003: 15) we might call 'companion species'.

Companion species, in Haraway's terminology, are species which are bonded in "significant otherness", her primary example being humans and dogs. To do justice to this significant otherness requires thinking and imagining beyond notions of human dominance, and to a recognition that dogs own humans as much as humans own dogs. Like walking-with, significant otherness relies on acts of empathy and imagination: to discover (or to work at discovering) what one species has in common with another; to 'make kin' with them. For Haraway (2016: 2):

> *Kin* is a wild category that all sorts of people do their best to domesticate. Making kin as odd kin rather than, or at least in addition to, godson and genealogical and biogenetic family troubles important matters, like to whom one is actually responsible.

Making kin is therefore a choice and an act: kin does not only describe a genetic, familial relationship; kin also includes those with whom we choose to make common cause, whose lives are bound up with our own, and to whom we are responsible.

Artists such as Jeremy Hastings, Cathy Turner, and Miranda Whall have walked with (and in some cases, walked *as*) donkeys, elephants, and sheep, respectively to de-centre the human in peripatetic artistic practices. These are modes of walking with (or walking-with) which seek to imagine the significant otherness of humans and animals, comparable to Haraway and her dogs. If it is challenging to make this imaginative leap in relating to creatures with whom humans have lived and worked over hundreds of thousands of years, even sharing a mammalian evolutionary root, how much harder is it to imagine the significant otherness of trees and humans? The arboreal team on Hampstead Heath, in their extended relationships with trees, are in a process of making kin with them. In their work, the arborists are accountable to human needs: the requirement that the Heath be a place of leisure with enough of a modicum of 'wildness' to satisfy the bunkered urbanite; to be safe, to be clean, to be beautiful. But they are also accountable to the trees and the meshwork of biological systems they support and are supported by. Balancing these, sometimes contradictory, needs is a delicate business. To take one example: in the absence of grazing animals on the Heath, ensuring that mature trees continue to have access to the canopy requires the arborists to clear any saplings that would take their sunlight, a task which is particularly unpopular with human visitors to the park. This messiness is the substance of making kin, of navigating the threads of accountability entailed in sharing a world with other beings. It is a form of work, moreover, which de-sacralises the natural. Rather than a sanctified or transcendent space outside of the human (to which we look for salvation), nature is the ground of human and non-human 'becoming-with'.

The insights of the arboreal team – of tree subjectivity and tree walking – are gleaned through their unusually intimate knowledge of those trees, developed over many years. David, for instance, has been working on Hampstead Heath since the late 1980s. Arborists and tree surgeons are more often contracted to work on a site; once a job has been completed, there is no guarantee they will be called back to work with a particular specimen a second time. The localised and long-standing service of the Heath's arborists means that they have the opportunity to develop deeper and more sustained relationships with specific trees. Even so, David's 30-year tenure at Hampstead Heath is a tiny fraction (less than 4%) of the lifespan of the Mother Oak, the oldest of the veteran trees we worked with on 'The Listening Wood'.

Tree time stretches out beyond the lifespan of any single human being. Human lives and human actions can have drastic effects on the lives of trees, but an individual human (if perceptible at all) barely registers in sylvan sense apparatuses. Ancient trees, though they change with the seasons, appear stationary at human timescales: monolithic (or monodendric) structures around which human activity flows. Yet if we are to accept them as walking subjects, trees have agency. As much as we act upon them, they act upon us. The Leaning Pine of Sandy Heath was sketched on multiple occasions by the English landscape painter, John Constable (1776-1873). From his drawings, it is clear that this specimen is the sole survivor of a cluster of similar pines. Dubbed '*Llundain fach*' (Little London), pine clusters such as these sometimes served as route markers and shelter for Welsh cattle drovers on their long walks to market. This group, however, came to the Heath as seed from la Pineta, Ravenna in the late eighteenth century, carried back to London by the industrialist Turner as a memento of his Grand Tour of Italy. Did Turner acquire these trees, or did la Pineta mobilise Turner? Seen another way, humans become the propagation vectors through which trees reproduce themselves in new habitats.

There is an eeriness to this thought: that the agency we think we have over the natural might in fact be a part of patterns larger than we (as individuals, at least) can discern. If tree time and human time are to become commensurate, it must be as interference patterns, the points of convergence, where the rhythms of tree lives and human lives intersect. Discerning these patterns necessarily implies a multi-generational, species perspective, and a dislocation of well-worn habits of thought. One medium in which they might be detected is in the accretion of human culture.

As a temporal marker, the Mother Oak would have been planted around the time that Shakespeare wrote *Macbeth*. The spectre of Birnam Wood marching on Dunsinane is one literary imagining of tree walking. Tolkien's Ents (lit. Giants) in *The Lord of the Rings* is another. Both of these images function through an appeal to the supernatural, and both render trees walking at a human pace. The Marxist historian Ellen Meiksins Wood (1991: 109) argues that only in Britain, where the traces of pre-capitalist urban life were so comprehensively erased by the early onset of capitalism, could the nostalgia for medieval social structures of the Arts and Crafts movement appear as a form of radicalism. In similar vein, for *The Lord of the Rings*, modernity has so disenchanted the natural world of agency that the text must literally render trees as animate – wooden people with legs, eyes, and mouths – to return it to them.

Shakespeare's walking trees point to a more complex way of imagining tree subjectivity. In Macbeth's second meeting with the Witches, they conjure an apparition, which tells him:

> Macbeth shall neuer vanquish'd be,
> vntill Great Byrnam Wood, to high Dunsmane Hill
> Shall come against him. (Shakespeare, *Macbeth*, lines 1633-1637)

Macbeth is indeed vanquished, the prophecy coming to pass in simultaneously fantastic and prosaic fashion: soldiers disguised with branches. This mixing of the impossible (spirits speaking of events which have not passed) and the mundane, or the manifestation of the impossible *through* the mundane, structures the relationship between the natural and the supernatural in *Macbeth*. The Witches, as Banquo and Macbeth observe, are human, natural, unnatural, corporeal and incorporeal, all at once:

> *Banq.* The Earth hath bubbles, as the Water ha's,
> And these are of them: whither are they vanish'd?
> *Macb.* Into the Ayre: and what seem'd corporall,
> Melted, as breath into the Winde.
> Would they had stay'd. (ibid: lines 180-184)

The earth becomes like a gas or a liquid, bodies melt and dissolve: categories which were fixed are set in motion. The staging of the play itself – the interplay of bodies, smoke, and mirrors – repeats this pattern. The march of Birnam Wood on Dunsinane, whether under supernatural impetus or not, could be staged identically: people holding branches; men dressed as trees.

Neither entirely explicable by natural, magical, or realist frames of reference, the ontological status of the apparition's prophecy is irresolvable. This suggests an imaginary opening to forms of agency whose purposes are opaque to human ways of being. In *Macbeth*, humans are subject to the whims of entities who are not only beyond control, and whose motives are beyond understanding, but whom cannot be represented 'face on'. Unable to articulate their nature directly (for they are literally unspeakable), the play presents us instead with impossibilities and lacunae. The fantastic if somewhat literalist character of Tolkien's Ents speaks to a dire need to break with the reifications of materialist conceptions of more-than-human entities. *Macbeth*'s haunted cosmos, conversely, suggests other routes to imagining the uncanny intersections between vegetal and mammalian purposes.

Root fibres vibrate to the pace of unseen steppers. Infrasound, a mosquito whine, an irritant, vibrates the soil particles. Sand agglomerates, smaller motes suspended and saturated, unaerated, clogged and compressed. Contents may settle in transit.

In the spaces between the trees, the shadows passed, pausing. Caught in the eddies, in the wood between the worlds. What were they drawn by, and what did they see?

Eyes on a cradled glow, scrying, then upwards to the canopy, listening. What did they hear? Was it a voice? A word?

Traces of an enchanted world-view cling to Renaissance culture. In *Macbeth*, the Witches are as much of the non-human as of the human world, and they act as mediators between supernatural entities and the world of people. This is a populated universe in which humans are not the only actors. With the Enlightenment, the humanist subject was placed at the centre of a modern world emptied of other and multiple selves. However, as communication technologies proliferate and the increasing cheapness of computing power enables more and more objects to become communicative, the centrality of humans is once again called into question.

The Internet of Things, in making objects speak, re-enchants the world; but technology is often thought of as a distraction and as unwanted in the spaces that we choose to delimit as 'natural'. Discussing his experience of walking with donkeys in France over several weeks, away from digital interference, Jeremy Hastings reflected on the 'necessary greed of the digital'. Not only does the digital interpenetrate human relationships to politically exploit and monetise them, there is also a sense in which these technologies are hungry for both attention and time. The all-absorbing pull of the screen is felt to prevent meaningful interaction with the world.

There is something unsettling about this technology as well. As with the staging of *Macbeth*, communication technologies are fleshy, corporeal things. Mobile phones are composed of lithium mined in South America, rare earth metals from Australia and Myanmar, and they are assembled in city-scale production facilities in China. The antennae which allow them to function are found, in western countries, in even the most seemingly remote regions. Yet what makes them work is ethereal: electricity and radio waves, undetectable to the human sensorium.

Mobile communication technologies privilege the instantaneous over the slow. 'The Listening Wood', instead, used technology to encourage people to walk the Heath and unlock poems with keywords inserted into the landscape. The team tried to repurpose the technology in this way to encourage a reflective, slow engagement with arboreal lives. On a practical level, it was not possible to attach technology to the trees for risk of damage or theft. In the mode of humans and trees as companion species, nor did we want to intervene and disrupt the habitats which they sustained. SMS messaging represented the least obtrusive technological intervention, while the words were etched into wood roundels that had been reclaimed in the day-to-day management of the woodland. The poetry then became the mediating element between the different material and temporal realities of humans, trees, and technology.

> *Washed by the lapping of the sun's waves, a pink-noise rumble, the fields had long been tranquil. In the leaves and branches, changes were felt: a flux, a knotting, a new pulse. The encircling threads of force, labile, invisible, began to thrum with new vibrations: spectral emanations at 300kHz, 300MHz, 3000MHz. Like and unlike the wind, like and unlike the sun: a storm felt in the mesophyll, visible as patternings in the cell walls, the cambium, in rhytidome encrustations.*

> *If this were a sound, where was its source? If this were the sun, what power might bend the stems towards it?*

The call-and-response structure of sending a prompt word and receiving a text message implies a kind of ventriloquism. However, as the severed sweet chestnut and its phoenix suggest, to speak of a tree as an 'individual' may be a case of mistaken identity. In both their conception and structure, the poems received by visitors to the Heath were less messages *from* a particular tree, and more a frequency or channel that could only be tuned to in their presence, through being with each tree, in the same place. The appeal to poetics and chance figured as attempts to resist the conversational tropes typical of 'chatbots', to work with the limitations of the software and lay bare the instrumental nature of the message exchange. Just as audiences to *Macbeth* may see the mechanics of the theatrical production and also invest in the imaginative world of the play, so a text message exchange can become a metaphor for much greater and more meaningful forms of human, nonhuman and inhuman interaction. It is in the space given over to the imaginaries of the audiences that the trees and technology were able to enchant one another, as the following response to the work suggests:

> I loved the slippage between things that using SMS gave me … using SMS as a sort of physical probe – like it felt as if I could use it to nudge the tree, or wave at it, or something, to have another level of depth to the encounter. And I guess knowing that there were more possible responses than I received helped it all seem like an encounter with a world bigger than me.

It is here that IoT and mobile technologies gesture towards new opportunities for walking and walking-with as means of transcending the limitations of species-being, leading to unexpected encounters and ways of imagining relationships between the human and more-than-human.

References

Haraway, D. (2003) *The Companion Species Manifesto: Dogs, People, and Significant Otherness.* Prickly Paradigm Press

______ (2016) *Staying with the Trouble: Making Kin in the Chthulucene.* Duke Univ. Press

Hoad, T. F. ed. (1996) *Concise Oxford Dictionary of English Etymology.* Oxford Univ. Press

Springgay, S. and Truman, S. E. (2018) *Walking Methodologies in a More-than-Human World: WalkingLab.* Routledge

Shakespeare, W. (2015 [c.1606]) *Macbeth,* ed. Sandra Cark and Pamela Mason. Bloomsbury

Tolkein, J. R. R. (2005 [1954]) *The Lord of the Rings.* Harper Collins

Wood, E. M. (1991) *The Pristine Culture of Capitalism: A Historical Essay on Old Regimes and Modern States.* Verso

Dancing-Walking with Trees

Vicky Hunter

In this essay I reflect on a tree-sound-walk workshop led collaboratively by the walking artist Rosie Montford, dancer and dance scholar Leslie Satin (New York University, Gallatin) and myself as part of the Museum of Walking's 'Sound-Walk Sunday' programme (1ˢᵗ Sept 2019). The on-line based Museum of Walking is an initiative led by walking curator, author and podcast innovator Andrew Stuck and Sound Walk Sunday is an annual volunteer-led event in which a series of walks takes place nationally and internationally. The events have a shared interest in drawing attention to space and place through walking, listening and responding to sounds encountered *en route*. The 'Dancing/Walking with Trees' workshop extended the sound walk format to incorporate movement, drawing and dance activities alongside listening as modes of doing and thinking that might bring individuals closer to an awareness of environmental features. Starting from the University campus, participants followed a section of the Chichester 'tree trail' route and engaged with a series of tasks involving drawing, moving, pausing and reflecting on experiences, sights and sounds gathered along the way.[1]

Informed by new materialist theory, I will describe what took place, how we worked and reflect a little on the human-nonhuman intra-actions encountered *en route* and the potential for this type of walking / dancing / moving practice to invoke human-environment relations in particular ways. The term 'intra-action' originates from Karen Barad's research in new materialism and acts as a neologism that signifies 'the mutual constitution of entangled agencies' (2007: 33). It moves beyond a customary conception of interaction which "assumes that there are separate individual agencies that precede their interaction, the notion of intra-action recognizes that distinct agencies do not precede, but rather

---

[1] Details of the trail can be found on the West Sussex county council website – search 'Chichester tree trail' for further information about the route.

emerge through, their intra-action" (ibid: 33). Through this approach I hope to give a flavour of what took place and what this type of work might bring to walking arts practice and scholarship.

Site-based Body Practice

My approach to the walking event and to the research that informed it stems from a form of movement practice that I am calling 'site-based body practice' in which different actors, material and entities come together and contribute to an entangled process of 'becoming-with' one another in a co-constitutive manner in which; 'all together the players evoke, trigger, and call forth what-and-who-exists' (Haraway, 2016). Exploring how bodies, sites and materials might 'dialogue' with one another through the medium of sited dance and movement practice I am concerned with pragmatic questions of: How is the body's design and function reflected in the environments in which it engages? What synergies of form and function exist? Coupled with more speculative questioning of what might happen if we prioritise bodily knowing over interpretation and analysis and what might site-based body practice reveal regarding human-environment engagement?

Researching and developing this movement practice has involved engagement with a range of sites from urban arterial routes to wide open spaces and watery sites and beaches. The practice employs movement improvisation, broadly defined as spontaneous embodied and kinetic responses to bodily engagement with a range of site-based phenomena and materials. It explores how material and functional analogies between bodies, structures and materials can be initially explored and subsequently developed beyond the analogous into an embodied realm. Through engagement with the materials of the body and the materials of real-world locations it aims to expose the body's in-built structures and processes as devices though which intrinsic synergies between bodies, and sites might be illuminated and explored. It does not, however, attempt to anthropomorphise particular non-human elements but does propose that parallels can be drawn and that such alignments and synergies might be worthy of closer inspection. In this practice-based research I tend to work with movement scores – a simple set of instructions – designed to lead participants and myself towards specific intra-actions between bodies and sites. Participants are presented with a score in a specific location that draws their corporeal attention towards particular site elements such as textures, forms, materials, tempos and rhythms. Once a process of tuning-in to a site has commenced, spontaneous movement responses are encouraged to emerge, these might include expressive gestures, pedestrian actions, running, jumping and dancing or stillness.

Walking acts as a partner or collaborator for this type of somatically informed movement practice. As a largely familiar mode of moving through space it renders the less commonplace practice of dancing (or moving in an expressive manner) more accessible and potentially less threatening. Couched within the pseudo 'guided tour' format, the Chichester tree walk housed and framed the exploratory movement 'episodes' encountered *en route* and helped to facilitate one of the key aims of this work, to get people out and about and away from passive environments and mediatised modes of engaging with the world towards hands on, corporeal engagements with sites and their material components. Such modes of doing and thinking inevitably involve unscripted and spontaneous encounters with real world phenomena, materials, people and things. It requires improvised responses and openness to being in the moment, whatever that might encompass, from which new discoveries might emerge. As Rebecca Solnit observes:

> The random, the unscreened, allows you to find what you don't know you are looking for, and you don't know a place until it surprises you. Walking is one way of maintaining a bulwark against this erosion of the mind, the body, the landscape and the city, and every walker is a guard on patrol to protect the ineffable. (2014:11)

Rather than walking being employed 'in service' to dance and movement practice, in this scenario, however, the workshop aimed to engage participants in a hybrid practice. As opposed to models of hybridity in which one dominant mode of practice is imposed upon or subsumes an other, I aspired to work with a processual model of hybridity that constantly negotiated the various elements of walking, drawing, moving, talking, listening and dancing in an entangled state of flux.

The Workshop

Participants were recruited via social media and word of mouth. The group of around twenty included men and women, a number of whom were members of local arts and ecology / eco-activist groups, members of University staff and artist practitioners interested in environmental arts practice. A small number had previous movement or dance experience and the majority regularly took part in walking activities but were new to movement practice and this type of hybrid workshop format.

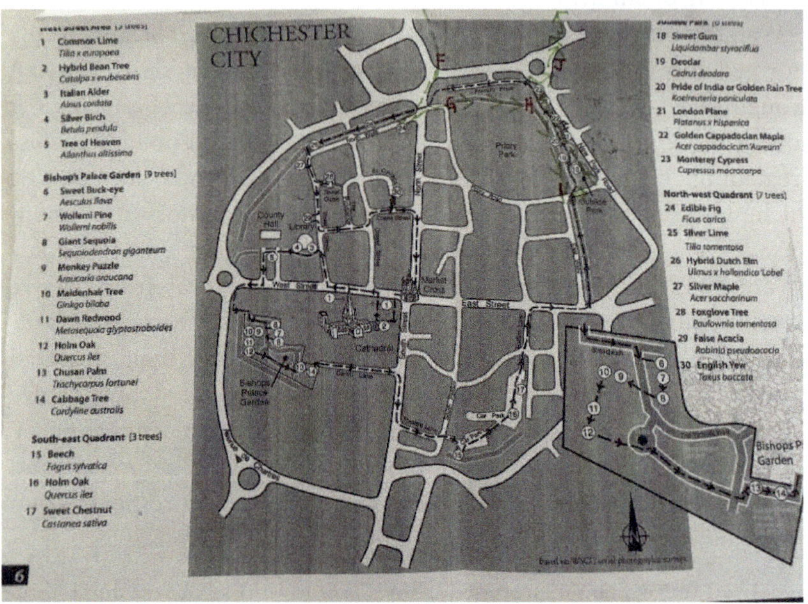

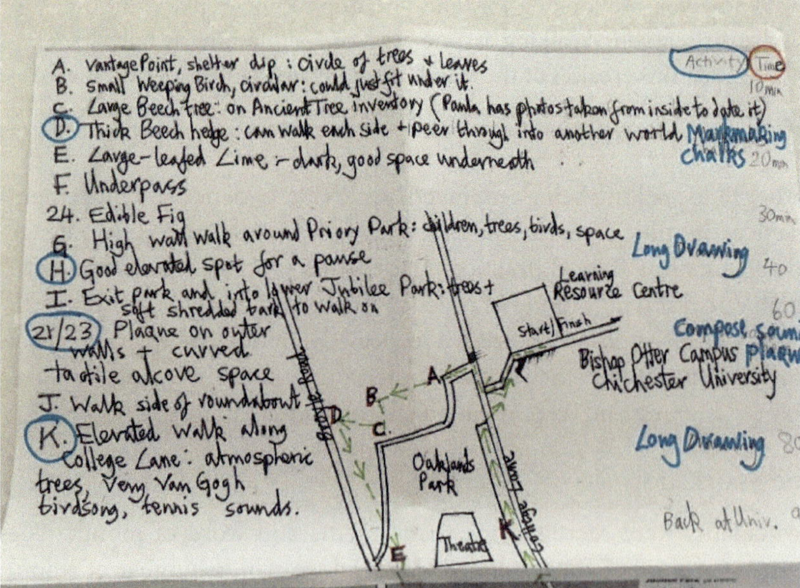

Tree Walk route designed by Rosie Montford

Planning for the workshop aligned with my own growing interest in creative arts practice as a means of engaging individuals with lived environments, in particular exploring nature spaces. This interest responds to a growing body of work in the sciences and environmental humanities exploring phenomena such as 'nature deficit disorder' (Kerret, Ronen & Orkibi, 2014) and 'plant blindness' defined as "…the inability to see or notice the plants in one's own environment" (Schussler & Wandersee, 1998). The potential for dance and performance work to draw attention to and engage individuals with trees and nature spaces plays out across the work of a number of artists such as Rosemary Lee's 'Calling Tree' (2016), French and Mottershead's 'Woodland' (2019), Annette Arlander's 'Stockholm Tree Calendar' (2019) and Nigel Stewart's 'The Dusk Wood' (2016). These examples provide a context for the workshop's design and implementation and evidence a growing sense of ecological and environmental concern within dance and performance practice that reflects broader themes of global environmental crisis.

The walk followed a circular route from the University campus and was designed by Rosie Montford in consultation with Chichester's tree warden prior to the workshop from which a walking map was developed that contained a variety of tree species, aural soundscapes and material textures (see previous page). Transitions between selected trees were conducted in silence to enable the movement, listening and drawing tasks to percolate and resonate with each individual on their own terms. Whilst the tasks were designed to bring attention to the trees' shape, placement, textures and features, they were also intended to bring about awareness of an embodied sense of self in relation to and emerging from each tree-body encounter from which a sense of co-existence might be proposed. As the author and artist Glennie Kindred suggests:

> Trees create an interface, and can be experienced through all our senses. They help us to expand into parts of ourselves that lie at the edge of our consciousness. When I am walking with the trees beside me I feel complete. Their wild beauty opens my heart and can move me to profound joy, and sometimes to tears. When I stand with them I breathe more deeply and become more rooted, and more fully present in the here and now. (2019: xvi)

Our first stop was a weeping birch tree. The tree offered a delicate canopy that drooped down to the ground and could be opened to one side like a curtain to create a temporary entrance for participants to pass through.

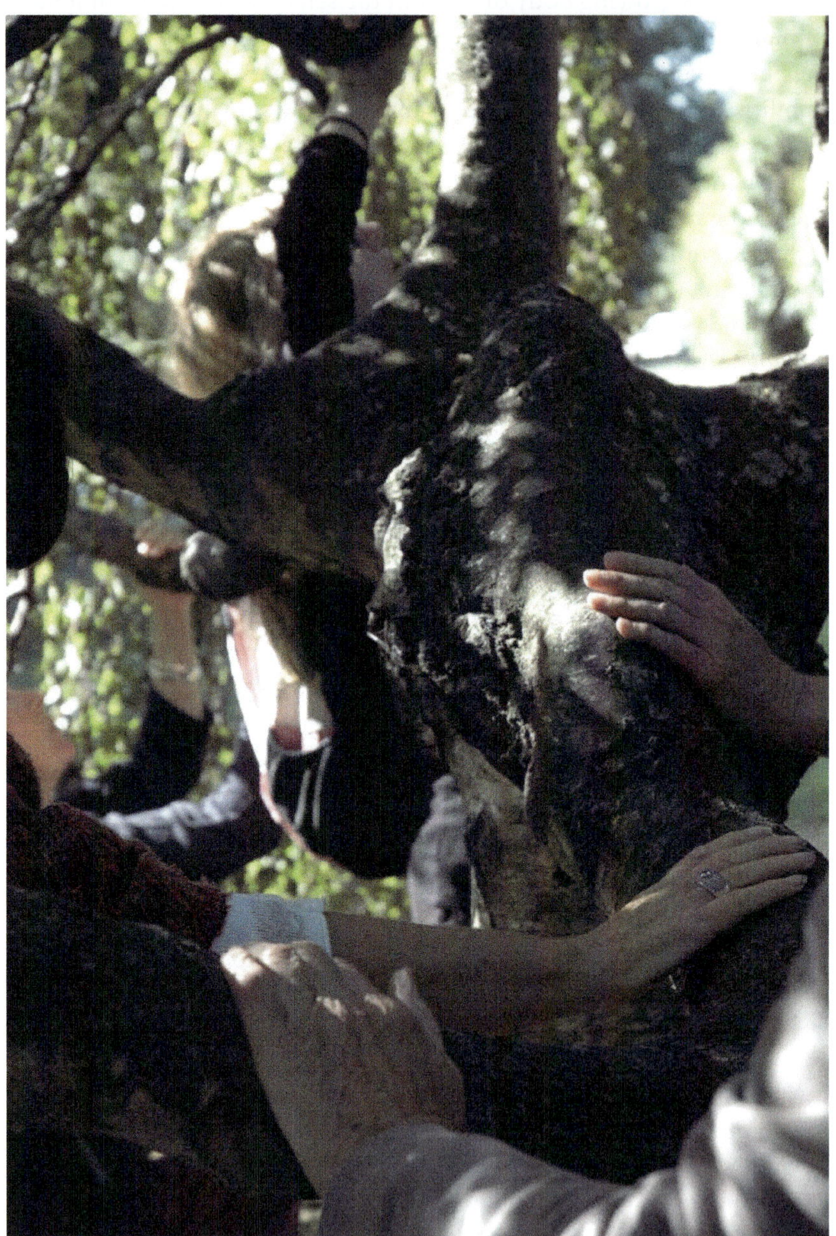

'Elephant's Trunk' Weeping Birch

Once inside the space we were enclosed within the canopy, which circled around its central structure. In my commentary the tree's trunk and interlaced branches were likened to an elephant's trunk and participants were invited to touch and engage with its leathery skin, to trace its forms with their hands and rest their bodies against its structure (see previous page). Following this intra-action we moved on to consider a large beech tree situated at the heart of a public park. The ancient beech is surrounded by a low protective fence framing the tree and creating a clearly defined border from which its size and scope can be contemplated. This arrangement informed the design of a short movement score in which participants were instructed to focus their attention on their solar plexus and employ a sense of 'looking' from their bodies emanating from this centre point. Participants were then instructed to walk the perimeter fence whilst maintaining a relational connection between their centre point and the tree. This task challenged participants to consider proportional relations and to explore felt senses of scale and size emanating from the body-tree engagement. Rosie then led participants in an experiential drawing exercise where they were encouraged to place their heads and peer into the dark interior of a beech hedge and listen to the sounds of this interior world (see below). Emerging from this immersive task, they were instructed to record their visual and aural encounters on a piece of black card using white chalk. These records were collected and used to construct a documentary 'score' that recorded and collated experiences and impressions encountered on the walk.

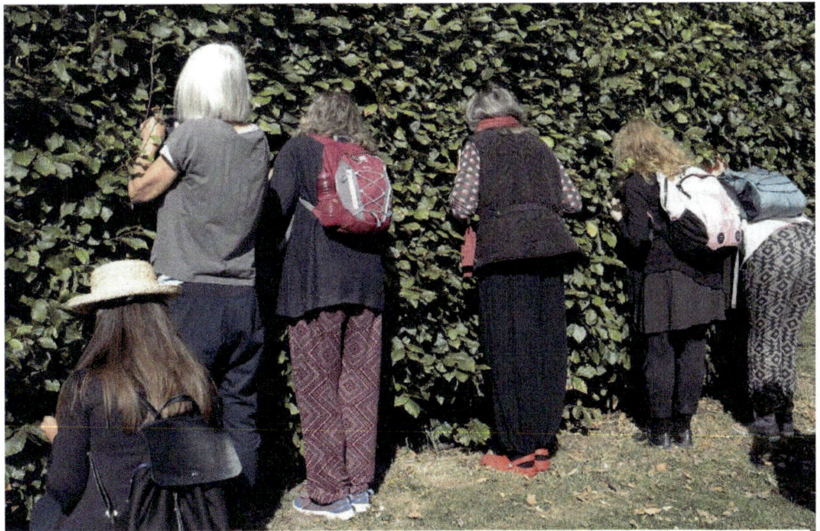

Beech-Hedge 'listening' and drawing task

The next stop *en route* took us to a large mulberry tree on the edge of the park where a more expressive movement task was set in motion. Participants were encouraged to trace the forms of the tree's winding branches with their arms and torsos and to allow this movement improvisation to gradually involve the whole body. From this task we moved, articulated and danced with the tree and with one another. The forms of twisted branches echoed through the contorted postures and flowing form of the dancers' movement patterns and their interlacing structures resonated through the groups' interwoven travelling patterns as a dance with the tree site gradually emerged. Following this danced episode we continued our walk into Chichester town centre and progressed along the city's wall walk to eventually arrive at a vantage point from which we stretched out a roll of paper forming our score and engaged in a collective wall rubbing and mark making responding to the brick and flint materials typical of the region. Crouched over the paper we collectively responded to the physical nature of the task and recorded our impressions of the site's sounds, materials and textures. Resuming our walk we circled the city's walls and rested against a giant leaning pine tree that provided a temporary space of contemplation. Individually we considered how our movement into and out of this exchange with the tree might be physically managed and considered and adapted our transitions accordingly. Collectively, bodies rolled into and out of the tree trunk support and hands, feet, backs and shoulders were molded into its contours and surfaces. Prior to returning to the University campus we reflected on our experiences by writing key words, thoughts and reflections on a series of cards that were collected and subsequently placed within our drawing score employed in the second part of the workshop on campus.

The design of tasks and activities employed on the tree walk drew on new materialist perspectives that challenge us to look closely into entangled human-world relations and consider what the immediately perceived life-world comprises. Haraway for example imagines a world of 'Terrapolis' in which 'companion species' engage in relentless processes of 'becoming with' a world in which "natures, cultures, subjects and objects do not pre-exist their intertwined worldings" (2016: 13). How such worlding processes encountered in embodied movement inquiry are articulated, reflected on and communicated through description, imagery, metaphor and theoretically informed perspectives requires careful handling, as Haraway warns:

> It matters what matters we use to think other matters with; it
> matters what stories we tell to tell other stories with; it matters
> what knots knot knots, what thoughts think thoughts, what
> descriptions describe descriptions, what ties tie ties. (ibid: 12)

In site-based body practice movement 'utterances' become the medium through which entwined worldings are produced, evidenced and (if required) communicated to others. Site-based body practice therefore calls for a considered and measured approach to movement research in which (in this instance) we move with the companion species of trees and related flora. This work requires concentration and focus on the intra-action at hand as opposed to the telegraphing of gratuitous expressive gestures or unrelated codified movement vocabulary that bears little relation to the nuances or subtleties of the body-site exchange. Tuning in to the affective vibrancy of the body-site exchange and the emerging moving with its complexity requires careful attunement and attention.

Haraway's work (and the work of new materialist thinkers such as Karen Barad, Stacy Alaimo, Bruno Latour and Iris Van der Tuin) calls into question the nature of matter itself, what we perceive and consider as human and non-human matter, what counts and *what matters* and, through doing so enables the fostering of new ontological dispositions towards the world and worlds at large. From these perspectives, the world, the body and their material actants are equally conceived as materially amorphous, unfinished and always on the move. Trees move, dance and communicate with each other and with the human actors who pass by, pause, linger and engage with tree time and space. This mobile perspective informs my reflection on the body-world intra-actions encountered through site-based body practice and facilitates the articulation of nuanced understandings emerging through the movement explorations born from kinaesthetic and corporeal mattering.

Embodied Reflection

Following our return to campus we moved into a dance studio where we attempted to reflect on the walk through the movement of our bodies through a series of tasks and exercises. This part of the event was designed to sediment the walk experience in some way, to imprint the experiential encounters within our embodied memory. In many ways we aspired to store or set this work down within the body as archive (Lepecki, 2010) by setting down layers, reinforcing experience and recalling sensation.

To begin this process Leslie Satin led us through a walking meditation where, collectively we walked back and forth from one side of the studio to the other in an act of physical re-call that engaged mind and body. In this task we not only recalled the event's central movement theme of walking but also reflected on the holistic, embodied nature of walking in general, as the movement artist and dance phenomenologist Sondra Fraleigh observes: "Most of the time, we take movement for granted; we just walk. But we can also walk consciously, concentrating on particular features as we go. The brain is not commanding the feet to move us forward. Walking is far more complex as involving the whole person" (2015: 66). In this seemingly simple task we brought the physical, automatic act of walking to our attention – heel, ball, toe, heel, ball, toe. Subsequently however, the simple complexity of this physical act became manifest – heel, ball toe, hip, transfer of weight, slight twist in the spine, connection of the shoulders, neck and head. Through embodied noticing we drew our attention in to observing and acknowledging the act of walking as a composite, whole body action connecting the heel of the foot to the crown of the head through a complex system of skeletal, muscular and fascia connections.

Following this meditation we returned to the drawing score we had made collectively throughout the walk. Comprising a series of sketches, wall rubbings, reflective drawings and written comments generated *en route* the score was laid out across the studio space as a device to instigate movement exploration. Through improvised dance we abstracted and amplified particular aspects or elements contained within the score. These spontaneous movement utterances responded to a range of features recorded on the paper including the pencil markings of texture, the record of shapes, forms and abstract references to energy, direction of travel and moments of stillness.

We used these markings as prompts to action and recall as we moved around the space, transferring the trace hieroglyphics into physicalised actions and movement explorations. In a sense, this task facilitated another way of knowing the walk – evaluating it from another angle. Transitioning from the real-world exploration outside the University campus and into the enclosed environment of the dance studio provided a physical and temporal space in which to process the affects and resonances of the walking practice. The relatively neutral white room offered sensory relief from the aural, visual and haptic stimulation encountered throughout the tree walk that, at times could have overwhelmed. The studio offered a space of reflection in which the affects of the practice could be acknowledged, noticed and processed through the body. Rather than rushing off into other modes of being and doing following the tree walk therefore, the studio time offered a more gentle re-entry into everyday modes of engaging with the world as we reflected on our experiences both through the movement practice and through a final group discussion.

Observing the movement explorations in the studio I began to question (in a fashion that owes a debt to Peggy Phelan and other theorists concerned with performance and ephemerality): What remains? What do we do with this experience once it has passed, how do we cling to its remnants and why – what purpose does re-call and the palimpsestic nature of these re-engagement tasks do here? Why did we (as a collection of artists) feel compelled to retain and preserve the 'walk as phenomenon' in this manner and what were we afraid of letting slip away? In some ways these are existential questions concerned with the preservation of experience and the capturing of a moment in time reflected in the requests from a number of parties (participants, facilitators, the Museum of Walking and the ubiquitous University publicity department) for photographs and sound recordings as markers of the walk and workshop providing evidence that this event took place.

However, as the requests mounted part of me remained resistant to this compulsion to document and record as I began to wonder why the ephemeral and phenomenological could not be left to lie, to sediment, to permeate and percolate within the body-self of the experiencer who had to physically be there, to attend and tend to the event, to acknowledge the walk itself, and its activities. The residual nature of this type of experience can only be known from the inside, from the doing and being and that, for me is more than enough, more than sufficient. Understandably perhaps, for others it is not, and the resonance of embodied experience alone is not a sufficient artifact, record or 'marker' of an event's event-ness. The cultural capital of the image and the documentation of an activity's reach and potential impact are important commodities that circulate around such events and mark their place within a broader, neoliberal event-experience economy.

Following this line of reflection, I was most interested in the participants' need to document – almost everyone asked to be sent pictures afterwards. This led me to question whether they were prioritising the visual record over the embodied and actually not trusting the corporeal over the ocular – an understandable anxiety in our contemporary 'selfie' obsessed visual culture. It was almost as if, without a visual marker of the event they wouldn't be able to remember it in the future and something of the outward shape and form of the event and its activities would be lost. Perhaps I needed to emphasise the corporeal, the sedimenting of embodied knowledge further as a means of processing the experience and employing embodied re-call as a method of remembering the event and its significance at a corporeal level. Perhaps I needed to do further work on articulating the ephemeral and encouraging others to access embodied knowledge as a vehicle through which they can tell of an event – or show physical echoes of it to an-other at a later stage supported by the visual record or image but not in place or in lieu of it.

To move towards a form of reflective conclusion, this work (and associated site-based body practice) is concerned with what dance and movement can do here, how it might bring us closer to environmental phenomena as a form of intervention or extra-daily practice. How might it encourage us to notice the world around us and gently foster a sense of environmental awareness and ethical responsibility? This work can encourage a form of messy exchange with the natural world and embolden us to reach beyond hermetically sealed sensibilities that discourage modes of touching unsanitised textures, surfaces and materials prevalent in both nature spaces and urban environments.

As a physical practice it encourages lingering, following circuitous routes and the exploration of movement patterns that contribute embodied modes of doing and being to the growing repertoire of walking arts practice. Dancing *en route*, dueting with trees, plants, textures and materials facilitates playful, sensuous and haptic exchanges within body-site intra-actions from which temporary worldings are formed, followed and subsequently, dissolved. Through these ephemeral moments of exchange we emerge with new-found knowledge and perhaps appreciation of often overlooked or ignored environmental features. We come to knowledge of other bodies, human and more-than human through their vibrant materiality that moves us, moves with us and shapes our perception of the world.

References

Barad, Karen (2007) *Meeting the Universe Half Way: Quantum Physics and the Entanglement of Matter and Meaning*, Duke Univ. Press

Fraleigh, Sondra (2015) *Moving Consciously: Somatic Transformations through Dance, Yoga and Touch*, Univ. of Illinois Press

Haraway, Donna (2016) *Staying With the Trouble: Making Kin in the Chthulucene*, Duke Univ. Press

Kerret, Dorit; Ronen, Tammi & Orkibi, Hod, 'Green Perspective for a Hopeful Future: Explaining Green Schools' Contribution to Environmental Subjective Well Being', *Review of General Psychology*, Vol. 18, No. 2, June 2014, pp. 82-88

Kindred, Glennie (2019) *Walking with Trees*, Permanent Publications

Lepecki, Andre (2010) 'The Body as Archive: Will to Re-enact and the Afterlives of Dances', *Dance Research Journal*, Vol. 42, issue 2, pp. 28-48

Schussler, Elisabeth & Wandersee, James (1998) 'Preventing Plant Blindness' *The American Biology Teacher* Vol. 61, No. 2, pp. 82-86

Solnit, Rebecca (2014) *Wanderlust: A History of Walking*, Granta Books

Walking with Elephants

Cathy Turner

Walking art, with its roots in *dérive* and *flâneurie*, conceptual art and nature writing, is necessarily self-conscious about the simple activity of walking. It is perhaps indicative of the sedentary and alienated nature of European culture that this everyday action is experienced as redemptive or resistant, as the newly-liberated psychogeographer unpicks the urban fabric, reenchants fictionalised spaces, transgresses boundaries and enjoys "A sense that they are once again a player in their own story; an artist on their own canvas" (Smith, 2016).

In his essay on 'Walking and Subjectivity' (2016), Phil Smith writes of the ways that walking has become an escape from the algorithmic takeover of a public self, in a culture of "self-exposure and mass intimacy", and that the 'psycho' in 'psychogeography' has become ever more important as the walker is empowered to re-possess a self overwhelmed by the spectacular media of late capitalism. Walking is recognised as an escape from the desk, both potentially life-transforming, and an activity that might be slipped between shopping trips. Written as an address to a conference on 'Asylum Topographies' the paper notes its contextual emphasis on the individual and concludes with some speculations on group subjectivities. It does, however, articulate the individualist allure of 'disrupted walking'.

In his essay, 'Psychogeography adrift' (2015), Christopher Collier suggests that during the 1990s, radical walking sought to avoid the risk of individualism and relativism through "innovative forms of collectivity", as Smith's essay would seem to confirm, two decades on. After Brian Holmes, Collier describes these loose networks as "collective phantoms" which aim "to found a deterritorialised resistive practice", yet he concludes that they might, despite this, "function simply as a mirror of the networked liberalism they [attempt] to oppose" (Collier 2015: 142). The problem, as Collier describes it, is the tension between the desire to provide 'structural antagonism' to Capitalism, while also being situated outside a leftist programme as a negative withdrawal, even a hidden and internalised alternative space: "Something subjective, something un-sharable, unexplainable" (Collier 2015: 143; Smith, 2016: n.p.). The negative and resistant quality of the *dérive* is in tension with any form of programmatic political organisation. Moreover, while the subjective significance of the performative experience is undeniable, I argue that the *dérive*'s self-identification with subjectivity cut loose from societal structures is dependent on illusion, and often on privilege.

There is a geographical bias to this walking discourse, which presupposes walking as taking place mainly in the interstices of the cultural and professional structures imposed upon us (both class and gender privilege is frequently implicit, as Dee Heddon and I have pointed out (2010, 2012)). Walking art emphasises the anarchic and disruptive, and has been historically disinclined to make wider reference to labour, care, procession or pilgrimage (it is "pilgrimage-*like*" Smith suggests (2016: n.p., my italics)). These latter types of walking are prevalent in parts of the world where urban dwellers are so predominantly pedestrians that this status is not significant in itself. In terms of species, too, there has been little consideration of other creatures who walk with us, despite animals having been our travelling companions for millennia. This raises the question, at the very least, of what can be learned from the culturally sanctioned walking that occurs in contexts where mythic and artistic spaces are entwined with others which are more problematic and even oppressive.

I will consider walking with elephants: specifically the walking that occurs in relation to the Vrischikolsavam, an eight-day Hindu festival at the Sree Poornathrayeesa Temple in Tripunithura, Kerala, which opens the festival season in late November. I draw on the work of the research network 'The Politics of Performance on the Urban Periphery in South India', which comprised researchers from performance, ethology and sociology[1]. In observing the Vrischikolsavam, we were particularly concerned to learn about the non-human actors and their keepers. This chapter is based on observation and interviews between our project team (Anindya Sinha, Jerri Daboo, Sharada Srinivasan and myself) and those directly involved in the festival, including network participant and NIAS doctoral student, elephant biologist Sreedhar Vijayakrishnan.

---

[1] This research network 2018-19, comprised researchers from the University of Exeter, UK and the National Institute of Advanced Studies (NIAS), Bengaluru, India. It was funded by the Arts and Humanities Research Council through the Global Challenges Research Fund.

The Vrischikolsavam is famous for its line-up of caparisoned elephants who process within the temple, with the effigy of the deity held by the elephant in the middle, accompanied by the jubilant music of the *panchari melam*. More than 200 artists participate in this *melam* with percussive instruments and horns, with each session lasting for about three to three and a half hours. The procession takes place every day of the festival in the morning and evening.

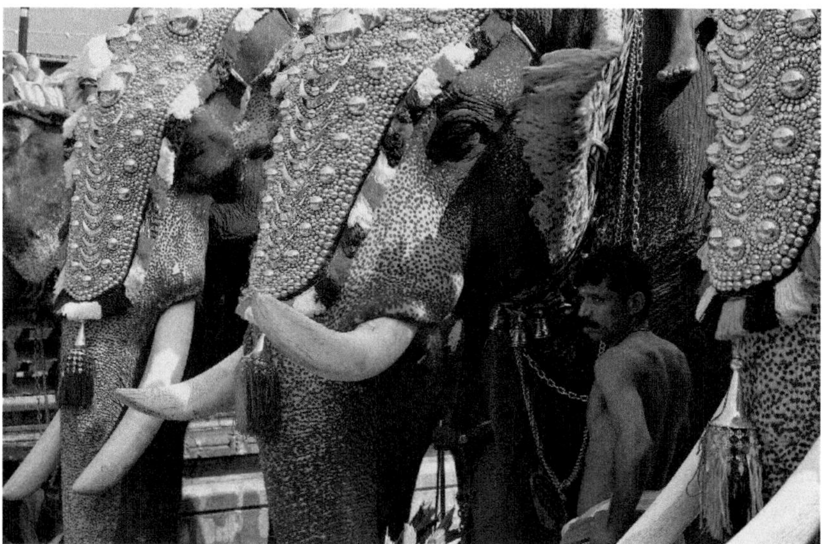

It would be neo-colonial appropriation to consider this as 'walking art', but there is art in it, and there is walking in it. This essay proposes that such a festival, drawing on traditions of Asian elephant domestication from 4,500 BCE, and perhaps 600 years of elephants in this temple, demonstrates the way that creative, communal and coercive spaces may be simultaneously produced through walking. When spaces of spiritual/ artistic practice, spaces of spectacle and everyday spaces overlap to this extent, it is hard to see any aspect of this walking as resistant or radical[2]. On the other hand, we should also note the creative, spiritual and

---

[2] However Vikash Singh (2015) argues that young, destitute male pilgrims find the space of pilgrimage to be one in which they can acquire performative status, resisting everyday erasure by global neoliberalism, despite the admitted right-wing ideological appropriation of pilgrimage in general by Hindu Nationalists. Singh's argument for a nuanced attention to the particular individuals while simultaneously acknowledging their entanglement in ideological frameworks informs my thinking here.

communal expression apparent within such institutional, but extra-daily contexts, and that while their more coercive and exploitative aspects might need to be dismantled, there is much to be learned about spatial transformation, the integration of community and the bond with the non-human, in positive as well as negative senses.

The elephant is a 'companion animal' in the sense that Donna Haraway intends, when she writes of relationships between humans and dogs. According to Haraway, such relationships demand, "the recognition that one cannot know the other or the self, but must ask in respect for all time who and what are emerging in relationship…" (2003: 49). Alongside this question of 'who' and 'what', one might also ask what spaces emerge. On a depleted and crowded planet, the answers to such a question have implications for the literal living and working spaces of people and creatures. However, this question, like Haraway's, cannot be given a stable and straightforward answer, because the relationship between humans and elephants is neither. Anthropologist Piers Locke observes of Nepalese practices, that the elephant handlers, the mahouts, relate to the elephants in shifting dynamics, where elephants are sometimes viewed as animals, lesser beings to be controlled; sometimes as persons, as equals; and sometimes as gods, to be venerated. He writes:

> Only the dynamic of companionship is balanced, the others place human and elephant in converse hierarchies, making a handler a master in one, and a devotee in another. How then might one make sense of the shifting states of being that mahouts attribute to their elephants? Here, the metaphor of the kaleidoscope might be useful for thinking about the fluid manner by which the relative salience of these attributed states continually shift. (Locke, 2016: 166).

These findings also hold good for the Keralan mahouts and elephants, so I will borrow his categories, though my focus is on the dynamism of spaces – practised, spectacular and social – in this kaleidoscopic shifting between one and another.

Gods

Even when there are no festival processions, the temple at Tripunithura uses at least one elephant daily, in ritual procession, *sivali*, carrying the idol around the sanctum, twice in the morning and twice in the evening. The idol represents Vishnu in the avatar of Santhanagopala Murthy.

During the festival, as we descended from viewing Kathakali (dance theatre), in the early hours of the morning, we witnessed the single elephant who marks time in this way, festival or no festival, accompanied by a small band of devotees.

When we ask a bystander at the festival what the elephants mean to him, his answer is simple and direct: Ganesha. Ganesha the benevolent, elephant-headed son of Shiva, whose image has mediated the human-elephant relationship for centuries.

What does it mean, to circumambulate? This is not the A to B walking of purpose, nor the deliberate evasion of purpose in the *dérive*, nor the sustained walking of pilgrimage, though closest to that. One story relates it back to the cheeky success of Ganesha himself, who outwitted his brother Karthikeya in a competition set by his parents to race around the world, by circumambulating his mother and father and claiming that they, themselves, were the world. The god is our world, so we revolve around him.

The festival itself is this practice writ large – more elephants, more music, a slower pace, a more relentless and ecstatic obligation. Slowly the elephants move in the temple precincts. Slowly the crowd backs with them. And slowly, such slow walking and its unaccommodating music produces the temple as world.

Haraway writes of the "negative way of knowing" God, God known only as *not* the projection of one self. Though drawing on Catholic experience, this is parallel to the Vedic concept of 'neti neti', that Brahman, the divine principle is 'neither this nor that', to be discovered not through recognition, but by recognising what it is not. Haraway suggests that "Another name for that kind of negative knowing is love." The strangeness of the sacred is epitomised by the elephants in spaces of awed contiguity and joyous celebration, pressing in under the tusks, bugles blowing, arms raised to beat time.

No doubt, the meaning of the event is lost on the elephant. What is shared is practice, a practice in which the command to process is unavoidable, for both human and companion animal, albeit differently obligated.

It is hard to know what the elephant's experience of the festival is like, or to what extent it varies between individual animals. Should they wish to resist the festivities, they could do so, and indeed, there are instances of elephants running amok (for instance, in this temple in 2017 (Staff reporter, *The Hindu*, 2017)). Such reactions can often be prevented by attention to elephant mood and welfare, however. The elephants we saw appeared placid, their swishing ears seeming to keep time with the drums. While this might be fanciful, retired mahout, Bhaskaran Nair, told us that his own elephant, Chandrasekaran, used to sway in time to the music. Another always responded to entering these temple precincts with an odd dancing motion, never repeated elsewhere. Some elephants, he said, seem to enjoy being looked at, others just enjoy the sugar cane (Nair & Varma, 2018).

Despite this, there was consensus in our interviews that 'the elephant would not choose the festival' (Nair & Varma, 2018; Varma, 2018). That there is restraint and tolerance is, perhaps, all one can really ask of a god.

Animals

Restraint is different, though, from being restrained.

The News Minute reported in November 2018 the death of a temple elephant owned by the Sri Poonrathrayeesa Seva Sangham:

> Once considered the pride of Thripunithura Poornatharayeesa Temple in Kerala, Sreehari the elephant met with a tragic death in September. Unknown to many, the elephant had lived through months of misery, before finally succumbing to internal and external injuries. When the autopsy report concluded that Sreehari had died due to sepsis from injuries, it sparked a furore among elephant lovers.

This is too often the cruel reality where the elephants are treated as objects to be exploited and traded, whether the accusations of insurance fraud are valid or not.

Even where the cruelty may not be deliberate, it is perhaps even more widespread. All elephants are shackled by law and injuries are often the result. The shortage of mahouts for the festival circuit means that untrained young men are employed, moving employment frequently. Lacking time or knowledge to build trust, short cuts are taken to gaining the creature's obedience, through excessive use of violence. This lack of knowledge leads to poor hygiene and resulting infections.

Well-meaning moves to reduce cruelty have had unwanted results. The insistence that elephants must be transported in trucks, to remove the stress of walking, has had a negative effect; transportation-led stress is estimated to increase overall stress by up to 350% (Laws et al, 2007), opening the elephant up to exploitation at long distances and causing a lack of mobility and impaction (Vijayakrishnan & Sinha 2019).

Given such scenarios, one could view the Keralan festival parade as a simulation, merely a procession of captives where wounds are disguised and backstage areas hidden. This could be described as a commercialised space of spectacular show, where a festival equals profit to the detriment of elephants and mahouts alike (for these elephant handlers often share the conditions of the elephants). While this particular festival is long established, it takes place now in a context which sees the burgeoning of new parades, fed by the needs of elephant owners wishing for status and profit. Commercialisation and overwork are rife. Twenty-four elephants died in Kerala last year alone, though Vijayakrishnan and Sinha posit that the use of trucks could be the biggest killer.

On the other hand, it is important to dig deeper than the headlines. Further enquiry revealed that the Sri Poornathrayeesa Seva Sangham was an advisory committee at the temple, and not directly associated with the temple management. Srihari was taken away for timber logging and was, at that time, seldom used for works related to Tripunithura temple. He died of an infection that resulted from wounds inflicted by an inexperienced mahout, against whom a case has been registered. Some of those we spoke to actually took over his treatment during his final days and gave him the best possible medical support. Medicines were brought from different parts of Kerala and transported to the elephant's treatment site for more than a month, almost on a daily basis. Unfortunately, elephant medicine and surgery in India is still in need of development, and it was too late (Private correspondence, anonymity requested, October 2019).

Informed by the captive elephant management regulations put forth by the Government, and increasing cognisance about welfare conundrums, improvements have been made. Roofing has been brought in to shade the animals. There has been an increase in the number of elephants on call, so that their participation can be rotated. Advice has been given on diet. Such moves are welcome, though insufficient, treating the elephant generically, adjusting the space according to rule.

Vijayakrishnan, significantly, is not an outsider, but a biologist who grew up in the festival community. He counsels attention to elephant individuality – a move to line up the elephants not according to height but compatibility. Another important factor is for the keepers to look for evidence of sickness, irritability or animosity and to exclude such elephants for the time being – similarly so when a creature is in *musth* (a periodic hormonal state, producing aggressive behaviour in males). In doing this, the modified festival space combines the biological view with interspecies communication, liable to more flexible judgements than scientific rule in the abstract.

In his open letter of 2015 Vijayakrishnan points to the impracticality of a straightforward ban, and the lack of knowledge such a position implies, instead advocating grass roots understanding, regulation, better training of mahouts and a slow phasing out of the practice. He concludes:

> We need to work towards changing these practices slowly and with reasoned arguments based on ground realities, backed by the science of management. We cannot expect an overnight change. But we must start and engage over a long-term to bring about these changes (Vijayakrishnan, 2015).

Persons

In Vijayakrishnan's understanding, the elephants are considered not only as other, as animal or god, but as persons, equivalent, if not the same.

The mahout-elephant relationship, when sustained and developed over years, is remarkable as a familial bond, often as great or greater than that of the same-species family, and taking more of the mahout's time.

Prior to the widespread use of trucks, elephants and mahouts would walk together more frequently. They walked between assignments, or to look for work. Trust developed between these individuals, of necessity, for an elephant that does not trust the mahout can soon dispense with him. We were told stories of walking and trust. An old mahout, Gopalan Nair, permitted to lean on the tusks of his companion elephant, Koodalattupuram, and it is also alleged that the elephant took care of the mahout, carrying him home after he had drunk a little too much toddy (Narayanan, 2011). Another who lay down to sleep by the roadside, prompting the elephant to lie down to sleep beside him, both awakening to a crowd of astonished bystanders, for this is not what elephants do.

Elephants were also important to the identity of Tripunithura, as they were led house to house to gather food during festival-time, rather than the food being carried to the temple. Such a mingling of elephants and people knitted that community together as one that included both. "What I got from the elephant was something very special", says Prasanna Varma, remembering her childhood "I can't put my finger on it. I get a lot from the elephant. It doesn't from me" (Varma, 2018).

Despite this rueful admission, it is clear that such an elephant-human natureculture tends towards less elephant-human conflict, whatever its limitations for ideals of the wild elephant (e.g. Baskaran et al, 2011). It reaches towards an understanding of shared *dandi* (wild elephant paths, also used by humans) and the potential for thinking human-elephant spaces together, rather than as ideally adjacent (e.g. Shaffer et al, 2019).

"Would you like to meet an elephant?" we were asked, and found, to our surprise that there was an elephant in the back garden. His name was Padmanabhan.[3]

The entanglement of walked spaces

The spaces that seem to be emerging through this festival-related walking include: a practiced space of restrained otherness in the walk around a sanctum; a spectacular, staged, commercialised parade space of hidden pain and occasional cruelty; a social street space where co-personhood and trust can exist.

Yet all these spaces are simultaneous. They are not separate, but co-existent, partially entangled and convergent with one other. The artistic (musical) component blurs, on the one hand, into ritual, and on the other, into the everyday, while also contributing to the spectacle (in all senses). To adapt any one of these spaces, or these modes of walking, or the artistry of each, is to adapt them all, and must be done with the care of a surgeon, whose cut endangers the whole body.

This makes it difficult. Policies fail when they do not take account of these difficulties, however well-meaning they are. Attempts to limit risk and exploitation can produce alienation and disrespect. Attempts to prohibit practices implicated in cruelty limit corresponding reciprocal practices, and damage the economic interdependencies of some of the poorest humans as well as elephants.

The challenge is to unpick and subvert objectifying and commodifying practices, while understanding the knock-on impact on delicate naturecultures, and not to presuppose an ideal state of unsullied wildness, or that innocent humanity can be obtained by restoring all elephants to wild forests, and re-training the mahouts. However desirable it might seem to take both out of the temple, it is firstly unfeasible in the

---

[3] His full title is Paramekkavu Sree Padmanabhan. Originally from Bihar, he is one of the largest elephants owned by the Paramekkavu Bagavathi Temple, Thrissur, Kerala.

short term, and secondly, there would be losses here too, in terms of creativity, knowledge, community and even the inter-relationship between species. It would be contemptuous not to listen to all those involved, including paying close attention to the elephants.

To return to walking art, this example demonstrates what Appadurai describes as 'the production of locality', entailing the 'imaginary work' of 'ordinary persons'. He writes 'I saw…that locality itself was a creation that required effort, imagination, deliberation and persistence' (2013:254). According to Appadurai, locality is constructed through customs, habits and practices (from the earliest 'tool-making, body art, ritual creativity, storytelling, and mythmaking of which we might well be envious' (2013:255)), amounting to an informal design of place. If we are serious about re-imagining our world through walking art and psychogeography, we must take account of the ways in which it is already walked, creatively, recognising the performative significance of walking even in conservative settings. Spectacular spaces are entangled with communal ones. We are entangled with others, human or otherwise. These entanglements are the products of inescapable histories and political realities. There is no independent, quasi-heroic walking. Therein lies both our tragedy and our opportunity for acknowledging the multiplicity and paradoxes of walking, by seeking mutual understanding and collectively-realised alternatives.

Acknowledgements

Many thanks to Sreedhar Vijayakrishnan and Anindya Sinha for their guidance, and to Anujan Varma, Prasanth Varma, Prasanna Varma and Bhaskaran Nair for their knowledge and hospitality.

References

Appadurai, Arjun (2013) *The Future as Cultural Fact: Essays on the Global Condition*, Verso

Baskaran, N; Varma, Surendra; Sar, C.K. & Sukumar, Raman (2011) 'Current Status of Asian Elephants in India', *Gajah*, 35, 47-54

Collier, Christopher (2015) 'Psychogeography Adrift: Negotiating Critical Inheritance', in *Walking Inside Out: Contemporary British Psychogeography*, ed. Tina Richardson, pp. 131-146

Haraway, Donna (2003) *The Companion Species Manifesto: Dogs, People and Significant Otherness*, Prickly Paradigm Press

Heddon, Dee & Turner, Cathy (2010) 'Walking women: interviews with artists on the move'. *Performance Research*, 15(4), pp. 14–22

_____ (2012) 'Walking women: shifting the tales and scales of mobility'. *Contemporary Theatre Review*, 22(2), pp. 224-236

Kavera, Megha (2018) 'Elephant's death in Kerala forces probe: Was a jumbo killed for insurance claims?', *The News Minute*, 03 Nov, found at bit.ly/wnm27 (Accessed 04 Jan 2020)

Laws, Nicole; Ganswindt, Andre; Heistermann, Michael; Harris, Moira; Harris, Stephen & Sherwin, Chris (2007) 'A case study: Fecal corticosteroid and behavior as indicators of welfare during relocation of an Asian elephant.' *Journal of Applied Animal Welfare Science* 10: 349-358

Locke, Piers (2016) 'Animals, Persons, Gods' in Locke, Piers and Buckingham, Jane (eds), *Conflict, Negotiation and Coexistence: Re-Thinking Human-Elephant Relations in South Asia*, Oxford Univ. Press, 159-177

Nair, Bhaskaran and Varma, Anujan (2018) unpublished interview with Anindya Sinha, Sreedhar Vijayakrishnan, Jerri Daboo and Cathy Turner, Tripunithura, Kerala, December

Narayanan, K. R. (2011) 'Irinjarakuda KoodalmaniKyam Temple: The Tusker Tales', found at bit.ly/wnm28 (Accessed 09 Jan 2020)

Shaffer, L Jen; Khadka, Kapil K.; Van Den Hoek, Jamon & Naithani, Kusum J. (2019) 'Human-Elephant Conflict: A Review of Current Management Strategies and Future Directions', Frontiers of Ecology and Evolution, 11 Jan, found at bit.ly/wnm29 (Accessed 04 Jan 2020)

Singh, Vikash (2015) *Uprising of the Fools: Pilgrimage as Moral Protest in Contemporary India*, Stanford Univ. Press

Smith, Phil (2016) 'Walking and Subjectivity', talk given at Asylum Topographies, Bethlem Hospital, 22nd September. Found at bit.ly/wnm35 (Accessed 07 Jan 2020)

Staff reporter (2017) 'Elephant Runs Amok', *The Hindu,* November 24th, found at bit.ly/wnm43 (Accessed 08 Jan 2020)

Varma, Prasanna (2018) unpublished interview with Anindya Sinha, Sreedhar Vijayakrishnan, Jerri Daboo and Cathy Turner, Tripunithura, Kerala, December

Vijayakrishnan, Sreedhar & Anindya Sinha (2019) 'Human-Captive Elephant Relationships in Kerala: Historical Perspectives and Current Scenarios', Gajah, 50, 29-35

Being Horse: walking as an impossible beast

James Frost and Sonia Overall

'Being Horse' (2019) is a film that places its viewer beneath the sackcloth of a hooden horse. The film articulates the experience of walking as a horse effigy, of becoming a creature which is no longer human but only partially horse-like. Orignally shot as continuous footage of a procession, using a camera mounted within a hooden horse, the final film draws upon elements of our individual forms of creative practice and research to produce a new collaborative piece that serves as both documentary and poetry film.

The Hooden Horse

Anthropomorphised animals and human-beast hybrids are a frequent feature of Morris sides and associated processions, but the hooden horse is a particularly regional Kentish figure. A hooden horse has a wooden head with an articulated jaw which shuts with a loud crack. The head is mounted on a pole, which is held by its operator who is covered in a large cloth, often of hessian. It is this cloth or 'hood' to which the old Kentish term 'hooden' most likely refers. The hooden horse was used in the East Kent 'hoodening' tradition, which was well documented throughout the 19th century and into the 20th century (Maylam, 1909). This was a house-calling custom at Christmas, and today several revival hoodening groups continue the custom in pubs and similar venues around Kent.

Although associated with Christmas, hooden horses had begun to appear in summer festivities in Kent during the 1930s, and May celebrations from at least the late 1940s, often alongside Morris dancers (Frampton, 1995: 744-745; Frampton, 2006: 65-66). The hooden horse of the 'Being Horse' film was made in 1976 by a Morris dancer, Jim 'The Ram' Bywater, for the revival of the Whitstable May Day parade. The horse fell out of use but was refurbished by James in early 2005 and reinstated for that year's May Day parade.

James shot the 'Being Horse' film footage while operating the horse during the 2018 Whitstable May Day parade. On the footage, through the sackcloth, one can make out momentary glimpses of other characters from the procession. Boris the Bear, performed in 2018 by a dark and hairy-costumed Trefor Owen, dances and makes mischief by sneaking up on and startling bystanders, growling and looming ominously at performers and audience alike. The second half of the event features Jack-in-the-Green, a (necessarily tall) performer who walks carrying an enveloping framework of foliage, flanked by assistants. From the appearance of the Jack onwards, two Morris dancers representing 'Robin' and 'Marian' become the key focus, leading the various Morris sides and musicians towards a fair at the 18th-century folly of Whitstable Castle. On the film footage, these figures can be seen from the point of view of the hooden horse as they circle it, move past in procession or dance ahead.

The Whitstable May Day parade was photographed in 1912. The Jack-in-the-Green is pictured and was apparently burnt at the site of a maypole as the culmination of the procession. A costumed male and female character dance in front of the Jack, presumably Robin and Marian (Doel et al: 25-27). It would be tempting to see this snapshot of a tradition as a vestige of the May or Robin Hood games of the early modern period: 'hobby horses' are well documented in May Games from the sixteenth century onwards alongside Morris dancers, a Summer Lord, King of May or Robin Hood and a Maid Marian, and often involving procession (Hutton, 1994; Cawte, 1978). However, the term hobby horse tends to describe a horse effigy worn around the waist with the operator as a literal rider. There is no evidence that the two agents of chaos we now see at Whitstable – the hooden horse and Boris the bear – were involved in the pre-WW1 custom. Rather, these two beasts appear to be revivalist additions that have now become part of the 'traditional' retinue of the procession.

The character of the horse

Like Boris the bear, the hooden horse is a badly-behaved creature given license to roam beyond the central body of the procession, within which the dancers and musicians must move together as connected units. Both James and Sonia have inhabited the horse at different times and have a long-standing relationship with the Whitstable May Day parade. Sonia's first experience of the procession was in the role of Marian, back in the late 1990s; as a Morris dancer into the 2000s; once as the horse, and more recently as a musician. Aside from Sonia's horse outing, James has undertaken the role of the horse annually since its reinstatement in 2005. This combined experience constitutes not only some site-specific knowledge of the processional route and its changing aspect over several years, but also an embodied knowledge of what it is to walk and perform in the parade, in costume or under sackcloth, traversing its different terrains in varying weather conditions. It has also led to the emergence of a specific character for the hooden horse, and one which is more dynamic than the rather static creature of Christmas hoodening performances. Our beast is unpredictable, barely contained by the expectations of public behaviour, and likely to run amok.

It is not that a particular character has been imposed upon the horse over this time, but rather that the horse's attitudes, mannerisms and behaviours have emerged through the investment of repeated performance – of walking-as horse. There is a playful mischief to the horse's engagement with the environment, making it feel at times like a reckless puppy or physically emboldened infant. The horse's chaotic behaviour has been partially tempered with the introduction of a stable-lad handler, our son Rowan, since 2016, introducing a new character to the parade that echoes the roles of 'rider' and 'wagoner' in the hoodening tradition. Further enriching of the hooden horse's character has come through our own hoodening practice and performances, including those with the Canterbury Hoodeners, featuring James as horse, Sonia as musician or wagoner and Rowan as rider.

There is also a sinister undertone to the hooden horse connected to its otherness and hybridity. Although it does not have the stately eeriness of its Welsh cousin the Mari Lwyd, with its ghostly horse-skull head, the hooden horse is nonetheless a weird and unsettling figure. Public reactions to the hooden horse vary, from amusement, to fear, to denial, as we will discuss further below.

Walking as hooden horse

Within the horse the performer can see their own feet, but has restricted visibility and a limited sense of the surrounding environment. The performer's feet are, notably, the only human element visible to the public. While inside the horse, James is acutely aware of his own movements but unable to see clearly. On the outside, from the perspective of the procession, Sonia can witness the horse's interactions with its handler and the public, and wider responses to the horse's appearance and antics.

Given these restrictions, how does the hooden horse navigate its terrain? At the beginning of the procession, the horse follows road markings. It walks in a space forbidden to pedestrians: the centre of the road. It navigates distances with some visual clues and by listening to environmental sounds. It takes small detours onto the pavement to snap at greengrocers' produce, to sit at a bus stop, or to jump on and off a static bus. It is pulled back to the centre of the road, partly by the stable-lad handler leading it by the reins, and partly by its responsibility to the procession. In earlier outings, the horse would run back into and through the lines of dancers, but now that it has a handler this movement has been restricted. The horse continues to steer around obstacles, street furniture, unmoveable members of the public, alarmed small children, and dogs who feel threatened enough to see off this strange bipedal horse-monster with their barking.

James began documenting the experience of 'being' the hooden horse in an ethnographic diary as part of his ongoing practice research. This extract gives a sense of the horse's character, managing movement and some of the physical discomforts and restrictions involved in performing as the horse:

> I enter the disorientating twilight world under the sackcloth; I become invisible. All that is seen from outside is an unpredictable creature… I have a sense of the space around me but not of objects very close, including my handler. I become a body without arms: I am still bipedal, but with a neck that I can extend and retract. So, nothing really like a horse. I am a monstrous hybrid form, made from the materials of farm and stable with leather ears, hobnail teeth and woollen mane. I am cantankerous and skittish, unpredictable and preening. I communicate by snapping and stamping. I quietly whisper instructions to my handler about slowing down or steering a certain way, or approaching a family. I gauge the distance from the dancers by sound, and will speed up or slow down accordingly.

> (Diary entry, 1 May 2017, in Frost, 2016-2020)

Revisiting the diary alongside the filmed footage of 2018 prompted the idea for a collaborative project, which might further explore and express the hooden horse's point of view and character. The tension of external and internal was central to the development of the final film. As the 'one within', James performs being and walking-as the hooden horse. Sonia's walking-writing practice uses ambulatory writing methods to explore concepts of walking-with, walking-in and walking-as characters (Overall, 2019). 'Being Horse' draws upon these complementary practices in an attempt to offer the viewer a first-person experience of walking-as a hooden horse.

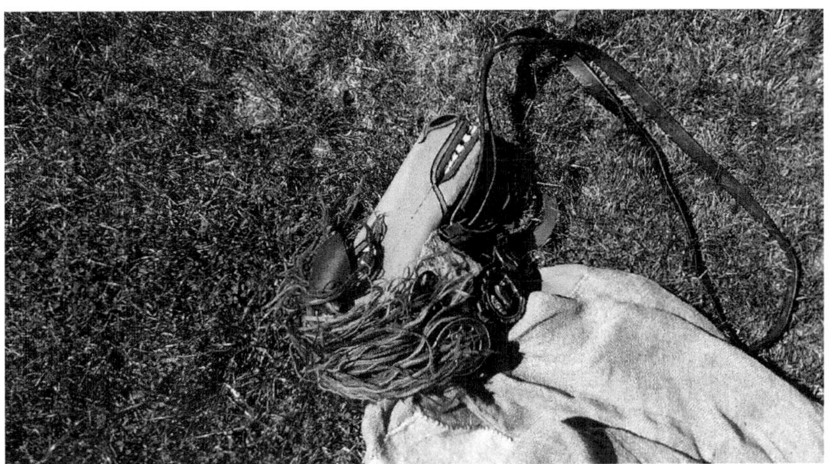

Making the film

The film began with the footage shot during the May parade, an experiment in recording something of the performer's visual experience from within the horse.

> I spent Sunday morning trying to attach a small Lumix camera to the horse's pole without it hampering the operation or obviously abtruding through the fabric. I tried unsuccessfully to gaffer tape a tripod to it before screwing the camera to a block of wood. I experimented and was happy with the recording but found that the camera display screen kept coming and going. Getting this to work was my main concern on Monday morning so I forgot to decorate myself with badges. It is the hottest May since the 1940s, it feels like high summer. I tend to rate whether we have had a good or bad spring by the weather on this May procession; however only a week ago the rain wouldn't stop and much of Kent was flooded. I think about how much this event punctuates my year. It anchors my perception of the seasons with winter before and summer ahead. The procession is on schedule, several attempts and I get the camera working.
>
> (Diary entry, 7 May 2018, in Frost, 2016-2020)

The resulting footage captured that 'disorientating twilight world' from within the hooden horse sackcloth, where flashes of light bring people and places momentarily into focus, only to disappear again beyond the weave of the hessian cover. Sudden jolting stops when meeting an obstacle, scampering forays beyond the central procession, the tentative steps along a narrow harbour wall and the regular bipedal sway of walking in time to music were all evident in the footage. Sound on the footage caught footfalls and the responsive snapping of the horse's jaw: as James noted of the snap in his diary, "I don't think about it at all really, but it is reactionary like a dog barking when it sees things that threaten it" (ibid).

The next challenge was to access and articulate the horse's ambulatory thoughts and feelings – to explore the inner world of this strange creature. What is in the mind's eye of the hooden horse? What might it sound like, and what would it make of the world around it?

Drawing on James's diary, a rough edit of the film footage, and her own experience as the horse, Sonia experimented with writing text using the first-person voice of the horse. This resulted in a body of prose poetry that gives voice to the otherwise voiceless creature, allowing the performed object to speak independently of the performer. The text reflects the press of walking, of footfalls in time to music, and of continuous forward movement, emphasising the inevitability of the advancing procession and the horse's part within this:

> I am a swaying pillar of sackcloth moving in steady time. I am coming towards you. I am immoveable. I go where I will….
>
> I am coming. Watch me, the prow of a ship, pressing a path.

> ('Being Horse', 2019)

The hooden horse is only seen from the outside at the end of the film, when the performer (and camera) are removed and the horse is viewed as a prone, lifeless effigy on a patch of grass. Preceding this reveal, the physical appearance of the horse is conveyed through moments of self-awareness in the text, countering the otherwise exclusively internal, first-person-viewer experience. This gives some context to the unseen figure that the viewer effectively inhabits while watching the film. As noted in James's diary, the materials of the hooden horse are those of the stable-yard, but when performed, they are given anatomical life, capable of sensory experience.

My flanks are creased. My mane is a tangle of yarn. Hawthorn
blossom hangs, flesh-and-honey sweet, at my leather ears. I taste
the rust of the sea between hobnail teeth.

('Being Horse', 2019)

The text also addresses the agency of the horse as an inhabited or
occupied form in relation to the performer inside it. The horse has will
and movement but is reliant upon its performing 'other' to carry out its
chosen actions. In the text, the human operator is the mechanically
labouring body, the horse the elevated mind, conscious of these actions
yet removed from them.

The one within cannot see its feet: tread carefully. Its arms grow
numb with weight and lack of use. Sweat gathers in its hairline.

('Being Horse', 2019)

While there is an obvious symbiosis between hooden horse and
performer – the horse-head effigy held high, clearly visible and with an
elevated point of view; the operator a hidden figure with limited visual
awareness; the two working together to create the hybrid being that is the
hooden horse – there is also separation between the human and non-
human. This is further emphasised by the use of a camera to capture the
experience of being the horse. To *be* the horse is not to be the operational
performer, but to be at a small, dualistic remove from them. The horse is
aware of the performer's physical tremblings, wrestlings and impacts of
movement, and the act of walking on a surface, just as one is aware of
one's own feet lifting and replacing themselves on the ground, and of
muscles propelling one's body forward. Sensory and mechanical
awareness is tempered by mental and emotional distance.

The ground moves, narrows to a point. A top-heavy, bipedal
balancing act. All feeling is there, in the soles.

('Being Horse', 2019)

The text complete, James recorded himself reading the part of the horse.
Variations in the voice were needed to create a sense of playful aloofness
particular to the horse's character; whispering the text worked best,
conveying a slight edge of menace beneath the skittishness. We then
edited the voice-over, footage and key foley together, using pauses, freeze
frames, refractions of light, and layered and distorted sound to reflect the
confusion, cacophony and visual interruptions experienced by the horse.

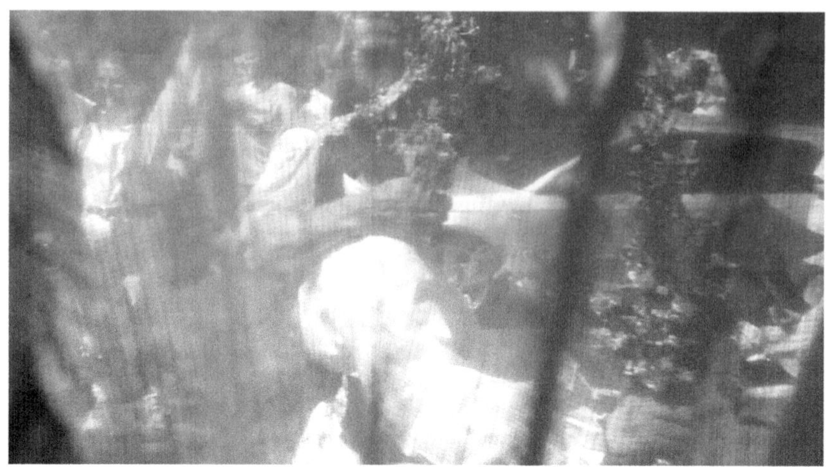

The horse enters your space

'Being Horse' also serves as a document of contemporary responses to the Whitstable May Day parade. Through the sackcloth the viewer can glimpse members of the public reacting to, engaging with and turning away from the horse's approach. Twenty-five years ago, the parade attracted local families who camped out along the processional route with deck chairs and picnics. The rise of Whitstable as a popular tourist destination saw the introduction of numerous cameras amongst the spectators of the early 2000s; the 2010s have been marked by a reduction in numbers and a switch to viewing the procession through raised mobile phones. The footage of 'Being Horse' shows many members of the public ignoring the 2018 parade, particularly at the harbour, where visitors gather not for the procession and dancing but for the fish and seafood stalls and outdoor eateries. The lack of engagement seems remarkable given the volume of dancers, the noise of multiple musicians and the unusual processional beasts that crowd into such a tightly delineated space. It felt important to mark this in the film by allowing the horse to comment on those who refuse to engage:

> You may not look at me now, but you feel me here. I am impossible. You refuse me, turn away…
>
> I am the mote in the eye, the unfeasible at the edges, unfathomable.
>
> Pretend you cannot see me if you must…
>
> ('Being Horse', 2019)

While some choose not to look, and some laugh with bemusement or amusement, there are others who are still genuinely frightened by the horse. 'Being Horse' captures the expressions of smiling children, the cries of spooked infants in pushchairs and the extended scream of a young woman surprised – and terrified – by the horse's sudden appearance at her side. That the hooden horse is sufficiently disconcerting to get such a reaction suggests that its presence falls between the recognisable (and customary) and the inexplicable (and unexpected): a gap that can be filled by laughter or terror. Little wonder that the horror genre continues to appropriate effigies and folk practices as shortcuts to fear.

Next steps: walking the hoodening way

In 1909 Percy Maylam, a Canterbury-based lawyer, recounted the traditional hoodening at Monkton in Kent during Christmas 1888-1892 (Maylam: 22-24). Maylam also photographed the team. These were the hooders of St Nicholas-at-Wade, a couple of miles away from Monkton; young male farm labourers and stable hands looking to make some extra money during the lean days of winter. The last surviving member of the old St Nicholas team, Tom West, was interviewed by the St Nicholas revivalist Tristan Jones in 1977. In the 1920s Tom had been the teenage rider who leapt upon the hooden horse's back during the performance.

The St Nicholas hooders performed for two nights during Christmas week, the first 'being devoted to shops, pubs and big houses in St Nicholas' and the second the 'great walk' (Frampton, 2006: 34). The act of walking remained at the forefront of Tom's mind and he vividly recalled the destinations. Despite their access to horses and carts, it seemed an important ritual that the hooders walked the whole distance of their tour, despite the trials and tribulations it involved. As Tom West recalled:

> That is why it took so long. We'd set out each evening straight after tea (about 5.30). We sang a lot more on the way home than in the houses… it used to be worse Christmases than they are now – used to be snow on the ground. And walking back from Minster or Monkton wasn't a joke really.
>
> (Frampton, 2006: 35-36)

George Frampton estimated that Tom West's 'great walk' was around 16km:

> Even allowing for a 6pm start, a brisk walking pace, and adequate time to perform and enjoy the hospitality of their hosts, the hike concerned looks like a challenge for getting home by midnight, with work beckoning the following morning.

> (ibid: 94)

The St Nicholas hooders' route covers an area close to our home in Sandwich, Kent. Many of the topographical markers of the great walk – farm sites, a windmill, country pubs – can be readily located. To take the experience of walking-as horse further, we plan to map out the route of the great walk and attempt to navigate it during the winter season. This will begin with small steps, locating pedestrian routes between sites that may have fallen out of use and exploring the terrain as it appears now. How has the landscape changed since Tom West walked it a hundred years ago? What differences have arisen through modern farming practices, the demise of rural pubs or the relocation of communities? How would it feel being the hooden horse of 1920 in the East Kent of 2020?

Our exploration of the horse's character continues. In 2011, James created a hooden horse for Sandwich, which has appeared at local folk events, on stage at The Gulbenkian Theatre (in the part of a cantankerous horse who throws its rider) and features in our own Christmas hoodening plays. James has also created a commissioned reconstruction of 'Satan', a hooden horse owned by the current St Nicholas-at-Wade hooders and thought to date from the 19th century. The Sandwich hooden horse remains a key cast member of our experimental folk laboratory, created to explore devised and site-specific approaches to traditional performance. We have learned much by walking-with, and walking-as, the hooden horse in procession, but it seems there is plenty more that this bipedal beast can offer our creative practices.

References

'Being Horse' (2019) [Film] Dir. Frost, J. and Overall, S. UK: James Frost and Sonia Overall

Cawte, E. C. (1978) *Ritual Animal Disguise: A Historical and Geographical Study of Animal Disguise in the British Isles.* D. S. Brewer

Doel, F., Doel, G. and Deane, T. (1995) *Spring and Summer Customs in Sussex, Kent and Surrey.* Meresborough Books

Frampton, G. (1995) 'The Return of the Hooden Horse', in *Bygone Kent* 16(12), Dec 1995, pp. 743-748

______ (2006) *Discordant Comicals: The Christmas Hoodeners of East Kent, Tradition and Revival.* The Faversham Society

Frost, J. (2016-2020) *Ethnographic Diary.* Unpublished

Hutton, R. (1994) *The Rise and Fall of Merry England.* Oxford Univ. Press

Maylam, P. (1909) 'The Hooden Horse: An East Kent Christmas Custom', in Maylam, R., Lynn M. and Doel, G. *Percy Maylam's The Kent Hooden Horse.* Stroud: The History Press, pp. 19-109, 2009

Overall, S. (2019) 'Walking into a Creative Writing Practice'. Living Maps Review, No 7. Available at: bit.ly/wnm44 (Accessed 09 Feb 2020)

pige*o*n steps

(change c*o*urse at the dr*o*p of a crumb)

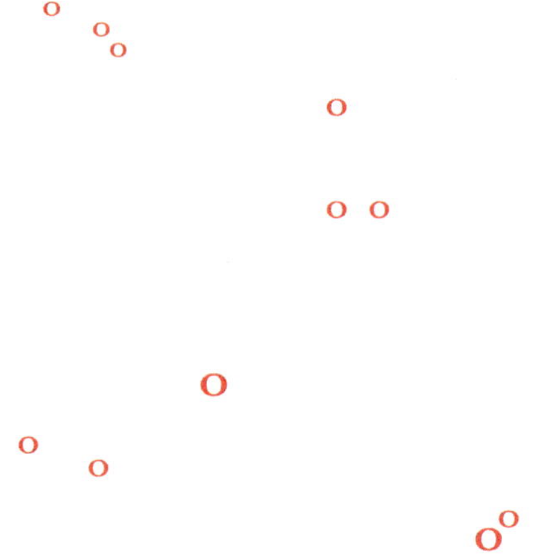

gabrielle h*o*ad & megan calver

a participat*o*ry pr*o*v*o*cation t*o* investigate
the walking m*o*vements *o*f feral pige*o*ns

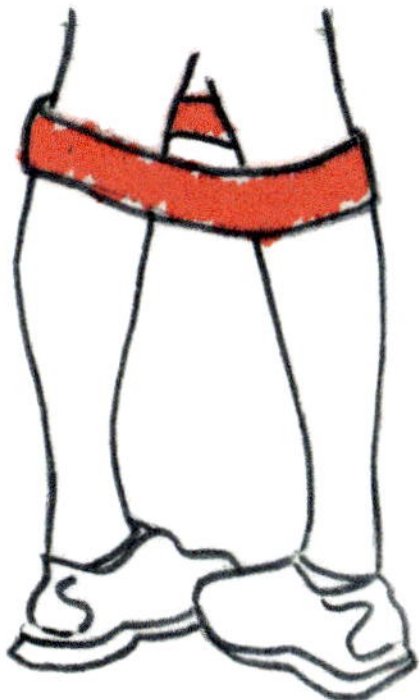

walk heel to toe
alert to the peripheral

gravitate with others
to potential gifters

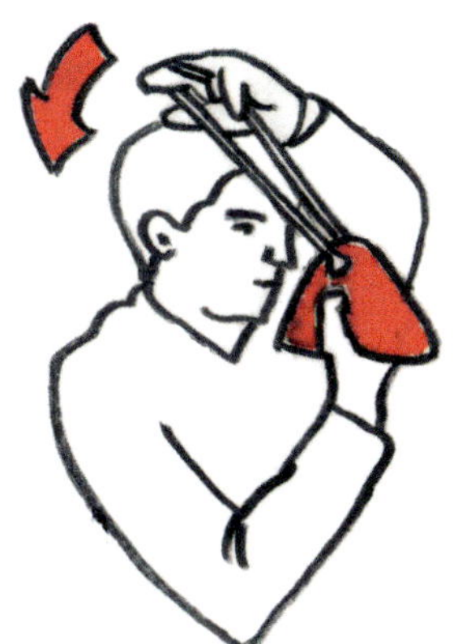

continue to inhabit
a state of expectancy

Fig 1: loop to enable smaller steps
(repurposed belt or sash)

Fig 2: mask to enable peripheral vision
(repurposed sandwich carton)

CROW

A short outdoor play by Matt Fletcher
Performed as a provocation by Matt Fletcher and Kevin Butler of
Out There Actions

*Music. A SCARECROW is discovered, a pole down his back
preventing him from moving.*

SCARECROW Here am I, rooted to the spot, rooted to the spot
A scare-crow
Nailed to this field by the pole at my back
Spelled, held, prevented from roaming
I shouldn't be moaning. It's a good life, really –
Nice view.
But all around me crows are flying
Crying their freedom - Caw! Caw!
Trying my patience with their gallivanting
Their taunts and zanting.
While me, I'm going nowhere, I just stand and stare
To be frank I don't even scare the crows.
Not much, anyway. Oh, look out!
Here's one now, all arrogance and power
I'll glower, let him know who's boss.
Who am I kidding? If it came to the toss
It's me who'd be doing his bidding.

Enter a CROW, who flies around and sings a song.

CROW (*Singing – to tune of 'Three Crows' in a minor key*)
Crow, crow, turning in the sky,
With my beady eye, watching everything that you do.
Crow, crow, wheeling in the blue,
But it's you who keeps me moving.

That's me, Crow, you see
Portent, oracle, omen, curse, and worse
Maybe it's because I'm black that people attack me
Tar me with a bad brush, rush to condemn me
Tremble when I'm near, what is it they fear?
Maybe they've seen too much
Of that old Hitchcock film
You know the one – 'The Birds'? Tippi Hedren?

Scared to go to bed then, worried I'll fill their dreams
But all's not what it seems.
Sure, I might have a habit of watching you
But with no evil intent
It's just my bent, I'm interested
Vested, you might say
In knowing the ins and outs of your rich lives
Marking who prospers, who thrives
Who makes worthy choices
Whose voice is loud, whose cowed.
I don't judge, I just record, seeking no objective
No reward, except to witness all you truly are
And for this privilege I'd travel far.
But wait, who's this?
Some old scarecrow, rotting on his post
I'll have some fun with this field's grubby host.
Caw! Caw!

SCARECROW   Oh no, he's spotted me! A laughing stock now I'll be
Life made a misery.

CROW   Hello, old stick!

SCARECROW   Go away, do you hear, get lost!
I'm fearsome, me, I won't be crossed!
There's no crows allowed around these parts
Now off you pop, let's have none o' your smarts!

CROW   Smarts? Is that what you expect?
I'll be nothing but respectful
Praise your fine attire – nice hat!
Only call you squire, refrain from low satire
Won't even mention fire (always a touchy subject
For someone stuffed with straw).
What's more, I'll express a strong desire
To acquire a stick like yours.

SCARECROW   Stick?

CROW   That pole down your back.

SCARECROW   Enough! That's one wise-crack too far!
Why must you mar my day with talk of this
hindrance
This affliction, this handicap to forward motion?
I've a notion to bop you on the beak
For speaking to me like that.

CROW   Come on then, if you think you're hard enough.

The SCARECROW attempts to move while the CROW taunts him from afar.

SCARECROW   Oh, it's no good! If I could I'd chase you down
                Beat you soundly
                Teach you roundly not to mess with me.
                But you're blessed with the power of movement
                What an improvement that would be
                If I were in your shoes?
                As it is, I cannot use these pointless pins
                And so I'm forced to suffer
                Your cheap jibes and grins.

CROW   Ha! You envy me? There's a turn-up!
                Let's just firm up what you're saying here.
                Without that post, you'd roast me for my wit?

SCARECROW   In a flash. Or I'd make a dash for the horizon.
                Straight as a die, as the crows fly
                Not looking back, but vacking my wayt
                With resolute gait.

CROW   And where would you go?

SCARECROW   All the way to tomorrow.
                Straight ahead, best foot forward.

CROW   Back up a mo! I hate to rain on your show
                But there's something you should know
                About a crow like me.
                We don't fly in straight lines. We circle, we wheel
                We feel our way with casual care
                Through town and country, ground and air,
                Haphazardly
                Flâneurs of the sky, you might say
                Drifters whose only aim is to continue the game.

SCARECROW   That won't suit me. I play to win, to take the prize
                And that lies in a straight line dead ahead.

CROW   I can tell you're not well read!
                Let me be the bearer of bad news
                These straight lines
                That you're so mad-keen to cruise

They don't in fact exist, they're just a ruse.
In true Euclidian space perhaps, but here
We're clinging to the surface of a sphere.
Here Bernhard Riemann's geometry holds sway
And orthodromic distance rules the day.

SCARECROW   What do you take me for – a fool?
I remember what they said at school
The shortest distance between two points is a line -
A straight line! Perhaps that will consign
Your specious din to the rubbish bin.

CROW   Not at all. Don't you recall?
That certainly could be the case in planar space
But can it on a planet?
Here, each line becomes a great circle
Working its way around the globe
Probing a curving path called a geodesic
Forming an arc at its most basic.

SCARECROW   An ark? Like Noah's?

CROW   Oh, stone the crows!
(Well, don't actually do that, will you?)
Everybody knows, an arc is a fraction of a circle
Measured from A to B, divided by 360
And multiplied by $2\pi r$. Alles klar?

SCARECROW   As mud. It's all Greek to me! But can't you see?
I don't care about the square of the hypotenuse
The quod ests and the demonstrues.
There's only one thing I've got my eyes on
And it's out there – the horizon.

CROW   What? That curved line between land and sky
Is crying your name?
Has you so aflame that you would up sticks
And go and mix it in some unknown clime?

SCARECROW   In double time! If to this one spot I wasn't charmed.

CROW   If that's the case, your wish is my command!

The CROW releases the SCARECROW from his pole. He dances around, elated, then fixes his eyes again on the horizon.

SCARECROW   "Distance ceases to be distance and to be blue

when we arrive in it. The far becomes the near,
and they are not the same place."[1]
Goodbye, good crow, I leave you gratefully
From here on in, you'll see no more of me.

CROW   We'll see.

*The SCARECROW heads off very forcefully in one direction, while
the CROW once again sings 'Crow, Crow'. The SCARECROW
walks a circle and arrives back on the stage.*

SCARECROW   What? I'm back! How has that transpired?
                I walked untiringly straight ahead
                And arrived back where I began instead.

CROW   You've travelled as the black crow truly flies
                In circles, with enlightenment your prize
                For here's the truth that you are forced to face
                Far and near are often the same place.
                And if on orthodromic paths you choose to dwell
                You'll get to wish this goodly crowd farewell.

THE END

[1] Solnit, R. (2017) *A Field Guide to Getting Lost*. Canongate

Walking away? From deep mapping to mutual accompaniment

Iain Biggs

By way of introduction…

The phrases 'walking' and 'walking away' reach far beyond the physical activity, just as 'sense of place' reaches so much further than our relationship to any particular physical location. In both cases, and for better or worse, the literal bodily experience becomes enmeshed in language, and so in psychosocial nuances, whole swathes of collective imaginal life, shared feeling complexes and a host of socio-environmental engagements. The phrase 'walking away' is intended in this expanded sense here.

What follows meanders for a reason. I need to proceed elliptically so as to keep side-stepping the strictures and assumptions of my own literal, academically conditioned thinking; to keep in question what is conceptually and administratively presented as 'given', 'fact'. These are assumptions that are so often predicated on a fantastically reductive binary thinking. I need to go forward in this way so as to edge into the shadow-patterned world of 'somewhere-else'; what, in Irish, is called *an saol eile* (roughly translatable as 'the other life'). Unlike the academic privileging of speaking/writing as authoritative, being open to *an saol eile* requires attending to multiple, often contradictory, voices. Particularly those whispered and marginalised voices that only join us in conversations that would otherwise be made impossible, or else drowned out, by the strident demands of categorical analysis.

Let me be clear. In many other non-Western cultures this listening constitutes a psychosocial or spiritual practice – a walking with the ancestors, with the dead or, as the ethnography of British folklore indicates, with 'the good neighbours'. The 'somewhere-else' is significant here as the ground onto which those of us who are drawn to multi-directional and other open walking practices are likely to stray; through psycho-geography, mytho-archaeology, deep mapping, or any related performative practice that, in William Blake's terms, seeks to keep both practitioner and participant from 'single vision and Newton's sleep'. Moving in and out of *an saol eile* (which is also, of course, always simultaneously very much in the 'here-and-now'), potentially expands walking into an imaginal act. For myself, a particular pair of works take me closer to the underlying sense of both walking-with and walking-away. These are Marlene Creates' *Sleeping Places, Newfoundland* (1982) and her partner Don McKay's poem 'Sleeping Places'.[1] Literally speaking, of course, this pairing does not reference the physical act of walking. None-the-less it illuminates our need to walk lightly on the land, with all that phrase implies about both living and dying.

For Hugo Ball

The presentation from which this essay derives was dedicated to Hugo Ball who, in 1917, broke with Tristan Tzara and Francis Picabia over their ambition to turn Dada into an international art movement. Ball then 'walked away', both from Zurich Dada and from the whole business of making art. Today, any number of artists – Jeff Koons, Lisa Yuskavage, Genieve Figgis, Damien Hurst, Luiz Zerbini (the list is endless) – have infantilised Tzara and Picabia's radical nihilism, pandering simultaneously to the most toxic and most trivialising aspects of the culture of possessive individualism. Ball's act of 'walking way' seems, in consequence, more resonant than ever. Ball rejected possessive individualism, believed in the ultimate unity of all beings and the totality of all things. But, perhaps as significantly, he also wholeheartedly accepted the need to live with the dissonances and contradictions that follow from that belief. Hans Richter reports that Ball ended his life living in poverty, even poorer that the peasants who were his neighbours, yet giving them whatever help he could. Fourteen years after his death, those neighbours still spoke of him with love and admiration.

My long involvement in a walking-based, open, deep mapping relates to Ball's concerns in two ways. Firstly, open deep mapping requires adopting ways of working that lead one towards that sense of unity and totality by, ironically, working with the particular dissonances and contradictions inherent in a particular place or region. Secondly, as indicated, it requires putting distance between yourself and the

---

[1] Both works are reproduced in (Garvey & Kunard, 2017)

assumptions that underpin the whole complex machinery of the art world. Distance, that is, from the complex of psychosocial and economic processes that makes up a culture industry that creates the poster boys and girls who sustain the aura of exclusivity and novelty central to possessive individualism. Establishing that distance now seems a necessary step in the process of finding – and here I am deliberately misquoting Les Roberts' (2018) views on deep mapping as bricolage - a 'space in-between' (a phrase also used by Ursula Le Guin in relation to art in her *Always Coming Home*), in which to wander in a deliberately undisciplined manner. An approach that seems necessary to letting go of the assumption of gravitas that both constrains and, simultaneously, lends authority to, creative practices sanctioned by the exclusive practices of an institutional, disciplinary, or 'cultural' habitus.

Walking with trouble in mind

Physical constraints mean I no longer have a walking-based practice, although for many years walking was central to my work. For example, on 15th April, 1999 – that is, exactly a month after Loyalist paramilitaries had murdered the solicitor Rosemary Nelson – I walked the streets of Belfast. Sometimes sectarian borders were visualised through red, white and blue painted kerbstones, sometimes they were not. Either way, the background fear and anger in Belfast was still palpable. Four months later, I began a fourteen-year-long open deep mapping project that follows one of the tributaries of trauma that fed into that city's fear and anger. A project that engages with the long-standing Anglo-Scottish Border culture of endemic violence later exported to Ireland.

That project took me to Scot's Dyke. This eroded earth bank marks the English Scottish border to the north-east of Carlisle, where it crosses the once-notorious Debatable Land. Historically, this was an area straddling the border and typifying the worst social consequences of wars between the English and Scottish crowns. Wars that locked the region into an unbroken cycle of violence and retribution that run from the late thirteenth into the early seventeenth centuries.

When I first visited Scot's Dyke I could still follow the fence that runs parallel to the remnants of the Elizabethan dyke that attempted to establish a fixed border in an area so violent that, in 1524, the Bishop of Carlisle and his entourage undertook a sixty-mile detour to avoid it. If it was possible to follow the dyke from west to east today, you'd hear little other than your own turning thoughts, distant agricultural sounds, and the occasional cry of a buzzard, at least until you approached the busy A7. You'd get no sense of that long period of historical violence, nor of the measures that brought that violence to an end. A series of mass hangings, the forced enrolment of large sections of the male population into mercenary regiments fighting in Europe, and the exile of whole extended families considered troublesome to an already troubled Ireland.

I've begun here because the Debatable Land gave its name to my long-term project. By excavating and contrasting narratives focused here and elsewhere along the Borders, I could uncover a deeply engrained legacy of anger, trauma and fear now conveniently repackaged, in no small part through the reiver heritage industry. A legacy exported first to Ireland and, from there, to the USA. Just one small, livid thread in the UK's contributions to what Amitav Ghosh calls, in his discussion of the culture of colonialism and its links to the environmental crisis, The Great Derangement.

It might seem morbid to focus on the repressed historical elements of the derangement that has led to our current, toxic psychosocial and environmental situation. However, I see that focus as a necessary prophylactic against the consequences of the large-scale denial of the undertow of violence and trauma that haunts so much of a land viewed through rose-tinted or heroic lenses. This denial has very real sociopolitical consequences, not least by sustaining the status-quo in terms of the ownership and usage of land. I recognise that by writing this I'm touching on a large and difficult topic, one that I cannot attempt to explore properly in the space available to me. I'll direct you, however, to the poet and essayist Kathleen Jamie's review – 'A Lone Enraptured Male' – of Robert MacFarlane's *The Wild Places*, in the *London Review of Books*, Vol. 30 No. 5, 6th March 2008. This casts a cool, clear light on the presuppositions that underwrite not only much of MacFarlane's work, but an entire genre of nature writing. Any reader who wishes to pursue this line of thought is invited to do the following.

Read both Jamie's review and MacFarlane's *The Mountains of the Mind: A History of a Fascination*, paying particular attention to his use of the first person singular and asking what this indicates about his presuppositions. Now read James Hillman's essay 'Peaks and Vales' (in *Puer Papers*, 1979), with its careful analysis of the traditional association of mountains with spirituality. Finally, read Sarah Jaquette Ray's 'Risking Bodies in the Wild: the "Corporeal Unconscious" of American Adventure Culture' (in Ray and Sibara's *Disability Studies and the*

Environmental Humanities, 2017), noting her careful exposition of the historical links between the 'frontier mentality', gender, 'moral purity' (with its direct links to Hillman's essay), eugenics, and the founding of modern ecology. Finally, read 'Bird's Eye View', the Introduction to Rebecca Solnit's *As Eve Said to the Serpent: On Landscape, Gender, and Art* (2001) and, if you have time, the first chapter: 'Lise Meitner's Walking Shoes'. By which point I'm reasonably certain that you'll understand my stressing the need to keep in view the violence and trauma that haunt the land.

The most critical point here, however, is open deep mapping's distancing itself from the culture of possessive individualism. Something achieved by setting aside the assumptions that flow from the monolithic, heroic ego, redressing the Cartesian splitting of self from other, mind from body, the perceptual from the imaginal, the material from the spiritual, the literal, supposedly 'outer' world from *an saol eile*. Open deep mapping enacts, that is, a desire to embrace and celebrate an ensemble self. A self that is aware of its own multiplicity and that of the multiverse to which it finds its various selves or persona related at every level.

The peripatetic basis of open deep mapping

Open deep mapping is fundamentally *peripatetic*, grounded by a walking, listening body getting to know a place in as many of its dimensions as possible. It's also, of necessity, intellectually peripatetic, wandering freely across disciplinary and conceptual borders in order to ask unexpected and unorthodox questions in spaces-in-between. Its practitioners also tend to be psychically peripatetic – to resist any long-term identification with any single genre or praxis by accepting the necessity to regularly 'move house'. A psychic nomadism necessary to resist the relentless process of co-option by the culture industry. Currently I see open deep mapping as a walking-with a multitude of voices of both the living and dead; a walking-with that animates differently a particular place or, increasingly, set of relationships between places. A walking-with that's alert to voices that dominant narratives have forgotten, marginalized or repressed. Alert to them so as to re-articulate their pressing and unanswered questions in the here-and-now.

There is, then, a psychosocially therapeutic element to this walking-with a multitude of voices. A process that is perhaps best indicated by paraphrasing an observation made by James Hillman, who suggests that we take care to avoid falling into the habit of mis-conceptualizing the unconscious as either a place or a state, and instead understand it as "a dark ironic brother, an echoing sister, reminding" (1988: 41). This psychosocially therapeutic aspect was clearly signaled in the title of *Between Carterhaugh and Tamshiel Rig: a borderline episode* (2004), the first book to come out of the 'Debatable Lands' project. The symptoms of a borderline episode or disorder include: unstable relationships with others, confused feelings about identity, feelings of being abandoned, and difficulty controlling anger. In 2004, my title was intended to signal something of what, for hundreds of years, the inhabitants of the Borders had enacted and suffered. Only some time later did it dawn on me that the same symptoms had gradually come to characterise my relationship with both the art world and the academy and that, as a result, they had led me inexorably to deep mapping as an ensemble practice.

In 2006 I became involved in a project called 'Living in a Material World: A Cross-disciplinary, Site-based Enquiry into the Performativity of Emptiness'. Mike Pearson was another participant and his work on deep mapping / theatre archaeology with Michael Shanks, Cliff McLucas, and the radical site-specific theatre work of 'Brith Goff', became one benchmark against which I measured my practice. In 2007 this project took us to what is now the Sennybridge Army Training Camp, formally the home of the upland farming community of Mynydd Epynt. The project's concerns with place as abandoned, degraded, disappeared or unmarked came to the fore in this contested, physically traumatised, environment appropriated for military use. I found myself plunged, as an Anglo-Scot visiting a highly controversial site in Wales, into reassessing what I value and remember. The result was a large wall-map piece 'Hidden War (for Anna Biggs)' (see next page).

This was made by intercutting, reversing, annotating and reprinting parts of two very different maps of the Sennybridge / Mynydd Epynt area: a specialist military map, obtained directly from the army, and the standard OS walker's map. Parts of each were juxtaposed together on the basis of copious notes made while walking there. The work is an attempt to address and visualise, by analogy, the cognitive dissonance I experienced as an academic/artist/researcher with a walking-based practice and as a carer for someone too ill to walk more than a few paces.

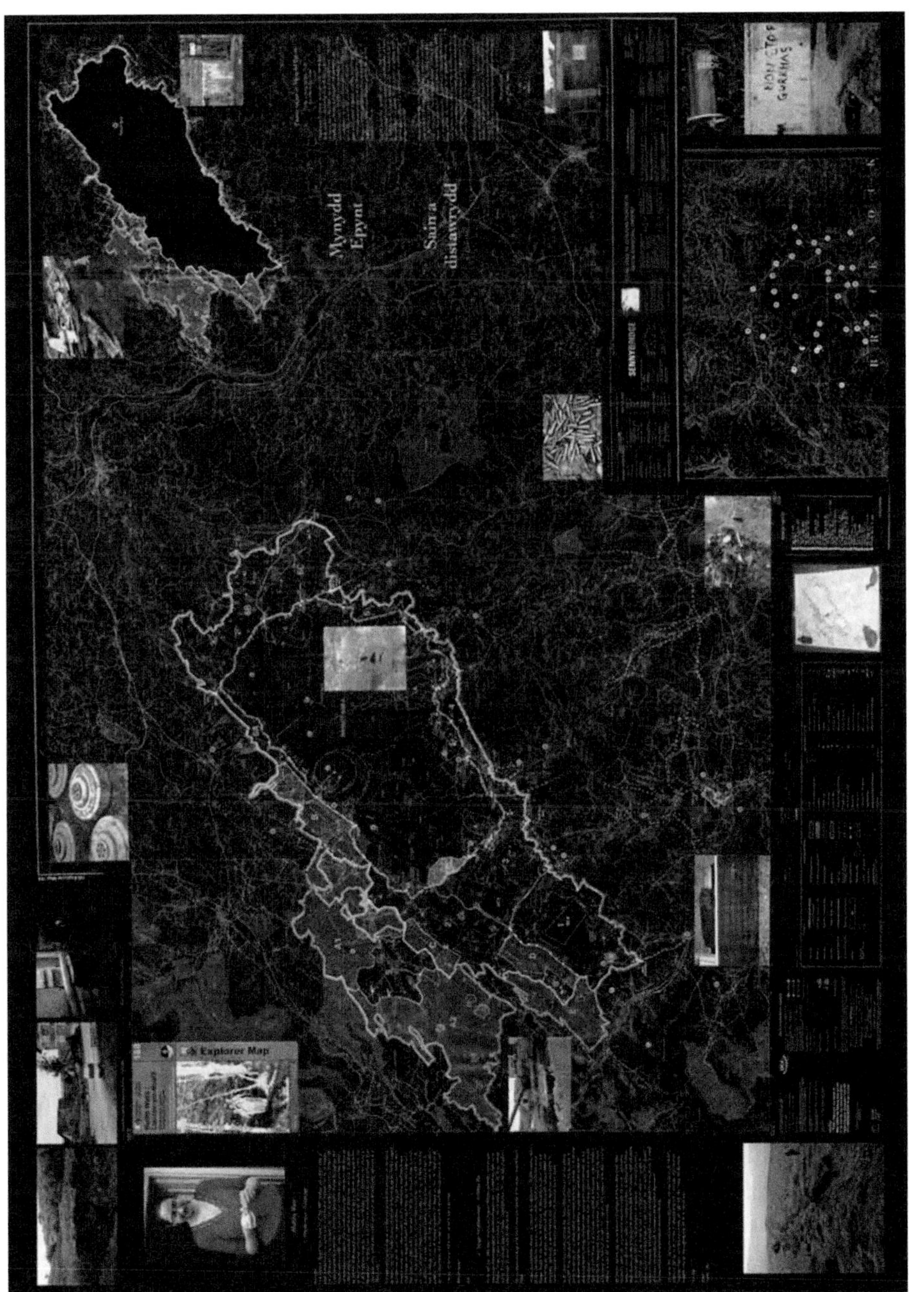

Hidden War (for Anna Biggs). Photo: the artist.

Making the piece further emphasised the need, in open deep mapping, for lateral thinking, for looking for connections where they're not expected – some would say don't exist. (I take this to be what Michael Shanks (2012) refers to as: "the rhetorical tropes of *parataxis* and *katachresis* – forced juxtaposition of dissimilar components and designed to produce frictions (parataxis— this and this and this and ...; katachresis – mixed, forced, what could be deemed inappropriate metaphor"). Like the 'Debatable Lands' project, it emerged from my listening to a range of narratives - of power, fear, loss, and anger – and to their counter-narratives. Walking in a military training area, where the land is still visibly marked with a complex of historical traces of violence, ranging from a Bronze Age boundary dyke to a firing range target area saturated over decades with spent ammunition, suggested the means to visualise the contested medical, psychiatric, and social contexts in which my daughter Anna lives with a chronic illness that, among many other consequences, prevents her walking.

Deep mapping as contesting and contested practice

Those engaged in critically alert, psychosocially engaged, ensemble practices like open deep mapping must act nimbly while moving in many dimensions if they're to avoid being co-opted by the disciplinary *status quo* for its own instrumental ends. Ends that always threaten to water down or undermine its primary concerns.

Tahmineh Hooshyar Emami's 'Alice's Alternative Wonderland' uses a similar sense of cognitive dissonance to my 'Hidden War (for Anna Biggs)', but in order to articulate a child's experiences on the European refugee trail. She does this through contrasting spatial and textual renderings of the world of Lewis Carroll's *Alice in Wonderland* and *Through the Looking-Glass*. Drawing on refugees' first-hand narratives and press reports, and inspired by a reading of Carroll's texts as political allegory, the work offers a critical analysis of the spatial politics of refuge. Carroll's Alice, always at odds with the physical and social space of 'Wonderland', provides a starting point for analysing how our bodies are defined, shaped, and influenced by space. Alice's fears and dispossession are, then, used to highlight the experience of refugee children in a contemporary Western 'wonderland' characterised by the on-going disputes over child-refugees and their right of asylum in countries like Great Britain.

I want to suggest that such open deep mapping projects provide both those undertaking them and the recipients with an education in what Bruno Latour calls Terrestrial politics. They teach us that a place, region or country is not *exclusive*, nor is it differentiated *by closing itself off*. Instead they enact Edward S. Casey's claim that places, despite their frequently settled appearance, are in effect essays in experimental living that are undertaken within the context of a constantly changing culture. They demonstrate why Terrestrial co-habitation requires us to think the global through our embodied engagement with specific places. Places experienced *as inclusive – as opening themselves up to* multiple, diverse, sometimes contradictory, relationships, attachments and connections. And they contest the presuppositions of unidirectional professional specialisation by suggesting that, if we want to survive in both the near and more distant future, we had better start to register, maintain, and cherish a maximum number of alternative ways of belonging to the world. However, there is now a concerted effort to co-opt the term deep mapping by the disciplinary *status quo* for precisely the type of instrumental ends that will water down or undermine what I take to be its primary, peripatetic, attributes and concerns. Far from being a portal to access multidirectional understandings of our relationship to place grounded in embodiment, it is now being touted as providing a digital access mechanism to spatial narratives so as to allow students to initiate a categorical inquiry. (I'm paraphrasing the Co-Director of the Institute for Advanced Technology in the Humanities at the University of Virginia). One might ask to what extent Michael Shanks' intellectual co-option of all forms of performance and performativity – those that re- iterate, re-mediate, re-work, re-store, re-present, and re-enact – to an expanded 'archaeology' has contributed to this, but that's not a question to be answered here.

However, I want to stress the contrast between instrumental, disciplinary views of deep mapping and open deep mapping, seen as a multidirectional activity involving observing, listening, walking, conversing, writing, exchanging, selecting, reflecting, naming, generating, digitizing, interweaving, offering and inviting. (Here I'm drawing on Roberts again, who is in turn quoting Jane Bailey's and my account of our open deep mapping work in North Cornwall). Fortunately, this second view has yet to be either co-opted nor wholly marginalised. My concern here is to draw attention to open deep mapping's constant mutation, it's capacity to walk-away from definitions of itself as having given qualities, a set purpose.

Open deep mapping and mutual accompaniment: Marega Pelser in Swansea

In 2017 Marega Pelser contacted me to talk about the potential possibilities of walking-based open deep mapping. Marega trained as a dancer, works with movement and drawing, and is half of the performance duo Mr & Mrs Clark. We spent a day walking and talking together in her home town of Newport. This eventually led to my supporting her project 'Framing the Transient NoW (An exercise in deep mapping)' in Swansea. My sense is that Marega's thinking is first and foremost bodily, so we arranged to walk the centre of Swansea together. As she has stated, she finds that walking enables her, draws her attention to the micro and to things easily overlooked. It's a way of paying attention, of observing and meeting the people that pass through a place, the objects that bang up next to each other, and the spaces in-between places. Her compound walking-based activity in Swansea generated drawings and assemblages that illuminate the city centre socially, historically, and geographically - a city centre she rightly describes as "somehow absent".[2]

Her particular take on deep mapping was to focus her attention on experiences shared with a whole range of local people. These included traders, allotment holders, the homeless, other artists, the partially sighted and the elderly. Many of these she actively accompanied into the chaotic mixture of decay and development being enacted in Swansea city centre. That *act of accompaniment* became mutual because, for her, it illuminated the multi-faceted mixture of the new, the trivial, the old and the traumatic – with a particular undercurrent of uncertainty and disquiet - that constitutes that somehow absent city centre.

A scribbled notation on one of her large-scale drawn maps drew my attention to an incident with a bollard. Marega had accompanied a group of local people – some blind, some partially sighted, and some wheel-chair users – on a walk through the city centre, using hazard tape to mark problematic obstructions as they went. When they reached the central square a city official challenged them as they marked a bollard as hazardous. Marega explained why they were doing so but was told that the use of hazard tape was (I quote): "*interfering with the structural integrity of the bollard*". As a result, the absent city centre appears through the notation of this event as present in the disconnect between the lived experience of

---

[2] See bit.ly/wnm50 and bit.ly/wnm52 (accessed 12 Dec 2019)

functionally impaired citizens and official concern for a groundless conceptual principle: namely, the structural integrity of a bollard.

Accompanying Marega during this project helped further shift my concern with open deep mapping towards considering the need to focus more specifically on post-disciplinary ensemble practices linked to other possibilities: practices that increasingly distance themselves from the dominant, hyper-professionalised, unidirectional mentality, rewarded equally (if differently) by both the art world and an academy in which authority is still underwritten by the *realpolitik* of disciplinary thinking. Today my concerns are increasingly with supporting a variety of people engaged in ensemble practices animated by commitment to *walking-alongside,* to mutual accompaniment. (A term I've borrowed from the liberation psychologist Mary Watkins). In Swansea, Marega walked-alongside, or mutually accompanied, those who enacted the lived reality of a hollowed-out, psychosocially dysfunctional, city centre. A spectrum of people who grounded her project in horizontality, interdependence, and potential mutuality. Her Swansea project as a whole – within which I see the final exhibition as served principally as an enabling device – points us away from the unidirectional approaches on which academic and professional art activity are increasingly dependent, and from the culture of possessive individualism that they ultimately reinforce.

Walking away?

So, am I advocating walking away from deep mapping (or indeed from art itself, at least as we currently understand it)? I'm not sure. 'Yes', if they are reduced to supporting mechanisms for a conceptually driven worldview caught up in serving the culture of possessive individualism. 'No', if they contribute to ensemble practices predicated on mutual accompaniment. We are now in desperate need of reviving Hugo Ball's commitment to the unity and totality of all things. But, increasingly, if we are to do so we must find new ways to live with the sometimes-overwhelming dissonances and difficulties that flow from any such commitment. Open deep mapping has led me to see the desire to 'mutually accompany' others as helping make that commitment possible. Despite the fact that it requires that we live with our own and others' fear, anger and the trauma that fuel them; that we "stay with the trouble", in Donna Haraway's terms. Speaking personally, I see no other way of working towards the Deep Adaptation that Jem Bendell believes is now vital to our collective survival as a functioning society.

References

Bendell, Jem (2018) 'Deep Adaptation: A Map for Navigating Climate Tragedy', bit.ly/wnm47 (Accessed 13 Dec 2019)

Garvey, Susan Gibson & Kunard, Andrea (eds) (2017) *Marlene Creates: Places, Paths and Pauses,* Goose Lane Editions / Beaverbrook Art Gallery

Hillman, James (1988) *On Paranoia,* Spring Publications

Roberts, Les (2018) 'Spatial Bricolage: The Art of Poetically Making Do' *Humanities,* 7(2), 43; https://doi.org/10.3390/h7020043

Shanks, Michael (2012) 'Let me tell you about Hadrian's Wall'… Heritage, Performance, Design. The Reinwardt Memorial Lecture, bit.ly/wnm48 (Accessed 12 Dec 2019)

Watkins, Mary (2019) *Mutual Accompaniment and the Creation of the Commons,* Yale Univ. Press

Web Walking

Helen Billinghurst & Phil Smith

We want to propose a new strategy called Web Walking. We are going to begin in Dunstable, a town in Bedfordshire, just west of Luton. There, we check in to our rooms in a guest house called Cherish End under a crackling pylon, in the shadow of the last ridge of the Icknield Way, the route that we have been walking. We are on an adventure we have spun out from a labyrinth in Plymouth to a web that stretches as far as Cardiff and, the other way, to Cambridge…

Beyond the B&B's astroturfed back garden is a colossal Amazon depot. We have just come from Royston, where the Royse Stone with its Rosicrucian associations marks a crossroads where the Knights Templar dug a bell-shaped cave and filled it with enigmatic graffiti. And from the springs at Ashwell where a ten-year-old boy was splashing in the water with his mum, a man meditated on a bench, a young couple arrived and started to strip off. Here at the Springhead in Ashwell there was something… a way, a collective and convivial way, without dogma, to access certain things, often old things – patterns, values, objects, connections, desires – and throw them forward into the future.

Through a practice we've come to call 'Web Walking' we want to map such affordances in privileged points such as Ashwell and a Glastonbury spring we bathed in or at the Uffington white horse where we imagined a ceremony of red on white, while volunteers crushed chalk and a red kite hovered over our heads. We want to avoid separating off the explicit nodes that still connect us to a certain 'magical mode' and reconnect them to a wider pattern that includes the places where capitalism is bottoming out. Dunstable is one of those; cut away from the rest of England by motorways, its vitality sucked out by the swirling grey vortexes of London and Luton. Disconnectedness is palpable in Dunstable. Genteel Georgian buildings stand in utter shock: they do not recognize their harried populace. People look traumatised, like characters with no idea what movie they are in. Things pass through the town, but, like the Amazon depot, nothing sticks.

We pass failed businesses, smashed windows, gaps where old inns used to be. The local *am dram* are playing a 1960s' 'bedroom farce'. Cards in the employment agency advertise jobs for minimum wage. Time is twisted; not in a good way.

In the lawns around what's left of the old priory, the shapes of missing buildings are marked out in white, like pitches for not yet invented games. A young woman approaches and suggests we look at the war memorial. Her smile is one of desperation. She gestures to the priory; but she can only tell us it's closed. We pass a cluster of people who seem at odds with each other, like a group of chairs that have been toppled from around a table. Two Polish men sit on the grass, one growls angrily at a woman who is standing with her back to the men, holding a baby. Another woman stands over a flower bed watching a tiny child play in the soil.

From Plymouth to Cambridge we have seen and felt the same sadness, isolation and division. We have picked our way through smack dens in heritage sites and along needle strewn paths in woodland. We have watched the harried looks on people's faces, trespassed into the pits ripped out by mining companies and ceremonialised in the killing fields where the last wild wolves were slaughtered.

These things are neither new nor unusual. Part of their horror is how repetitive they are. In Brexitland the seas rise, the temperatures edge up, but the only things that are new are the levels of anguish and anger. In the face of these longstanding but accelerating crises – of populism and authoritarianism, failing globalism, misinformation and digital invasion, misogyny, fundamentalist reaction and species extinction – we want to propose a new emphasis for walking.

Changing the default mode of our 'drifts' from solo walks or group wanders focused on affect and ambience, to make walks of conviviality and togetherness for a collective world building. *Dérives* based on experiencing are vulnerable to apocalyptic thrills and the consumerist charms of the eerie; to go beyond the affect, we want to repurpose psychogeographical walking as a means to connectivity, not just with each other and the past, but with the future and with the unhuman. We call this 'Web Walking'. Putting hyper-sensitised walking at the heart of a multi-modal practice that fires out threads and routes and lines of communication to form webs, which in turn, attach themselves to a wider Pattern.

Web Walking starts with a familiar site-specificity, with attention to materials, to scuzz and grime and soil, to the plastic in our gut. We need to love that fucked-upness, if we're going to do anything about it. Like good Butoh dancers, get our noses in the mud; moving from the grot to re-enchantment without dogma; unearthing the signal within the signal in the abject landscape.

These hidden signals, curled up in tiny dimensions within consensus reality, are messages through time from when life was in a so-called 'magical mode'. We want to understand them, then throw them forward as a challenge to futuristic techno-exterminism's claim to be the only possible and inevitable future... we want to mix up times. To shift scales; to throw ourselves upwards, while sinking into the ground. To make art that unveils patterns that shift through different planes. To be sparing in our use of representations, but rigorous in our specificity to the qualities of found materials, and enthusiastic for diagrams that show relations.

Working across disciplines, we use actions, drawing, painting, written and spoken word and installations, drawing threads together into a web, which we then throw out to others – to other people, to other things, to other webs. For our 'Plymouth Labyrinth' project we used the myth of the Labyrinth, Ariadne and her red thread to investigate the way a city weaves together. On one walk we went to giant white clay pits on the edge of the city. After trespassing into one of the pits, we climbed back over the fence and found an entire sheep's skeleton spread out on the grass, picked clean by crows. Without talking we began to gather up the backbones and then threaded them onto red and white woollen threads we had with us. Picking up the ends of the threads, we jangled the bones and began to swing them gently, then, like a skipping rope, we whirled them around. Afterwards, Helen wrote a poem, called 'Lee Moor':

Two crows.

A sheep's bones picked clean

on the grass.

A painting, or perhaps a game:

red

removed from white

by black

on green. (excerpt)

These became rules for making a series of paintings, which became part of our first exhibition. Meanwhile we whirled the bones, as we had done on Lee Moor, on a walk with dancers, for poetry nights in pubs and cafes, and in the streets of the old red light district where we had our exhibition. Winding desire and death, vitality and change, around each other.

Other artists picked up on the signals within our signals. Dancers created a site-specific performance piece using red thread to connect one dancer to another and then to weave the whole group together in a web. Later on, on the Isles of Scilly and at Leo Camp in Norfolk, we added the white thread and entangled these two colour codes, asking walkers to walk between the blood red hunting lines of desire and the bony deathliness of the white... for between the white and the red there is a connectivity in the moment of crisis, as when a bone breaks and the bleeding within the fracture begins the knitting of the broken parts that forms new bone. Similarly, we apply the mortal body to the landscape, death as part of life, not separate from it... together the red and white bring the walker to the gate.

By letting things have their own life, and their own death, we saw them combine and fix themselves in different webs, flows and diagrams. And these became our first models for web walking ... emerging, like the threading of the sheep's back bones, without planning. We'd go to the suburbs or to a modern tungsten mine and there we'd find wolf packs, hidden forests, arks, giants, and the Syrian founder of Albion, because the terrain is the most powerful force in our walking, uncovering itself in different forms, as gods of the earth, as environmental pollution, as amphitheatres... in response we put our bodies into the landscape and our selves at the mercy of it, so the land guides us and we trust what we feel there.

We take inspiration from Butoh dancer Alkistis Dimech, who advocates "the retrieval of the body and its inherent potentials from the bonds that have been put on it". Allowing the un-inhibited moving body to become a "vehicle for the manifestation of the interior landscape, and the realm of images". This is how, as walkers, we connect with the myths and stories of place; how we drop down through the privileged points to the signal within their signal. Not just by research or turning experiences into poems, but by skulking around in places where few people care to go, or care about. And listening to what we are told there. And we talk endlessly – about the walk, the places, we share memories, theories, and fictions... and we are silent...

We make actions: lie down in fields, lean against trees, scry in pools, wash in holy wells, light fires by the sea. And we fiction what we do, and this is crucial to the spinning out of things. We inhabit stories as we walk, we put ourselves into fantastic or futuristic narratives that challenge the fixity of where and when and what we are. Old lamp posts take us to Narnia, deserted villages to Dr Who, Pan appears in a playground in the Plymouth suburb of Southway, UFOs from the future came into view, and wolves from the past crept forward on Dartmoor; and when all these things start to spin together – the philosophising, fictioning, collecting, touching, listening, dialoguing, learning – what develops is a web walking. Not one story, but a cat's cradle of stories and ideas and things and feelings, a linking of one place to another, connecting Lee Moor white clay pits to Stonehouse red light district, connecting one kin to another; drawing diagrams and walking them into landscape, taking up threads and drawing them together, crossing from thing to feeling to story to crow.

We walk, we connect, we spin yarns. With feet on the ground and eyes open, through observations and encounters with people, animals and unhuman things, we construct complex models of how things connect ecologically, socially and economically. We draw from Donna Haraway's ideas about 'string figuration' and 'Cat's Cradle', the playground game in which skeins of thread are passed back and forth between collaborators, to make different combinations of intricate patterns.

We have a powerful emotional attraction to theorising these models – we call it Sexy Theory because it respects the erotic drive in thinking. Thinking that is done with the whole body. And through the body, the places and the things and beings and forces that accompany our walks direct our thinking and think us, write us, draw us.

For a long time in 2019 we walked in the winter, in the rain, we rejected anything to do with the sun; to us airy solar spirits were distorting phantoms, deceptive anti-materialist idealisms, but then, in the spring, we began to find things – and equally they began to find us – a sun wheel, rusting in clay and sinking into the mush of a clay pit, old bits of motor car in the woods. One night we lit a fire and blazed alongside it, gathering up its ashes in the morning and next day, on our walk, found a new sun wheel, a rusty metal dustbin lid in a bush, and we used it as a stencil sprinkling the ash round it and leaving a sun shape, a sun in the ground for others to find… then in the depths of a suburban wood we found a huge "sun wheel" and humped it up a slope and installed it in our exhibition. We found the sun in the ground, to be left in the ground; oil, wood, gas, coal, rusting products returning to the soil. Each of these solid things were living nodes along strings or threads, parts of a web, just as the sheep's bones were nodes along the hunting lines of the last wolves in England.

Imagining ourselves as plastic/human hybrids, we learned to find empathy with the materials of the greenhouse-gas-creating-industries. Similarly, we were coming to understand the significance and importance of the hunter's empathy with the hunted. We began to grasp the complexity of the web and how restoring and re-wilding was a work of things and organisms and amoral forces and materials and wolves, and that these were already organising themselves in complex webs; and that if we would touch the threads of these webs we might feel the tugs of their different agencies.

Some of these agencies are very, very old. Like 400-million-year-old limestone making calcite processions in the White Spring at Glastonbury or 300-million-year-old desert dunes that redden the Devon footpaths. Some are very new. Like the Brazilian theatre artist who came on a walk and married a wolf. She took our labyrinthine web from Plymouth and transferred it to São Paulo, mapping out her city in hunting lines in resistance to what the authoritarian regime of Bolsonaro is doing there.

In this spirit of connectivity, we invited all the people we walked and workshopped with to send us a postcard with a drawing or a poem or whatever, and then in the exhibition we used the corridor of the gallery to link its different rooms with long threads to which we attached the over one hundred postcards we received. We called this corridor Linketty Lane after an old lane we found in Plymouth. People came into the exhibition to take part in making sessions, adding their work to the exhibition and contributing to a giant hybrid sea monster which then swam off to be exhibited at the Fish Factory gallery in Falmouth. Student dancers took the threads of the exhibition out into the streets around the gallery.

We drew from the myths and images that had stepped forward during our walking to create a red room with a scrying mirror, like the body of a spider, from which legs of silken thread worked around the room and escaped through the window to another web on a roof top. Ariadne had been joined by Arachne. Then, in the 'Plymouth Pantheon' we collected, in book form, some of the ideas and fabulous images that had emerged, sharing rules for new games, definitions of zones, theories about thinking and art making, a bestiary of local mythical personalities, and so on.

These constituted a web. Threads from which we then span out across more of the country – walking to Cambridge, Dunstable, Glastonbury, Cardiff, Ashwell, Bristol, Exeter, Wells, Scilly Isles, Avebury, Cheddar, Draycott, and so on, extending the lines of our wandering, each time connecting to more and more threads, and drawing them together to make new webs. And we will describe all that in a new book, called *The Pattern*, which we hope people will use to connect their own threads to the threads of others, to make their own pantheons and fire out their own lines of desire and flight, to connect one web to another... so, that just as our visual works constitute one big picture, the many webs entangled connect to one big Pattern of desire and resistance.

The new book, *The Pattern*, is very much a practical handbook. But it is also a description of moving warily towards something we have chosen to call 'the pattern', a tattooing of the land that we have found to be far more intense, connected and intricate than is generally acknowledged. A combination of affordant landscapes and the subjective markings on them; a pattern for navigating by, for mental manoeuvring and for living in what the philosopher Gilbert Simondon (2016) called the "magical mode".

The magical mode is the life of connectivity – of human and unhuman – pre-dating any division between subject and object in culture, pre-dating human exceptionalism. A mode in which an increase in being free is done, paradoxically, by entanglement with other forces so that agency is magnified by connection. In seeking this mode we are following Simon O'Sullivan's (2018) pairing of Raymond Williams with Gilbert Simondon; taking Williams's (1980) argument that an old or ancient dominant culture may continue to live in its remnant traces in such a way that offers a resource of alternative nodes for reconstruction now, and that such revenants – what Williams calls "residual culture" – can constitute the DNA of future oppositional cultures.

We make this idea geographical by linking it to Gilbert Simondon's argument that this mode is founded in a network of 'privileged points' – places where there was an especially intense exchange and entanglement of ancient humans with their cosmos, where this entanglement was compacted and landmarked for repeated use, privileged in the calendar as parts of a scrolling network of routes to be physically travelled at particular times, and stories to be held in the mind throughout the rest of the year. Places like the Royse Stone, the Chalice Well and the Uffington white horse, and with contemporary and unexpected examples, like the plastic copy of the bones of 'Cheddar George' our black ancestor, at whom visitors throw pieces of metal, mostly coins, in a ritual action practised for thousands of years. Or the sweet chestnut tree in Hyde Park, where we found people gathering to feed clouds of green ring-necked parakeets. Putting the ideas of Williams and Simondon together, in our web walking, we are threading together old and contemporary 'privileged points' as lines in a larger pattern, a map of a future that is alternative to the mode of the present one.

This pattern is experienced most intensely at sites that were once foundational to the magical mode; but we can add to them, because the old places were never just human constructions, but also natural and random affordances. So the springhead at Ashwell is modern compared to the Iron Age shrine to the goddess Senuna discovered in 2002 a few hundred metres away; likewise the White Spring at Glastonbury which is all the more powerful for being housed in a former town reservoir.

The network that joins these points is like a spider's legs without a single organising body, like an orrery without a sun in the centre; it constitutes a way of reverencing things without the need for dogma. A way to live and walk in hyper-connectivity as well as hyper-sensitivity; a way to learn how to live with the plastic in our guts alongside excited invasive species.

Our quest is for a connective and immersive 'mode', slipping the binaries of human and unhuman, self and cosmos, me and you. It will not solve any of the problems of cruelty, desire and community that the myths and fairy tales describe (but do not resolve). Instead – like the myths and fairy tales – we seek a mode that rubs thin the subjective-objective and self-world distinctions. Which makes the route the agent of the walk; makes a stranger just as responsible for a place as its residents, makes the crow our partner and our witness, makes the squid an ideal and an ecstasy, makes the world a web in which we are always *in loco parentis* and always children.

References

O'Sullivan, S. (2018) Myth-science as residual culture and magical thinking. *Postmedieval: a Journal of Medieval Cultural Studies*, 9 (4)

Simondon, G. (2016) *On the mode of existence of technical objects*. Univocal Publishing

Williams, R. (1980) Base and superstructure in Marxist cultural theory. In *Problems in Materialism and Culture: Selected Essays*. Verso, pp. 31-49

The Artist-Scholar Walks: Passage to Else-Where

Ishita Jain

This walk is conceptualised as a formalist performance to carve out a passage to 'Else-where'. Keeney defines Else-where as "An intentionally archaizing representation of a non-place that inhabits all forms of representation that involve spatial metaphors and a form of future space-time given to the artwork. [It is] indicative of both the form of time and the space-time continuum inhabiting art" (2010: 165). The walk as performance is staged in an improvised theatre constructed for the walk. A camera is set to record the theatrical walk. Word-images are made to report the cinematic record of the walk. These assemblage record makes the walk a transmedia event. It is also Badiou's Event. It becomes a dance that can never be a walk again. The dance has however always existed within the walk, like art has always existed within scholarship. The emergence of this walk transforms the space of academia into a theatre to produce new myths. It transforms the academic into Artist-scholar.

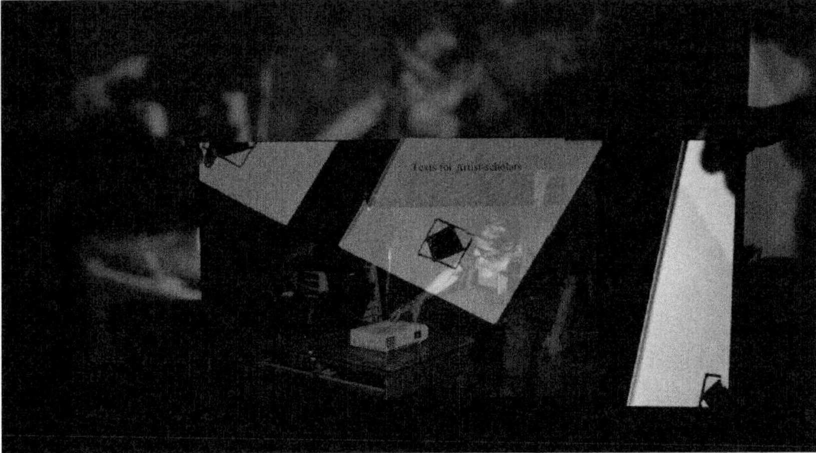

Through the performance of *this* Walk, the Artist-scholar transforms. These transformations are generative, and iterative. They also dynamically change through space and time. The iterative dynamism is an ouroboros infinity loop of time and space. This infinity loop is mapped through the performative walk. This transformation of the walk to Event is a discursive passage from text to record, *through* a performance and re-performance. Keeney argues for the necessity to privilege the archaic and/or out-model modalities of discursive and non-discursive scholarship in order to "escape the circularity and claustrophobia of the Arts and Letters today" (2015: x).

PASSAGE = THEATRE

THEATRE = SPACE FOR BEING + DOING

WALK THROUGH PASSAGE = BEING + DOING

PASSAGE = ARCHAIC DISCURSIVE SPACE

Verb-tenses:

INVOKE - WALK - MAKE

Proper nouns:

VENUSIAN - ARTIST-SCHOLAR - ELSE-WHERE

Time-senses:

FUTURAL - NOW - THEN

The settings of the stage are re-projected into a formalist layered stage-set. Three white screens are hung vertically, spaced apart in three directions such that the fragmentation of the surface create a space. The landscapes from which the quest has emerged are re-projected within this formalist stage-set. The walk is staged inside these fragmented re-projected landscapes. This re-projection leads to a performative reading of the theatrical walk.

N.B. All italics are notations of the theatrical cinematic re-performance of the Artist-scholar's walk.

N.B. All bold-faced are the landscapes against which the walk is seen.

ACT 1

INVOCATION TO THE VENUSIAN SHAPE-SHIFTER

INTERVAL: A scene from Derek Jarman's 'Blue' becomes the plane of invocation. Shadows dance inside the 'Blue'. We realize that the inside is a tomb.

SCENE 1 | WALK

Two sentries guard a doorway with their sticks making an "X" on the doorway. On a fragmented screen behind, their headless silhouettes guard themselves guarding the screen. We see the screen move slightly.

Voice begins to read to the screen.

"We shall now tune into the frequencies along which the temporal scale operates.

We shall reach into the space that is called the Past.

It might be found along the horizontal time-axis and can be located by following more of the same.

To the keen observer, sometimes an arch may be visible that reaches into the future. To the believer, the arch shall present itself into the Now."

Words merge close together to become a chant.

The sentries fragment on the screens.

Voice is static in space.

The visual fragments dissolve in darkness.

We have not walked at all.

***

INTERVAL: A scene from Derek Jarman's 'Blue' becomes the plane of invocation. Shadows dance inside the 'Blue'. We realize that the inside is a tomb.

SCENE 2 | PAUSE

The sentries give way. We are in front of a tower made of foam-boards, each of the boards inscribed with High-Romanticist ideals, and magical realist transformations.

"Under this arch is the space of the 'Present'. We may choose to call it the 'Archive'.

We will stop to look at a locked closet called Evidence.

We will reach into our dark pockets and change the lock.

The lock shall now read - Chance.

The changing of the lock will lead to a change in the closet itself.

It shall no longer be a wooden closet, opaque, filled to the brink with documents – historical detritus.

We will see it transform into constellations;

knitted like the verses of a poem, and not tied like the beads of a rosary.

We shall weave ourselves within the Evidence."

Half of the tower is intact.

The other half is fragmented on fragmented screens.

Voice becomes its Shadow.

It is seen within the fragments.

Shadow walks behind the intact tower and disappears.

Voice can still be heard.

> "The Present shall be freed, slowly, becoming the here-and-now.
>
> The Archive shall no longer be bound to the past."

***

INTERVAL: A scene from Derek Jarman's 'Blue' becomes the plane of invocation. Shadows are dancing inside the 'Blue'. We realize that the inside is a tomb.

SCENE 3 | WALK TO CIRCLE

> **The foam-board tower succumbs to a black shadow that envelopes it from above. The High-Romanticist ideals and magical realist transformations are still visible. They are within our reach amidst the debris.**

> "A winged angel guards the gates of 'Now'.
>
> The angel shall appear to be a hologram.
>
> The digital origins of this angel shall be mysterious.
>
> A debate will ensue over the identity of the angel.
>
> Some of us will refuse to recognize it.
>
> As we stand there, we shall bear witness to its changing forms;
>
> Klee's Angelus Novus to Benjamin's Angel of History to Scholem's Angelus Satanus.
>
> Its wings shall seem inadequate for flight of any kind.
>
> It shall appear suspended like a marionette.

The uncertainty shall put a lot of them off.

They shall call it Chaos."

The broken tower is fragmented into debris.

Voice is still disembodied.

The chant slowly becomes dense, almost illegible.

Voice becomes Body momentarily.

Body passes through the opening of the fragmented screens and disappears again.

Voice appears as Shadow again.

"We shall call it Chaos."

Shadow dissolves into the black.

This is Milton's Chaos – an "abyss", "a gulf" and the "vast vacuity" in which all the elements "in their pregnant pauses mixed/Confus'dly" (2001: 39).

***

INTERVAL: A scene from Derek Jarman's 'Blue' becomes the plane of invocation. Shadows are dancing inside the 'Blue'. We realize that the inside is a tomb.

SCENE 4 | PAUSE TO REVER

The debris becomes a poem. We see fragments of the poem captured as an image. The poem walks as a silhouette within the image. The Artist-scholar walks into the poem and becomes a silhouette again.

Shadow walks out from behind the blue tomb and stands meditating.

"The few who decide to stay shall witness the angel change its form.

It is no longer recognizable.

We may decide to put some distance between the angel and ourselves.

One of us shall decide to stay a moment longer.

In that moment, we discover the angel's origins.

We shall be able to see through a man.

He had allowed himself a moment longer with the angel.

The angel and the man looked the same.

Both with a churning core.

And a transparent outline on their bodies.

We shall all huddle closer and become outlines.

The gates open."

Shadow is now walking across the breadth of the stage-set, in and out of the fragmented screens and becomes partly corporeal.

The walk around the screen allows it to be multiple.

At times, it is Shadow. Sometimes, Body.

Sometimes Voice becomes both, simultaneously.

Body stands behind the image of the poem, reading it out.

The chant becomes less dense.

The screens and the poem move.

***

INTERVAL: A scene from Derek Jarman's 'Blue' becomes the plane of invocation. Shadows are dancing inside the 'Blue'. We are inside a tomb.

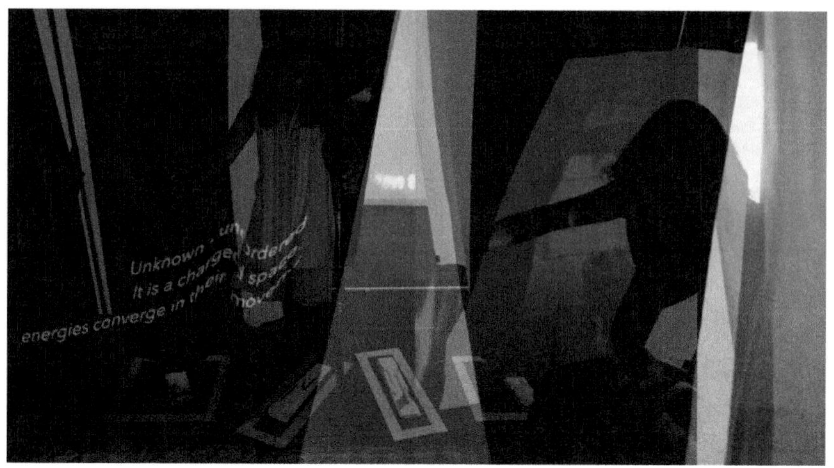

SCENE 5 | PAUSE TO PAUSE

A shapeshifter appears on the screen as a spectral image. The Artist-scholar recognizes and stands in devotion. The screen becomes a sacred space. We begin to walk into it.

We shall endeavour to occupy the "Now".

Standing at its gates, we will see that shadows, silhouettes and reflections populate it.

The shadows from beyond the gates might tell us that the "Now" is the densest in the timescale. Bachelard calls it the "poetic instant", from where the vertical time shoots off,

Releasing occupants from a chronological movement along the horizontal time-axis.

Free of causation, we shall become aware of "irruptions" – solar flares.

Body has again walked out of Voice.

The walk de-laminates the screen.

Voice walks down the stage, alone.

A spectral image haunts its path.

The surface is now an altar for transformations.

The surface becomes a space.

The altar dissolves into a black shrine.

Voice walks out of the darkness and becomes the spectral body.

***

INTERVAL: A scene from Derek Jarman's 'Blue' becomes the plane of invocation. Shadows are dancing inside the 'Blue'. We are inside a tomb.

SCENE 6 | PAUSE TO WALK

The Artist-scholar walks into the black shrine. It is lit up by a candle at the centre of a cuboid frame, inside a half-cube. He holds an empty foam-board against the flame. The flame begins to dance on the surfaces of the shrine.

One shall become many, and many shall be compressed into one.

We shall catch a glimpse into the nature of generative narratives, *narrativity itself.*

Tales shall be born of the same womb but become very different animals.

Man, and animal shall become one, as in archaic illuminated manuscripts of Paradise.

In the "Now", we may become limbs of these beasts, enabling them to walk or fly,

or we may sometimes become the bigger beasts, and full of ourselves, consuming the narratives to satiate our present hunger.

In the "Now", we shall discover the lives of these narratives when they live *in* Us.

Perhaps, we may fill the voids in the wings of the angel at the gate.

Perhaps, it may fly again, and with it, so shall we.

Body joins Shadow.

They walk inside the shrine.

Chanting becomes words.

Voice moves into a glowing space.

In the darkness, Voice cries,

"…with it, so shall we."

***

INTERVAL: A scene from Derek Jarman's 'Blue' becomes the plane of invocation. Shadows are dancing inside the 'Blue'. We are inside a tomb.

SCENE 7 | WALK TO PAUSE

The Artist-scholar is back in front of the screen. The sentries have relaxed their guard. One of the sentries opens the screen door to reveal a space of transformations. The Artist-scholar walks into it.

Inside the "Now", we shall experience simultaneity.

We will have been enabled to experience the chronological horizontal time,

while crossing over into a vertical, non-causal time.

We will ascribe it to the spatial experience
of being in the secret garden called
Archive.

We will use the theatre to register the
various agencies that make visiting the
archive a type of séance and call out to the
source, the space, the extensions;

all incomplete without the lost subjective
states of those who created the record,

with their internal landscapes,

activating presences with their being
present in the "poetic instant" and creating
it, simultaneously;

the rupture of the screen between the
individual and collective landscape.

Voice continues to walk the darkness.

The screen on the screens invites Shadow to inhabit it.

The screens on the stage transform the walking shadow into a body.

Body and the screen move together.

Rhythm overtakes motion. The walk becomes a dance.

Dance absorbs the Walk.

ACT 2

THE ARTIST-SCHOLAR WALKS

[The Artist-Scholar makes art and shares scholarship…]

1…2…3…4

2…3…4…5

[… makes scholarship, and shares art.]

1…2….3…4…5…6…

[THE LAST DANCE]

The sentries have given their guard sticks to the Artist-scholar. The sticks have become props in his hands. His walking body has become the receiver of the High-Romanticist ideals projected through an invisible source. His half-lit body is partially corporeal, and partly spectral. The screens behind are animated by this split dance.

The foam-board from the shrine makes an appearance. The walking bodies have hidden in the darkness, the foam-boards are the only recipients of knowledge. An unknown hand animates the surface of the screens.

The Artist-scholar and sentries decode messages received from inside the shrine. They walk into a forest. The Venusian shapeshifter had assembled a forest from the debris.

The forest sends out these coded messages. The Artist-scholar walks amidst the debris, touching them to transform them into images and then enchanting them to move. The enchanted forest is now made of trees.

The shrine has moved into the forest. The forest has moved into the theatre.

The foam-board tower of High-Romanticist ideals materializes in the forest. The walk is a circumambulation.

The forest becomes the theatre again. The theatre is made of black and white screens, each of them receiving fragments of messages from the Venusian. A sacred symbol appears.

It is a rotated Black Square inside a White Square. This appearance transforms the screen into a shrine.

The sacred symbol disappears. The forest disappears. The Artist-scholar walks back and forth in the same rhythm inside the theatre.

The Artist-scholar walks out the theatre. They reconfigure the screens that make up the thick space. The Body parts a large black screen, and a grey space is revealed. A passage is seen in the distance. The Artist-scholar has paused, longing for the passage through the grey space. The black and the grey and the white together are the Theatre. The Passage. The Archaic Discursive Space.

Shadows of past and present selves are seen walking through the grey space. In the depth of the black screen, the image of the candle inside the square frame haunts this passage.

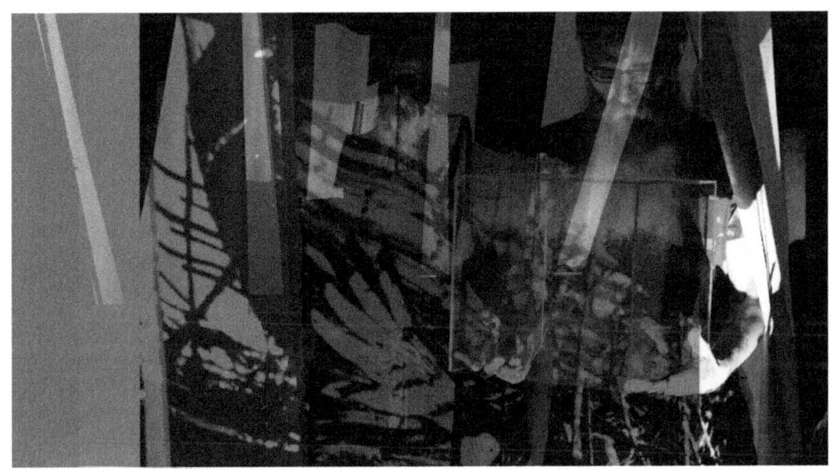

[A SILENT WALK]

The screens on the stage are static.

Shadow moves across it.

Body picks up a set of found tarot cards from the darkness and holds it against the quickly disappearing images of the prophecies of the new myths.

Body and Shadow together try to capture the making of the new myths.

The tarot cards on the stage fan out to re-inforce the new myths slowly vanishing.

Theatre becomes a shrine again.

The walk is now a passage between the theatre and the shrine – realms separated by bodies and shadows, tied together by the Voice.

ACT 3

LOOKING FOR ELSE-WHERE

[VENUSIAN SHAPE-SHIFTER = ARTIST-SCHOLAR]

The Artist-scholar has collected the foam-board pieces of the broken tower of High-Romanticist ideals and magical realist transformations.

He can be seen laying them flat on the floor and perusing their non-structural configurations as puzzles.

He stacks them into two groups. The pieces of the tower are now Tarot Cards. Both the stacks are framed on the black floor with glowing white borders.

The screens part to reveal that the Artist-scholar has been working in the passage between two realms. A place to walk has become a place to make new myths, between being and doing.

She joins the Artist-scholar's reverie with the Tarot Cards. She walks in circles around the spots that have been marked to carry the tarot cards. Her dance consecrates the site.

The passage begins to get populated as the Artist-scholar begins to read the Tarot Cards. People from all over flock to see the spectacle. New myths are constructed out of High-Romanticist ideals already inscribed on the tarot cards. The darkness becomes a fertile ground for the myths to walk upon and into.

The first myth glows white in darkness - "Text for Artist-scholars". Two shadowy hands hold it. A rotated black square inside a white square mark the myth.

The next myth is churned out. It reads, "Transmedia as event + catalogue + archival record + technical/existential report + re-performance…". A shadow behind visually chants, "Theatrical cinematic conceptual formalism". A corporeal hand is holding both these myths in the dark. The rotated black square inside the white square seems to be floating in the distance.

A hand appears glowing. She was kneeling in front of the Artist-scholar as he held out the Tarot Cards in front of her to choose from. Their shadows loom large behind on the screens. The screens remind us of the theatre they are in.

Two hands hold out another tarot card. One holds it, and her hand points to "Post-view, pre-view…"

The Artist-scholar holds yet another card in the path of the light. "…post-rationalization" shines bright. "Romantic formalism" is partly visible.

Silhouettes of hands hold a Tarot Card like the conducting stick of a music conductor. In the background, a stormy sea is crashing against stones. The only myth that appears on the Tarot Card under the shadowy hand reads "The right to have no rights."

The Artist-scholar seems to have found an answer. He begins to walk out with the sentry's stick in his hand. A shadow of a sea-siren with sixteen fingers is seen crying out from within the grey space he has just left.

The shadowy self of the Artist-scholar reaches his boat. His corporeal hand barely does. The boat leaves with the shadow. There is no reference to where the boat goes.

The forest and the theatre are empty.

The Venusian shape-shifter walks into the shrine. The Artist-scholar sits meditating. Words float above his head.

"The Edge, the crossing,

Where one is both there and not there,

Where one is united with this and that

One…"

The gates to the shrine cross again with the sticks making an "X" again. The sentries have disappeared. Only their hands remain holding the "X" in place.

[AN EXCEPTIONAL TRANSFORMATION]

We now recognise she is the shapeshifter charged by darkness.

The darkness lifts.

Shadow becomes Body, completely.

Body dances on the theatrical stage.

The dance enchants the Artist-scholar studying the High-Romanticist ideals.

The shape-shifter – Body, Voice and Shadow together – picks up parts of magical realist transformations and highlights them on the stage.

She swiftly transforms from Body to Shadow, silently.

She only walks between the screens on stage and the screens on screen.

The walk transforms her Walk into a new myth.

She stops.

References

Keeney, G. (2010) *Art as 'Night' – An Art Theological Treatise,* Cambridge Scholars Publishing

______ (2015) *Knowledge, Spirit, Law,* Punctum Books

Milton, J. (1667) *Paradise Lost: Book 2.* Global Language Resources DJVU E-Book, 2010. Available at: bit.ly/wnm45. (Accessed: 01 Jan 2020)

How do our bodies act as instruments of sensory navigation? A study through 'shared acts of sensing'.

Emma Bush

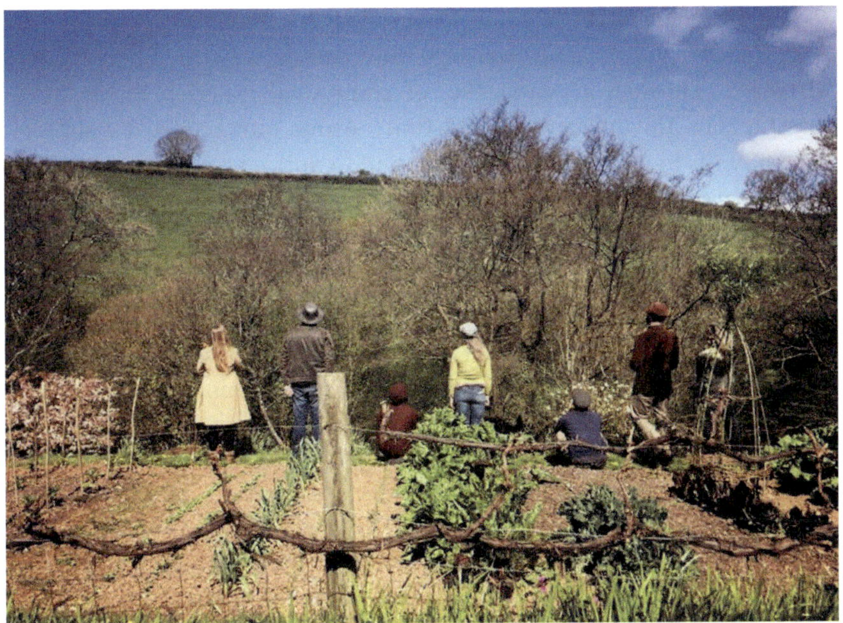

'warm-up'. one. May 2017, Coombe Farm Rural Arts Centre, Dittisham.
Photo: Lara Lloyd

Navigation

I am interested in using performance walking to invite the senses to become more alert to 'thing power', the unceasing motion and responsiveness inherent in objects including those usually considered inert or dead. Past works – 'Fields', 'City Walk' and 'Village Walk' – have worked with observation, twilight, the animal gaze, and translating shared oral histories into performance. Recent works place 'shared acts of sensing' in a central role with a shift towards a more participatory embodied way-finding.

'warm-up' is a research group I began in 2017; a series of small-scale research gatherings with a low-key intimate atmosphere, encouraging reciprocal learning and teaching. Over the past two years we have had twelve day-long events hosted at various locations. 'warm up' explores embodied approaches to place, and extended modes of sensing by using a variety of methods. We gather together with around 6-12 people from a group of (around 40) arts and ecology professionals working in areas including visual arts, sound, radio, voice-work, somatics, ornithology, naturalism, statistics, botany, choreography and performance.

Night Walk[1] is an ongoing project which offers an opportunity to experience 'shared acts of sensing' on a coastal walk to Elberry Cove, Brixham. Through a gentle play of communal experience, we arrive together in this place at night-time, using our bodies as sensory instruments to navigate the darkness and to notice what is already there. I will share some fieldnotes reflecting on this collective orientation:

Fieldnotes: Night Walk, Mary Loveday, Sept 2019

I read a book once where the author surmised that the origins of dance were in a bunch of single smaller organisms (people) getting together in order to look like a bigger organism, either for protection from large predators, or to chase large animals like mammoths off cliffs for food. Moving together in unison would make the group of smaller organisms into one large one. I think this is something like what you are trying to accomplish, and it fits into the whole focus-pulling (or focus-changing) underpinning of the walk – from individual to group energy, from internal to external, from interiority to awareness of other sentiences. With this section of the walk we are paying attention to our interior speeds; with the walk to the trees we are paying attention to a kind of group pace. I think the 360° turn is a good way to change from an interior awareness of ourselves, to the awareness of a larger field of attention, in order to be able to attend to a group sense. By the time we get to the trees on the hill we are about to enter into ourselves again, but on the way there we have been the one monster, so to speak.

---

[1] Night Walk is a project commissioned by the Eyeview Cultural Programme based in Torbay made in collaboration with artists Mary Loveday and Anna Keleher.

In writing about materiality and sensory perception within archaeology practices, Linda Hurcombe writes: "Traditionally sensory perception is described in relation to five senses; visual, auditory, tactile, olfactory and gustatory. This division is argued to be a convenience of analysis but not part of the reality of a holistic sensory system where sensations perceived by one mechanism act as cues for the receipt of other sensations and where inter-sensoriality is recognised." (Hurcombe, 2007: 537)

Recent collaborative walks in my practice-led research –'warm-up walk', Feb 2019 and 'Night Walk' – have created space for 'shared acts of sensing': a term I have invented to describe collective acts of looking, listening and more broadly the orientation and perception of the senses. Focusing on particular ways of framing communal observation these are performance acts aimed towards a radical permeability, offering insight into embodied encounters between 'self' and 'other.'

Cultural anthropologist Anna Tsing states: "To listen to and tell a rush of stories is a method. Its research object is contaminated diversity; its unit of analysis is the indeterminate encounter. To learn anything, we must revitalise arts of noticing and include ethnography and natural history. A rush of stories cannot be neatly summed up; they draw attention to interrupting geographies and tempos." (Tsing, 2015: 37)

I am interested in making time for 'arts of noticing' through direct material sensory experience and framing this participation as central to the life of an artwork. The embodied trans-sensual fluidity proposed here in attending to matter, the body and sensation encourages "combining different senses with a generalised intuition that seems to be a kind of webbing, so there is a relation, overlayed by an overarching 'feel' for the multiplicities." (Smith, 2019)

This participatory embodied way finding is informed by performance training in embodiment, somatics, and kinaesthetic awareness, through developing 'shared acts of sensing' I aim to find out more about using the body as a tool for sensory navigation. For the purposes of this paper I will look more closely at the term, 'shared acts of sensing' and attempt to begin creating a definition.[1]

---

[1] A definition will support my own modes of reflecting on shared acts of sensing, by attempting to articulate practice more precisely I aim to find out more about what is happening here. This reflecting occurs through my own experience of making and doing and through feedback gathered from participants' fieldnotes. It provides a jumping off point for further dialogue and investigation.

Introduction

I entered an old cream house with a green door in Plymouth (UK) where recently I visited an exhibition by Helen Billinghurst and Phil Smith titled 'Plymouth Labyrinth'. This exhibition brought together elements of their walking practice, mapping, sculpture, word-smithing and myth-making. Whilst sitting talking to Helen and Phil, I was given a lump of clay and invited to make an imagined extra-sensory organ. I enjoyed the feel of the clay, its cool damp surfaces, moulding and shaping it in my hands, not knowing what it would become, feeling out the folds, apertures and curves … which eventually formed an imaginary sensory organ. I was invited to place this 'organ' on an altar to join others in an accumulated collection. Through haptic memory, the strong physical impact in recollection of the act of touch and the remaining physical presence of the object in the room, this act offered me lasting material contact or participation with the exhibition beyond the duration of my visit.

I work with an approach that creates pockets of time, or spaciousness, and potentially frees us from our habitual patterns of observation – using tools from performance, including non-linear story-telling, gesture, and repetition to guide attention and to make an invitation. To stand still and simply look at the sky, a snowdrop, or a stone wall for five, ten or fifty minutes is an unusual act. To do this looking, really looking – especially in a group, is something we don't often do, perhaps because we do not have time or capacity, perhaps because we are so often lost in thought and a large part of our lives is now constantly screened or mediated by technologies. This practice is concerned with making spaces available for intimate encounters with materiality, meeting points between self and other, in a way that relies on sensual lived experience and remembering how to refine our receptivity.

John Berger's extraordinary capacity to paint creaturely, precise, felt images in words teaches us how to look at the world again. In the film, 'The Art of Looking,' Berger explains, "The removal of cataracts of the eyes is comparable with the removal of a particular form of forgetfulness, your eyes begin to remember first times, and it is in this sense that what they experience after the intervention is a kind of visual renaissance". (Berger cited in Dvorak: 2016)

In her essay 'Against Interpretation' Susan Sontag says:

> Ours is a culture based on excess, on overproduction; the result
> is a steady loss of sharpness in our sensory experience. All the
> conditions of modern life – its material plenitude, its sheer

crowdedness – conjoin to dull our sensory faculties. What is important now is to recover our senses. We must learn to see more, to hear more, to feel more. Our task is to cut back content so that we can see the thing at all. In place of a hermeneutics we need an erotics of art. (Sontag, 1964: 13-14)

Definition

I will begin to explain what I mean by 'shared acts of sensing,' in a series of points:

1. There will be an emphasis on sensory contact with materials and thus a direct 'lived experience' of materiality.

2. This 'collective observation' will have a particular set and setting and the collective attention will be guided by a clearly marked temporal and spatial frame.

3. The shared act will be performed by a group of people in the same location, enacting the same task, at the same time.

4. The experiences I am referring to will most often take place outdoors, though not exclusively. Exercises can be tailored to different locations in a site-responsive mode – words and instructions will adapt and refer to the specific material qualities of each place visited.

5. Language will operate through instruction or score as a mode of storytelling, priming or guiding aimed at inviting participants to particular spaces of collective encounter. The language used will be a blend of fact and fiction and will suggest, emphasise, and frame notions on which the continuity of the walk lies.

6.

7. Shared acts of sensing will potentially reacquaint us with familiar territory by re-examining our experience of place and our relationship with our surroundings.

8. Shared acts of sensing will alter our experience of time, for example in the act of slow walking and thus could be viewed as techniques for time travel.

Point 6 in the above list represents an intentional lacuna, to make space for the un-known or in-expressible element. A large part of what renders these acts interesting or enjoyable is the shared experience of the unknown encounter that cannot be pinned down or tamed into a definition. The participation encountered invites a shared language of experience, a felt understanding that we are learning all the time with small subtle shifts and adjustments, a return to our creaturely selves.

Of course what we can 'know' about the specific sensory experiences of another, be they human, animal plant-based or inorganic in origin, is limited and problematic. It is good to be sceptical about just how much of these activities is shared and who with. In the example of groups of humans sharing directed activities, any attempt to verbalise these experiences is obviously flawed, but nonetheless interesting and valuable. There is intrigue in the 'not-knowing'; we stand together in tentative anticipation that we have a shared intention to perform an act together. This sharing does not imply an equivalence of experience – what we notice and how we notice it will vary and those differences in what draws or attracts our attention are revealing.

Sensation

A shared sense of time opening up or slowing down can create space in which sensory attention is given room to notice small details or events; the constant flux of change about and within us is given the opportunity to arise. Calvino describes this process of noticing as the invisible becoming visible he reflects on the epic poem the 'De Rerum Natura', On the Nature of Things (first century BCE), in which Lucretius describes "the little motes of dust swirling in a shaft of sunlight in a dark room" (II.114-124); the minuscule shells, all similar but each one different, that waves gently cast up on the *bibula harena*, the "imbibing sand" (II.374-376); or the spiderwebs "that wrap themselves around us without our noticing them as we walk along." (III.381-390)' (Calvino, 1988: 9)

Shared acts of sensing can give rise to a space in which our perception is invited to slow down, to look anew without preconceptions and indeed to attempt to see "as if for the first time" (Whitehead, 2017). I suggest that these shared acts bring us closer in affect to Bergson's theoretical position of pure perception. This attempt – albeit impossible – to get closer to a spontaneity of vision is encouraged in Goethean observation[2].

---

[2] As Brook (1998: 68) states; "It should be noted that what is represented here as the method is a combined interpretation of Goethe's methodology being practiced in Britain. As with any live tradition there are constant reinterpretations, developments and debate about what Goethean Science actually is."

A spontaneity of vision or more widely sensory perception is impossible because we come with our histories, memories, our 'life-worlds,' placing a filter, between us and all that we meet, or come into contact with. When we look, listen, touch, taste or remember anything – in those first flickers of a moment's encounter – in the instant that a space of recognition opens up the possibility of seeing things in themselves as they are begins to close down.

Goethean observation provides a scientific method with clear experiential methodologies for inviting a visceral, bodily and sensual experience of the other through qualitative modes of observation. (Brook, 1998; Myers, 1997; Bortoft, 1996). So, for example, this would be the start of one set of instructions to describe an approach towards observing a plant or flower[3]:

1. Allow the plant or flower to select you as much as you are selecting it – for example, while walking across a field or lane try to be alert to which plant 'calls out to you.'

2. When approaching the plant or flower try not to categorise your specimen as part of a known family, for example, 'I am now holding a nettle', but rather try to see this specimen as an individual and try to look closely at its details without allowing preconceived notions or information to interrupt or foreclose your sensory receptivity.

3. Take an extended moment in time, ten minutes, to look closely at this specimen, with the naked eye, firstly close-up, and now hold it further away.

4. Keep returning to this looking and tactile observation. Hold it, smell it, touch it, listen to it – let the object and the information it contains present itself to you. Notice varied colours, shades, lines, textures, markings.

---

[3] This set of instructions for observation is my own re-writing from memory based on activities led by other specialists on a number of occasions: botanist Richard Lewis and Artist Mark Leahy's workshop 'Herbarium' as part of 'Language Landscape and the Sublime', 2016 at Dartington Hall Estate, also multiple exercises led by Richard Lewis and Tony Whitehead as part of the 'warm-up' series of transdisciplinary workshops 2017 – ongoing, curated by me.

We look and we look again, we draw the details, try to describe in words, we listen with our touch and our eyes, then we use a hand lens to magnify the details 10 times more. We let the information come to us, present itself and wash over us. Going out like hunters, we try to become more porous and open to our more-than human selves.

Movement artist Paula Kramer stresses that "whilst perception, awareness and attentiveness might reach out from the body into the world, receptivity emphasises receiving information and allowing it to seep into the body". (Kramer, 2012: 86) Within performance training, sensory data does at times seem to present itself to meet our awareness anew, momentarily the world rushes in with all its material vitality and presence. At this juncture, the balance between self, mind, memory, thought and perception is somehow re-struck or trained to behave otherwise.

Cultivating alternative modes of observation which are akin to Goethean observation, Berger's 'ways of looking', and Sontag's 'Against Interpretation', we are offered the opportunity to be surprised by details; patination, shine, transparency, smoothness, speckling, veins, hairs, sparkle. In this way we see something which cannot ordinarily be perceived, or habitually is not perceived; we see the world which surrounds us all the time but which is so often hidden from our eyes.

This mode of observation offers insights from the viewpoint of a world in which agency is more evenly distributed allowing for an approach which acknowledges networked processes of perception which can reside in, deflect from and be triggered by 'object'[4] and further encourages a decentralising of the object/subject dualism. Blassnig states 'Bergson attempted to bridge the dualism between external and internal states through the notion of extensity – the extension of consciousness placing itself into the things to be perceived.'[5] (Blassnig, 2009: 47) and further:

---

[4] object: I use the term fluidly to refer to multiple things –

(a) significant material objects encountered, e.g. sky, stone-wall, invertebrate, bacteria, electricity, ocean.

(b) The human body itself can be sensed interchangeably as a subject and an object through various means and media including somatics and other performance training methods.

[5] Bergson said: "My perception can, then, only be some part of these objects themselves; it is in them rather than they in it." (cited in Blassnig, 2009: 43)

Bergson also referred to this as an intellectual sympathy, if only very briefly, in which we coincide ('co-inside') with the object'. This action, Bergson claimed, takes effort and cannot be sustained for long; the mind usually oscillates between the two states, between the movement of the intellect and intuition, which constitute a collaborative, complementary entanglement serving the creative evolution of human consciousness.

(Blassnig, 2009: 189-90)

Fieldnotes: Anna Keleher, warm-up. one. May 2016.

"Choose a patch of sky, this big and this wide," she says. And her five-minute bell measures the sky. Mind rays shoot from six times two eyes. Mind hovers above our gaze. Our gaze hovers beyond, shuttles. Holds steady, expands. Cloud grows, disperses, leaves. Am I sky? Or in the sky? Six humans looking up at me. Pinpricks of light in their eyes. The bell brings us back down. Minds spool home. Sky again becomes sky. We again become we, not Sky.

Emma says to take off our shoes, for a slow walk. Warm bare earth, soft sponge, sharp water, grit, rushing water. Our eyes that have been in the sky are now in our feet.

Cognition

Reading on social and embodied cognition in the *Stanford Encyclopaedia of Philosophy* offered some insights on collective observation, agency, and self:

"If the mind is not skull-bound but at least embodied, and perhaps even extended, then what view should we adopt of the self, subjectivity, and consciousness?" (Wilson & Foglia, 2017)… "where mind goes, the self follows: if the mind is extended, for example, so too is the self". (Clark & Chalmers cited in Wilson and Foglia, 2017)

One way of looking at this problem would be to imagine an *extended* biological system, "such as spiders and the webs they spin – these organisms are bounded, roughly speaking, by their cohesive, organic bodies, but still act in the world through the extended biological systems they construct". (Wilson, 2005 cited in Wilson & Foglia, 2017)

Perhaps sensory observations might guide us to consider our individual selves as multiple, our bodies as collectives. We are made up of flesh, bones, organs, micro-bacteria, virus, toxins, blood, fascia – all these parts of our selves combine to allow cognition, perception, attention, sensing, in this regard, sensing is always a collective effort. I am interested in viewing these shared acts of sensing as a kind of standing to attention, a showing up for and experimenting in collective world making.

Bratman defines conditions necessary for 'Shared Cooperative Activity' (Bratman, 1992: 328) including:

1. mutual responsiveness
2. commitment to the joint activity
3. commitment to mutual support

Bratman states "our activity could be co-operative despite differences" (ibid: 332), the shared acts of sensing being explored here are a mode of collaboration and attuning the self in readiness for the unknown encounter. This willing acknowledgement of differential experience and the unknown underpin the shared or 'mutual commitment' encouraged in the guiding language used on a performance walk: "Let us use our efforts collectively as a group today to stay focused and committed to the tasks we are performing, engaging together in some 'serious play' …" (2019: Night Walk) I borrow Turner's phrase here to begin thinking about the way this 'serious play' (Turner, 2001) is organised in my practice as research –through shared acts of sensing.

Formation

What then are the are rules for this 'serious play'? A group of human bodies will be organised and placed into a considered formation – with a chosen distance setting them apart, in a chosen position e.g. standing, sitting or lying down. The intended formation provides a *tension* or a resistance for the activity, a set and setting outside our habitual experience, functioning as a design which holds and gathers the experience. This modelling provides a formality or a disciplined structure and for some participants is part of a strengthening framework which may bring a more relaxed merging into the activity and/or a frustration or resistance. The *tension* perhaps exists in the pull between the orderliness and constraint of formality alongside the (sometimes) welcome relief offered in moments through a movement towards stillness and a listening to all that is sounding in silence. I will list some of the formations commonly used in shared acts of sensing:

1. Cluster (gather behind) within designated proximity

2. Horizontal line

3. Circle or Semi-Circle

4. Vertical line (sometimes joined together by an invisible golden thread or rope)

5. Scattered for example in a forest each standing beside a tree

6. Two adjacent packs facing one another across a field

7. A random constellation is formed which creates its own effect

Intention

If there is a shared intention in these performative acts then how can we begin to articulate it without inhibiting the performance of these embodied actions? In the work I am discussing here shared acts of sensing have actively enabled the formation of a temporary community through shared intention;

- To arrive into place more fully
- To touch. To meet. To come to know the material of the place
- To relax and enter into the body more fully

An immersion into or return to *the body* is a vital component in this work and the types of exchange or sharing allowed move beyond and besides words. This language of sensation is one which shifts and responds sensitively to subtle changes, such as weight distribution, dropping the left shoulder, the weather, including the touch of breeze, rain or sun on the skin, group re-positioning, and, most importantly, to sensory re-alignments offered in the presentation to the group. The overarching framework of the walks uses specific language through storytelling, instruction, rhythm and atmosphere guiding each participant deliberately back towards somatic experience through cues which foreground sensation, touch and materiality. For example, at the start of a coastal Night Walk we say:

> There are edges and cliffs that fall away to sea and gaps in hedges … if you go astray … you could stumble or fall. So, we will stick together. In a pack. We will each help to create a safe space … not wander off. We will hold the space together keeping it safe, focused and contained. We will become collectively an imaginary beast with many eyes, hearts, mouths, heads, tentacles spreading out into and gently touching the night. So, in other words when we move together, we may heighten our capacity, we may sense more, we may feel more of the sensation in our own organs, turning, responding, listening.

Bergson talks of the body as an 'obstacle for perception' and perception as a 'filter or screen'. What then is the role of the body in these circumstances? It must include the difficulty in standing still, the ache in the small of the back, the challenge in coming back to the task of attending to a particular object or state, the meeting place where our foot meets the ground. This accepting physical discomforts, and manifold distractions alongside ease, loosening and receptivity is part of the challenge offered here in this 'education of the senses.' (Bergson cited in Blassnig, 2009: 181)

I would suggest that framing and experiencing these events as a live performance offers heightened focus internally and this operates in connection with the affect or 'idea' of being witnessed. Over the last 18 years I have led collective acts of looking at the sky in which many human bodies stand together in a vertical relation between ground and sky[6]. Standing in formation for various durations of ten, twenty, fifty minutes, we closely observe a patch of sky together. Participants have often remarked on the effect of being witnessed as a kind of crystallising of presence, giving heightened intensity to the shared activity. Paula Kramer observes this happening in her movement practice "I was also working in the presence of an audience of one (a witness) …, which often helps to clarify my actions and heightens my sense of presence". (Kramer, 2012: 88)

---

[6] Some of these sensory observations were developed in 'propeller performance' – a collective I co-founded in 2003. They have since been shared in many contexts with many people across educational institutes, festivals, in the woods, the village and the city. propeller were Emma Bush, Neil Callaghan, Augusto Corrieri, Pete Harrison and Timothy Vize-Martin.

At the simplest level I propose performance as a work of art that is staged as a live event or has live presence. In *Performance in Contemporary Art*, Catherine Wood suggests the "*liveness* is not just an attribute of the human actors involved but a state of *potentiality* embodied in how all the elements of a work might move or change." (Wood, 2018: 10). I use the term performance here to indicate a range of '*live*' events, covering a whole scale from the human body placed in space-time before an audience to the invisible, shimmering, effervescent, vibration of atoms inside a metal structure, taking place already on its own without witness. Or perhaps the moment when something becomes hinted at, framed, gestured towards or offered as a site of interest so that it has a witness to 'perform' for. Or perhaps the notion that if we earnestly accept the agency and independent liveliness inherent in 'thing power' the sky could be performing for the ground or vice versa…. thus raising the question: how would we know? Or why is this interesting? Or perhaps anything can be viewed as a performance or narrative if it is framed with intention and an audience's attention is directed towards it within a guided setting.

We may consider shared acts of sensing as artworks in their own right, although small scale interventions they are also offered as acts for the 'environment' (field, city, garden, town square) in which we are co-present fully aware of the possibility of the reciprocal gaze. In this regard 'performing' plays provocatively with the notion of reciprocity or exchange across human and non-human actors. Shared acts of sensing can give a sense of temporary community, solidarity, or shared common ground which heightens focus and gives rise to an expansive sense of belonging with the matter of the world.

> While we might agree that every action is a micro-political act, Bergson's insights go even further in considering every perception as a political act, precisely because of the inherent political agency in the beholder's engagement with the present.
>
> (Blassnig, 2009: 201)

Fieldnotes: Tony Whitehead, warm-up. three. October 2017

> A Dartington garden. An entrainment. Simply sitting back to back. Breathing. In. This garden. Out. With thousand eye birches. Fuzzy-edged oaks, shedding leaves, becoming lighter. Opal dusted petals revealed in glass (10x, 20x). Lichen coastlines folded in infinite length. Soft meows of distant buzzards, closer croaks of raven. All in good company. All in good time.

References

Berger, John (2016) *Confabulations*, Penguin, Random House

Blassnig, Martha (2009) *Time, Memory, Consciousness and The Cinema Experience, Resituating the 'Spiritual' Dimension in the Perceptual Processes of The Spectator*, Rodopi

Bratman, Michael E. (1992) *Shared Cooperative Activity, The Philosophical Review* Vol. 101, No. 2, pp. 327-341. Duke Univ. Press. Available at: bit.ly/wnm181 (Accessed: 01 Oct 2019)

Bortoft, Henri (1996) *The Wholeness of Nature: Goethe's Way of Science*, Floris Books

Brook, Isis (1998) 'Goethean science as a way to read landscape', *Landscape Research*, Volume 23, Issue 1, March 1998, p51-69. Available at: https://bit.ly/wnm179 (Accessed: 04 Feb 2020)

Calvino, Italo (1988) *Six memos for the next millennium*, Random House

Dvorak, Cordelia (2016) John Berger: The Art of Looking, Documentary film, Dir. Piotr Rosolowski. Deckert Distribution GmbH

Forgas, Joseph, P. (2011) 'What is social about social cognition?' June 2011, British Journal of Social Psychology, 22(2): pp129-144, Available at: bit.ly/wnm191 (Accessed: 29 Oct 2019)

Hurcombe, Linda (2007) 'A Sense of Materials and Sensory Perception in Concepts of Materiality', *World Archaeology*, Vol. 39, No.4

Kramer, Paula (2012) 'Body, Rivers, Rock, Tree – Meeting agentic materiality in contemporary outdoor dance practices', *On Ecology, Performance Research*, Vol 17, No 4

Myers, Natasha, 'Exploring Goethean Science', Available at: bit.ly/bitly48 (Accessed: 28 Sep 2016)

Sontag, Susan (1987) *Against Interpretation*, Andre Deutsch

Smith, Phil (2019) Email to Emma Bush 20 Dec

Tsing, Anna Lowenhaupt (2015) *The Mushroom at the End of the World: On the Possibility of Life in Capitalist Ruins,* Princeton Univ. Press

Turner, Victor (2001) *From Ritual to Theatre*, John Hopkins Univ. Press

Whitehead, Tony (2017) 'warm-up' six, Landmatters Permaculture Co-op, East Allington

Wilson, Robert A. & Foglia, Lucia (Spring 2017 Edition) 'Embodied Cognition', *The Stanford Encyclopedia of Philosophy*, Available at: https://stanford.io/2XS87nW (Accessed: 29 Oct 2019)

Wood, Catherine (2018) *Performance in Contemporary Art*, Tate Publishing

Serpentine Gallery, London (2018 ongoing), 'General Ecology; The Shape of a Circle in the Mind of a Fish', Avail: bit.ly/wnm180 (Accessed: 05 Mar 2019)

Suriashi as a ceremonial, subversive act

Ami Skånberg Dahlstedt

Plymouth. She finally arrived. Rain pouring, feet soaked. Finally Plymouth. She was invited here four years ago but she had to cancel. Had a breakdown in London. Got frightened of universities, of speaking in English. No way of moving forward, just backwards. Her teenage son was diagnosed with a deadly but manageable disease. She was awake in the hospital with him breathing into a mask. The ground was shaking.

But here she is now in Plymouth. Rain pouring, feet soaked. Frightened of speaking English, but will speak English, frightened of speaking, but will speak. She walks through rain to find her bed. She walks many stairs until the floors have no numbers, and the walls have no light. Even the painters have left the building. No rise in salary, so they just left the buckets of white paint, the bills they never paid, drips, stains of paint on the grey carpet. She finds the key to her room in darkness, she finds electricity. All windows face the University of Plymouth. One window is healed with silver gaffer tape. One cupboard has a sign asking to please not open as it will break and never come together again. Her apartment is huge and awkward. It is perfect. Alphabet City in the 1990s.

She is frightened, but she is in Plymouth. She is in the university, where someone puts red tape on the floor. The tape creates a user-friendly nomadic labyrinth for anyone to calm down with. A table starts to be covered with books on walking. She engages with the corners of those tables; she rests in the margins of the space. Talks to some people who kindly come to her presentation.

Zen primate Takashina Rosen writes in 'Sermon without words':

> There is an ancient saying: "Better an inch of practice than a foot of preaching". He refers to the sermon without words, preached by the body itself, through action and without speaking. The finger points to the moon. The fist knocks at the door. See the moon, and not the finger. Knocking is not important, opening the door is.

But she is not doing Zen. She is a Swedish dancer practising suriashi, a key movement for Japanese dance: as carefully as she pushes her feet into the ground to develop a point of departure, allowing theoretical practice to facilitate a formulation of the artistic practice, and to communicate this research in a wider context. The PowerPoint is up now with a photo of her walking in suriashi with students in a corridor at Université de Lorraine, and she speaks:

I am very happy to be here, thank you so much for organising this. I really look forward to learn and hear more about walking. I come from dance and performance. But I have a walking practice, walking work, which is called suriashi that I am happy to share with you. I am usually the one in conferences who offers walks, but I wanted to challenge myself and just talk this time.

The next image shows a group of people walking in suriashi. The group walks in the suburbs of Karlstad, a small town a fifty-four hour walk from her hometown Gothenburg, and a twenty-four hour walk from the Norwegian border. The walk is framed as a pilgrimage in the micronation Lorenzburg, an artistic project created by the artist Frei von Fräähsen. In this parallel universe they walk four point forty-four metres per minute. In total, four hundred metres for ninety minutes. Frei wears a fairy tale crown and a pink sash with a grand star.

She raises her hand to demonstrate a well-known posture.

This posture usually signalizes the activist: you lean forward, stretch upward, and raise your hand. Is there a way to act, and to move forward at a slower pace, and without this steam engine? Is there a body posture which can be positioned in past tense, presence and in the future at the same time? I would like to propose an alternative activist posture: suriashi.

She shows how to walk in suriashi. Reading, bending legs, walking slowly, sweeping the floor, leaning backwards, breathing in, breathing out. One foot in front of the other, without lifting the feet. One step, one breath. Walking. Talking. Four point forty-four metres per minute.

In the dance studio, students walk slowly forwards in suriashi, but lean backwards to acknowledge past times, while being fully present. This practice shows almost literally the scientific view of time: a linear progression of past, present, and future. Suriashi is written with two different kanji: 摺足. These kanji combine a verb and a substantive – the verb 'creep'/'rub' and the substantive 'foot' – thus pointing out an activity performed by the foot, that is something that the foot does. Suriashi translates as creeping/rubbing/sliding foot. However, suriashi involves the whole body, and ideas of where spirits are placed. My teacher Nishikawa Senrei explained to us that our most important audiences are our ancestors, and that we should lean back in space and through time to acknowledge them, while practising suriashi. Suriashi – a ceremony for ancestors.

The next image shows the Iaido-master Momiyama Takao practising with his sword.

Suriashi is part of a method for acting on stage. It is one of the foundations for how the dancer/actor positions him/herself on stage in traditional Japanese theatre and dance. My work asks whether suriashi could also be a method to act, as being active, or to activate, in spaces outside the theatre.

Suriashi is also a method for fighting. In martial arts the goal is to become a better and stronger warrior; in dance the goal is to become a better and stronger performer. You can practise suriashi really slow and really fast. My teacher focused more on the slow version of suriashi, and this is also my choice for this project. On stage, suriashi often represents the traveller in constant flux, either travelling between geographical places or travelling from a spiritual to a human state. The practice not only depicts geographical places, it also depicts metaphysical and liminal spaces and time. Suriashi moves in places and moments that are both material and immaterial with the portrayal of nonhumans, spirits, and ghosts, and the psycho-physical space to acknowledge your ancestors while leaning back.

Who is walking behind you, who was here before you?

A photo showing suriashi with her teacher Nishikawa Senrei. They practise on a light wooden floor in front of a folded screen (Byōbu). They both wear kimono and white split-toe tabi socks. She continues:

Practising suriashi connects me with my teacher Nishikawa Senrei. I have walked with her for nineteen years. We would begin the class by practising suriashi for thirty minutes, side by side. A considerable amount of energy is generated by this intense muscle activity. We walk at the same pace, and we turn at the same time. Our tabi socks brush the floor, which creates a smooth rhythm, while our bodies tremble from keeping the posture. Suriashi is all about action. But this is not easily noticed with sight only.

Nishikawa Senrei died in 2012, but she still walks with me. Movements are abiding references that we continue to quote with and through our bodies. They are everlasting melodies continuing their music through our limbs. A body can house knowledge from people who have passed away. Suriashi is a repeatable construction that holds 'presence' from the past. Now that my teacher has passed away, my walking alone also represents my loss, the necessity of walking alone, and the absence of that connection I had with her.

She shows black-and-white photos of Nishikawa Senrei. One is from Senrei's favourite temple Kosan-ji, where Senrei enjoyed walking. One is of them both, looking young and healthy. She continues:

Nishikawa Senrei held the degree of shihan, Master of Dance. She toured with performances and lectures to France, Germany, Switzerland, Italy, Poland, and the US. She was interested in French culture, the Japonism, and Jung's analytical psychology. She performed several times in the Jung seminars in Ascona. My teacher is gone, and I feel the responsibility to continue what she has taught me. How can I do that? One way is of course performing, and teaching.

Photos of suriashi with graduate acting students at University of Essex. And of Disa Kamula and actors suriashing in a shopping centre in Tampere just before Xmas in 2014.

For my PhD, I decided to see how suriashi could be framed as a walking practice. Suriashi is already defined as walking in many writings, for example the anthropologist Origuchi (1887-1953) wrote that 'the essence of traditional Japanese dancing is wandering around the stage, which originally signified sanctifying the place by treading down the evil spirits'.

Walking scholars Deirdre Heddon and Cathy Turner point out how walking as an aesthetic practice is confined by 'two enduring historical discourses:

One is the Romantics and Naturalists, tramping through rural locations', where I have explored suriashi as walking in 'nature', in parks, in temple grounds, and 'in the wild'.

Photos of rural suriashi walks through lovely heaths in Wales. Her students performing suriashi in Gothenburg Botanical gardens. Solitary suriashi walk in the evening through the tunnel of thousands of vermilion-coloured torii gates at the Fushimi Inari Taisha. Solitary suriashi walk among mosquitos and gnats in Sápmi.

A well-known romantic Naturalist and metaphysical hiker was Rousseau. Nishikawa Senrei took a strong interest in him. Her very last performance that premiered four months after her death had the title 'Reveries of a Solitary Walker' and was based on his writings. I see here an unpredictable encounter with history where practices meet and merge through time and space. Nishikawa Senrei was indeed trained to be a metaphysical hiker, through her expertise in suriashi, and through her practicing and studying Zen, and she directed her last performance while dying in the hospital, and somehow continued directing 'from the other side'.

Her PowerPoint shows a booklet with the title 'Senrei meets Jean-Jacques Rousseau'. In the middle there is a black and white photo of Nishikawa Senrei. This performance premiered four months and six days after Nishikawa Senrei's death. She remembers now how the students would fold these printed leaflets together, kneeled in seiza next to tiny wooden tables, in the winter cold dance studio in Kyoto. They were folded in silence, mourning a dead master. Their joints were sore.

The second enduring historical discourse of walking is defined by the avant-gardists; drifting through the spectacular urban streets of capitalism, where I have explored suriashi on very busy streets, on plazas and outside cafés in big cities.

She shows a collection of photos from her solitary suriashi walks through Paris. On an empty street in Montmartre, next to the river Seine, outside a café, on a roof with Sacré-Cœur as the background. The next slide she shows is a well-known photo by Ruth Orkin from 1951. It has the title 'An American girl in Italy'. Some say the photo is about street harassment, some say it is about women's independence and self-determination. The photo shows Ninalee Craig in a Florence street corner passing fifteen men of various ages. All of them have their eyes directed at her and at least four of them catcall her. The photo is not arranged.

There is also gender. Heddon and Turner write there is the assumption of the universal walker – 'whose experience is uninflected by gender'. This universality did not exist, and it does not exist today. Nineteenth-century Western cities offered very different spatial possibilities for men and women, and they continue to do so. George Sand knew that she had to dress up as a boy to have the same access to space as men did. She was not exaggerating. The French historian Jules Michelet commented in his 1860 essay 'La Femme (Woman)' on the hindrances to women in Paris: 'How many irritations for the single woman! She can hardly ever go out in the evening; She would be taken for a prostitute.' 'She would constitute an event; she would be a spectacle: all eyes would be constantly fixed on her, and she would overhear uncomplimentary and bold conjectures.'

As a young female dance student in Paris, I learned quickly that even in the twentieth century it was not possible to be a flâneuse, neither to follow the male situationists nor to engage with the city's utopian potential. It was neither possible to drift, nor to practise psychic landscaping. I differed from the male situationists and I differed from male flâneurs, since my contract with the city was not the same as theirs. I could not dérive, i.e., I could not drift, certainly not in Paris where my potential street drifting would be stopped many times by catcalling, drink offers, and unwanted invitations. In Paris, and in other European cities, I had to isolate myself spatially from the city.

She sits in seiza vis-à-vis her teacher Nishikawa Senrei on a light wooden floor in front of a folded screen (Byōbu). They have their dance fans on the floor in front of them. They are about to bow to each other. This is how the dance class at Senreinokai begins and ends.

I identify the need for a different choreography that does not claim to represent the universal: a gendered suriashi for gendered spaces. There are many variations of suriashi, and all of them are gendered. For this investigation, I have chosen the male-to-female variation. It was created by male Kabuki actors and dancers to represent the feminine stereotype, however in Nishikawa Senrei's studio, it was the general practice. By general, I mean that it was not singled out as gendered; the stereotypically feminine suriashi was instead made universal in her studio. One answer to why the feminine construction has become so essential in Buyō and Kabuki is simply because women were banned from stage in 1629 by the Tokugawa Shogunate. Only men were allowed to perform in public. My choice to practise the feminine suriashi on the streets makes a clear statement: I will not walk the streets like a man. I will walk the streets like a woman.

A photo of Japan's most famous Onnagata (female impersonator), the Kabuki actor Bando Tamasaburo. He is wearing a wig and a dazzling red kimono. The photo shows his exaggerated posture, leaning backwards, squeezing his shoulders. She squeezes her shoulders and encourages participants to engage with the Onnagata.

Let us try the body alignment for becoming Woman. You can decide if you want to sit or stand. Please create an arch in your upper body, by squeezing the back of your shoulders. You maintain your elbows tightly pressed against the waist. Knees and feet are collected closely, inner thighs active. Your palms rest on top of your thighs, your fingers are held together, pointing inwards. You tilt your pelvis backwards, squeeze the lumbar spine, and push your chest forwards and upwards. You will notice how all muscles along the spine are activated. This body posture is a tool for male actors to look smaller as they pursue performing as women. It can also be a tool for gender fluidity, and for performance of non-binary genders. To make oneself smaller in order to perform the idea of the Woman demands a lot of muscular strength, but this is not easily noticed with sight only.

Please rest.

There was a nice connection made with the work of the gendered posture, with different ways of walking, and with each other. There is a feeling of responsiveness and safety in the room. The participants are generous and curious. They follow her to the frightening walk on the métro platform of Place Pigalle.

I was about to discover; walking the streets in suriashi like a woman was efficient. I did not even have to ward anyone off, as no one even dared to approach me.

It is as if I am hovering the streets in a spaceship. The slow walking creates a safe space for myself, an oddness that blocks flirting, catcalling and assault.

Finally, I can be a flâneuse.

I decided to invite more people to walk with me in suriashi, as a friendship act, political act, a conversation, an instead of coffee or wine-act, a birthday gift.

I will stop and rest a bit here, to make sure that you are able to follow me. For this text, I wanted to experiment with how to write a conference proceeding, where you were able to walk with me as I got off the train, arriving to Plymouth. I wanted to begin with the loneliness of the presenter and ask whether you also felt lonely upon arrival. I also wanted to identify when the lonely presenter becomes part of the conference community. I identify this happened when listeners stood up and tried a bodily practice from Japan. I still struggle with how to introduce 'doings' in conferences – but here in Plymouth we were gathering in order to walk together. Our minds and bodies were already familiar with, longing for, and were passionate about movement. Walking as scholarship, walking as research, walking for causes, walking with other, dancing as walking, walking as dancing. How can we create these passionate atmospheres elsewhere? Indeed, we need to present ourselves, and promote our ideas, and produce quotable knowledge. We also need to be together and create possibilities for togetherness. What are your own struggles here, combining walking and talking? Please have a moment to reflect on this.

I remember my heart beating while planning a suriashi walk for University College of London in 2016. London was so stressful, expensive, crowded, and I did not know where to begin. I practised by myself in order to time suriashi. I slowly passed two men speaking Japanese, but they might not have known suriashi. I was frightened. Finally, I found the in-between-spaces through walking and re-walking. I realised I rested in the backyard of the British Museum – so crowded at the front, so empty at the back. I found the silent pathways, an unimportant garden, with the tiniest kiosk for coffee. The unimportant garden was Virginia Woolf's garden. Not the one with her official statue, the other one. A secret. Because she wrote AROOO. I rested there too, with Woolf. I dragged a whole conference to this tiny, not famous garden. The participants walked, experienced their ancestors, and they wrote together. It made sense. I also walked in suriashi with librarians and archivists at the SIBMAS Conference in Copenhagen in 2017. We left the conference room at the library, and moved slowly together in a hall, shaped like a circle. They told me they felt how the whole archive rose and came alive and showed itself to the people in the library café.

Walking alone works for many reasons and in various ways. Walking together works for many reasons and in various ways. In Walking's New Movements Conference in Plymouth we were claiming how walking works together. Walking works even though we are not walking for health, for collecting plants or objects, or for drifting. For example, C.Y. Cheung who teaches at the Chinese University of Hong Kong, learned suriashi from me (with Nishikawa Senrei directing from the other side). He made a political act by himself when he walked in suriashi as a peaceful act at Yuen Long Station in Hong Kong. This was on 27th July 2019, when almost 300,000 people were marching in protest at the mob attacks, and in protest at Hong Kong's extradition bill. C.Y. Cheung has continued to present suriashi as a nonviolent, feminist protest, arguing that authorities could never label suriashi as a riot. C.Y. Cheung recently wrote that researchers in Taiwan also have started to do suriashi for the same purpose.

Doreen Massey has helped me a lot in my work, for example how to see suriashi as ceremonial, but understanding that the ceremonial can be subversive. Earlier in this text, I described Nishikawa Senrei's request – that the most important dance, the most important suriashi, should be dedicated to our ancestors. When I compare her request with Doreen Massey's – that we must work (and walk) to escape the 'grand narratives' related by the modernist prioritisation of time and the frameworks of Progress, of Development, and of Modernisation – I see how suriashi can be a subversive act. Suriashi is a micro activism, and it helps keeping space open, playful, strange and fun, however it is also a spiritual activism, engaging with spirits, ghosts and deceased walkers. I don't know yet if and how you wish to proceed walking with your ancestors. After having resisted Nishikawa Senrei's request for many years I started to practise suriashi in cemeteries, near gravestones of my ancestors, and inside buildings where they had lived and worked. I walked in a house I had not known. I walked inside and outside hospitals. I read brutal stories in the archives. Not about 'the people out there', but about people I should have known. My slow walking research finally surprised me in a productive way. I found them. They are with me now, and I always bring them with me. I recommend you try walking with whoever you call your ancestor. It is encouraging and shattering at the same time. Thank you for reading so far. My presentation ends here.

She shows the last photo of her and Nishikawa Senrei bowing to each other after dance class. Thank you for teaching me.

Otsukaresamadeshita. You must be very tired.

Acknowledgements

Ami Skånberg Dahlstedt wishes to express her gratitude to the conference organisers and Triarchy Press for facilitating walking, talking and writing together. She also wants to thank David Overend, Elisabeth Belgrano, Astrid von Rosen and David Dickson for helpful comments on her walking writing.

FROM WORKING TO WALKING AND THE LIFE (OR LOSS) OF LEISURE

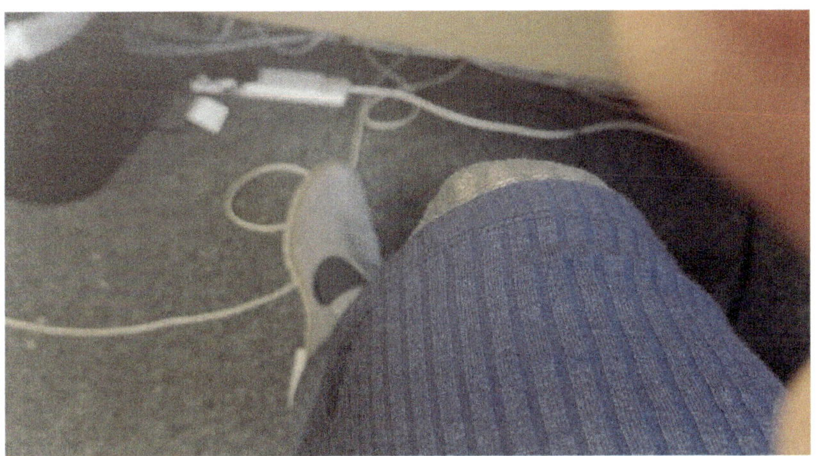

FROM *WORKING*

This story starts with me working in a job. An administrator at a redbrick university, exchanging forty hours of my week for a decent wage (and a hefty dose of work-related stress).

The university could be a challenging place for all types of workers. It was imposingly hierarchical, deeply colonial and increasingly neoliberal.[1] Fears of job precarity and joblessness, as well as huge pressures around productivity pervaded the staff and student body.

It was also an extremely rich environment. Through my contact with the academic world, I was introduced to such ideas as 'neoliberalism' and 'decolonisation', and texts that helped me understand some of the issues that I was grappling with.

[1] 'Neoliberal' here meaning the system of deregulated global markets, privatisation and austerity. Or, put another way, seeing society as a marketplace, life as a race, and people as profit/loss.

Such texts opened my eyes. I had imagined that the work of earning an income ended when I left the office each day. In fact, there was a great deal of (unpaid) labour that needed to be done at home in order for me to show up physically and emotionally available to perform my duties and fit into the professional box that had been outlined for me.

In full time employment, I had less time to walk, but more money for Ubers. Less time to relax, but more money for wine. Less time to fix my clothes, but more money for new ones.

As well as bargaining with my mental health, this exchange of time for money caught me in a shitty contract with privilege, oppression and global exhaustion. 🌿🔫

And all the while, time rushed by in a cramped haze. It became harder to distinguish the days, weeks and months from each other.

The wonderful kids book *Momo* describes the 'men in grey', who descend upon a town and encourage adults to save their time by paying it into the bank. This quote sums up how I had come to feel about my working life:

> *People never seemed to notice that, by saving time, they were losing something else…. For time is life itself… and the more people saved, the less they had.*
>
> Ende (2001, p.41)

TO *WALKING*

So I saved up my wages, expended my privilege, and I quit. And that clock, and that routine, stopped. For the last 5 months I have been living and working outside in the UK with a strange, nomadic project called Land in Curiosity (LiC). Walking and wild camping as an alternative to paying rent, and experimenting with something we call 'regenerative cultures'.[2]

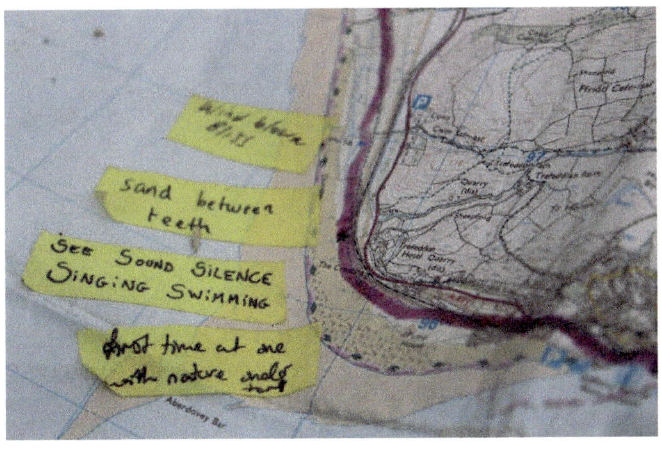

[2] *'Regenerative cultures' recognise human and ecological interdependence in order to create resilient, adaptable and healthy societies. At LiC, these ideas inform how we relate to members of our community, how we respond to conflict, how we make decisions, plan, etc.*

Sometimes people are surprised to find out that as a walking project we rarely walk for more than a couple of hours a day.

People we met (2019)

Walking is not our purpose; it is a method that supports a different pace and way of life. It's a cliché but it's true to say that the focus really is on the journey rather than the destination. Because of this, we can take it slow. We can stop to nap beneath a tree if we feel the need, or to watch a slug dangle from a thread of mucus, or for a cup of tea, if someone is kind enough to offer.

Today's jobs expect us to work on schedules like machines: we clock in, produce, we clock out. And again the next day, all of us like clockwork.

On LiC's walks, we try to account for the fact that people have different paces and rhythms. We have route-markers, who lead the way and mark a trail for people behind to follow in their own time. We designate a timekeeper, who holds the time for anyone who doesn't want to keep checking their watch.

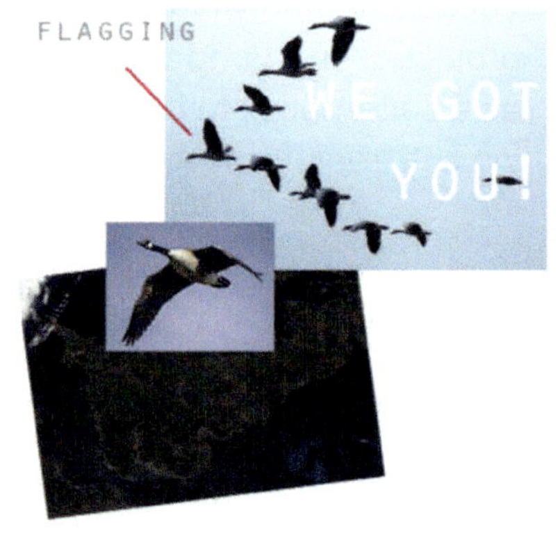

Most female bodies know – if only we listened – that productivity is part of a cycle rather than a constant mode. As a female led organisation, when we bleed, we slow down, prioritise ease and comfort. We have the opportunity to see rest and recuperation as part of the work of our project – not something that people have to scramble to do in their evenings and weekends.

The clock has taken on a different quality. We rarely know which day of the week it is, but we are acutely aware of the changing seasons. **Major events are when the sun comes up and goes down; when the full moon is bright enough to light up the night; when the nettles seed, when the beech nuts drop, when**

the mosquitos die down. We bustle like the birds on sunny days, and like them, damply shelter when it rains.

TO *RESTING*

So, what's all this about the loss of leisure? It sounds idyllic…

Well, not entirely. Nomadic life involves plenty of labour. Of course there's the physical work of carrying heavy bags and finding a place to sleep each night (like fugitives in a country where nearly all land is private), making fire and daily missions to fetch water; not to mention the emotional work of living in close community. After all this, we hardly had any time to properly rest, let alone work on the creative, personal, and organisational projects we had set out to do.

Despite the ideals and values that I'd set out with, I found myself getting frustrated when emotional responses got in the way of our productivity. I even missed the days in the office when I would get SO MUCH DONE! Without clearly marked boundaries between work and leisure, I found it even harder to switch off the sense of responsibility, to the extent that I struggled to prioritise or even acknowledge my most basic needs (e.g. nourishment, sleep, expression, warmth, movement) over that of the project.

Here I was replicating the very systems I was trying to escape. The walk became a mirror that showed how deeply I have internalised one of the worst aspects of patriarchal, colonial, high consumer capitalism: the notion that my value equals what I produce or achieve.

This belief fuels with our obsession with growth, and is therefore behind much of the damage that we humans create, and the crap piling up in landfills, chemicals flooding our rivers, harmful gases clogging up our air. And the very same thing within our bodies, and the bodies of people across the globe, which are overworked, stressed, abused, drugged and ignored. All in the name of *productivity*.

So what can be done? At LiC we don't have the answers; we are babies in this work, learning as we go. But we have some great teachers. We've been hugely inspired by Adrienne Maree Brown, who suggests that what we embody and enact in our interior life, in our relationships, in our organisations, echoes out, for better or worse (Brown, 2017). And of course, our great guide, nature, who reveals endless wisdom through her work, including countless examples of systems that tend towards balance.

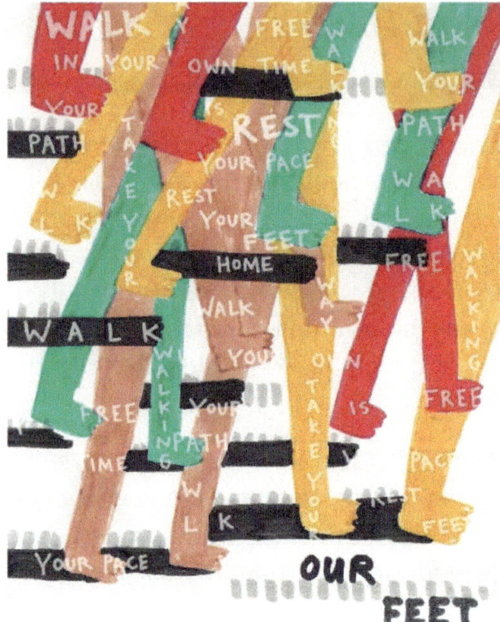

One thing I have become sure of is that the answer to this problem will lie, at least in part, in our ability to reconnect to that which capitalism has made a project of discrediting. That is, the wisdom of our physical body and our wider bodies.[3]

This time I'm listening. After a long summer of walking with LiC, our bodies are telling us, slow down! It's autumn now and as the leaves fall, it's time for blood to sink back to the earth.

[3] By 'wider body' I mean our environment, our communities, our family, friends, conscience and intuition, spirituality or God if we have one.

Rest. Reorientate. Integrate. Take time. Listen to a body (*especially* if it has been marginalised) and know that this is a radical and regenerative act.

References

Adorno, T.W. (1991) Free time, in Bernstein, J. M. ed. *The Culture Industry: Selected Essays on Mass Culture*, Routledge

Brown, A.M. (2017) *Emergent Strategy – shaping change, changing worlds*, AK Press

Ende, M. (2001) *Momo*, Trans. Brownjohn, M. Available at: bit.ly/wnm79 (Accessed 20 Dec 2020)

Frayne, D. (2015) *The Refusal of Work: The Theory and Practice of Resistance to Work*, Zed Books

Federici, S. (1975) *Wages Against Housework*, Falling Wall Press

Gregg, M. (2018) *Counterproductive: Time Management in the Knowledge Economy*, Duke Univ. Press

Mama, D. & Anderson C. ed (2018) *Breadlines*, 1, Community Centred Knowledge. Available at: bit.ly/wnm80 (Accessed 20 Dec 2020)

Rilke, R.M. (2005) *Rilke's Book of Hours: Love Poems to God,* Trans. Macy, J. & Barrows, M., Riverhead Books

InspiralUndergrowth

Rachel Gomme

13th October

In Japan, dandelions grow close to the ground.

I

Fresh from this morning

Starting at the beginning

Circling around King's Cross

bare flat paving, dry sooty road

turn the corner to find

      tiny campanula   plantain

      dandelion   moss   ferns in a drain

Caledonian Road – dry grass at the base of a signpost

turn again:

      moss everywhere

      tiniest dandelion   chickweed
      hawkbit

      dandelion   chickweed

dandelion   chickweed

dandelion   chickweed

   spurge

Caledonian Road

   grass in the kerb in the bus lane

   chickweed, dried grass in a drain

   grass squirting from a paving corner

   plantain

Left again

   ivy marching up the trees

   buddleia high in a wall

   willowherb in the kerb

   mossmossmossmossmoss

   cherry tree sprouting from its base

   creeping toadflax – groundsel – nightshade

Crinan Street between tall buildings

   dry grass, fresh groundsel in the cracks

   a moss not seen before

Goodsway and the canal

   tidied, spruced and manicured

   with dandelion beneath the planters

Virginia creeping under the fence

buddleia up the wall

rich moss in cobbles

lichen sliding up the trees

geese swim along the canal

opposite the London Wildlife Centre, willowherb nibbles
at the manicure

Midland Way

grass-groundsel-willowherb bouquet

for a lamp-post

turn the corner again to quiet and voices

grass   dandelion   chickweed   moss

in stones and drains

winter jasmine peers through a fence

Purchase

a streetfull of moss and grass

locust resprouting irrepressed in a corner

chickweed, hawkweed flowering

buddleia from the ground up

green green moss

ragwort in the underfoot leaves

hawkbit, grass flowering, tiny willowherb alone

Flashing past in Tavistock Place

      a London plane buckles the pavement

Japanese dandelions grow close to the ground.

II

Eighteen months ago, somewhere in the middle

      dandelion

      chickweed

      shepherd's purse

      dandelion small dandelion tall

      goosegrass

            also known as cleavers

            also known as Sticky Willie

      clover

      speedwell

      meadow geranium pink in the grass

      lichen coating a letterbox

      bramble   nettle   willowherb
      dock

      periwinkles through a fence

      brambles and nettles

      green alkanet flowers blue

Japanese dandelions flower close to the ground.

III

Fresh from this afternoon

The end in Gravesend

dandelions, daisies, shamrock, clover

an enterprising nettle in Jury Street

      geranium, chickweed, mallow, shepherd's purse

      elder out of a wall

      groundsel, thistle, buttercup, spurge

      dandelion dried dark

      yellow wood sorrel (or black medick)

      grassgrassgrass plantain grass dandelion grass moss

      grassgrass

      dog's mercury

      deadnettle

      goosegrass

      shepherd's purse

      toadflax creeping

all around the dockside, salted and furred

      stunted and lush

      alone and in crowds

bindweed   bramble   buddleia   sycamore

hogweed   hawkbit   herb Robert

yellow corydalis

creeping down the streets to the river

buddleia cramponing up the slope

        one after another

campanula with a feather for a flower

aquilegia sows itself at the foot of a wall

lichen licks the locked gate

moss in the cracks, grass in the road

a fern under a cobweb

chickweed tumbles down the kerb

ragwort-honeysuckle-deadnettle-dandelion-mallow-nightshade-grass

all in one

dusty corner

cut back and sprouting

tall and barely there

hidden and proud

flat-growing grass, low-lying moss

        in the middle of the shopping street

        tiny dandelion under tramping feet

mini-snapdragons in the car park

       self-sown

dead fridge, live grass

toadflax   dandelion

In Japan, dandelions live close to the ground.

The Sight of the Walker

William Sharpe

> I see it feelingly.
>
> Gloucester, *King Lear*

When art is made from the action of walking, the sight of the walker, in a double sense, is often a focal point. What does the sighted walker see—conceptually, visually, in terms of both insight and/or eyesight—and what does an audience see—again conceptually, visually—when it looks at a walker walking? And is this visual information overvalued? Or could the sight of a walker change a life?

In 1907 the poet Rainer Maria Rilke walked up to the truncated remains of a Greek statue in the Louvre Museum in Paris. As Auguste Rodin's secretary, he knew walking's radical artistic possibilities through the famous sculptor's 'Walking Man' (1900), a dynamic yet flat-footed, headless, armless composite of two earlier statues. Now Rilke faced the 'Archaic Torso of Apollo' and, stunned, wrote a poem of the same name. The torso, probably fashioned by Miletus in the early fourth century BCE, represents a giant step in the development of Western art. For the first time, a sculptor has presented a 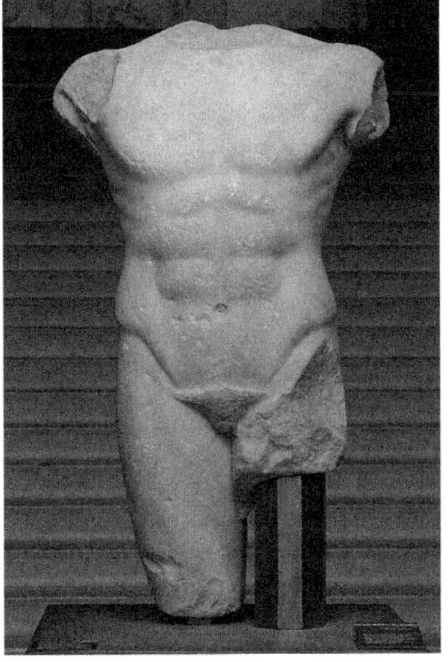 physically realistic modelling of the human body in motion. The artist has discovered how to use *contrapposto*, an unequal distribution of weight on the feet, and the subsequent adjustment of the whole body to bring it in balance. The subtle visual information provided in the tension of the torso muscles tells the story of the step taking place. Describing his experience, Rilke's poem asserts the power of the object over the viewer: "here there is no place that does not see you." And in his famous concluding line he announces the inescapable power of the sight: "You must change your life." (Rilke, 1907)

The torso is nearly legless, but as a precursor of Western art's naturalistic portrayal of human motion, it strides forward into history. The torso walks even if the body parts that can accomplish the step are missing. It is a symbol for the subsequent art of walking, implying motion and communicating the walk in the absence of a fully present body.

Visual images of walking, as the statue shows, can be compellingly beautiful. And yet they are so clearly incomplete. Because the ever-altering engagement of body, mind, and environment necessitates a hopelessly complex imagining of interior and external stimuli just to evoke the sensation of taking a few steps, images cannot convey the totality of the walk. Or even the whole of the walker, as the Torso shows. The spectator must fill in what's absent, an act that creates the pleasure and frustration of viewing walking images. Rilke's mutilated sculpture, eloquent in its absences, is not an aberration; rather, it is typical of what visual images of walking demand.

***

For millennia, images of walkers have played a central role in representational art, participating in a history of carefully crafted material objects. But contemporary walking art, art that regards the act of walking as artistic in itself, has from the start been concerned with its own immateriality. Each step vanishes as the next one comes into being. One cannot grasp the totality of a walk from a single point of view or a single point in time and, as Hamish Fulton asserts, one cannot erase the line made by a walk.

Complicating the challenge of how to "see" a walk is the question of whether visual artifacts generated by the walk are incidental or integral to the art-walk "itself". Does the "art" reside in the walk, the walker, or the documentation? Furthermore, concerns about ocular-centrism, about the inadequacy and selectiveness of visual images, have led many walk-makers to focus on senses other than sight. Sound walks, tactile walks, unsighted walks, smell walks, memory walks have proliferated in recent years. Perhaps ironically, discourses addressing these concerns have produced a sea of words whose relentless waves suggest that printed text, itself a visual medium, claims the final authority to tell the truth about walking.

Indeed, the sight of the walker, what the walker sees, has been an incessant subject of writing about walking since ancient times. In perhaps the greatest of all walking texts, James Joyce's *Ulysses*, Stephen Dedalus sums up how most writing about walking works: "Ineluctable modality of the visible: at least that if no more, thought through my eyes." This is what walking literature provides readers who turn pages as they would corners: the gradually unfolding look of the world and thoughts about it, from the walker's point of view. Although he briefly experiments with unsighted walking by closing his eyes, proving that thought does not require sight, Stephen Dedalus opts for a textual definition of vision. The world is like handwriting to the walker, he decides, "Signatures of all things I am here to read" (Joyce, 1922).

If there is a new movement in visualising walking, it must find its way amid the push-and pull of current theories and practices, where sight and the other senses jostle for attention. Critiqued or admired or puzzled over, visual images and encounters continue to play a vital role in walking art, as this essay will show. This is particularly true in the case of artists who want to make more visible two interconnected groups of "watched walkers," the disabled and the surveilled.

***

With roots in Surrealism and Situationism, walking art emerged in the 1960s in conjunction with the rise of conceptual art, performance art, land art, and new definitions of sculpture that not only required involvement from the spectator but also interacted with natural and human-made environments in site-specific ways. In a world cluttered with lasting masterpieces, the process-oriented art of happenings and performances sought to create something spatially ephemeral and ecologically advanced, works that might take up just a moment in time and only the space needed to hold an idea.

Walking art offers its proponents a choice: do I make my body visible in this work, as a painter might, so that my audience may have a sight of the walker, or shall I shape my work in such a way that the audience, perhaps as participant, sees something else, "thought through my eyes," as Joyce puts it?

Since walking is a natural, everyday activity, its use as a material for art-making accords with the Russian formalist understanding of what art does: it *defamiliarises* the world we know. The artist imposes an unusual, thought-provoking itinerary or bodily constraint or underlying conception that signals difference, that marks the walk as art, not life. Documentation forms part of the estrangement. Immaterial though it may be, walking art emerged in part from the actions of artists tied by training to a visual arts tradition, one that produces objects to look at, from gallery-ready textworks or photos and films, to retrieved objects, casual drawings, and illustrated books, that artists employ to record the passage of their bodies through space and time. Whether art walks are done privately or presented as public performances, material traces and pictorial images of them convey part of the artistic experience, but never its entirety. In an art of process, an art involving mind, body, and landscape, the image will never be enough. It will always be suggestive rather than complete.

Perhaps for this very reason, strong images have acted as place-holders and evocations of actions now completed or that may never have had an audience. The desire to have an "image to hold on to" seems to be felt more strongly by critics and art historians than by the artists themselves.

If the question had been posed a generation ago as to whether walking was a visual art, the answer would have been fairly clear. Not only did Hamish Fulton and Richard Long, two of its best-known proponents, make arresting images from unwitnessed walks, but other artists with a performance orientation enacted striking works that produced indelible images. In contrast to the unseen "heroic" efforts of Long and Fulton, they showed that it's not the length of the walk but the strength of the idea animating it that counts in making provocative, illuminating art. A strong alliance between concept and image has been essential to their success.

To offer just a few examples: after ninety days of walking the Great Wall of China from opposite ends, Marina Abramović and Ulay approached each other in 'The Lovers (Great Wall Walk)' (1988). Francis Alÿs playfully displayed what walkers might gather from a walk in his performance 'Sometimes Making Something Leads to Nothing' (1997) when he pushed a gradually melting block of ice through the streets of Mexico City until it vanished. Mona Hatoum invoked tactility, vulnerability, and race in 'Performance Still—Roadworks (Brixton,

London)' (1985-1995), while Kubra Khademi's walk in Kabul wearing steel armour to resist that vulnerability (2015) drew attention to how a walking experience depends heavily on gender and location. And since 1994 Hamish Fulton has located his group walks, which challenge participants to maintain slow, equi-spaced progress, in historically and politically charged settings that have potent visual impact.

Given the staying power of certain images, these documented sightings of creative walkers may, for all their shortcomings, actually have *more* political, social, and/or aesthetic impact than the "real" walks they have emerged from.

✳✳✳

Since the beginning of a new millennium, however, a growing number of practitioners have argued that walking art needs to challenge ocular-centrism, to pay less attention to objects that can be visually consumed without engaging other senses. They seek to explore a body intermeshed with the landscape and with other people. A greater emphasis on walking as a collective, activist form of art has emerged, together with less certainty about the value of tying the meaning of the art walk to representative images. If the all-too imperial power of the masculist gaze could be compressed into a phrase, it might be Caesar's *veni, vidi, vici,* a domination by sight and physical force that progressive walkers seek to dismantle through a de-centring of the image, through a greater emphasis on haptics, sound, memory, and orality.

Summing up this new mix of walking art and activism, Stephanie Springgay and Sarah Truman write that "the focus on the proximal senses has disrupted ocularcentrism [. . .] Over the past few decades, qualitative research has been re-shaped by sensory studies, non-representational theories, and affect studies making way for non-visual experimentations and techniques."(2018: 38, 48) Or as the authors of an article on 'Cripistemologies' put it, they favour work that "invites audience-participants into embodied experiences of the world beyond the visual that generate non-normative ways of walking/traversing together, thereby 'cripping the flâneur'" (Chandler et al, 2019).

Necessary as it is, the corrective, anti-ocular position does not sufficiently recognise the somatics of looking. The sighted eye activates the rest of the body's senses in a number of ways, as pornographers and visual artists have always known. Seeing other bodies in motion, whether in real life, in a live performance, or filmed, produces a powerful bodily effect known as kinaesthetic empathy, an effect that can produce physical sensations of fear, desire, revulsion, anger, sorrow, and so on. "As a viewer, my perception of a moving body cannot be usefully separated from my imagining, or attempted imagining, of what it might be like for my body to move that way" (Profeta, 2015: 147). Non-moving images can also produce a somatic effect. Art historian Nancy Forgione, for example, has analysed the "corporeal situatedness" guiding the spectator's reaction to Impressionist views of Paris (2005: 666). Speaking of a picture called 'Buzzard' (1987) Hamish Fulton explains, "the title does not mean that this is a photo of a buzzard. It simply says 'buzzard'. What comes into play is the simultaneity of senses. There is a certain sight, we hear the birds, we smell the brush and the wind whistles in the corner of the eyes from the direction of the setting sun" (Fulton, 1989, cited by Tiberghien, 2000: 246).

Today more than ever, the sight of the walker is related to the words that surround or appear in the image, since walking images rarely circulate without language to sustain them. Psychogeography, which could be said to bridge the perceived gap between sight and sense, is a heavily textual mode of walking art, since its rambles seem most amenable to documenting in semi-novelistic form, most saliently in the work of Iain Sinclair. Psychogeography is said be about feeling ("the sudden change of ambiance in a street within the space of a few meters" in Guy Debord's words), but it is often directed by sight since that sense operates over longer distances and pulls the walker toward far-off enticements. Recent reinventions of the *dérive*, such as Phil Smith's 'mythogeography', delight in visual discoveries, ripples in the space-time of ordinary-looking buildings or vacant lots, that then open up into layers of history, community, and physical situatedness. Smith often speaks of the "big picture" but it is a multi-media one, whose receptivity to all forms of experience is its defining characteristic. "There can be no finished mythogeography, so a provisional one – one that proposes big pictures based on disorientations not orientations – is the best kind." (Smith & Schott, 2018: 45). Smith's walks present themselves to an audience as a series of unanticipated discoveries of texture, feeling, thought, and organic matter that are notated visually with a quirky eye for detail but that, in their post-walk presentation, are most eloquently elaborated in texts whose sinuosity mirrors the twists and turns of mind and body through a space densely packed with material encounters.

In his role as champion of "the latest generation of performative, postmodern walkers", Smith notes approvingly that "where there is product, other than walking itself, it often takes the form of documentation, handbooks, and exemplary objects *designed to encourage others to further exploratory walking* rather than of commodities for new markets" (2018: 44, my italics). Today, these mostly non-commercial records of an art walk are in a sense *dispersed* over a variety of 'containers', which may include text, sound, maps, internet postings, blogs, and perhaps most especially the bodies and memories of the participants. The hybrid works that are 'handed on' in various media serve to remind audiences that the most compelling current goal is not to recreate an absent walk but to participate in a present one.

Following that path, a walker can consult Clare Qualmann and Claire Hind's *Ways to Wander* (2015), a compendium of fifty-four sets of instructions for intellectually stimulating, physically 'eye-opening' walks in town and country. Only about ten walks request the performer to engage in drawing, making photographs, mapping, or other forms of visual art. These are balanced by an equal number that focus on how the body senses the walk and the environment. Most of the proposed walks guide the ambulating performer through a variety of mental or physical landscapes and actions, without having the walker producing anything tangible.

And that may be the most significant point. In 2018 walking artist and historian Blake Morris performed all the walks in *Ways to Wander*, most often in company with others whom he invited and later cited via a running internet commentary, 'A Wander Is Not a Slog'. The blog and its extended walking community reached around the world, thanks to remote participation. With photos, posts, discussions, and images of pre- and post-walk documents, Morris pictured a walking world whose very being is "medium specific" – a medium that is *not* the internet. Morris proposes that "the central gesture of the artistic medium of walking is the walk itself" as it creates "direct connections between the body and the social and physical landscapes it traverses" (Morris, 2018). Allowing for the ways in which walking is a multipurpose, multifaceted medium, Morris argues that walking creates aesthetic events whose further life may turn them into a painting or a film, but whose essence resides in the walk itself as it is shared with others.

And yet even a shared walk needs company; it does not communicate its artistry by itself. "Just as there are many ways a painter can apply paint to a canvas," Morris writes, "artists . . . integrate various media into their work. Walking is not a stand-alone medium, it requires interaction with other media to communicate the specific design that structures the walk"

(2018). The walking medium is not monolithic: it can touch, smell, taste, and hear, engaging time and space and its own thoughts. Visuality forms an inevitable part of this communication, as walkers see, while others see them, and the camera eye, human-pointed or fixed in a surveillance stare, sees both. Whether it is 'captured' 'only' in memory, or whether it is represented in various media, the walk is 'seen' on many levels.

***

Two kinds of walking art – disability art and surveillance art – are concerned with new movements in a literal way as they question the meaning of public space. Above all, they are animated by a desire to make their subject matter visible, and visibly felt, to get the spectator to "see feelingly" like the blinded Duke of Gloucester in Shakespeare's *King Lear*.

In Carmen Papalia's 'Blind Field Shuttle' (2010, ongoing), the artist leads a long 'accordion' of sighted people behind him. While each participant, eyes closed, holds the shoulder of the person in front, Papalia leads them on a walking tour through urban and rural space, providing commentary as he goes. In so doing he challenges in an embodied way Michel de Certeau's notion that walkers in the city are "blind" wanderers unable to read the script of their own steps (1984: 93). Instead of the blind leading the blind to disaster (as in the famous Breughel painting of 1568, whose composition Papalia's performance mimics), here a blind man leads the sighted to discover another way of moving through the world.

A complement to the unsighted walker who shows the way is the crawling 'walker' who fearlessly confronts the painful friction of urban surfaces. A short film, 'One Morning in May', follows artist Noëmi Lakmaier as she leaves her wheelchair behind and crawls, dressed in a business suit, from the domestic space of Tower Hamlets towards the financial district in London, a mile away. Battered, exhausted, her clothes in tatters, she abandons the quest after a day-long struggle, asking, "can I see the map; I want to see how much I didn't do." (Lakmaier, 2012).

One of the most significant pieces of American walking art also employs crawling as a tactic. Although not disabled in the conventional sense, William Pope.L brings metaphoric disability to a powerfully embodied performance. Over several years he crawled the length of New York City's longest and most famous street, Broadway, whose nickname gave the title to his performance: 'The Great White Way, 22 Miles, 9 Years, 1 Street' (2001–2009). Dragging a black body dressed in a Superman costume through "the great white way" of American culture, his work makes visual in an indelible way the "out-of-placeness" and paradoxical invisibility of black people in America. Despite the ideologically inflicted disability of racism, the super-heroic struggle that his work represents manages to traverse space and time with unrelenting determination.

The flip side of being overlooked and yet pushed from public life by being stared at when entering it, is being constantly monitored and silently recorded. In recent years, mapping art that uses voluntarily activated GPS tracking systems has evolved in ingenious ways that 'picture' the surveilled body's path through life. One of the most striking is a single composite image, 'My Ghost (Sixteen years of mapping my life in London with GPS)' (2016) by Jeremy Hunt, which shows all of the artist's movements over the course of many years, presenting him with the spectre of his past. More complex, and tied to the history of women's tapestry-making that goes back to antiquity, is 'Running Stitch' (2006) by Jen Southern & Jen Hamilton. Participants in Brighton and Hove, UK, carried GPS tracking devices that the artists turned into sewn lines on fabric, tracing the intermeshed routes on a material rather than digital screen. In such works the walker becomes a mark-maker, a stylus, a stitch or line physically distanced from the recording medium that accretes signals which will eventually represent the scope of a walk. The sight of the walker in its double sense, whether in motion or at rest, is definitively split between locales, no longer sharing the same space. The viewers of the artwork do not see the body of the performer, a metaphor for the contradictions of distance-collapsing technologies.

But these are technologies that walkers use. What of technologies that use walkers, often without their permission, either to entertain them or to point out their vulnerability to darker devices?

Like disability art, surveillance art seeks to turn the tables, to make visible the repressive gazes that threaten watched people, bringing those gazes into fuller human contact with the spectator. In 2001, Steve Mann, an inventor of wearable technology and also a strong privacy rights advocate, designed the 'Invisibility/Aposematic Suit'. Its portable screens can show what's on the far side of the walker so that the wearer can be 'seen through' or rendered invisible, a defensive gesture that also renders visible the metaphoric desire of all surveillance, to 'see through' appearances. In its 'aposematic' mode, the suit reflects potential predators back at themselves, subjecting them to the warning gaze of a surveillance apparatus. With its dual modes of concealment and observation, Mann's work queries contemporary art that relies on or exploits the presence of pedestrians, works that range from the apparently innocuous to the aggressive and deeply troubling.

Some projects use data captured from passers-by to reflect traffic patterns and human presence in the form of large-scale visual displays on nearby structures. Among them are Christian Moeller's 2006 'Nosy' (2006) in Osaki City, Japan, and Camille Utterback's 'Abundance' (2007) at the city hall of San Jose, California. More focused works track individual walkers. In Mexico City, Marie Sester created a work called 'Access' (2003) that allowed anonymous website users to pursue individuals with a spotlight through the liminal public space of a building lobby, while an acoustic beam sent sounds that only the subjects could hear. Caught in the spotlight, they did not know if they were singled out as celebrities or victims, selected for approval or punishment.

One of the most troubling works is by Belgian artist Dries Depoorter, who exploits publicly accessible surveillance cameras across the globe. In 'Jaywalking' (2016), he asked gallery visitors if they would like to report a walking activity that in many places is a crime, crossing the street without the permission of a traffic signal. "Would you like to report the jaywalker?" reads the headline on a screen that shows a defiant pedestrian. "By pressing the button you are sending a report of the jaywalker to the closest police station" (Greenberg, 2016). Depoorter pushes the psychological buttons of a society often told that undergoing constant surveillance is a fair price to pay for public safety.

In one of the earlier works of surveillance art, 'Trust' (2004), Jill Magid established a connection between disability and being watched. Becoming a self-watched disabled walker for artistic purposes, she closed her eyes and walked through crowded downtown Liverpool. She asked for guidance not from a nearby person who could lend her an arm, but from a surveillance camera operator with whom she had previously established phone contact. She made her way forward by depending on his verbal instructions as literally he watched over her from above.

Magid also brought observation technology together with disability in earlier projects when she described her experience wearing a 'surveillance shoe', an upskirt camera she designed to wear on her leg during the performance of 'Monitoring Desire' (2000). While Magid walked with the camera in one location, a video monitor showed the view from her ankles upward to spectators at a nearby site. Magid's audience, by implication voyeurs all, had the choice to watch the artist or a remote image of a more private part of her. Speaking of 'Legoland' (2000), a night walk through the city wearing the camera shoe, she remarked on "the image's distortion and the body's appearance of being crippled… The space appears to be tied to the body, even as a victim of it" (Magid 2000: 31). Part literal, part metaphorical, the prosthetic camera impinges on the walking body to produce a disabling exposure, even in a work designed to undercut the male gaze by broadcasting it.

Stationed above or below, the cameras and camera-watchers subvert one of walking's most heralded attributes. In the eighteenth century, Jean-Jacques Rousseau brought recreational, restorative, self-revelatory walking into prominence. The progenitor of modern autobiography, Rousseau was forever haunted by how he thought people were looking at him. He used his long walks to discover himself, to renounce the watched performances and artificial roles that social life imposed on him. He walked to become, he thought, a free man. Today's Rousseau must assemble instead an array of defamiliarising techniques, an artistic wardrobe of masks and disguises, to get free of a gaze that presumes to know all the walker's secrets.

***

Furnished with text and links, the online photo-poster announcing the University of Plymouth conference 'Walking's New Movements' (2019) provides an instructive picture of walking art today. At first glance, one sees walkers on a rural trail moving forward toward the viewer. The photographer employs the powerful visual motif used by Giuseppe Pellizza da Volpedo to depict 'The Path of Workers' (1900) striding forward on the march of history, a motif used to great advantage in photos of Clare Qualmann's 'Perambulator Parade' (2014), where prams, children, and mothers bear down on the viewer. But the conference photo shows on closer inspection that the walkers do not march as a unit;

they face in different directions. Some have stopped; others turn backward, perhaps to check on companions fallen behind. If these movements are new, they are also plural, individual, loosely coordinated, concerned about others sharing the same road.

At the conference itself, there was a small but significant focus on the making of visually creative aesthetic objects. To mention only a few: Ali Pretty's 'Kitchen Table' (2015) builds communities by the collaborative fabrication of colourful flags and banners that make ensuing walks around the Thames estuary stunningly vivid and beautifully unmissable. Tom Spooner produces dense, haunting drawings of what he calls 'transsubjective walking' at twilight. Sam Kemp curves his poetic lines through creative space in his mythogeographical poems.

Simple yet symbolically revelatory, Monali Meher's 'Visiting Sutton Pool' perhaps best sums up the complexities explored in this essay. In her Plymouth performance, the artist turned the sight of the walker in an unforeseen direction, creating a dangerously trustful action that incorporated elements of disability and surveillance, sustaining community and solo risk. The silent walk through Plymouth's streets, across busy streets and down steep steps, was remarkable, like the rest of her 'Visiting' series (begun 2011), because she did it walking backward. Refusing to look where she is going, holding aloft burning incense sticks whose smoke and smell map and mimic the walk's vanishing trail, and whose remains will testify to the event's realization, Meher moves slowly toward water, always the goal of these short-term pilgrimages. Looking to the eyes of the audience for mute guidance, she displays not only the vulnerability of the walking body, but also how it can be protected and encouraged by visual cues, wordless instructions, caring gazes. Walter Benjamin described the angel of history as facing the past while the wreckage of history piles up at his feet, blasting him into a future to which his back is turned. Meher reroutes this scenario, investing the backward look with the power to generate a more positive vision of humanity's prospects. She shows how guardians of sighted compassion can steer the artist, and themselves, toward a safe arrival at an unseen destination.

Where walking's new movement will lead, as we step into a future invisible to us, is anyone's guess. It may be that an ever-more feeling form of walking perception will thrive in coming years, resurrecting the lesson of Shakespeare's Gloucester, even in the face of an emotionless camera eye. But touchingly or remotely, the art of walking will have to deal with the fraught and ever-shifting sight of the walker.

References

de Certeau, M. (1984) *The Practice of Everyday Life,* trans. Steven Rendall, Univ. of California Press

Chandler, E., Johnson, M., Gold, B., Rice, C. & Bulmer, A. (2019) 'Note to Cripistemologies in the City: "Walking-Together" as Sense-Making', *Journal of Public Pedagogies,* no. 4, online at bit.ly/wnm60 (Accessed 12 Feb 2020)

Forgione, N. (2005) 'Everyday Life in Motion: The Art of Walking in Late-Nineteenth-Century Paris', *The Art Bulletin* 87.4: 664-687

Fulton, H. (1989) *Des Pierres Levées et Des Oiseaux Chanteurs, en Bretagne.* Cited in Tiberghien, G. 'La Marche, Emergence et Fin de l'Oeuvre' in: *Un Siècle d'Arpeneurs* (2000), ed. Fréchuret, M., Réunion des musées nationaux, 225-252. My translation

Greenberg, A. (2016) *Turning Live Surveillance Feeds Into Unsettling Works of Art.* Available at: bit.ly/wnm55 (Accessed 12 Feb 2020)

Joyce, J. (1922) *Ulysses* [3] Available at: Project Gutenberg eBook of *Ulysses,* bit.ly/wnm54 (Accessed 12 Feb 2020)

Lakmaier, N. (2012) *One Morning in May.* Available at: bit.ly/wnm66 (Accessed 12 Feb 2020)

Magid, Jill. *Monitoring Desire* (2000) Thesis, MIT. Available at: bit.ly/wnm71 (Accessed 12 Feb 2020)

Morris, B. (2018-2019) *A Wander Is Not a Slog.* Available at: bit.ly/wnm67 (Accessed 12 Feb 2020)

______ (2018) *The Artistic Medium of Walking,* Interartive, Available at: bit.ly/wnm58 (Accessed 12 Feb 2020)

Profeta, K. (2015) *Dramaturgy in Motion,* Univ. of Wisconsin Press

Rilke, R. M. (1907) 'Archaic Torso of Apollo'. Trans. Stephen Mitchell. Available at: bit.ly/wnm65 (Accessed 12 Feb 2020).

Smith, P. (2018) 'Radical Twenty-First Century Walkers' in: *The Routledge International Handbook of Walking,* ed. Hall, C., Ram, Y. and Shoval N., Routledge, 37-45

Smith, P. and Schott, J. (2018) *Rethinking Mythogeography in Northfield, Minnesota,* Triarchy Press

Springgay, S. and Truman, S. (2018) *Walking Methodologies in a more-than-Human World,* Taylor & Francis

Walking Diagrams was a collection of artworks shown by Helen Billinghurst at the Walking's New Movements Conference (2019). They were selected from a larger body of work that was made as part of her final doctoral submission and initially exhibited as English Diagrams (2018) in the Royal William Yard, Plymouth.

This research explored ways of making artworks in the studio in response to walking the landscape. Between 2014 and 2018, Helen walked across England; each walk a fragment of a single route between her home in Plymouth and her childhood home in Cambridge. She explored a country politically and socially at unease with itself, a terrain increasingly fragmented, urbanised and spectacularised. She also found a sense of a vital 'other'; a repository of strata of history and story still available in the gaps and edges of the hypermodern, twenty-first century landscape.

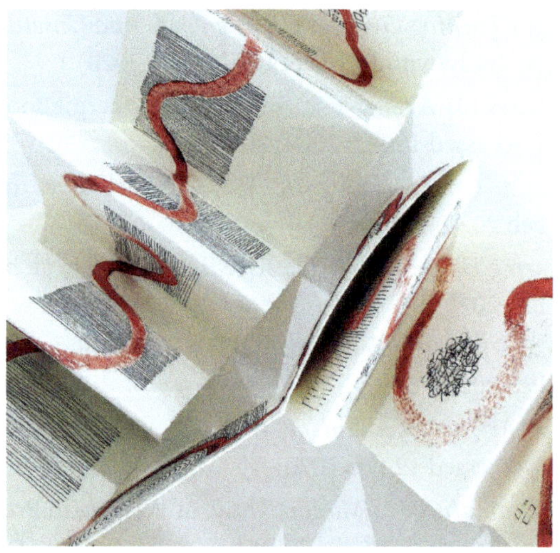

Toothache Drawing (2017). Folded paper, egg tempera & inkpen.

In the studio, a variety of 'voices' emerged in response to the unfolding and enfolding walked route; autobiographical memory, childhood games, stories, and personal mythologies became interwoven with histories, tracks, traces and places explored in the landscape. A bricolage of visual and painterly languages was drawn together, reflecting the variety of terrains negotiated.

During phases of making Helen broke her foot, worked through periods of illness and a bereavement, and these events became entangled in the work. Narratives shifted scale and repeated their patterns between human and non-human embodied, to social, political and ecological organisational fluxes and flows of the landscape.

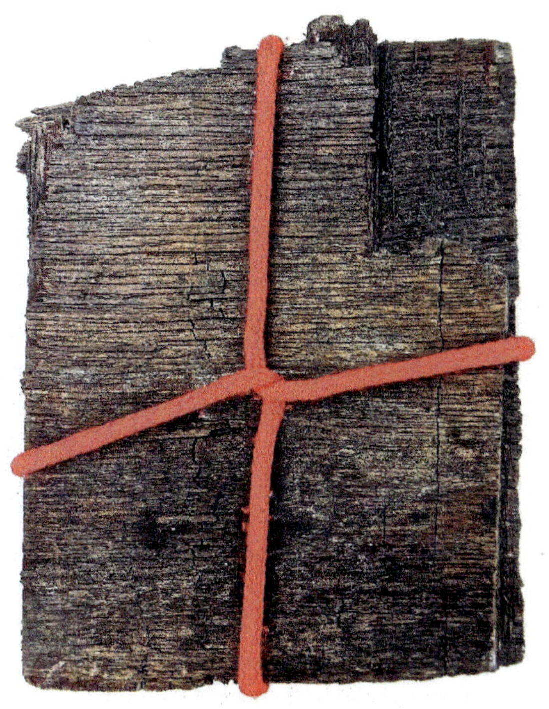

English Memories (2015). Found plywood & bootlace.

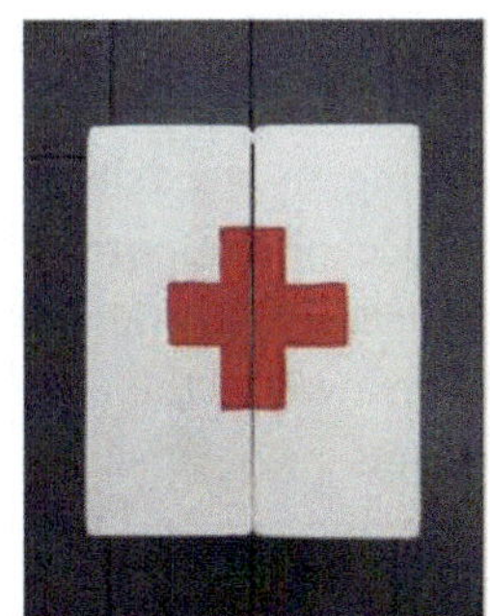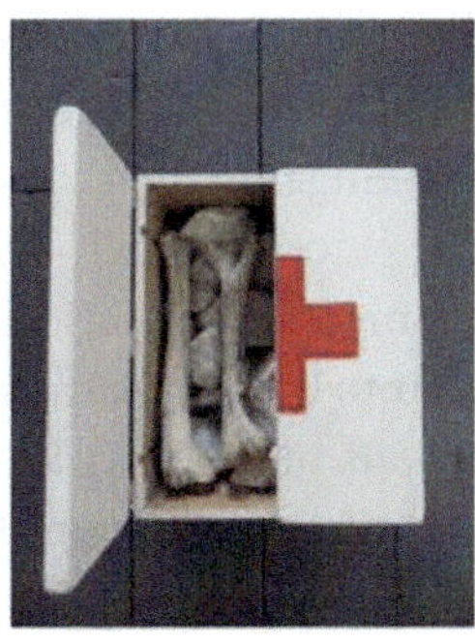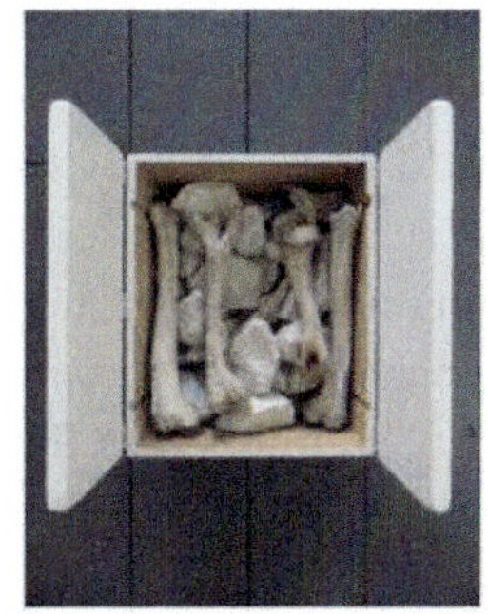

Cabinet of English Medicine (2017). Painted box, found chalk & deer bones.

Visiting Sutton Pool

Monali Meher

2nd of November 2019 at 5pm, outside Roland Levinsky Building, exit to Drakes Circus, North Hill; a small group of enthusiastic people gathered to participate in my 'backward walking in silence with incense sticks' performance. The weather wasn't that good. It was rainy and already getting dark.

For the first time I was manifesting this 'backward walking' performance called, 'Visiting Sutton Pool' in the evening twilight.

The act of walking backwards with incense sticks is a kind of exercise and challenge. Not necessarily to make an entertaining show of excitement or drama of heroism but this is how I perceived the initial idea when I strolled through Xiazhou village in Guangzhou, China in year 2011. The narrow path had its forward and backward movement while I observed the surrounding, walking back and forth, keeping the rhythm, a cinematic choreo-graphy and a motion picture is how I imagined it. In every new place I apply the same theory, observe the paths, the streets, the surroundings and trace my route towards the water.

Walking backwards in such a way that I could face and meet the eyes of my audience as they begin to navigate space with a passed-on emotion of trust. I follow my path by looking into their eyes, judging my steps slowly and steadily while leaving a trace of smell and sense of temporarily mapping journeys. The perfumed smoke has its movement; it's neither stagnant nor fluid but merges into the air and gets blown away by the wind into the atmosphere. Further on it fades away from its hazy thickness combined with intensified fragrance to thin air of remembrance and then disappears. I distinguish this temporary aspect as metaphor close to life as to live art. The use of the incense as a gentle, ephemeral tracing of spaces, a short-lived remnant, an unexpected sense. Incense has been used in various cultures as part of rituals, ceremonies and cleansing. The tracing of the route is significant depending on the site, city and its history. Walking backwards becomes a moving theatre where I perform guiding my audience intuitively under their subtle gestures of instructive expressions.

Signboards, traffic instructions, buildings, zebra crossing, traffic poles, spray painted markings, tactile ground surface indicators are also important guides and useful references in the streets of the city landscape.

'Silence' is an invisible aspect of walking, walking is connected to breathing; when one is aware of breathing, then the 'walking' becomes conscious meditation.

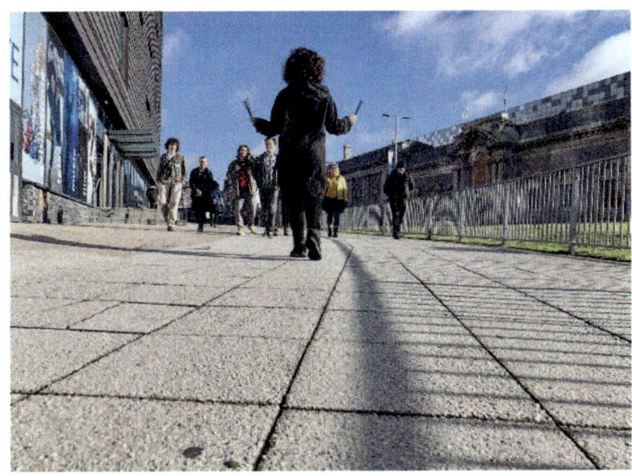

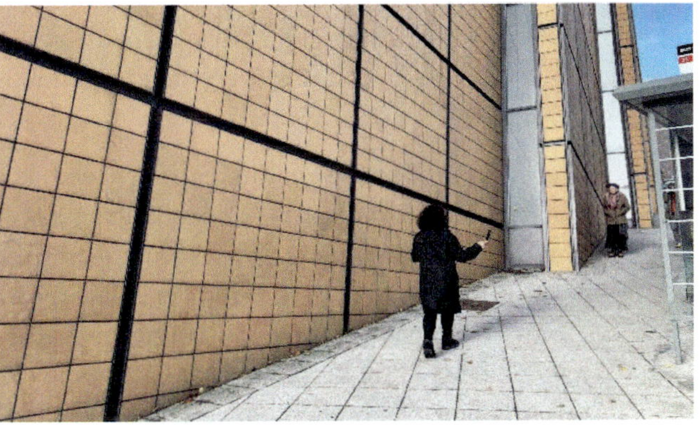

The 'walk' on the evening of 2nd November was challenging and unforgettable. Due to the darkness and rain, the participants happened to walk very close to me leaving not much distance between us. I concluded the walk at Sutton Harbour, North Quay by turning and facing the water. I repeated the performance on the 3rd of November at 10am with another group of participants when it was bright and sunny.

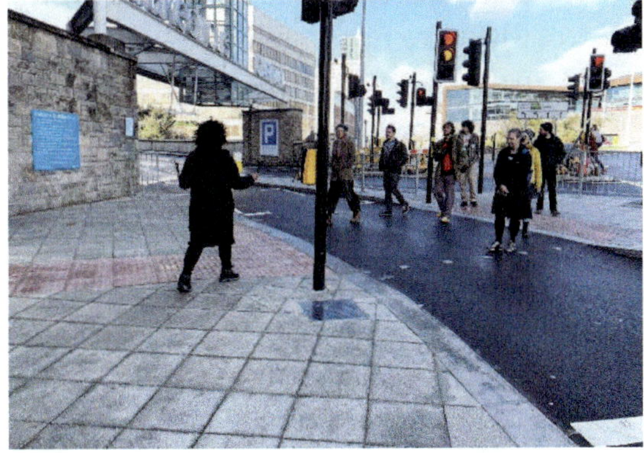

Object Place Walking

Jody Oberfelder

Object Place addresses the inner energy of people and things and their relationships. Participants were asked to bring portable objects to the site:

- An item which has personal significance
- Something to lighten your load
- A thing you use every day, or something you happen to have with you

A movement procession and ritual ensued, connecting one's object, its materiality and value, and our selves as physical beings, as signifiers in ever shifting relationships. We illuminate the things we *hold* (have within our grasp) and *behold* (see, inspect, view, regard, contemplate) anew.

Movement is my primary language. Rather than having this occur only on stage, I'm stimulated to devise new scores that move audiences towards an embodied experience, while creating a forum for interactivity. Inviting engagement, we recognise our relationships to place, space, self and object. We invite participants into this Object Place, where we recognise our relationships to things, via contemplation, and personal connection.

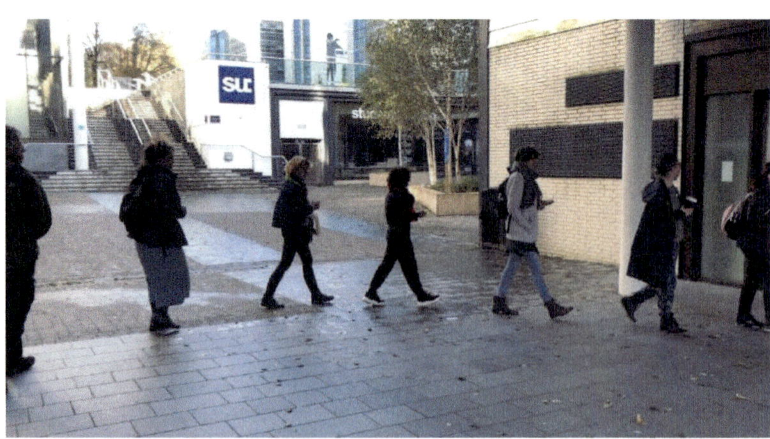

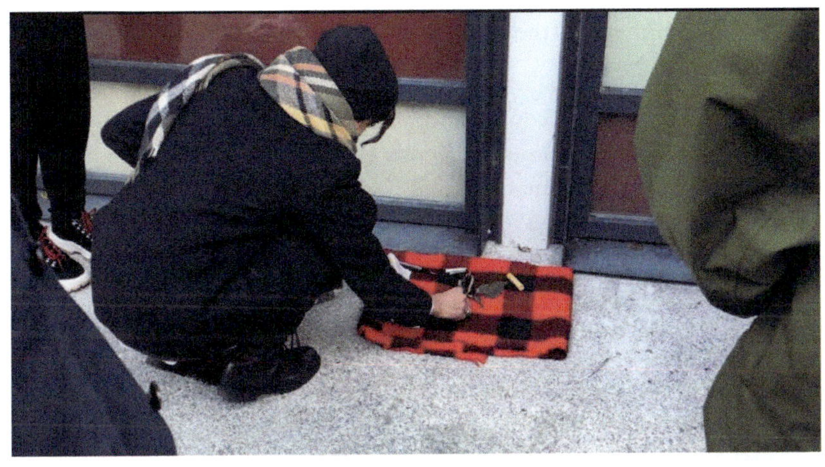

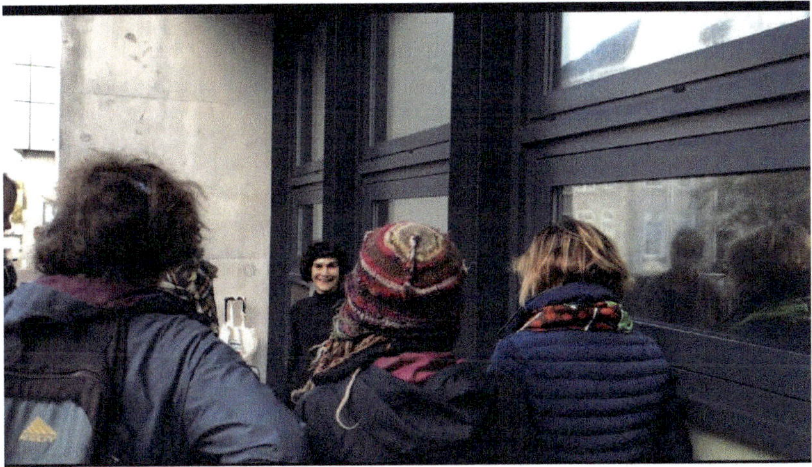

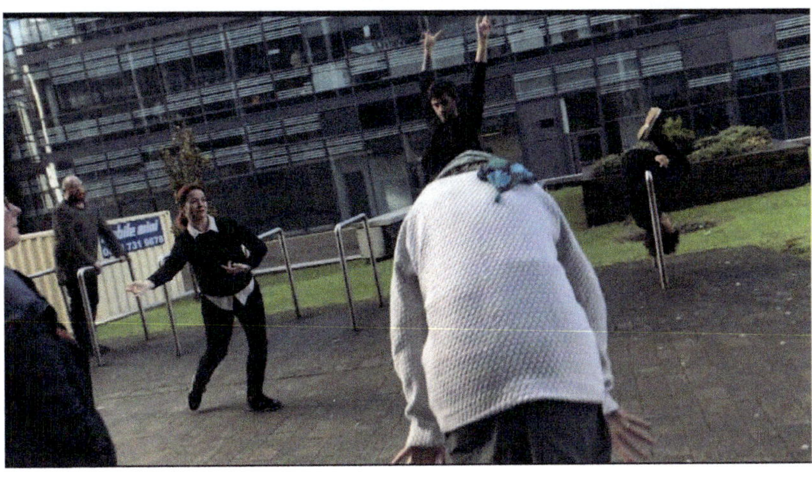

Guides: Christopher Matthews Hutchings, Jody Oberfelder and Andrew Sanger

I really enjoyed the construction of your work, how it 'held' a space for the participants and gently encouraged participation in a seemingly simple manner that, in reality is very difficult to engineer. So thank you!

Dr. Victoria Hunter, Reader in Site-Dance and Choreography,
Dance Department, University of Chichester

Rain, wind, darkness (a gale!),
Precious objects,
Pen, lip balm, diamonds, coin, peel,
Each with a story and a resonance that rippled out across the night,
Movement, touch, kinetic bounce, a twirl,
Reflection, connection.

Rebecca Johinke, Department of English,
University of Sydney

Your start of the day provocation attuned my bodymind first to mark making and unmaking, reminding me of embodiment and finally in a suitably destabilized questioning movement towards affective shaping and carving of space, time, matter. An enjoyable and challenging energized embodiment, what a way to start a day's conference with walking artists!

Richard White
Artist / Researcher

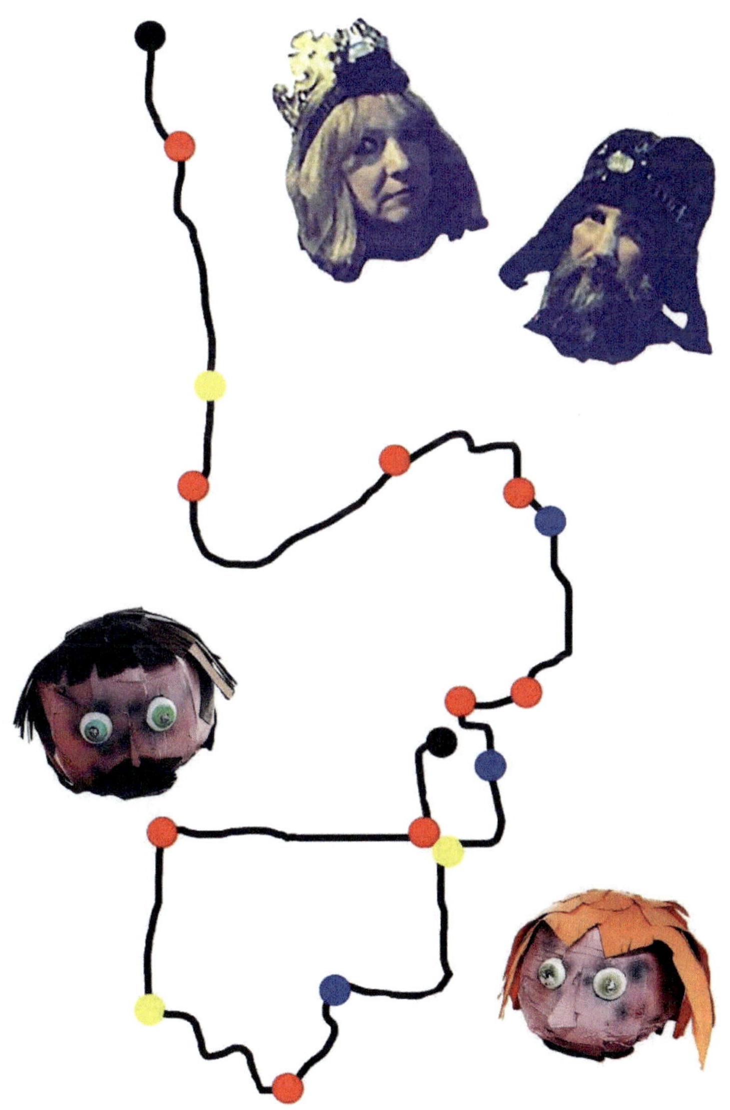

A Route Unscrambled

Gary Winters and Claire Hind

Ramble

This is a provocation kit bag, packed with prompts to write a performance walk.

We offer a framework from out of the *Dream Yards* performance (Plymouth), for you to compose your own walking performance.

Dream Yards was performed weekly across several months in the city of York and then remapped elsewhere; for S.T.E.P New York, the Lord Mayor's Celebrations Norwich, and for Walking's New Movement, Plymouth.

Our walk relates to dreaming, sleeping and reimagines Shakespeare's King Lear for a modern city. It is a walk with pauses and stop off points. It is not a direct path to the pub; there are places to discover and get lost in before a good local ale and choice conversation.

We designed and composed a script where repeats happen. It is also designed for two people to conduct the tour. The text is made up of a dialogical relationship between King Lear and her Fool, it is also a way to inform the audience of what is going on in the five stages of sleep. The story is interwoven with dream donations from the public and discussions with a neuroscientist. There is an unpacking of what is going on in the moment of the walk itself and the job of the dream to map site with a conscious experience of lucidity. The formulaic that follows includes different ways of describing this composition and how it unfolds at each place.

When we composed our walk for Walking's New Movement Plymouth, we searched for a variety of contrasting places that have a particular quality; somewhere busy, somewhere quiet, some type of landmark, the service areas of a restaurant or business, intimate spaces such as a nook or a cranny, a yard, some street furniture that can be used for a platform or mini-stage, a special place, somewhere calm - that is the city but does not feel like a city; a cat's hideaway. This route gives you an opportunity to occupy such contrasting places. If you can't get to Plymouth, trace this route over a map of another city and appropriate.

How do you compose your own walk from the shape we created?
What is it like to experience the qualities of each different place?
How do the sites we map inspire you to write creative material?
What lens might you put upon this route?
Is there a story you want to adapt?
What happens in each site and how do you define moments?
Is your walk experienced as a politically engaged activity?
What walk can you write for both an invited and incidental audience?

Think of the route as a desire path, we propose this idea to keep up momentum of the walk so that it may be ghosted. This an offer, open to interpretation. Think of other established pilgrimages or routes; paths are made, journeys encountered, rituals performed. We offer a structure to make your own ideas for performance.

Preamble

Avoid walking on an empty stomach but leave room for a nice supper afterward.
Prepare nine music loops to play during the wandering between sites, set up to tease and keep the audience guessing the familiar track.

Prepare for rain, prepare for smells, prepare for the
emotions, make room for humour and invite in the other
worldly (this applies to everyone, both performer and
audience).
Know your route like the back of your hand, and accept that
you might get lost.
Have some prepared writing in hand.
Have a portable prop bag with you for little interventions and
surprises so that the walk's journey is easily recountable.

A m b l e

Arrange a time for your audience to meet, allow them to
gather before your arrival.
Arrive together wearing something recognisable.
Have a sign that promotes the title of your work, and have
some music playing.

Take your audience on a walk and ask them to follow.
Gather at the pedestrian crossing, the appropriate signal will
guide you and check all bodies made it across.
Allow for the slowest pace.
Find a free-standing boulderstone and stand up onto it, name
this place, know why you have named it.
Acknowledge public space.
Set the context of the walk through a reveal.

Walk on.

Walk through the shopping mall, plant an uncanny image
that distorts the world that you propose, a fleeting moment,
something that may pass you by. Do this quickly for security
purposes.
Be aware that you are disrupting the normal flow, and no
animals are allowed.

Emerge from the shopping mall, breathe again.

Find yourself at an oasis in the town, find non-native foliage, get amongst it and make a declaration.

Walk on.
Music playing.
Make sure you are noticed by people in the windows, those who are busily engaged in eating and drinking, allow for the odd lewd comment.
Walk for a longer stretch so the music loop playing really sinks in as an earworm.
Walk on.

Walk to a dimly lit spot that provides a focus and perform a surprise, have something up your sleeve, or in your backpack, or in your pocket.
Stand there in the fire exit at the back of a fast fashion retailer and invite your audience to make suggestions for alternative shopping habits; for example, that the retailer hosts a 'recycle your clothes day', in a Swap Shop format. Step out of the fiction of the text and speak directly to the audience, tell them what you think is going on. If it is raining behave as if it is raining. Accept the conditions of situation, whatever. Don't worry too much about those who moan about it, they will find a way through this and it is ok to be wet, despite the titters.

Walk on to the pedestrian crossing, note you have two crossings to deal with, are they in sync? Press the button to stop the traffic, the music loops can fill the gap as they wait.

Walk toward the car park and settle for a short while in a blue room, it is the lobby but you may wish to call it a vestibule. This is a nameless place, name it.
Draw upon the fiction of your diegesis.
Recall the face of an animal.
This space deserves more attention that it currently gets in its accepted state.

If there is an odd smell, behave as if there is an odd smell.
Accept the conditions of the situation.
Let one performer disappear from out of sight, leaving the other to talk in detail.
Step out of the fiction of the text and speak directly to the audience, tell them important stories that signify a change of habit, or a shift in experiencing the world.
Allow one performer to lead the audience to find its compadre.

Walk on.
When you have found the other accept the instructions to walk on from them.
Even if things appear broken keep walking and walking, allow for the split.
Walk on as a lone performer and take your audience to a back alley to make a note of the bins, the neighbourhood, the paving, the silence.

Turn the audience's gaze up the alley to frame a view into the neighbourhood that has depth. The image of this place is ripe for others to pass through, silhouetted anonymous folk, or an urban fox.
Foreground a rhetorical question and if an audience member responds behave as if they have responded.
Acknowledge the appearance of your compadre who arrives into frame and walks towards you.
Create a change of tone and walk whilst speaking, be aware that you are inviting your audience to walk and listen simultaneously, create a sense of overload.

Echo a protest march of some significance, set up a sense of heightened togetherness. The relationship to the place is changing because you are walking and chanting, an assault.
If someone slings a lewd comment, act as if a lewd comment has been slung.

Walk on.
Find yourself in a back street.
Gather from the city's fabric the debris and detritus found there.
Create a temporary assemblage that somehow illustrates the thinking behind your personal walking diegesis.
Are you doing enough? Where do your responsibilities lie?

Walk on.

En route, plant an uncanny image that again distorts the world that you propose, a fleeting moment, something that you try not to pass by.

Step out onto the road with care, allow your compadre to stop the traffic, there is no rush, allow the music loop to fill the gaps. Accommodate the slowest pace. Restart the flow of the traffic with a nod and a wave to the drivers - you will be surprised at how patient they can be.
Walk on.

Find an intimate space where a hidden landmark can be viewed. Take the performance to ground level, create a lasting image. Be aware that you are inviting your audience to slow down.
If it feels emotional,
behave
as
if
it
is
emotional.

Walk on.

Up a narrow ginnel, in the distance, there is a gin shaft.
There is a bend in the passage and it disappears into

darkness. Reach for the portable prop bag for a little intervention and make a pact for the audience to witness. Here, headlights turn on and a car pulls out of a gate and drives into the performance space; someone else's business interrupts and everyone moves to the side, take care of yourself. They lock up the gates and get in the car and hesitate. They wait, we wait. They wait in the car, we wait on the street. The bright red brake lights are now the main focus of the moment. Soon as those lights drop off it's an indication to restart the performance as the vehicle drives off into the darkness.

Walk on.

Arrive at special place, somewhere calm that is the city but does not feel like a city; a cat's hideaway.
Plant an uncanny image that again distorts the world that you propose, a moment from the pact that is simply too beautiful to pass by.
If it tears at your heart, let it tear your heart out.
Set the tone of the moment, there are no words here, just a song:
Silhouette the washing lines
Let the ancient glacial boulder bubble through the pavement
Mix the Wensum with the Tud, dip your head before the Yare
Train the geese
Blow smoke rings
Stay pendulous.

Walk on.
Find a recess, refer to the site, the neighbourhood and its buildings.
Walk on.

Allow for the split. Your compadre walks away, the last music loop fades into nothing.

Create a change of tone signalling the end, recap, remember, reappear. If the mundane everyday humdrum happens; the flicking of a switch, the boiling of some water, the opening of the curtains, let it happen, it is important. Bring your audience back around. Propose a way back in. Acknowledge there is no way back in. Name this moment.

Walk on to find local ale and choice conversation.

Shamble

Buy a round, settle in a snug and allow for responses, they will come thick and fast. Allow for different forms; comments on the snug. Grunts. Sighs of comfort coming in from the cold. Folk comparing their cask ales. Questions, observations, confusions about a coat. Random thoughts. Petting a passing animal. Listen for prompts. The writerly aspect of your walk and the considerations you had for your audience will eventually be called into frame, because the shambles stir up something. When the conversation turns to immediate experiences of the walk, remember those moments, they tell about how affective walks are for each individual and the communal experience of gathering and witnessing. Soon, the conditions of the night, the state of the streets and route you took hold much attention, there will be detail in the back alleys. The incidental will be shared from different points of view. When the elements of what was specifically tuned into are spoken of, note how they tuned in. Others will talk about their own walking projects and compare yours to their feats of danger. One might ask what walking performance is, one might ask what one of the sound loops was. If someone slings an unexpected comment, act as if an unexpected comment has been slung. Allow for communal conversation to shift into more localized chats where multiple topics in the room amplify the sound.

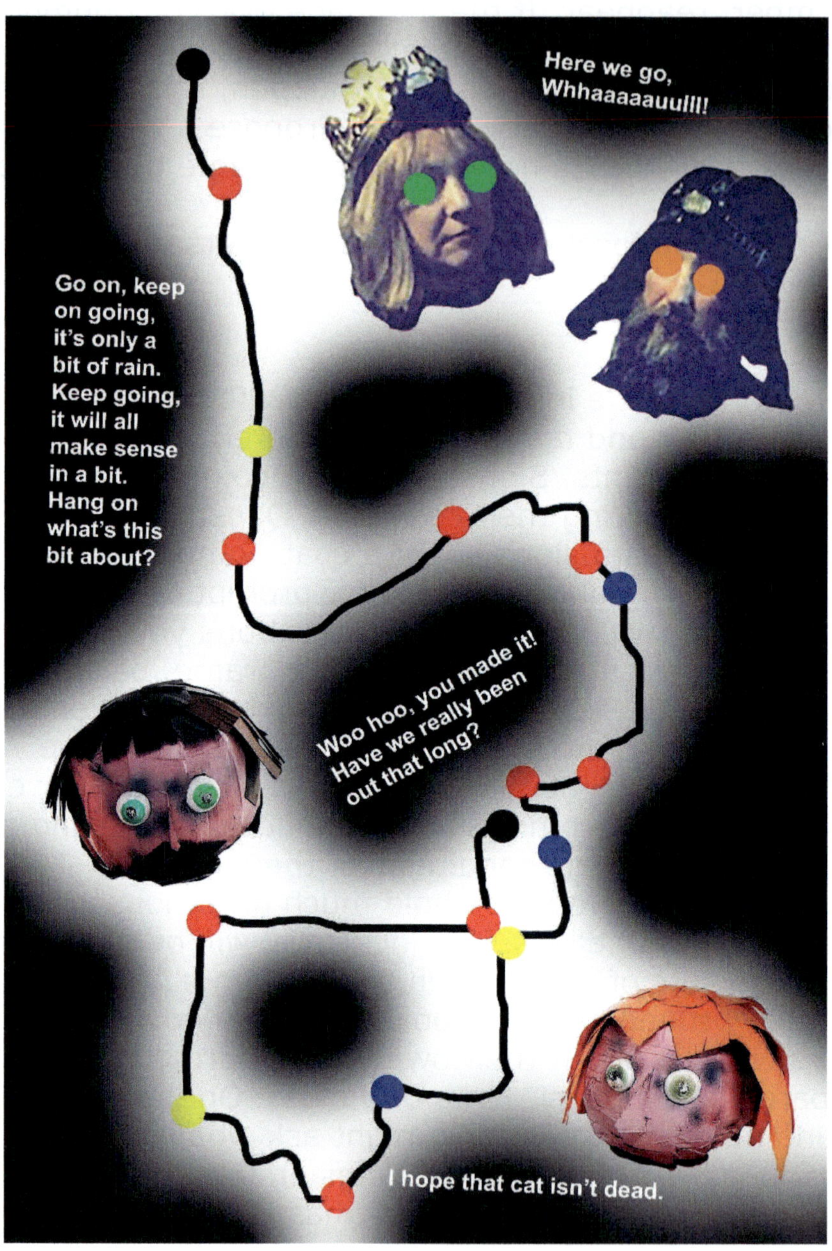
Here we go, Whhaaaaauulll!
Go on, keep on going, it's only a bit of rain. Keep going, it will all make sense in a bit. Hang on what's this bit about?
Woo hoo, you made it! Have we really been out that long?
I hope that cat isn't dead.

WORDS FROM WALKS

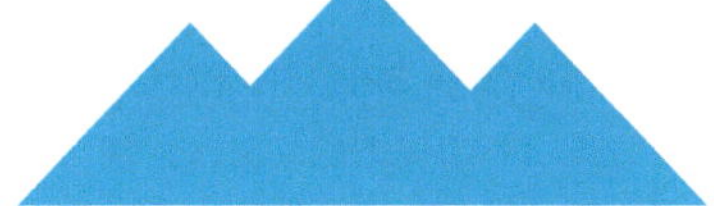

HAMISH FULTON

WORDS FROM WALKS

'Never write anything,
you'll only regret it'.
(Don Whillans, English mountaineer 1933-1985.)

I understand that the artist may not be the best person
to provide an objective, art historical overview
of their own life's work.
However, in the absence of any in-depth writing,
and in an attempt to prevent misconceptions
continuing without comment (the complicity of silence)
I present here, in leaflet form, for the record,
a few points
regarding my general outlook.

I exhibit words as a walking artist, not a conceptual artist.
I am not an author. I'm 'uneducated'.
Learning without being taught.
Words are independent
of any one material, size or colour.

The sovereignty of languages. The histories of nations.
In the English language,
justice is a seven letter word.

THE NEWOLD WAY

Walking is ancient and contemporary.

I describe myself as 'a walking artist'.
Walking art is the bringing together
of two entirely separate activities.
Walking and art.
I transform ideas
into physical experiences.
My self-imposed rule is:
If I do not walk I cannot make any art.

**THE ENJOYMENT OF WALKING
THE PLEASURES OF CREATIVITY**

I recognise the fact that not everyone
is physically able to walk.

I am not a fast walker, but I can keep going all day.

I am an artist who walks, not a walker who makes art.
Not every artist enjoys walking
and not every walker is tolerant of contemporary art.

An 'artwork' may be purchased,
but my walks
cannot be sold or stolen.
A Walked Line Unlike A Drawn Line Can Never Be Erased.
Duration. Ten toes. Counting by hand.
Mark time… *not the land*.
Measure, is a se7en letter word.
Reading from left to right, but walking in every direction.
Up hill
down hill.
From and to THE TENT.
Tent doors opening to the east.

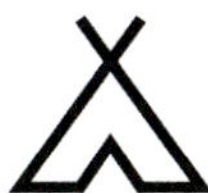

Brain Heart Lungs. Breathing. Walking Rhythms.
Different walks different rules.
My walks range from...
7 barefoot paces walking on grass towards the rising full moon,
to...
multi-week solo camping treks (on the Earth under my feet)
to...
coast to coast walks (sea to summit to sea) and...
road walks (walking with a light pack) to...
'high altitude trekking' (guided mountain ascents),
and,
1-2 hour unique shared urban walks
(building experiences, not objects)
involving up to several hundred participants.
(Participation corroboration).
Repetitions of the same walk ideas
in different locations with different people.
The Walking Participants Are The Art Observers.

Images of the land.
I walk on the land, not in the 'landscape'.
I do not take walks, I make walks.
'Walk texts' are about past events.
Walking 'in the moment',
is walking now.

AN OBJECT CANNOT COMPETE WITH AN EXPERIENCE.
A completed walk is like an invisible object.

Out of respect for the abilities and standards
of world-class mountaineers, The Marathon Monks,
and unrecorded foot travellers from the past and present,
I describe my few artwalks as short and easy.
I compete, only with myself.

Walking Is The Constant The Art Medium Is The Variable.
Every piece of art I materialise contains a 'walk text'.

I make art exclusively
from **walks that I have personally experienced.
WORDS FROM WALKS.**

**When a walk has been completed, the text can be written.
('Earning the right' to record the event.)
The basic facts of the walk cannot be altered,
but as time passes and the quantity of walks increases,
the walks may be re-evaluated, re-contextualised,
and the 'walk texts'...
recycled.**

**In choosing a text 'title' with the same number of letters
as the days walked,
the graphic elements are 'locked' together.
Numbers. (Old Norse, meaning: a report, narration).**

**My walk texts are like a pack of playing cards
which I can rearrange into a variety of categories.**

'When the time is right'.
I took a gamble, and placed my bet on just the one horse,
walking.
1973, my year of the unknown **road ahead.**

**In a 21st century internet world overflowing with words
I do not provide the relief of wordless abstract art.
Conversely, I am not an urban 'primitive'.
Internet research** ⟶ ⟵ surveillance capitalism,
all in contrast to our private intuitions.

Make a walk, write a text, read it to an audience.
By word of mouth. The spoken word. Oral history.
Memory is selective.
**The retelling of stories. A good story well told.
Verbal interpretations for the meaning of visual symbols.
Picture writing. Sign language.**

 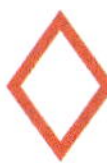 

The Winter Count (from snow to snow.)
Quipu, knotted string records.
Moon counting sticks.
The length of a journey, remembered by the number of sleeps.
Beyond the word. There are no words in nature.
Written-in-the-earth, fresh tracks of a grizzly bear.

A walk may exist purely as a walk,
but my 'artwork'
cannot be created without the walk.

IT'S WHAT IT'S ABOUT,
NOT WHAT IT LOOKS LIKE.
The surrounding 'imagery', the graphic design of my artwork,
is what I call the 'container' for the 'walk text'.
I date my artwork, by the date of the walk.
EVERY WALK IS UNIQUE.
Walks are facts for the walker and 'fiction' for everyone else.
An Artwork Cannot Re-present The Experience Of A Walk.

Walking Art.
Neither of these two words
specify an art medium,
thereby suggesting openness and potential
for anyone.

The separation of experience and object.

The history of walking...
'from walking to... sitting and riding',
'from necessity to... choice'.
'On the path, to go off the path'.
A tree at its birthplace, a boulder at its resting place.
Distance and time.
Direction
of the rising sun.
Summer solstice.
Winter solstice. Darkness. Silence. The call of an owl.
Sound of the wind through pine needles.

Walking against the traffic.
Not-by-car. The width of a footprint.
Side stepping. Walking in the age of vehicle dependency.
'Park your car, ride a bike. Stash your bike, take a hike.'
The consistency of walking.
Childhood, old age. Ancient and contemporary.

Uncontacted Peoples. Walking without a smartphone. Uncontactable.
(There are no photographs of Crazy Horse).
Walking without talking.
Springtime listening. Arrival of the first cuckoo where you live.
The Southern Hemisphere. The South Face.
Walking backwards in mud. Walking In any direction.

Walking
is the interconnecting experience
for a wide spectrum of possibilities, disciplines and research...
slow travel, SLOWALK, walkability,
restorative walking disentangling the mind,
walking and talking, mental health, HEALING is a 7 letter word,
creative thinking, into the trees (shinrin-yoku),
the experience of purposeless walking,
freedom of movement, freedom of expression, free speech,
non-violent protest marches, refugees on foot...
the electronic identification of walking styles, (facial-ID) AI,
escapes across the Nangpa La, Journalists Without Borders,
the right of assembly, walk the talk, not rule-by-law,
walkabout, the right to roam, public pathways, footpaths,
pedestrian road crossings, indoor walking,
egoless pilgrimage, Kailash is a 7 letter name.
The Tibetan Kora (both outdoors and indoors),
seated mechanistic society's missing rituals,
meditation, 'performance', 'movement', visual art...
'the wandering haiku poets of old',
and contemporary mountaineering expeditions:
'the walk-in',
the climb... 'ROUTE AND STYLE'... descend and, 'WALKOUT'.

Walking Between Walks.

Weaving the walks,
layer on top of layer, 'woven time'.
Connecting the invisible footsteps of my previous walks,
crossing and re-joining.
The starting place: dawn of the day.
The ending place: euphoric exhaustion.
Energy from deep sleep.
(Physical energy provided by a strong idea.)
Walking Through.

Oxygenating the brain,
lost memories rising to the surface like tea leaves,
opening the mind, a change of mind,
transforming perceptions, relaxed but alert.
Walking is magic. Walking is 'good medicine'.
Walk-In-Nature.
Organic is a 7 letter word.
Walking In Relation To Everything.

MY ART IS A COMMENT ON THE WAY WE LIVE TODAY. INDOORS.
Outside.
Seeing The Bird That Sings.
Antidote: fresh air for children
as they stride out across the hill tops.

A DECISION TO CHOOSE ONLY WALKING.

Although I made my first 'artwalk' with other students
during 2 February 1967,
step
by
step
it took me a further six years of trial and error
via several short walks,
to arrive at a total commitment to walking.

In October 1973 at the age of 28,
after completing one coast to coast walk
of just over a thousand miles,
on Scotland, Wales and England,
I made the single most important decision
of my creative life:
To Make Art Resulting Only
From The Experience Of Individual Walks.
7 the universal readymade.
The 7 days of the week, the seventh wave,
The 7 principles of 'Leave No Trace'.
Rainbow. No-thing is a 7 letter word.
The seven colours of a rainbow
transformed into a heap of grey dust.
Mandala, is a seven letter word.
Bardo. Transition, rebirth after 49 days.
The Seven Stars. 'The moon lives for 28 days'.
Index finger of the right hand.
'Seven steps, rest. Seven steps, rest.
I knew that should I try 12 or 13 steps
I would lose consciousness'.
(Jerzy Kukuczka. My Vertical World. 1992.)
In the English language,
WALKING IS A SEVEN LETTER WORD. **(Bipedal)**
The seven names of women
who ascended to the 8848 metre summit of Everest
Phantog Schmatz Allison Pittman Boskoff
Araceli Segarra.
Habeler• Messner• Mandela• Thoreau• Jokhang•
Leonard Peltier•
Arapaho• Arranda• Dongria• Quechua• Inupiat• Huichol•
Dzambha •
(Google: Naglha Dzambha, a sacred mountain in Tibet).
HABITAT.
Oceti Sacowin, The Seven Campfires. 'For the Seventh Generation'.
The United Nations Declaration
On The Rights Of Indigenous Peoples. (2007)

In 2016 I voted to remain in the EU.
In 2019,
it is the Indigenous Peoples of the world who may guide us
to a more reverential relationship with what they call,
Mother Earth.
Changes, is a 7 letter word.

'We need to remember that the work of our time
is bigger than climate change'.
(Rebecca Tarbotton.
Quoted by Naomi Klein. This Changes Everything. 2014.)

———

idlenomore.ca

———

www.honorearth.org

———

'...to transform human laws to match natural laws,
not vice versa'.
(Winona LaDuke. All Our Relatives. 1999.)

———

'...the democracy of all life, the little beings and the big beings
with no hierarchy
because you have no idea
ecologically how things fit into the web of life'.
(Vandana Shiva. Restoring The Balance. 1997.)

———

'Man is part of nature and his war against nature
is inevitably a war against himself'.
(Rachel Carson. Silent Spring. 1962.)

———

'We have somehow contrived to discount land
as a significant subject for public debate'.
(Mark Cocker. Our Place.
Can We Save Britain's Wildlife Before It Is Too Late? 2018.)

———

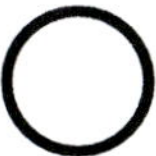

1969 boot prints on the moon.
Our lack of respect
for the diversity of life forms
on
This Planet
is the root cause of the ecological crisis.
BIGDATA or, eye WITNESS? Lithium is a 7 letter word.
As we gaze down
into our smartphones (nomophobia)
we simultaneously turn our backs on all non-human existence.
Either 'game' or 'vermin'...
SHARKS WOLVES BEARS ... SERPENTS
(slugs, spiders, rats, leeches, mosquitoes, termites, flees...)
The life-force even in the smallest of insects.

See: Chatral Rinpoche (1913-2015). Fish release ceremonies.

Migration of the Arctic Tern. The pollination of plants...
Migration of the Monarch butterfly.

Mountains that look like clouds,
clouds that look like mountains.

Moving and seen to be moving,
moving and seen not to be moving.

The altitudes of high mountains... gravity.
Let the rivers run free and 'wild'.
Flowing energy.
Animate
and inanimate 'beings', 'the other peoples'.
The Uncarved Block.
A glacial boulder transported by ice and shaped by erosion.
The-rocks-are-alive-in-their-homeland.
Scale and Quantity● Weight and Value● Marble and Diamonds●

A MOUNTAIN IS NOT MADE OF STONE IT IS STONE

THE RIGHTS OF NATURE

———

History is not neutral.
A case of mistaken identity.
There is more than one story to be told.
From the 70's to the present time,
some art historians have categorised me as a Land Artist.
From my side,
in 2019, as a symbolic gesture of respect for nature,
I wish no association with a dominant order of art
that intentionally re-models
the naturally evolved form of the land,
or introduces natural-objects into the international art market.
The means do not justify the ends.
LAND ART CONTRADICTS WALKING ART.
My disagreement
is with the limited focus of art historians...
not the diversity, freedom and creativity of artists...

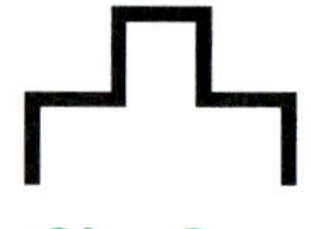
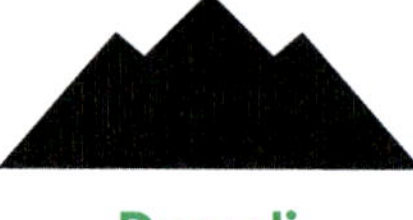
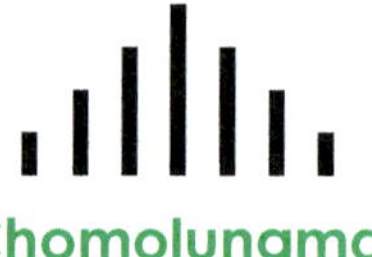

Cho Oyu   Denali   Chomolungma

My rule for high altitude mountain art is to mention only
those few mountains that I have ascended (with assistance.)

'My truths are not universal,
which is one reason they are so difficult to express.
My ice axe may be your paintbrush.
One man's Slovak Direct is another's West Buttress'.
(Steve House. Beyond The Mountain. 2009.)

———

An Object Cannot Compete With An Experience.
Movement in contrast to stillness.

All my art begins with the walking experience,
not nature as material for human use,
not ancient monuments and ruins,
not the history of agriculture and 'landscape' gardening...
not the history of 'landscape' painting...
Conversely,
some Indigenous Peoples,
sense that particular natural locations are 'sacred'.

(I do not consider myself to be a world traveler
in search of diverse 'scenery'.
Scenery coming from the Greek word meaning, stage.)

'...the idea of history is itself a western invention whose central
theme is a rejection of habitat. It formulates experience
of nature and tends to reduce place to...
only a stage upon which the human drama is enacted'.
(Paul Shepard. Nature and Madness 1982.)

Sometime in the mid-seventies, I defensively coined the term
'walking artist'.

But the true beginning for my intuitions,
was when, as 13 year old, I read the life story of Wooden Leg,
(born c 1858)
a Northern Cheyenne from the Black Hills,
in what was later to become South Dakota.
Nakota, Lakota, Dakota.
In the summer of 1969,
with Nancy Wilson I visited those places that I had read about,
among others,
The Greasey Grass, The Black Hills and Wounded Knee.
In 2005, I had the privilege of meeting Dennis Banks,
an Ojibwa
and co-founder of the American Indian Movement (AIM)
who led the occupation of Wounded Knee in 1973.
'The Black Hills Are Not For Sale'.
(Public Sculpture At Mount Rushmore and Thunderhead Mountain.)

The worlds oldest ongoing art is
re-painted
Indigenous Australian cave art.

Flyweight = the weight of a fly.
My decisive restraint in the use of art materials,
is merely a symbolic gesture.
Eco-nomics.
Art materials: every 'thing' has to be made of something,
and everything comes originally, as 'free goods' from nature.

Didactic-sanctimonious-hypocrisy.
As an international artist,
I identify the fact that I generate a carbon footprint.

Zero emission flights? Rising sea levels, footprints at high tide.

I have read, that we have lived as hunter-gatherers
for 90% of human existence.
The light of day and the darkness of night.
'Moon - the night sun'.

Contributing to the life
of a footpath.
Hooves, paws, claws, feet, shoes, boots, rain, melting snow.

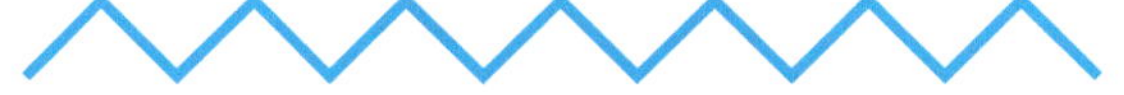

Mountain skyline,
a gap in the distant horizon.
Over the pass, between the hills, down beside a river,
the flow of air.
FIRE   FIRE and WATER.   WATER
A blackened shelter rock.
Out on the plateau, a few scattered nomad tents.
Regrowth green. The seasonal rounds.
"Space generates time".
(Vine Deloria Jr. God Is Red. 1973.)
Spring Summer Autumn Winter Spring.
East South West North East. The Four Winds.

The Numbers: Four And Seven. DUST[4] SHADOWS[7].
Lowlands and mountains. Odd and even. Yin and Yang.
7 14 21 28. The number of days to be walked
may be set in advance,
but not always.
Twenty one walks, walking from one to twenty one days.
(Various locations 1971-1989.)
49 seven day walks. (Various locations 1978-2019.)

Unpredictable timing of the first seven steps and the last seven steps.
All my walks are related, from the shortest to the longest,
from the first to the most recent.
Then and there, here and now.
My walks collectively constitute 'a journey'.
I am the storehouse of all my walks.
The satisfaction
from earlier walks
contributing on reflection,
to the appreciation
of present day walks.

Walks
are like clouds,
they come and go.
In the memory
nowhere to be seen.

Walking into the distance
beyond imagination.

When I say that 'the walk is the art',
I simply mean
that 'the walk',
is my contribution to contemporary art.

A WALKING ARTIST
1 2 3 4 5 6 7 1 2 3 4 5 6 7

A FOURTEEN DAY WALKING JOURNEY
FROM SALTWOOD BY THE STRAIGHTS OF DOVER
TO THE STIPERSTONES IN SHROPSHIRE BY THE WELSH BORDER
ENGLAND SPRING 1972

HONOUR THE EARTH
1 2 3 4 5 6 7 1 2 3 4 5 6 7

FOURTEEN DAYS WALKING FOURTEEN NIGHTS CAMPING
WIND RIVER RANGE WYOMING U.S.A. SUMMER 1989

WALKING
SEVEN DAYS WALKING SEVEN NIGHTS CAMPING
THE WALK
CENTRAL HOKKAIDO JAPAN JUNE FULL MOON 1989
1 2 3 4 5 6 7

Above: Walk texts for mailing cards and wall paintings.

Words From Walks
2019 © Hamish Fulton (Born 1946)
Outsider   Survivor   Lefthander

Printed on 100% recycled paper.   **Revised Version V.**

15

Quipu

Elspeth (Billie) Penfold

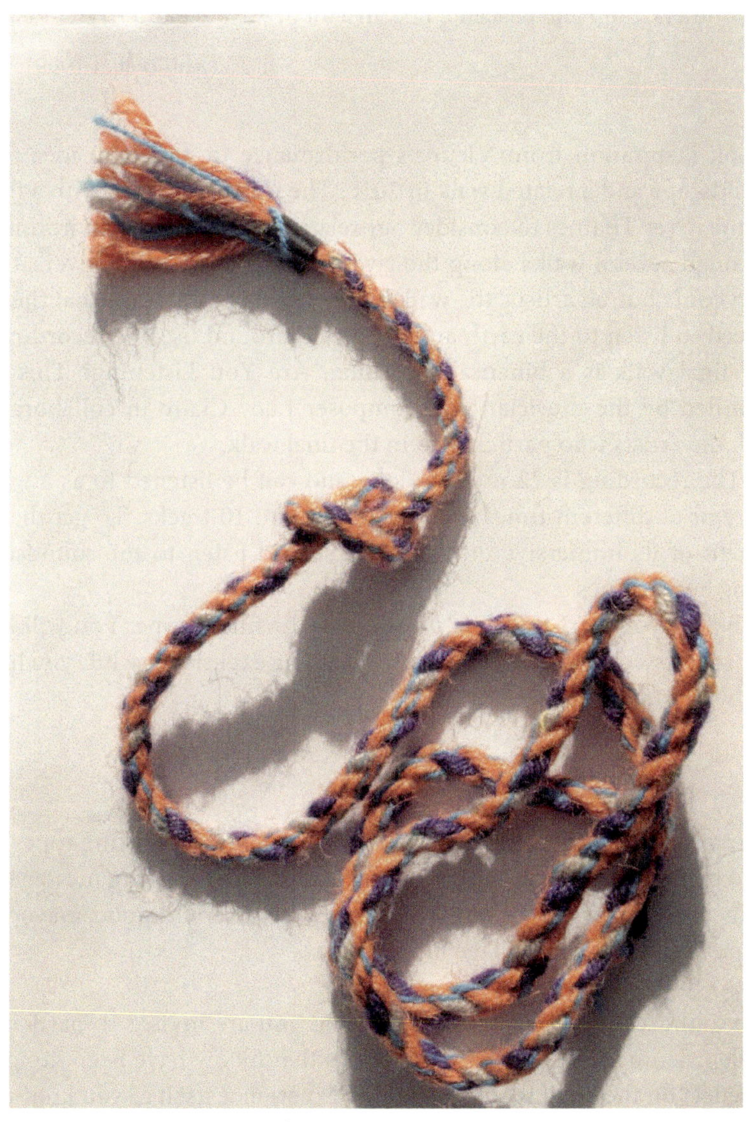

Photo: Anna Bowman

The Chilean artist Cecilia Vicuña conducted a performance by the Mapocho river in Santiago Chile in 1970 titled 'Listen to the River':

> The water wants to be heard. Everything is falling apart because of a lack of connections. Weaving is the connection that is missing, the connection between people and themselves, people and nature. Life is a winding adventure. At times it is rough, at others, calm and peaceful. Life, in a lot of ways is like a river.

> (Rubio et al,1999)

I took inspiration from Vicuña's performance to create an idea for a soundscape and a related walk in 2018. The walk developed with a focus on the River Thames to consider our relationship with the environment. Through several walks along the river embankment and conversations with contributing artists, the walk highlighted an awareness that there is a need to listen to the earth and the world around us. The recording of our final walk is a binaural recording, Are You Listening? This was recorded by the musician and composer Lucy Claire in collaboration with the artists who participated in the final walk.

The recording is 22 minutes long and can be listened to as a whole piece or at different times as it is divided into 10 tracks. To get the full benefit of its immersive qualities you should listen to the soundscape using headphones.

Before you start to listen, please make or find a rope. You will knot this rope as a quipu of your visualised walking experience while you listen to the soundscape:

Are You Listening?

Quipu is a Quechua Andean dialect word for a knot. Knotting ropes was used by the Incas primarily for record keeping and sending messages by runner throughout their empire. There were several quipucamayocs or quipu keepers in each village in the Andes.

The soundscape has poetry readings and you are invited to participate while listening. The associated activities that follow have been designed to reflect on the quality of the listening experience itself as you knot your quipu rope.

Start with a warmup exercise to listen. Our walk started in Battersea Park in the Courtyard of the Pump House. If you know the area you might visualise that specific place, or you can stand or sit in a room hum tunefully, discordantly, softly or loudly, imagining a space of your choice. You might choose to do this in a group. This is your first action to experiment with listening to sound.

As you hum meditatively knot your rope.

Now play the soundscape bit.ly/wnm114 and, holding your rope, start to listen.

Track 1 – Trees can Talk. This is a recording that used string attached to tins to transmit sound. The conversation you hear is a performed conversation between two trees in the park. Use your rope, stretch it tight between your two hands and create a taut line. Visualise a tree of your choice and what you would like to say to it. Listen to the track and, when it has finished, knot your rope.

Track 2 – A Late Blackbird. A poem by Owen Lowery read by Virginia Fitch.

Listen to the poetry reading and knot your rope.

Track 3 – Go with Your Creative Flow. Devised by Julia Riddiough. Listen to Laura Shawyer as she guides you through this short yoga practice. As you listen knot your rope. At the end of this action you might like to continue to track 4.

Track 4 – Visualising Orange. This has an explanation about the colour orange and annatto seeds with a final meditation led by Laura.

Track 5 – Blackbird as you Fly Out. A poem by Owen Lowery, read by Virginia Fitch. Listen to the poetry reading and knot your rope.

Track 6 – Miracle. Susan Sciama. During this track you should visualise yourself walking with the group and knot your rope as you listen to the poem and the sounds of walking.

Track 7 – Volcanic Paradox. A poem by Susan Sciama. Listen to Susan reading her poem and knot your rope. You can use your rope to create drawings making shapes of the sounds you hear. At the same time you will hear the sounds made by the group as they draw, followed by an explanation of Sumak Kawsay by Elspeth (Billie) Penfold.

Track 8 – Blackbird at The Stretton Fox. A poem written by Owen Lowery. Listen to the poem read by Virginia Fitch. This is followed by 'My Heart Leaps up When I Behold' by William Wordsworth, introduced and read by Sue McCLymont. Listen to these poems back to back while you meditatively knot your rope.

Track 9 – London Calling. A song by The Clash 1979. Listen to a protest poem, song and shout out concept by Julia Riddiough enacted by Elspeth (Billie) Penfold and fellow walkers. Feel free to join in and shout out.

Track 10 – Listen to S.O.S. Recorded by Julia Riddiough in Deal. Draw S O S with your rope as you listen.

Now look at your quipu rope, feel the knots and reflect on what you have listened to.

End.

References

Rubio, P., Vicuña, C., Zegher, C. de and Allen, E. (1999). *The Precarious: The Art and Poetry of Cecilia Vicuña / QUIPoem*, World Literature Today, 73(1), p.123

Unlimited. (n.d.). Owen Lowery – Transitions. [online] Available at: bit.ly/wnm192 (Accessed 07 Mar 2020)

The Clash (1979) 'London Calling' (CD). CBS

The S Project

Carly Butler and Gudrun Filipska

'S' is a project about transatlantic communication and virtual journeying between two artists who have never met, Carly Butler (Canada) and Gudrun Filipska (UK). The title of the project references the first transatlantic wireless signal sent from Cornwall to Newfoundland in 1901. The message was simply the Morse code signal for the letter 'S'.

Tracked by pedometers, the artists' steps, taken around their domestic locations are translated to a digital map where avatars walk carefully designed routes between UK and Canada. Butler and Filipska have mapped trajectories to find a variety of halfway points where their avatars will one day 'meet'. Using combinations of celestial, nautical and gnomonic mapping techniques the project embraces a variety of cartographical practices and Google maps alternatives. Exploring the radical potential present in the circular, repetitive domestic walk, set against colonial adventuring narratives and the contemporary art world's jet setting travel practices.

The S Project; Pedometrics and Vicarious Travel

Gudrun grew up excited by the possibilities of rave culture, happenings that necessitated sporadic travel, walks to woods, caves and warehouses; it all seemed very egalitarian at the time. As she became more versed in walking as act of 'research' or as 'art' she began to notice the lack of women, people identifying as female or people of colour.

Carly grew up immersed in the lore of the (white male) wilderness adventurer/voyageur that makes up much of what passes for Canadian history. Her recent research follows the routes of David Thompson, who mapped Canada on foot in the late 18th century and is generally known as the greatest land geographer who ever lived. What is less well known is that his wife, Charlotte, half Cree, accompanied him on many of his travels, bearing and looking after five children as they walked. Thompson

"

surveyed a total 3 million square kilometres of wilderness. Charlotte, though rarely mentioned by Thompson's biographers, has been helpfully described as 'an excellent housekeeper'. (Gordon, 2011)

Together we have interest in raising questions about why the inherent privilege of some practices would be seen as more desirable or significant than those where personal limitations mark the boundaries and parameters of the work. For example, why is walking alone such a common trope of most revered land/walking art practices?

The idea of taking time out to 'jump over the back fence' as wilderness explorer John Muir (2001) famously said, and setting out on a long walk alone seems downright indulgent when you have children (or any adult responsibilities for that matter). Sometimes it seems that the whole history of the 'walking artist' and their attendant, often banal readings of psychogeography are the documented experiences of a large bunch of anorak wearing toddlers, hopping over fences looking for adventure. Rather than trying to join this male fraternity of wanderers, psychogeographers, explorers, and urban strollers, as female artists working with journeying and walking, we have come to the conclusion that *not-walking* may be a far more interesting proposition.

Musing further on our society's fixation on travel and the genuine 'lived' experience, we started wondering if there was a way to transform the experience of our domestic and local spaces and create an avatar who could travel for us. We began counting steps and embarking on a virtual journey towards one another from our respective homes (from Fordham in the UK, to Ucluelet in Canada). Every day we count and log steps as we go about our daily lives.[1]

We were not interested in making an argument in favour of cultures of dual distraction, e.g. watching TV while playing on your phone. Rather we saw this as a proposition to use technology as a conduit to thinking, learning and fantasising about other places. This may have implications for those unable to travel (due to caring responsibilities, economics, agoraphobia or disability).

---

[1] There are a number of examples of travelling without leaving home or travel by proxy in literature, notably De Maistre (2004) and Proust's (1913/2003) flights of allegory and metaphor, as well as Andre Breton's 'Nadja' where the character vicariously (and dubiously) lives through Nadja's vision of the world to subvert his quotidian existence. Contemporary examples include the agoraphobic photographer Jacqui Kenny who uses Street View to travel the world.

It has become very common to rely on proxies when navigating the info-sphere and, in many ways, technology has made *standing in for* something else a matter of ordinary, and often overlooked experience. The word proxy from Latin *procuratio* means 'a caring for' and is a Middle English contraction of 'procuracy', translating as 'legitimate action taken in the place of, or on behalf of, another'. In our technological age, the term 'proxy' is likely to evoke thoughts of websites accepting requests for services: 'proxy server' for example.

Devices enabling the counting of steps have existed for at least 500 years[2] and the contemporary commodification of human ambulation exists within a complicated nexus of marketing, health, and governance. Naturally by extension, devices skewed to a male centred bias, which make female routines and use of space seem odd and non-conforming, perpetuate the historical normative already established, that men's use of space in the public sphere is somehow more valid.

Male-centric design bias of course stretches far beyond pedometric devices, embedding the urgent need for women, those living and identifying as female, and people of colour, to be involved in the design of algorithms in order to counter trends, which, as society becomes more reliant on AI technologies, may deem any non-white male a less valid member of society.[3]

In a culture of 'learning analytics' and the pitfalls of data harvesting, if any new meaning is to be ascribed to step-counting through pedometric devices it may involve re-inscribing step count data to other uses, routes, journeys, diversions and cultures of lending and borrowing.

Walking is often described by artists and writers as a thinking process. Using proxies and avatars (as we have in the S Project) who walk our

---

[2] Thomas Jefferson introduced the pedometer to the American public in the 1930s where it was, unsurprisingly, very popular with long distance trail walkers and branded the *'hike o meter'*. Pedometers have also been a big feature in the 1960s' Japanese walking model and programme, based on 10,000 steps, called Manpo-kei.

[3] Artificial intelligence can also be prejudiced due to its design and according to the bias of those who 'train' it. An algorithm used by Amazon to sort through applicant CVs was recently found to be discounting female CVs altogether, this was not done consciously on the part of the designers but had arisen due to the way it had been taught by men using male colleagues' CVs as examples of successful candidates. Original source, Dastin, J (2018) bit.ly/wnm83 (Accessed 18 Dec 2019).

steps but on different trajectories, opens up a dual walking/thinking space where the everyday A to B routes may parallel the long-distance avatar journeys. Here, walking's meanings may move between the quotidian and the symbolic. We may be on the school run while our avatar crosses the Bering Strait, or food shopping while walking across East Iceland. The presence of the two narratives within the same step count opens up interesting temporal propositions.

The histories of the 'non spaces', which often make up the point-to-point of practical journeys, are now also spaces of presence and non-presence. The 'non spaces' designated by Auge (1992), transitional zones such as supermarkets and airports, are rapidly being by-passed through digital means. The idea of 'Junktime' is an extension of this as discussed in a recent article by Hito Steyerl (2019) who outlines an ethical position for 'non-presence' in a contemporary art world which places increasing demands on artists to 'be there' in person. Her position is developed through Heidegger's Dasein.

Lefebvre writes about a 'constrained time' (2014), which are moments somewhere in between work and leisure, including travel and time for official formalities. Of course, school runs, dog walks and domestic tasks can't really be designated as 'non' or 'Junktime', they can be complicated and relational, more so, we would argue due to their repetitiveness, but the model still holds as they are not licensed spaces of either productivity or pleasure.

Bjorn Nansen (2008) states:

> the pedometer participates in mediating and (re)configuring the meaning and rhythm of this in-between time in a way that reshapes physical activity, as well as experiential and embodied modes of comportment... this questions the possibility of an in-betweenness to time as it blurs distinctions between the rhythms of times and places – there is less of a temporal demarcation between the free time of leisure, the enforced time of work, the dead time of commuting, and the liberating time of play or exercise. (p. 801)

Step counting, in its compulsiveness, represents an erosion of the idea of 'in between time' altogether, the back and forth of the commuter, the steps while shopping or at the park become 'useful' in the sense that they add to a step count in exactly the same way as playing, getting lost, working or setting out to dérive the city. The mundane/domestic walk may reside in the same territory through this egalitarian model as the high-handed psychogeographical game *or* the epic walking adventure.

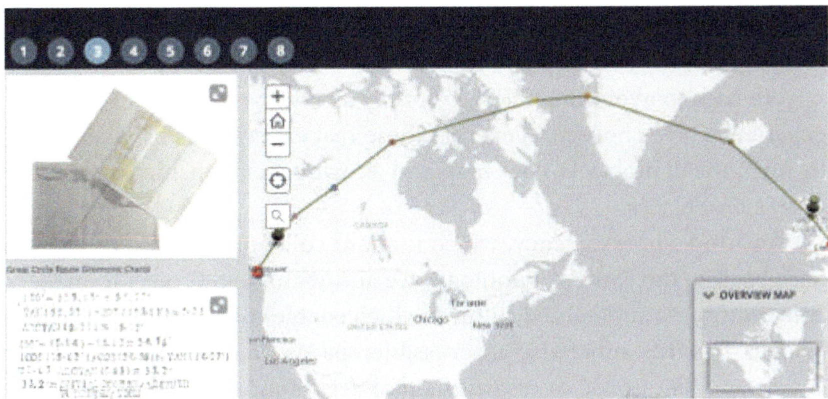

Still from the S Project Interactive Map. Butler/Filipska 2018.
Created with Esri Storymaps.

There may be something in the everyday, embodied, repetitive, self-consciously performative practice of counting and recording steps. Everyday walking, therefore, slips out of the net set for it by the demands of the *dérive* and the masculine walking history that suggests that interesting moments can only happen if the everyday is left behind.

The act of counting steps and the possibilities of lending and borrowing as a re-appropriation of the device's intended use is an intriguing one. Nansen further states "the pedometer extends walking practices and routines from monochronicity and modularization to polychronicity and modulation". (p. 793)

This polychronicity and modulation could swing perhaps towards a neoliberal culture of population monitoring. Yet, through the self-aware act of lending steps to other uses by avatars and others we may abstract linear time into a further splitting and create the possibility of being in more than one place at once, to be going somewhere and going nowhere. To be able to travel without inserting ourselves physically into a distant landscape may offer a small step towards de-stabilising an established and stale male-centric, techno-political walking framework.

The dual material/digital proposition within our project is essential. The materiality of our own territories and the active interest in each other's locations hang around items exchanged through the post and objects and images lent by people in the places our avatars pass through.

The concepts of borrowing and lending are particularly pertinent in relation to land ownership, the problematics of which are all too present in Carly's home, Ucluelet on unceded First Nations territory and the insanity of the real-estate bubble in the UK, which for many makes the idea of 'home' ownership an impossibility.

We seek to avoid the notion of proxy as ersatz replacement for 'real' experience. We choose to generate these real experiences in other ways, through the digital veil of our map and vicarious relationships with other people and places.

Creating a proxy agency, which is about collaboration and caring (to hark back to the word's etymology) we aim with the S Project to make a contribution to augmented cultures which enable collaboration and form bridges towards otherwise inaccessible spaces of experience, towards generating, in our age of environmental degradation, new ways to think about and engage with place.

References

Auge, M. (1992) 'Non Places', Introduction to an *Anthropology of Supermodernity*. Verso

Breton, A. (1994) *Nadja*. Grove Press

De Maistre, X. (2004) *A Journey Around My Room*. Hesperus Press

Gordon, I. (2011) *People of the Fur Trade: From Native Trappers to Chief Factors*. Heritage House Publishing

Kenny, J. (2019) *The Agoraphobic Traveller*. Available at bit.ly/wnm82 (Accessed 15 Dec 2019)

Lefebvre, H. (2014) *Critique of Everyday Life* Vol 1. Verso

Muir, J. & Way-Teal, E. (eds) (2001) *The Wilderness World of John Muir*. Houghton Mifflin Harcourt Publishing

Nansen, B. (2008) 'Step-counting: The Anatomo- and Chrono-politics of Pedometrics' in *Continuum Journal of Media and Cultural Studies*. Vol 2

Proust, M. (1913/2003) *In Search of Lost Time*, trans. D.J. Enright, Modern Library

Steyerl, H. (2018) bit.ly/wnm193 (Accessed 20 Dec 2019)

White Man Walking: Settler Ambulation in Colonised Spaces[1]

Ken Wilson

At a press conference at the 2009 G20 summit in Pittsburgh, Pennsylvania, Canada's then-Prime Minister Stephen Harper said an extraordinary thing. Canada, he stated, has "no history of colonialism" (Wherry, 2009). What made this statement so strange is the simple fact that Canada is a colonial country: it has colonised and continues to colonize the Indigenous peoples who lived on this land before Settlers arrived. This colonisation has been pursued through a variety of government policies and practices, including residential schools (Milloy, 2017), deliberate starvation (Daschuk, 2013), the pass system, which confined First Nations people in western Canada to reserves (Barron, 2009), the so-called 'Sixties Scoop', which took Indigenous children from their families and communities, a process that continues today (McKenzie *et al,* 2016), and rates of incarceration of Indigenous people by the legal system that far exceed those of the Settler population (Johnson, 2019). As a descendant of Settlers, I am unavoidably one of the colonisers. I have benefitted, however unwillingly or unknowingly, from all of these attempts at erasing Indigenous people, languages, and cultures; they have been carried out in order to justify the presence of Settlers, including me, on Indigenous territory, a process Patrick Wolfe describes as "the logic of elimination" (Wolfe, 2006: 388).

Like other Settlers, I am one of the beneficiaries of that logic: I have always lived on land taken from Indigenous peoples. Land is the key to understanding settler colonialism. Wolfe notes that "settler colonizers" –

---

[1] This essay is a revised and expanded version of '*Wood Mountain Walk* and the Possibilities of Decolonization Through Relationships with People and Land in Solo Walking Performance', published in *Canadian Theatre Review* 182 (2020).

that is, people like me and my ancestors – "come to stay", and for that reason, their "invasion is a structure not an event"; moreover, since Settlers "come to stay", settler colonialism "strives for the dissolution of native societies", because as long as those societies exist, the legitimacy of Settler possession of and residence on the land is called into question (Wolfe, 2006: 388). That "dissolution" might mean the erasure of Indigenous cultures and languages through various forms of forced assimilation, or it might mean the physical destruction of Indigenous peoples themselves; Canada has an ongoing history of attempts at both forms of dissolution.

Land is central to decolonisation as well. Eve Tuck and K. Wayne Yang contend that the end goal of decolonisation, for Indigenous peoples, is "the repatriation of land and life" – "all of the land, and not just symbolically" (Tuck & Yang, 2012: 7). For Settlers, such a process of repatriation will, as Eva Mackey writes, "require engagement with the difficult yet necessary task of unsettling attitudes and practices based on settled expectations" (Mackey, 2016: 38). However, the question of what decolonisation will look like, or how it will end, is unclear, as is the place of Settlers within that process: our presence on the land may be illegitimate, but at the same time, we have nowhere else to go. For that reason, it is essential that we find an ethical basis on which we can justify being here, which might exist in the treaties between First Nations and the Crown.

I live in southern Saskatchewan, on Treaty 4 land. In September 1874, Cree, Saulteaux, and Nakoda Chiefs, and representatives of the Crown, negotiated Treaty 4 at Fort Qu'Appelle, then a Hudson's Bay post located in the Qu'Appelle Valley northwest of what is now Regina, the provincial capital, where I live. Two stories are told about Treaty 4, and about all of the nineteenth-century numbered treaties: one by Indigenous Treaty Elders, and the other by Canada's federal government. The federal government claims that the numbered treaties – including Treaty 4 – were real estate transactions in which First Nations Chiefs surrendered their lands in return for assistance with the transition to an agricultural economy and small reserves. That story relies on the so-called "surrender clauses" in the written treaty texts by which First Nations allegedly surrendered their land. As historian Sheldon Krasowski points out, however, there is no evidence that the Crown negotiators ever mentioned those "surrender clauses" during the negotiations that led to Treaty 4, or in the negotiations of any of the other numbered treaties, acts of lying by omission which call the validity of the treaties into question (Krasowski, 2019). Nor have governments over the past 146 years lived up to the commitments made in the written text of Treaty 4 (or any of the other numbered treaties), never mind the oral understandings of the agreement held by Treaty Elders. Given this history, if all we have to rely on to justify the presence of Settlers in western Canada are the written treaty texts, then it's true, as the Anishinaabe writer Leanne Betasamosake Simpson argues, that treaties are simply a vehicle for settler colonialism, and that their intention was simply to clear the land of Indigenous bodies prior to settlement (Simpson, 2017: 99). This view of the treaties ends up concluding that Settlers have absolutely no right to be on this land.

Treaty Elders tell a different story. For them, the treaties were sacred agreements meant to establish mutual and ongoing arrangements of sharing and caring between First Nations peoples and Settlers, including a sharing of the land (Cardinal & Hildebrandt, 2000: 15). The Cree (*nêhiyaw*) writer Harold Johnson goes even further: he states that the treaties were ceremonies in which First Nations adopted Settlers as family. Johnson uses the word *kiciwamânâwak*, "our cousins", to refer to Settlers, and assures us that, because the treaties were negotiated according to Indigenous ceremony and protocol, they are valid, and Settlers "have a treaty right" to share the land (Johnson, 2007: 13-14). Anishinaabe legal scholar John Borrows agrees:

> The laws surrounding Canada's formation in many treaty territories are profound because they are meant to encourage the spiritual, moral and legal capacities of all the people who would come to live here. The sacred nature of the treaties is one reason why many First Nations would not consider abandoning them despite generations of government neglect. It would be a violation of the Creator's law, sacred law, to turn away from their promises to him and others in maintaining peace and order throughout the lands on which they lived. (Borrows, 2010: 26)

If Borrows and Johnson are correct, the treaties could provide an ethical justification for the presence of Settlers on this land, although we would have to honour our treaty obligations and relationships. For instance, only 1% of the land in Saskatchewan is reserved for Indigenous peoples, a situation that can hardly be described as sharing; that would have to change.

Nevertheless, if we believe in this story, it's possible that an acknowledgement of the Indigenous perspectives on the treaties and commitments to share the land fairly and to honour and develop our treaty relationships might constitute decolonisation. At the moment, though, there is little recognition among Settlers of the need to think of the treaties this way. How can the range of acceptable political ideas in Saskatchewan be shifted to include the possibility of decolonisation – even this mild, attenuated version of decolonisation, which is far from the call to return all the land to Indigenous peoples? I don't know. Individual Settlers can't overcome the structures of settler colonialism by themselves; that kind of political action would need to be collective (Lowman & Barker, 2015: 16). But could walking, as an artistic practice help to open possibilities, if only symbolic ones, for decolonisation? Could walking be a way of symbolically revitalising the treaties?

Those are the questions my performative walking practice in Saskatchewan asks. And, I have to admit that to some people that practice is frankly ridiculous, or worse. They ask whether Settlers walking on the land aren't just colonisers inspecting their property. That perception is a real possibility – a serious risk. Nevertheless, walking remains part of my creative response to the ongoing history of colonisation in Saskatchewan, and to the possibilities of decolonisation, along with developing relationships with Elders and others, including by walking together, and beginning to learn the Cree language, *nêhiyawêwin*.

My 2018 walking performance, 'Wood Mountain Walk', was the first of a series of walking performances – some solo and durational, and others convivial and relatively short – that I intend to make in Treaty 4 territory in Saskatchewan over the next couple of years as a way of exploring these questions. 'Wood Mountain Walk' was a nine-day, 250-kilometre walk from Regina to the village of Wood Mountain in southwest Saskatchewan. During that walk, I was the only pedestrian in sight on that walk: no one walks anywhere in southern Saskatchewan, as Matthew Anderson points out, "unless they walk to or from a vehicle, they are in trouble, or they are too young or too poor to have a car or truck" (Anderson, 2018: 153). In fact, 'Wood Mountain Walk' was partly a test to see if walking was even possible in a sparsely populated province where towns and villages are far apart. However, it was more than just a test of practical considerations. It was also an attempt to see if walking alone over long distances could be a way of attending to the land, and if that kind of attending to the land might bring me into a different kind of relationship with it, a relationship which might be a way of beginning a process of decolonisation, or at least of gesturing towards that goal. As writer and walker Craig Mod has suggested, "the grand, pervasive boredom" of a long, solo walk leads, perhaps surprisingly, to "a heightened sense of presence" (Mod, 2019). That heightened sense of presence might be a prerequisite for developing a relationship with the land that is not extractive, one that recognises the land's agency and its life. In an interview with Naomi Klein, Simpson suggests that while an extractive approach to the land, which is part of colonialism and conquest, "removes all of the relationships that give whatever is being extracted meaning", non-extractive approaches to the world, which involve responsibility, relationship, and "deep reciprocity", can be intimate and loving (Klein, 2013). Developing a non-extractive relationship with the land could be an essential first step towards decolonisation, and walking might offer a way to develop that kind of relationship – the kind of walking, at least, that Springgay and Truman describe as "walking-with", a walking that "is explicit about political positions and situated knowledges, which reveal our entanglements with settler colonisation and neoliberalism" (Springgay & Truman, 2018: 11).

Such walking would acknowledge the land's sacred character, bringing a walker closer to an Indigenous perception of the land as sacred and alive. I often think of something the late Métis artist Bob Boyer told writer and naturalist Trevor Herriot during a panel discussion on the spiritual importance of the Qu'Appelle Valley in southern Saskatchewan, the subject of Herriot's first book, *River in a Dry Land: A Prairie Passage*. Boyer said that he didn't understand what made that particular valley so important to Herriot. "It's no more important than any other place", he stated. "It's all sacred ground. All of it" (Herriot, 2014: 16). Boyer's words reflect an interconnected epistemology and ontology of relationality and an apprehension of the sacred that are part of an Indigenous understanding of the world (Lowman & Barker, 2015: 49-50). They also echo something I learned from a Cree (*nêhiyaw*) Elder this past summer. We were walking together down a gravel grid road. I told her that walking alone sometimes leaves me feeling separated from community. Oh, she said, even when you're walking alone, you're still part of a community, because walking involves developing relationships with everything around us: plants, animals, the land, the sky. That's the meaning of the *nêhiyawêwin* expression – it's a prayer, really – *kahkiyaw niwâhkômâkinak*, "all my relations". Our relationships aren't only with other humans; they are with the more-than-human as well, and those relationships are sacred. This belief reflects one of the foundational principles of *nêhiyaw* law: *wâhkôtowin,* or relationship, which applies equally both to relationships between people and to relationships between people and the land (McAdam, 2015: 61). According to Borrows, *wâhkôtowin* "is viewed as the overarching law governing all relations", and it "is said to flow from the Creator who placed all life on earth" (Borrows, 2010: 84). By developing a relationship with the land, one is also recognising the jurisdiction of *nêhiyaw* law.

Thinking of the land as sacred is, in some ways, difficult for me; my rejection of my early Baptist training has left me resistant to practices that smack of religiosity, and my atheism sits awkwardly alongside discourses that speak of the Creator as a source of laws governing human conduct or notions of the land as something sacred. Nevertheless, when I walk on a remnant of the grassland that once covered the southern third of Saskatchewan – and it's important to remember that less than 14% of that grassland still remains; the rest has been destroyed to make way for fields of wheat and canola (Sawatsky, 2018) – I do think that I apprehend something of its sacredness. That might be an aesthetic reaction to the beauty of the grasses and wildflowers and the sublimity of the sky's apparent endlessness, but perhaps it's something more. Whatever the roots of this response might be, I've learned the names of the grasses and forbs that constitute the flora of that ecosystem, and I know when they blossom and where they grow; in that way, I think I am at least beginning to develop relationships with them. But when I walk all day past cultivated fields, I find that idea of relationship much harder to practice. Perhaps that's because I'm not a farmer and have no connection to farming; but perhaps it's because those vast industrial farms, the foundation of the province's economy, represent an extractive economic model in which the land is an object available for limitless exploitation. And yet, developing a relationship with those fields of wheat and barley and canola shouldn't be impossible: walking all day in a space means spending hours in it, experiencing in an embodied way its topography, sounds, smells, and weather, and watching the constantly changing sky. Surely that kind of experience presents an opportunity to relate to the land. Besides, as Simpson tells Klein, thinking of oneself as being in an intimate relationship with the land doesn't mean abandoning it because it's been damaged; if anything, one needs to intensify that relationship of love for the land, and to try to see its beauty despite the harms inflicted on it (Klein, 2013).

One of the things I learned at the Walking's New Movements conference in November 2019 was that there are non-Indigenous theoretical discourses – posthumanism and object-oriented ontology – that, while they begin in very different places than Boyer, Simpson, or the Elder I was walking with on that sunny summer afternoon, might be considered to arrive at a similar destination. In *Down to Earth: Politics in the New Climatic Regime,* for instance, Bruno Latour (whose work I was introduced to by Ian Biggs's paper at Walking's New Movements, "Walking Away? From Deep Mapping to Mutual Accompaniment") argues that territory has agency and actually possesses its apparent possessor (Latour, 2018: 40-41). That's not quite the same as arguing that the land is sacred and that we need to develop non-extractive relationships with it, but it's getting close. According to Latour, a materialist epistemology does not "reduce the world to objects", but rather extends "the list of movements that must be taken into account", and terrestrials – a term that encompasses more than just human beings – "have the very delicate problem of discovering how many *other beings* they need in order to subsist" (Latour, 2018, p. 87). "To track the terrestrials" – and, remember, these aren't just humans – "is to add conflicts of interpretation regarding what a given actor is, wants, desires, or can do, to conflicts about what other actors are, want, desire, or can do – and this applies to workers as well as to birds in the sky, to Wall Street executives as well as to bacteria in the soil, to forests as well as to animals" (Latour, 2018: 87). It's not a question of living in harmony with these other creatures, Latour insists; it's a question of "learning to be dependent on them", and "all our powers of investigation are needed if we are to begin to find our place among these other actors" (Latour, 2018: 87).

Being dependent on something implies a relationship with it, and by granting agency to all beings defining the term "actor" so broadly, Latour is getting close to the insights of Indigenous thinkers – but, as the Métis anthropologist Zoe Todd argues, perhaps not close enough, and without recognising the fact that those Indigenous thinkers were there first. The European academy (of which Latour is an example) continues to be reticent about addressing both "its own racist and colonial roots and debt to Indigenous thinkers in a meaningful and structural way" (Todd, 2016: 10). So, while I am interested in learning more about posthumanism and object-oriented ontology, I want to be cautious about ignoring Indigenous thinking that points in similar directions. At the same time, as a Settler I can't simply adopt Indigenous theories or methodologies, since they are part of a holistic approach that is inseparable from "Indigenous peoples' worldviews, lens, location and experiences" (Absolon, 2011: 161). It is a delicate balancing act: learning from Indigenous theories and methodologies without appropriating them, and working with posthumanist theories and object-oriented ontologies without ignoring the importance of Indigenous concepts such as *wâhkôtowin*.

Complicating any attempt at developing a relationship with the land of southern Saskatchewan during 'Wood Mountain Walk' are the "power-geometries of space" (Massey, 2005: 130) that are present everywhere in that territory, above all in the colonial grid of settlement imposed on the land, a grid that defines many of the roads on which I was walking. Massey contends that exposing those power-geometries of space is possible: one has to listen for the voices that resist them. Such resistance is hard to hear in Saskatchewan. Even the roadside weeds, most of which have been introduced from Europe and Asia, testify to the colonisation that has reshaped the land. However, I could reframe my response to those weeds: perhaps their exuberant growth suggests a flourishing of life beyond the herbicides and genetically modified crops of industrial agriculture. Perhaps there are other voices of resistance as well. The screams of the Swainson's hawks that followed me as I walked to Wood Mountain may have been voices of resistance, and perhaps even conversation, since those hawks were likely warning me to stay away from their nests. Maybe even the crunching of my own footsteps was a voice of resistance, since walking is a deliberate attempt to move through the land differently, in relationship with it, as Springgay and Truman's term "walking-with" suggests, rather than over it or through it. Perhaps such walking could even be a way of responding to bell hooks's call to enter the space of marginality, an "inclusive space where we recover ourselves, where we move in solidarity to erase the category colonized/colonizer" (hooks, 1990: 152). I am aware of the audacity, the temerity, of a White, male, cisgendered Settler placing himself within hooks's space of marginality, but at the same time, walking in rural Saskatchewan is, as Anderson suggests, a way of deliberately marginalising oneself, both literally (one walks on the margins of the road) and figuratively. In any case, the decolonising thrust of hooks's words, the suggestion that I could somehow renounce my position as a coloniser, draws me to them. I hope such a renunciation is possible.

Was my attempt at addressing decolonisation by developing a relationship with the land during 'Wood Mountain Walk' successful? Not entirely: the practical challenges of the walk – the heat, the traffic, the difficulty of finding potable water, and the distances I was walking every day – tended to overwhelm my intention to come into a relationship with the land and to experience it as sacred. However, there's no question that I learned more about the territory I walked through than if I had driven to Wood Mountain, a journey of three hours rather than nine days. Walking is a place to start, a way to begin to understand the land and enter into a relationship with it, and it is certainly a more intimate way of travelling than motorised options. While a Settler walking on the land in Saskatchewan could be easily misunderstood as making a claim to ownership, my intention, and my hope, is that walking will provide opportunities for developing a different kind of relationship with the land, one that acknowledges Treaty 4 in an embodied way, and that this new relationship might even point towards the possibility of a decolonised future.

References

Absolon (Minogiizhigokwe), K.E. (2011) *Kaandossiwin: How We Come to Know,* Fernwood

Anderson, M.R. (2018) 'Pilgrimage and the Challenging of a Canadian Foundational Myth', in McIntosh, I.S., Quinn, E.M., and Keely, V. (eds.) *Pilgrimage in Practice: Narration, Reclamation and Healing.* CABI, pp. 148-63

Barron, F.L. (2009). 'The Indian Pass System in the Canadian West, 1882-1935', in Marchildon, G.P. (ed.) *Immigration and Settlement, 1870-1939.* Canadian Plains Research Center Press

Borrows, J. (2010) *Canada's Indigenous Constitution.* Univ. of Toronto Press

Cardinal, H., & Hildebrandt, W. (2000) *Treaty Elders of Saskatchewan: Our Dream Is That Our Peoples Will One Day Be Clearly Recognized As Nations.* Univ. of Calgary Press

Daschuk, J. (2013) *Clearing the Plains: Disease, Politics of Starvation, and the Loss of Indigenous Life.* Univ. of Regina Press

Herriot, T. (2014) *The Road Is How: A Prairie Pilgrimage Through Nature, Desire, and Soul.* HarperCollins

Hooks, B. (1990) "Choosing the Margin as a Space of Radical Openness", in *Yearning: Race, Gender, and Cultural Politics.* Between the Lines

Johnson, H.R. (2007) *Two Families: Treaties and Government.* Purich

_______ (2019) *Peace and Good Order: The Case for Indigenous Justice* in Canada. McClelland and Stewart

Klein, N. (2013) "Dancing the World into Being: A Conversation with Idle No More's Leanne Simpson". Yes Magazine. 5 March 2013. Available at: bit.ly/wnm78 (Accessed: 22 June 2019)

Krasowski, S. (2019) *No Surrender: The Land Remains Indigenous,* Univ. of Regina Press

Latour, B. (2018) *Down to Earth: Politics in the New Climatic Regime.* Trans. C. Porter. Polity Press

Lowman, E.B. & Barker, A.J. (2015) *Settler: Identity and Colonialism in 21st Century Canada.* Fernwood

Mackey, E. (2016) *Unsettled Expectations: Uncertainty, Land and Settler Colonization,* Fernwood

Massey, D. (2005) *For Space.* Sage

McAdam (Sayseewahum), S. (2015) *Nationhood Interrupted: Revitalizing* nêhiyaw *Legal Systems,* Purich

McKenzie, H.A., Varcoe, C., Browne, A.J. & Day, L. (2016) 'Disrupting the Continuities Among Residential Schools, the Sixties Scoop, and Child Welfare: An Analysis of Colonial and Neocolonial Discourses'. *The International Indigenous Policy Journal* 7 (3), article 4. doi:10.18584/iiph.2016.7.2.4.

Milloy, J. (2017). *A National Crime: The Canadian Government and the Residential School System, 1879 to 1986.* 2nd. edn. Univ. of Manitoba Press

Mod, C. (2019). 'The Glorious, Almost-Disconnected Boredom of My Walk in Japan'. *Wired.* 29 May 2019. Available at: bit.ly/wnm77 (Accessed: 5 Sep 2019)

Sawatsky, K.D. (2018). "The State of Native Prairie in Saskatchewan". *PrairieCommons.ca.* 1 October 2018. Available at: bit.ly/wnm76 (Accessed: 24 May 2019)

Simpson, L.B. (2017) *As We Have Always Done: Indigenous Freedom Through Radical Resistance.* Univ. of Minnesota Press

Springgay, S., and Truman, S.E. (2018) *Walking Methodologies in a More-Than-Human World: WalkingLab*, Routledge

Todd, Z. (2016) 'An Indigenous Feminist's Take on The Ontological Turn: "Ontology" Is Just Another Word For Colonialism'. *Journal of Historical Sociology* 29 (1), pp. 4-22. doi: 10.1111/johs.12124.

Tuck, E., and Yang, K.W. (2012). "Decolonization Is Not A Metaphor". *Decolonization: Indigeneity, Education & Society* 1 (1), pp. 1-40. https://jps.library.utoronto.ca/index.php/des/article/view/18630/15554.

Wherry, A. (2009). "What he was talking about when he talked about colonialism". Maclean's. Available at: bit.ly/wnm72 (Accessed: 15 Jan 2020)

Wolfe, P. (2006). 'Settler Colonialism and the Elimination of the Native'. *Journal of Genocide Research* 8 (4), pp. 387-409. doi:10.1080/14623520601056240

Walking-with whiteness: story carriers, affect aliens and reluctant heritage

Richard S. White/Walknow

Introduction: speaking with my body

As my sixtieth birthday came and went it occurred to me that I have been walking a long time. Apart from the odd twisted ankle, blistered heel and painful toe, my legs have carried me a long way; yet it is only recently that I have thought about the years of mobility that they have provided me with. I have no conscious memory of a pre-walking mobility nor of the trials and errors of achieving pedestrian competence, my walking ability has become quite literally embodied and normalised. Engaging critically with walking practices as an able-bodied white English man, I recognise that for me race, gender and ability are as embodied and normalised as walking, and inscribed in it. Garnette Cadogan, in his seminal essay, *Walking While Black* (2016), describes walking in New York, marked and othered by the prejudice invoked by the colour of his skin. In Bath, and elsewhere in the UK, a white man walking passes unnoticed, his gender and skin colour as normalised as his ability to walk. Questioning the normalisation of injustice through the immanence and instability of walking is the wobbly corporeal foundation of my creative practice.

This paper develops from a presentation reflecting on Cadogan's essay I gave at 'Walking's New Movements' in 2019. I refer briefly to papers and provocations I was fortunate to be able to experience there and consider resonances with my own practice. I outline an iteration of a *walking-with* approach through a short case study of a project I hosted in Bath, 'Sweet Waters', 'sense-ing' legacies of slave-ownership. I consider how a walking arts engagement with heritage might attend to whiteness and the normalisation of privilege.

In developing a critical walking practice, I have been exploring catalysing moments of affect and triggers of involuntary thought. Jill Bennett cites Deleuze's comment that profound truth emerges from involuntary thought arguing that, "the affective encounter becomes the means by which thought proceeds and ultimately moves towards deeper truth" (2006: 33). At the conference I was drawn to those practitioners working in a space that combined criticality with a focus on the body, memory and affect. I was fascinated with the way Jody Oberfelder's exercise in physical storytelling became a powerful encounter. Easing me into the edgelands of my comfort zone, Oberfelder's workshop drew on our collective somatic creativity. The activity built trust and attunement to other presences, invoking our relational or peripheral intelligence (Little, 2013). I was inspired, again, by Vicky Hunter's account of site-based body practice, 'Moving with Trees'. I found useful resonances concerning movement as a questioning and disturbance that I am translating to walking.

I am interested in strategies facilitating the rapid development of attention and relational intelligence amongst a group of walkers. Both Oberfelder's workshop and Claire Hind and Gary Winters' performance, 'Dream Yards', enabled me to experience the participatory potential of stimulating affective responses and holding the space for them. Whilst other papers and presentations offered powerful insights and challenges, the approach of my fellow panel presenter, Ken Wilson continues to resonate. I admired his slow and gentle solo walking approach developing a non-extractive relationship with space and place, humans and non-humans; a white settler walking respectfully on stolen land, finding expression to the uneasy unbelonging I too am working with.

Sweet Waters

'Sweet Waters', was a series of participatory performative walks in the City of Bath (UK) and along the River Avon. The cycle of walks involved durational and location-specific interventions generating affective responses, curated to disrupt and question official heritage accounts. Whereas in Bristol the slave trade and the ownership of captured and enslaved Africans has become part of a contested sense of place, in Bath, although manifested in the Georgian architecture, these past injustices are seen as unconnected and happening elsewhere. In many ways little has changed since novelist Jane Austen described a conversation on the matter being closed down in a 'dead silence'.

Today this forms part of what I describe as a 'reluctant' heritage, a heritage that is painful or shameful, in which something of the past has become obscured or hidden in the present. I am exploring a walking, questioning, doing, process attending to that reluctance and in this context specifically addressing issues of racialisation and whiteness. 'Sweet Waters' took place as the Windrush scandal unfolded and in the week of the Grenfell Tower fire; one walk began at Bath Abbey following the minute's silence for those who had died in that fire.

Walking precariously

> When we first learn to walk, the world around us threatens to crash into us. Every step is risky. We train ourselves to walk without crashing by being attentive to our movements, and extra-attentive to the world around us. As adults we walk without thinking, really. But as a black adult I am often returned to that moment in childhood when I'm just learning to walk. I am once again on high alert, vigilant.

> (Cadogan, 2016)

Cadogan contrasts the experience of walking in his home neighbourhood in Jamaica with walking in New Orleans and New York City. From a place where his main source of fear and anxiety came from a violent stepfather, to walking in places where, as a black man, the streets became a minefield for him. "Despite my best efforts", he says, "the streets never felt completely safe. Even a simple salutation was suspect".

I keep returning to this essay, for me it is a reality check on the unspoken privilege bound up in my experience of walking as a white man. In Cadogan's reminder of the experience of vulnerability and risk in learning to walk, he implicitly references Brian Massumi's invocation of the classic idea of walking as a controlled act of falling (2017). Cadogan's essay raises fundamental questions on embodiment, particularly with regard to the sectional perspectives through which we make sense of and construct worlds, notably of race and gender. In Massumi's account, moving forward involves a harnessing of constraints; for Cadogan, as a black man walking, moving in a place where he is racialised as black, an uncalled-for alertness is generated by a sense of vulnerability. He references the experience of walking to engage with the experience of racism; developing Massumi's perspective, for Cadogan walking becomes an act of resistance.

Walking While Black directs me to consider the ways in which white supremacism is learned, manifested and policed. Donna Haraway's key question, "With whose blood were my eyes crafted?" (1988: 585) takes this beyond passive embodiment towards considering gaze and power, and the agency of matter. The question was a powerful provocation with which to open a walk, orienting walkers towards contested ways of seeing as well as the visceral and corporeal material awareness I am seeking to stimulate. Used as part of the first intervention in the 'Sweet Waters' walks, the question generated conversations on learned ways of seeing laying useful reference points for the first day of walking.

Revealing affective attachments

Walkers were invited to become agents in a slow reveal of the seductive normalisation of white supremacy as a legacy of slavery and slave-ownership. We walked to an iconic tower high above Bath funded and used by slave-owner William Beckford. In today's official version, the white William Beckford, whose family name was imposed on generations of captured and enslaved Africans, racialised as black, is described as a reclusive patron of the arts, a wealthy eccentric. The source of the vast fortune he inherited and the funds he lived on are glossed over; they were derived from the labour of those captured and enslaved people on his Jamaican sugar plantations. Alongside many Bath residents he received a share of the £20million compensation pay out when slavery was abolished in the British Empire in the 1830s. None of this compensation was passed on to those released from the bonds of slavery.

'Sweet Waters' passed the former residencies of slave-owners and the remains of mills where goods were made for the 'Africa Trade', we walked along the river to Bristol where those goods were loaded on the slave trading ships. Curated provocations along the way included readings from archives and contemporary statements by slave-owners. Walkers were invited to record and share their thoughts and observations in notebooks and as social media. Each walk began with introductions and an attunement exercise alerting the senses, engaging attention and focusing thoughts; each walk ended with a group sharing. In this walking and questioning approach, the developing somatic sensibility and its ethical context, an iteration of *walking-with* emerges.

Introducing walking-with

Inspired by the poetry and actions of the Zapatista liberation movement in Mexico, my approach resonates with the *'Preguntando caminamos'* process, walking and asking questions or *walking-with* questioning the words and world of the powerful (Sundberg, 2013; de la Cadena & Blaser,

2018; Springgay & Truman, 2018). The Zapatista movement was formed in alliances and solidarity actions of the indigenous peoples of the region and grounded in their knowings. Since the 1990s the movement has engaged with progressive international anti-capitalist networks worldwide, their understandings, approaches and techniques have been taken up by critical scholars and artists.

> Walking-with is accountable. Walking-with is a form of solidarity, unlearning, and critical engagement with situated knowledges. (Springgay & Truman, 2018: 11)

Walking-with is an ethical practice building solidarity, respecting dignity, valuing the contributions of all, in this way of knowing walking becomes an immanent practice, a speculative act of somatic questioning, attending critically to shared and embodied experience.

My practice involves a somatic and material questioning, a *walking-with* "unlearning and unsettling what has gone before" (Springgay & Truman 2018: 15). On this path our questioning is an embodied convivial activity, there are somatic skills and sensibilities we can alert, engage, learn and develop. Little (2017) refers to movement as a critical interference in space, a questioning through reaching and touching. *Walking-with* implies such an interference in time and space developing key capacities of attention and alertness. Reflecting on Hunter's paper and Oberfelder's workshop, I recognise this relational intelligence emerging through movement with humans and non-humans. Through questioning and embodied criticality *walking-with* develops, articulates and enacts what Barad describes as 'response-ability': "listening for the response of the other and an obligation to be responsive to the other" (2012: 69).

Alert to concerns about cultural appropriation, I acknowledge myself as a white European with all the embodied baggage and privilege that brings. I am walking a path towards social justice and in doing so I recognise the need to return to past injustices as a way of beginning social repair; in that context, working towards response-ability I offer this creative practice as an iteration of *walking-with*.

Sunrise and high tide

A dawn provocation, a modern white man's voice reading words that shock opened the last day of walking and sensing. On midsummer's day 2017, having walked the journey sequentially down the River Avon, we met at sunrise on Avonmouth bridge for the long walk back to Bath. As we imagined the slave ships leaving on the high tide, I read the instructions to one such ship's captain on the captured people he was to buy, who to deliver them to and what to sell them for. Curated content offered ways of seeing the wealth of the slave-owners in the present, as the walks continued and walkers attuned and became alert we started to attend to the uncannny stuff that pokes through, noticing embodied memories surfacing. Learning from each other, listening to our bodies, out of messy materiality and through involuntary thought cognitive knowledge formed. A walker, having had time to gather his thoughts shared this comment,

> It completely transformed the way that I saw and understood the city that I grew up in and now live in as an adult. It is fascinating to see how we can make a huge aspect of history disappear because it is uncomfortable. It also led me to have insights about current day exploitation in completely different ways by people who have large amounts of money around the world.

> (Respondent 9: 'Sweet Waters' Walker survey response 2017)

Walking-with in Bath

Bath is a city still holding the story of the origins of its wealth in 'dead silence'. In this enchanted city, manifesting the wealth generated by captured and enslaved people, many walk blind and deaf. In Bath I would add a particular kind of *building* blindness to Hunter's description of plant and tree blindness; *walking-with* developed a visual and haptic alertness to these buildings inscribed with the story of slave-ownership and resonances of racialisation. The unstated assumption in the book jackets, films and television shows, is that Jane Austen's Bath was white. In the city's marketing and world heritage orientations the Romans who popularised the hot springs nearly 2000 years ago are racialised as white. Whiteness is not only normalised in this City, it is the racialised form of aspirational success, the authorised heritage of Bath has become an enchantment concealing racialised privilege and past injustices.

'Sweet Waters' involved walking Bath's iconic crescents and promenades, stopping and delivering a gentleman's visiting card at residencies of former slave-owners. I gave short performances listing the plantations, numbers of enslaved people owned and compensation paid out. After one such provocation, on the Royal Crescent, a fellow walker shared that he had grown up in Bath and that he had never been taught anything about slave-ownership or the origins of the wealth inscribed in the city. He went on to disclose that as a young man, racialised as black, he had been stopped, searched and humiliated by white policemen just where we were standing. We learned something in that moment of (dis)enchantment as the past crashed so poignantly into the present, setting off conversations on institutional racism in school and police. As Cadogan (2016) notes, "For a black man, to assert your dignity before the police was to risk assault". The layered tissue of time and experience now intra-act each time a 'Sweet Waters' walk revisits the Royal Crescent and I share the story. I suggest that one of the social justice contributions of this process is that each walker subsequently holds that story and has agency in sharing it thereby drawing out the thread of racism as legacy of slave-ownership.

Walking (enchantment and dissonance)

Fellow walkers on the 'Sweet Waters' walks were engaged though walking networks, artists networking and a local natural history festival, most were white, many were local; although not all were middle aged the demographic was perhaps typical for a walking festival. This was my intended audience as it is this demographic who in some way have internalised the values of, and often embody, white privilege. These were walkers who at the outset, without recognizing the irony of such a suggestion, might suggest I offer 'Sweet Waters' as part of Black History Month .

At the core of my practice is an interest in registers of walking and an exploration of tactics that provoke involuntary thought. I curate experiences of temporal and spatial dissonance into a walk seeking to generate empathic responses. I use somatic attunements and such factors of duration, distance and pace to generate alertness and sensitivity. On a previous walking project, 'Honouring Esther', I had begun to work with dissonance and juxtaposition using curated interventions and provocations to catalyse involuntary thought and out of that empathy. Drawing on the work of artist Paula Levine, (Levine, 2014) I observed that empathic dialogues emerge in the process of resolving dissonance and involuntary thought. The core walking strategy in 'Sweet Waters' drew on that experience, the dissonant juxtaposition of registers of walking. Walking for pleasure in a beautiful city and alongside a river, whilst being reminded of a register of walking as coerced, in the case of

'Sweet Waters', the forced migration of captured and enslaved African people across the Atlantic ocean. In this way the experience of 'Sweet Waters' was based on a juxtaposition of registers of walking as a provocation to think and feel differently.

Sara Ahmed's view (2010) that historical injustice does not fade over time is embedded in this work; the injustice of slave-ownership manifests today as normalised white privilege. Injustice lives on if we don't address it, in order to begin the repair work and bring about change we must make the return. The juxtaposition of an enforced migration with a walk for pleasure in a city and countryside inscribed with the wealth of slave-ownership was an act of making the return. At the very least injustice was acknowledged by the walkers, some have taken it further, sharing the story and their responses. Ahmed argues that 'bad feelings' should not be forgotten as it "allows historical forms of injustice to disappear" (2010: 50). In this view, to forget is an act of complicity to the persistence of injustice. Taking this further to the questions and provocations of the walking process, participation has further empowered walkers to continue to question. Ahmed refers to an affect alien as someone who might, for example, at a family gathering challenge the normalisation of patriarchy. Here, I suggest the possibility of walkers becoming *heritage* affect aliens empowered to ask difficult questions of a reluctant heritage, to interrogate the silence.

White Fragility

As an affect alien intervention, the 'Sweet Waters' walks had a powerful impact on the walkers, it also stirred something through its performativity. There were several occasions when white people we encountered told us it was time to 'get over it', to 'forgive and forget' or to share a view on the benefits of empire and in one case to defend slavery. At times it felt as if we had hit on the raw nerve of reluctance, especially with regard to slavery and the issue of white superiority. I experience the continuing 'dead silence' of Bath and these encounters as manifestations of white discomfort (Di Angelo 2011:54). *Walking-with* in this context developed an embodied experience of confidence and solidarity towards countering white fragility, eroding reluctance to engage critically with this particular heritage narrative.

Levine argues that, 'bringing hidden stories and stories of place to the surface… transform[s] participants into story bearers' (Levine, 2014: 144). Participants became active story tellers, expressing a desire to stand up and be heard, breaking the 'dead silence' of Bath. A supportive space for questioning heritage and responding to the instances of white fragility described above was established. In this way, through new insights and ways of seeing, walkers took ownership of the story, generating affective attachments to a new co-created heritage narrative. The silence was broken, however temporarily, and the story of the walk and the spirit of questioning is shared, networked again and again.

Conclusion

Haraway reminds us of the embodied nature of all vision, drawing our attention to the gaze that, "makes the unmarked category claim the power to see and not be seen, to represent while escaping representation". (Haraway, 1988: 581) Walking and questioning the 'Sweet Waters' participants reflected on this observation, I shared the view that as Richard White I am always walking while white. Unlike Cadogan, however, walking in New York, marked and othered by the prejudice invoked by the colour of his skin, when I walk both my gender and skin colour endows privilege and leaves me unmarked. *Walking-with* in Bath we reflected on our response-ability, a conversation was heard.

'Sweet Waters' was an opening towards a somatic creative activism manifesting new ways of attending to whiteness and revealing privilege. In this regard *walking-with* may offer a non-confrontational embodied approach to addressing other 'wicked' problems and complex social justice issues. At a time of deep dislocation and as an ugly romance with empire and white supremacy emerges, I believe that collective and somatic acts of making the return to past injustice are vital precursors to the social repair needed for a just and sustainable future.

References

Ahmed, S. (2010) 'Happy Objects', in Gregg, M. and Seigworth, G., J. (eds.) *The Affect Theory Reader*, Duke Univ. Press, pp. 29-51

Austen, J. (2010) *Mansfield Park* ebook. Project Gutenberg. Available at: bit.ly/wnm194 (Accessed 04 Apr 2019)

Bennett, Jill (2006) 'The aesthetics of sense-memory: theorising trauma through the visual arts', in Radstone, S. and Hodgkin. Katharine (eds.) *Memory Cultures: Memory, Subjectivity and Recognition*, Transaction Publishers, pp. 27-39

Cadogan, G. (2016) *Walking While Black.* Available at: bit.ly/wnm86 (Accessed: 20 Apr 2018)

de la Cadena, M. and Blaser, M. (eds) (2018) *A World of Many Worlds*, Duke Univ. Press

DiAngelo, R. (2011) 'White Fragility', *International Journal of Critical Pedagogy*, 3(3), pp. 54-70

Dolphijn, R. and van der Tuin, I. (2012) *New Materialism: Interviews and Cartographies. Ch3 Interview with Karen Barad.* Open Humanities Press

Haraway, D. (1988) 'Situated Knowledges: The Science Question in Feminism and the Privilege of Partial Perspective', *Feminist Studies*, 14(3), pp. 575-599

Little, N. (2013) *Another Politics of Attention: Shifting Self-Sense, Shifting Time* (unpublished, text supplied by author)

Little, N. and Dumit, J. (2017) *Articulating Presence: Attention is Tactile* (unpublished)

Massumi, B. *Navigating Moments.* Available at: bit.ly/wnm84 (Accessed: 10 Feb 2017)

Springgay, S. & Truman, S. E. (2018) *Walking Methodologies in a More-Than-Human World: Walking Lab.* Routledge

Sundberg, J. (2013) 'Decolonizing Posthumanist Geographies', *Cultural Geographies*, 21(1), pp. 33-47

White, R. & Brunstein, L. (2017) *Forced Walks: Honouring Esther.* Available at: bit.ly/wnm88 (Accessed: 17 Oct 2018)

The Meaning and Importance of Refusals: is walking as accessible as we think?

Sarah Harper

'La Grande Traversée' (The Great Crossing) was a participatory art walk, which I was commissioned to create in 2018, in collaboration with community groups from seven towns in the Nord-Pas-de-Calais in northern France, where the vestiges of the mining industry have recently been recognised as a Unesco World Heritage Site. This large-scale neighbourhood project was to re-kindle community and celebrate Unesco's recognition by rediscovering the landscape and neighbouring towns through the collective act of walking. I sought to engage two publics: one of pre-existing community groups invited to participate not only in the walk, but also in its conception, route, and story, and another, more 'general' public invited to join the final walk by local council and community networks.

As a participatory project, this 'Great Crossing' was deemed hugely successful: I met regularly with ten community groups, co-creating performative interventions involving over 100 people, while another 450 participants took part in the walk itself. The walkers revelled in their achievement at completing the hike; they wondered at the natural and architectural treasures they discovered along the way; they were delighted by the interventions; it was a joyful event. Rather than make a celebratory case study however, I propose here to scrutinise the limitations of the practice, looking at where it failed to engage, why that matters, and what could be learned from it. I will ask whether walking as a participatory art practice can be racially exclusive, and what value we could give to its refusal.

The current French cultural and socio-political climate encourages, invokes, and puts a high value on participation, and as artists, we can tend to be complicit with that demand, without necessarily addressing whose interests that participation might serve. I would argue not only the inevitability of refusal in certain contexts but also its utility for those who refuse.

I'd like to focus on the value of *non*-participation, looking at some of those who did *not* walk and why, and in doing so re-assess the comparative cultural value of everyday activities, by which I mean what people are already doing before an artist turns up to invite them to go for a long walk, collectively, in the name of social cohesion. Exploring this act of walking together, walking through, and *walking past,* through the lens of refusal, I will focus on those for whom walking was problematic: physically, psychologically, culturally or for religious reasons, as well as those too angry with the economic desert they were born into to participate in celebrating a major aspect of their heritage with any kind of collective action.

Walking is something I take for granted and is key to the practice of witnessing that I have developed. I start all participatory projects walking around a neighbourhood, hanging about and being seen, in a slow immersion process. I walk to meet people and so when creating a walk for others, I am looking to meet neighbours, who may later be willing to become *hosts* to strangers passing through. But when does walking, walking past or walking through, become an *ex*clusive rather than an *in*clusive activity, reinforcing a community of sameness, of like-ness, reserved for those who are financially able, or who have the cultural or social capital which puts pleasure, sport, well-being, or risk-taking easily within reach?

The project was commissioned by *Le Boulon,*[1] one of France's fourteen centres of excellence for urban arts located in the small town of Vieux Condé, within the ex-mining heartlands of Nord-Pas-de-Calais. The core of their mission is to favour social and cultural inclusion through the arts. The walk was to be a cultural strategy to re-activate links between populations who, due to poverty and unemployment, are highly sedentary, many rarely venturing out of their neighbourhoods, let alone their towns. It was to reframe participants' lived experience of the territory, and re-infuse contested or disaffected sites with expressions of story, history or ownership. The Unesco recognition (a title which comes with no direct financial investment) had left many inhabitants non-

---

[1] *Le Boulon, Centre National des Arts de la Rue et de l'Espace Public,* Vieux Condé, France, www.leboulon.fr

plussed or confused. What was the point of celebrating an industrial *past* when the economic future is so bleak and uncertain? It was a delicate exercise, therefore, celebrating the mining heritage in an area which has since suffered such devastating unemployment, and proposing a *walking* project within a culture of limited mobility.

Le Boulon introduced me to existing community groups, with whom I slowly built up a relationship, including a women's do-it-yourself group, a knitting circle, a senior scrabble group, a residents' committee, a seniors' computer class, an amateur theatre troupe, a children's art club, a youth club, a job re-insertion centre, a drop-in house for isolated adults, two puppet groups, a miners' history association, and a brass band.

The territory is dotted with ex-mining estates, *cités minières*, built hastily for an imported workforce, isolated in the countryside, on the sites of coal. Since the closure of the mines in the 90s, these *cités*, their slag-heaps, and towering lift shafts, considered painful and depressing reminders, were demolished or left to rot by local councils until recent eco-tourism rehabilitated the *cavalières* (mining railway tracks) into cycle paths, the slag heaps into havens for biodiversity and walking or mountain bike trails, and caved in the underground pit tunnels to create lakes for watersports. So it *is* a walker's paradise, but social relics of 19th-century patriarchy mean that, after generations of being provided for (and controlled), initiative is lacking on mining estates and people find it hard to do things outside their comfort zones. Many families are third-generation unemployed and have never known a working family member. When the mines closed in France there was little or no protest from the miners, previously such powerful figureheads for social revolt. Paid off, in effect, by a generous government deal, redundant miners over the age of forty-three, received 85% of their salary until forty-five, and then 80% until retirement, conditional on not taking another job.[2] The isolation that resulted, meant a sharp rise in watching television, alcoholism and suicide.

Ali Ben Yaia, deputy mayor of *Beuvrages*, is quoted in the post-event souvenir booklet, as saying "This hike decompartmentalised the limits of our territory…it allowed us to go where hitherto the *a priori* had created exclusion", and a participant contributes: "It's the first time I've taken the

---

[2] *Le Pacte Charbonnier*, 1994, le congé charbonnier de fin de carrière (CCFC), bit.ly/wnm92 (Accessed 02 Jan 2020).

tram...in fact the town's not as far away as I thought", indicative of the prevailing negative assumptions about neighbouring towns.

In this context, I was forced to observe that walking for pleasure might be an exclusive activity. The first problem was the length. The project involved seven towns, strung along twelve kilometres of long straight road, gutted by the tram and lined with boarded-up shops, hairdressers or *friteries* (chip-shops), whose stark *FOR SALE* signs punch gaps in every block. My search for the intimate and bucolic led me to weave across this main axe into backstreets, over slag heaps and through mining estates, penetrating into the heart of the region's story, but lengthening the route. However the project's numerous institutional partners[3] proved only half committed to the idea of an artist revealing 'the poetics of the everyday', a precious and well-explored terrain of many walking artists. Ordinary was not their priority. They wanted to bring this *Great Crossing* past their expensive new arts centre, or renovated town hall. And the subtle, poetic rediscovery of sidestreets, corner cafés or unsung front-gardens was sacrificed to tourism and municipal pride, as the route lengthened again...to nineteen kilometres.

The Nord-Pas-de-Calais has the highest obesity rates in France,[4] reflected in the local LIDL, copiously stocked with frozen chips, pizzas, mayonnaise, bread, potatoes, fast foods, pork and cream. So to make it easier for many people who would visibly have great difficulty walking that far, I included hopping on and off the tram into the walk's protocol. But tramfares are too expensive for the large, low-income families we particularly sought to engage and although the long awaited tram has had mixed reception (aimed at improving access and reducing isolation, it has proved slower and more expensive than the buses), the tram company refused free tickets, offering tote-bags emblazoned with their logo instead, and leaving councils scrabbling to finance some tickets for *some* low-income families.

---

[3] The project was realised by *Le Boulon* in partnership with Valenciennes Métropole *Contrat de Ville*, la Mission Bassin Minier, Transvilles, Valenciennes Tourisme et Congrès and the towns of Anzin, Beuvrages, Bruay sur l'Escaut, Fresnes-sur-Escaut, Onnaing, Condé sur l'Escaut and Vieux-Condé.

[4] 25.6% obesity in the North compared to 10.7% in Paris in 2016, France Info TV, figures from INSERM, Institut national de la santé et de la recherche médicale, bit.ly/wnm118 (Accessed 07 Jan 2020).

For each community group I worked with, the decision to walk or not was usually based on the group's physical capacity to walk far. Groups who opted out on these grounds were invited to be 'hosts' along the route, harnessing their existing cultural activities to punctuate the walk with performance. Along the way walkers discovered the knitting circle dressed in an elaborate collectively knitted costume, knitting all afternoon to airs from *The Magic Flute*, the Miners' History Association who shared treasures from their archive *des gueules noires* (miners) and stories from the pits, or the community group singing bawdy mining songs while serving sharp, black coffee from a kitchen set they constructed. The pensioners club moved their scrabble afternoon outdoors, gracefully dressing in billowing lace and floppy hats, to re-activate the one-time mansion-gardens of a mine owner, now the municipal park, while actors incarnated the shadows of passengers waiting for a train that never came at an abandoned station and a brass band played all afternoon in period costumes in the grassed-over moat of the château of Condé-sur-Escaut.

For the walkers, these theatrical interventions served to revive flagging energies. The guide-maps in their hands became visible signs of belonging to this ephemeral community of adventurers, an invitation echoed in the local myths or stories that hosting residents confided to them, or in the soundscapes whispered from trees or letterboxes along the way. The amateur actors from Anzin threw themselves into *dis-organising* the walk's *DÉPART*, playing a team of over-enthusiastic, maladroit coaches, taking walkers aside for impromptu physical warm-ups, complex orientation instructions, or alarmist survival tips in the event of major accidents or disasters along the way. There were intentionally confusing tannoy announcements for each group's departure, with flag-waving, whistle-blowing and cheering to emphasise the challenge. Complicity was maintained along the way through a system of stamps logged onto walkers' maps, red wool tied to 'certificates of competence', surprise appearances of the overbearing trainers and the staged *ARRIVÉE* at *Le Boulon*, decorated by the do-it-yourself group who sat on tiered seating units, waving football rattles and blowing horns as each group crossed the finishing line.

Some groups, however, were excluded. In Condé-sur-Escaut I was introduced to a group of Algerian women who attended a twice-weekly sewing club. Although they've lived in France for over forty years, they speak little or no French, communicating to the world through their children or husbands, in Arabic or *Kabyle*[5]. The cleaner of their social centre translated for me, keen to encourage their participation, and sharing her disquiet that the women's daily routines were largely restricted to their flats and this centre, just down the road. But my questions inviting opinions about the town, or their lives, were met with shy shakings of heads from the women: a reticence to expand on subjects that might incriminate them through 'wrong' answers, and my proposals to participate in 'La Grande Traversée' were met with blank confusion or vague 'maybes'. Significantly engaging this group would have demanded several months dedicated to them alone, as going to another town or on the tramway was, for them, unimaginable. The project's focus was too wide to be meaningful for them, their isolation too great, and yet their particular story of immigration and family regroupment for the coal industry was a key part of the region's history that would remain unembodied and silent.

Another group excluded *themselves* in reaction to their experience of exclusion from society's workforce. I recorded, one day, the fuming discussion of a group of young, mostly third generation, North African immigrants in Bruay-sur-Escaut: a feedback session concluding a week's work experience as municipal gardeners. Anger was mounting at their endless round of work traineeships, unable to get a job without experience, or a car, unable to learn to drive without a job… *"On est pas des feignants!"* they railed "We're not skivers! We want to work!" Faced with their rage, a celebratory walk seemed an inappropriate suggestion. These young people are only tenuously connected to the memories of the mines. Their *grandfathers* were miners. The much talked of solidarity among mining communities is part of a distant story for which they continue to pay a price. A fortnight later I returned, bringing a tightly edited version of their rant for them to listen to. Fired up, they suggested rapping it to music to diffuse on social media, an idea that grew into a short film, with this track as its core. The walk is obliquely referred to: youths walk through a town, gathering in number, seemingly armed with forks, picks or spades, which cites a famous scene in Claude Berri's (1993) film of Zola's *Germinal,* depicting hundreds of angry miners marching on neighbouring strikebreakers. While that scene ends in extreme violence, in ours the gathering kids are revealed to be neither violent nor *feignants*. Symbolising their wish to be trusted to contribute to society, a

---

[5] Berber language spoken in Kabylie in Northern Algeria.

subject much discussed during our sessions, they gather to dig a hole and plant a tree for an old neighbour.[6] Their film played in Bruay's youth centre, in a triptych with the scene from *Germinal* and 1980s' archive images of local miners' unrest. The kids did not join our walk, though physically they were able, but many hung around their *cité* that day to watch the audience watching their film, that held a cruel, but necessary, mirror of reality up to our otherwise celebratory day.

A third group that *found themselves* excluded, was a collective of North African women in Beuvrages. Welcoming me with tea and cakes, they were keen to participate, and their mediator assured me confidently "If I tell them to come, they will be there". So we embarked on building a model of their town, in which they planned to sit and host walkers with cakes, spices and stories, before joining the walk themselves because it would be an adventure. But the last fortnight of this year-long project fell during Ramadan, when fasting invariably impacts participation. The *cité* is deserted during the day, teenagers are sleeping and mothers are busy cooking for the feasting at sun-down. The date of *Laïd*, depending on the position of the moon, is not known until the day before and it fell the day after the walk. So the previously enthusiastic Muslim women's attendance fell drastically towards the end, as they would not *and could not* commit. They could not go on the walk because they had to be home to cook, and they were evasive about their presence on the day. So the model village was finished and installed hastily by our technicians. The women visited the installation but did not 'own' it. Although they and the town were very happy with the event, I found it uncomfortable as the women became consumers of our 'animations'. Someone had the idea of engaging a local farmer with a horse and cart that seated twelve, enabling the women to take a short ride to the next town and back. But none of them went further, and amongst themselves in their cart, they remained isolated from the wider community the walk was designed to connect with.

Care and reparation are central to the relational aesthetic, within which I firmly base my practice and James Thompson (2015: 438) argues that in an aesthetic of care "[d]ecisions about accessibility (whether in terms of the appropriateness of the space for disabled people, the location

---

[6] *On est pas des feignants!* [Film internet] directed by Sarah Harper and Nadir Bouassria Available at: bit.ly/wnm119 (Accessed 07 Apr 2020).

in terms of costs of travel or the timing for people with different commitments) are not mundane organisational matters, but crucial ethical propositions." In my compliance with the commissioners' conception of this project, little space was made for those for whom walking out of their neighbourhood was physically or mentally impossible, nor for those whose experience of the territory was one of anger, or rejection, nor for those who would be celebrating Ramadan at the time. With an assumption that 'walking together' would be an accessible and cohesive act, the project ultimately appealed to white working families, with social and physical mobility, for whom the weekend *could* be devoted to leisure, or those whose memories or family ties still rendered the, now historical, mining heritage meaningful. People tend to see the results of a project, so the refusals become invisible and, concerned with how to share, frame, and give weight, to what has *not* happened, I return to my question: "What is the value of refusal?" For the women of Condé's sewing club, I propose that their regular intimate activity within a community of support, friendliness and comprehension has more value than 'walking without purpose' (Minamore, 2018) to celebrate a mining heritage which exploited their husbands forty years ago and left them adrift in a country which continues to demand their integration, while according them little attention or respect. The resentful reaction of the youths in Bruay, rejecting any celebratory ownership of 'their industrial heritage', shifted the focus firmly back to the impenetrable barrier of unemployment, sharing a bitter layer of story so fundamental to this region, though recently glossed over in its touristic and tech-valley re-branding. The Muslim women of Beuvrages were privileging their religious community and family responsibilities over and above their already strong sense of belonging to their town. So the refusals discussed here, can be seen variously as acts of affirmation of community, as expressions of identity and belonging and above all as defence against any cosmetic celebrations of locality which are not on their terms.

In conclusion it seems important to ask whether the act of walking is itself racially exclusionary? In the Nord-Pas-de-Calais, black, North African or Muslim populations are in a minority, so the local demographics allow for a certain imbalance. However I cannot avoid the reflection that the three groups, whose refusals I have examined, were made up almost entirely of people of North African descent. And looking back over the hundreds of photos that were taken that day,[7] of the walk and its participants, I can see two faces of colour; the vast majority of the 450 walkers were white. From my anecdotal evidence of this lived experience (Gallop, 2002), this act of walking *was* racially divisional, through racism deeply embedded into the region's history. I would argue that the walk produced, for the sewing group, exclusion based on an experience of belonging too fragile for them to perceive or make relevant meaning from this walk. The Muslim women of Beuvrages, although physically and vociferously demonstrating a sense of ownership and belonging, found themselves only nominally in control of the event. When a lack of attentiveness and failure of care, on the part of the organisers and myself, meant the timing of the walk clashed with their religious calendar, religion took precedence over art. The mixed-race youths expressed the confusion of simultaneously feeling at home in their town and yet finding themselves economically excluded from, in the words of one participant, "building a good life here". In addition, for all three of these groups, the unfamiliar act of walking a long way, in a group for pleasure, surrounded by others they did not know, with whom there was to be some undefined inter-action, would have needed mediating, accompanying or adapting.

Shaw and Sullivan's (2011) case study of artwalks within a context of urban regeneration in Portland, Oregon, conclude those walks to have been racially divisional, with black residents participating less than white residents. They specify that this was not because of differences in art appreciation, but "much to do with people associated with the arts" and "perceptions and experiences of belonging" (p. 242). Black residents perceived the event as something that white people went to, that it was 'not for them', and they spoke of the event amongst themselves as 'White night'. In the UK, a group of black male hikers, '100 Black Men Walk for Health'[8], set up in Sheffield in 2004, is so uncommon it seems, that it inspired Eclipse Theatre's play *Black Men Walking* by the rapper Testament, whose 2018 tour included the Manchester Royal Exchange, and the Royal Court. After joining the original group for a hike, Bridget Minamore, of Ghanaian origin, writes (2018) "The more we walk, the

---

[7] Photos visible on the project's website: bit.ly/wnm121

[8] Now called *Walk4Health*, as the group have diversified to include women and young people. bit.ly/wnm120 (Accessed 07 Jan 2020).

more I wonder why the idea of black people hill-walking seemed so strange to me". Thinking of her family permanently on the move, rushing from one job to another, this hill-walking 'without purpose' feels for Minamore 'at odds with [her] blackness'. The history of the black body so painfully linked to walking under duress, and the contemporary black body still economically bound to walking by necessity continues in non-urban contexts to make it unusual or difficult to imagine black families walking out of choice. One of the group, filmed climbing Scafell Pike (Scafell Walk, 2017), points out that though the environment is for everybody "it can be intimidating out here, because you don't see a lot of people out here who look like us".

Looking around me at the recent 'Walking's New Movements' conference at the University of Plymouth, I couldn't help observing that, while the mix of projects and participants evidenced the wideness and richness of the movement, the vast majority of participants, and artist or academic presenters were white, mostly older and middle class. The thing about walking is that it is, in theory, so accessible. Anyone can do it. But if its afficionados are so distinctly lacking in diversity, it begs the question, has walking become, or remained, a *white practice,* something elitist, potentially exclusionary, belonging to the last century? It used to feel, a few decades ago, radical, or counter-cultural to reclaim the streets with our feet. To stay relevant, we have to hope that as a movement it embraces, and is embraced *by,* diverse artists for a diverse public. Minamore affirms that "Walking is a reclamation. Of moving slowly enough to say this is a land you can take your time with; these peaks are safe, I won't need to run."

In my research I argue against my own practice, recognising non-participation in order to highlight inbuilt conscious or unconscious bias, and systematic contradictions of intent. For the last decade, I have developed and honed strategies to facilitate and encourage participation, to circumnavigate or transform refusals, but there may be more genuine social advantage in accepting refusals as an integral part of the work and attending more closely to the messages they contain. Examining these refusals to walk, reveals that people are *doing something else* that has value and that walking may not be as accessible as we think. Observing what it is that people are participating in, when they refuse to participate with 'us' we could, as Harpin and Nicholson (2017: 14) suggest, blur the boundaries of invitation and response, and consider rather, an "ecology of mutual doings and beings", acknowledging the implications of how participation is recognised and by whom.

References

Gallop, J. (2002) *Anecdotal Theory*. Duke Univ. Press

Germinal. (1993) [Film/DVD] directed by Claude Berri. France/Belgium, Renn Productions /France 2 Cinema / DD Productions

Harpin, A. & Nicholson, H. (2017) *Performance and Participation. Practices, Audiences, Politics.* Palgrave, p.14

Minamore, B. (2018) 'Black Men Walking: a hilly hike through 500 years of black British history'. *Guardian Online.* [Internet], 23 Jan. Available at: bit.ly/wnm94 (Accessed 07 Jan 2020)

Shaw, S. & Sullivan, D. M. (2011) White Night: Gentrification, Racial Exclusion, and Perception and Participation in the Arts, *City and Community, American Sociological Association.* 10 (3), pp. 241-263

Sheffield Environmental Movement. 2017 *Walk for Health Scafell Residential 2017.* 2'15", [Internet video] Available at: bit.ly/wnm95 (Accessed 07 Jan 2020)

Thompson, J. (2015) 'Towards an Aesthetics of Care', *Research in Drama Education: The Journal of Applied Theatre and Performance.* 20 (4), pp. 430-441

Access Denied? Walking Art and Disabled People

Morag Rose

> Once I went for a walk. I thought it would be The Walk, but it
> was just my walk, and I still don't know where it will take me….

This article aims to share a part of my own walking art practice but is also a call for a more inclusive and accessible walking art movement which values different bodies and is genuinely open to disabled people.

Last year I wandered to Plymouth for 'Walking's New Movements' (WNM). There is great pleasure to be had in a gathering of kin; I likened entering the conference to an exhalation, a sinking into a blissful pool because there is no need to begin with an explanation of why walking, how walking art. We may take many different paths, but all share at least one common theme: that the ordinary can be transformed and our footsteps can be creative. I've experienced the warmth of solidarity and shared experiences before, of course, on a crowded dancefloor, in the middle of a protest, at seminars, festivals, conferences when common ground is established in the invitation to participate. However, too often I find myself asking awkward questions about whether I am going to be excluded in subtle (and not so subtle) ways because of how my body works. As a disabled person will I have to ask about access? Must I spend energy and risk becoming "the conference crank"? Morris (2019) used this term to describe the participant whose awkward questions create the space to discuss who, and what, is being overlooked or marginalised. (This crank is kindred of Ahmed's (2010) *Feminist Killjoy* and any conversation on the power of complaint, of naming and becoming problems owes a huge debt to her brilliant work). True friends can be critical, contradictory and acknowledge the multitudes within each other and themselves, but this can be very hard to listen to. It is dangerous to assume and we need to stay open to new ideas. I left WNM with my head buzzing and body tingling but I also had a lingering unease. Morris (2019) helped me articulate this and on reflection I want to ask Walking

Artists to make a few small changes to ensure their work is welcoming to all.

But first, a step back. My route to walking art has been appropriately convoluted and I never intended to get here – but I am glad I did. In 2006 I co-founded The Loiterers Resistance Movement (The LRM), a Manchester based psychogeographical collective. We walk together to start a critical conversation with the city we love but often despair at, to instigate creative mischief, to uncover hidden power lines and join dots between people and places. We want to disrupt business as usual, mapping the city according to our desires and conjuring visions of a glittering anarcho utopia, or at least an uncommodified ginnel. The LRM manifesto states "Our city is wonderful and made for more than shopping. The streets belong to everyone and we want to reclaim them for play and revolutionary fun." (The LRM, online) We drift together on the First Sunday of every month, engaging and connecting with hidden stories, adding new layers to the palimpsest (see Rose, 2015 for more details).

Over the years The LRM, like psychogeography itself, has mutated, evolved and created a peripatetic community. There haven't been any SI style feuds that I am aware of, but people drift in and out, and each has their own motivations. For some we are a pedagogical device, for others a convivial curiosity, a creative exercise, a political stance or something else entirely I have never even dreamt of. This is to be welcomed, as is the sense now that, although I do the necessary admin, I don't control where we will go. I cherish Smith's (2014, 2015) thoughts on the *dérive* as a leaderless swarm and the undercurrent of radical subversion implicit in his (mis)directions on political walking. I will confess though not every LRM expedition is a joy, and I am fearful it may become a chore or a habit; should this be so I will retire and see what happens next. There's another issue too; the revolution we walk for feels no nearer and sometimes it feels as if all we are doing is bearing witness to change. Is that enough? Can any ever of us ever resist the spectacle? Recently I've been thinking, theorising and talking about The LRM; it had begun to feel somewhat abstract and dislocated, not a good thing because psychogeography is a practice above all else and it should never be static or boring.

Rather than discuss The LRM at WNM, I wanted to take the opportunity to explore a new, more personal project. I felt the need to re-connect to my own psychogeographical secrets, linking 'New' to a project that gets to the heart of a paradox in my work. I've made walking a mission, but my passion is not uncomplicated. I came late to not just walking art, but walking itself. As a child there were endless parades in front of doctors who wanted to analyse my gait, diagnose my painful walking and frequent falls. There were operations, callipers and care. This isn't a story that deserves pity or praise, but by necessity my walking has always been problematic and contradictory. I felt the word 'patronised' before I ever heard it and I longed to be able to roam the hills I saw out of the hospital window. Today I walk thanks to the NHS, to prescription medicine, orthotics, physiotherapy and an extended network of care. There is still pain, and tiredness, and falls but also stubbornness, joy and a deep sense of gratitude.

I haven't really spoken or written much about being an artist whose chosen medium is my nemesis because I didn't want to, and I was too busy with other things. Trying to reconcile this paradox, without making myself a spectacle, a superhero or an object of pity, has often felt hard and not something I wanted to give time to. My broken feet are not the most interesting thing about me, and having always lived with pain I don't really want to give it more energy. A truth: chronic illness is boring, really boring. Also exhausting, expensive and dull. Pain is painful.

However, I have also always loved the personal is political because, yes, it is, and I wanted to reconnect and develop a more intimate praxis that explored my embodied relationship to walking. After years of misdiagnosis I know now my condition is hereditary and degenerative. It's another psychogeographical cliché perhaps, the longing to join the dots with the past, make connections, uncover secrets, but this year I created time and space to find my mother. She died when I was 13, and with her silence fell. No doubt it was a loving, protective and well-intentioned erasure, but there are ties I want, need to untangle. Retrospectively I realise we share a mutant gene, but her pain was hidden, dismissed, and she became agoraphobic. I can't find her literally, of course, but I am searching for resonances and have been wandering where she was born, lived, and died.

This work, tentatively called "Desire Lines, Debored and DNA" was the work in progress I wanted to share at WNM. It remains unfinished at the moment, but the themes of the work are clear. The focus is on gender, disability, memory and hauntings. The spectre of eugenics looms large too, as the gene I share with my mother is on a hit list and we live in a time of medical advances which often fail to consider the humanity of disabled people. Even as I write this, the political environment I live in is shifting and the urgency to learn from the disabled people's movement, our fights and our lived experiences grows daily. The wider context of austerity is crucial here as is the disabling environment in which we all live. I don't particularly want to be focusing on materiality but inequality is very hard to ignore when there are barriers everywhere and policies encourage your demise.

It is of course essential to take an intersectional (Crenshaw 1989) approach to access and inequality. As a white cis woman there is much I cannot understand and we all need to pay attention to other people's testimonies and our own preconceptions. Here I am focusing on disability, and a very personal account; of course, disabled people are not a homogenous group, and I cannot speak for anyone but myself. That important caveat aside, I want to encourage walking artists to think about how we can recognise the needs and experience of disabled people and find ways to open up our work. There has been some brilliant work on women who walk and challenging the myth of the flâneur (for example Norcup's 'Geography Workshop Presents 'Er Outdoors' radio shows (2016-2018), Elkin's *Flâneuse* (2016) and Qualmann and Sharrocks' 'Walking Women' (2016) events) but the archetype is not just male. He is able bodied, wealthy, heteronormative, urbane and white; all aspects we need to address collectively. Improving access and valuing different bodies takes effort and means encountering uncomfortable truths.

At WNM I detected several threads woven across papers and events which spoke of embodiment, sensations, collectivism and connectivity. I appreciated the effort organisers put into finding a truly accessible venue and keeping the costs to participants as low as possible, cost being a serious barrier for so many. I was moved and inspired by my time in Plymouth. I was also struck by the realisation that I don't engage with walking art outside of literature, conferences and galleries, because my experience has been so painful. Hypocrite that I am, I read, listen, watch and discuss other artists' work, but seldom do I walk it for fear I will ruin it. Some constructive debate led me to post a message to the Walking Artists Network (WAN). This was not in direct response to WNM but rather to more negative experiences over the years, and I chose to share it on the mailing list as it seemed the best way to reach the largest number of other creative walkers. I am reposting my original post, with just a few edits for clarity and to correct typos.

Dear friends and fellow artistic wanderers

I'm writing here as (amongst other things of course) as a walking artist and a disabled person. I have had the privilege of walking and talking with some brilliant fellow artists in a variety of contexts this year, both online and in the real world. It feels like a recurrent theme is (unsurprisingly) the embodied nature of our art and the challenges of walking in, and with, different kinds of bodies. We all also seem to share a desire to create work which engages with diverse audiences and I am sure we would all like to increase participation in creative walking.

This is a plea to think about how we can get better at doing this particularly in relation to disabled people. It draws on my personal experiences but is not just about me, and to be clear I am not attacking any specific artist here: I have spoken directly, and privately, to some but will not engage in public shaming when we live in a society riddled with ableism.

Please can we all try and be explicit, and honest, about who is welcome and able to participate in our work. It can be really difficult to find out access information for many venues and events, and this labour should not have to fall on our audience. I'm sorry to say on several occasions I have found myself literally left behind during performance walks because the pace was too fast and nobody noticed or the terrain became very hard to navigate and this was not made clear from the off. I am sure this is oversight rather than design, but it is, to put it mildly, unfair and unpleasant. I've also been invited to perform in many venues where the stage is inaccessible, often despite being told the venue is open to all – the message the environment sends out is we crips aren't expected to actually be the artist, the speaker, or active participants. Regrettably I have become reluctant to attend events unless it is clear disabled people are welcome – because I assume otherwise there will be an uncomfortable struggle and my body will be constructed as a problem for others. I will not apologise for my pace or my body. This is, amongst many other things, exhausting and unfair.

To be clear I am not saying all our walks must be for everybody, this is clearly inappropriate and I have no desire to censor fast or long or physically arduous walks. I also recognise the environment we live in is disabling in many ways and we may not always have the power to choose or change a venue. However, there are things we can and should be better at and as a bare minimum please, please, can we start adding access information to publicity. I'd also like to encourage everyone to think about whether there are changes we can make that would enable more people to join in or access our work in other ways if they cannot physically be there. Perhaps most vital of all please be respectful of our audiences and reflexive to their needs. I don't ever want anyone else to be left behind, abandoned or excluded by creative walking due to someone else's thoughtlessness and / or bad planning. Allies of all kinds are needed if we want to walk in, and together with, disabled bodies.

In the past I have been criticised for continuing to talk about "walking art" as the term itself is exclusive. I absolutely disagree with this, and want instead to expand the term to be as inclusive as possible. My belief is that if we are making something enchanted out of the everyday it should be for everyone and "walking" can, should, must include sticks, wheels, orthotics and other enabling technologies. I follow a path made by many others here of course and I'd like to thank them for their inspiration. I also acknowledge there are many dimensions to improving access and this is just one; disabled people are not homogenous and there are many other factors which exclude and oppress. I know I have made mistakes and still have much to learn, and I hope this post will be taken in a spirit of friendly criticism and a desire to start a conversation. Thank you to all who have read this, especially those who take the time to reflect and respond.

The response was overwhelming, and overwhelmingly positive with many people responding with thoughts on walking as and with disabled people. I was reminded of the need to be active campaigners but also of the expectation that the hard labour of diversity work too often falls on those fighting for their own rights. I really appreciated the response from allies but declined offers to provide (free) audits for specific projects. I was also shocked, although I shouldn't have been, to realise the social model of disability is not integral to many peoples understanding of prejudice and exclusion. I sent the following public response, again lightly edited for clarity.

For some of us our walking art has to be inherently political because we simply aren't supposed to take up space / make noise / demand rights, but that is for another debate. More pertinently here the tension between enchantment and material reality has, regrettably always been central to my work. I believe – as stated in The LRM manifesto – "The streets belong to everyone", but I know today, certainly in Manchester where I live and work, they don't. I've spent many years campaigning in various ways, most recently this year focusing on two areas which illustrate the problem perfectly at a micro level. Together with disabled people's organisations and allies I have been fighting to make Jeremy Deller's Peterloo memorial accessible (for the record we support the importance of the memorial per se). A monument to equality, democracy, working class struggles and participation actually reifies segregation and oppression because it is a flight of stairs to be ascended. I have also been working with homeless people's organisations, GM Law Centre and others to oppose the PSPO (Public Space Protection Order) which is a social cleansing policy that will effectively criminalise homelessness (details here: bit.ly/wnm122). Whilst I am proud of these fights I am desperately sad they are needed and would much rather be writing, performing, sleeping, creating or seeing friends. These choices do come at a cost of time, energy, opportunity and reputation; I fully recognise they are not appropriate for everyone but I would love to hear about other people's activism and how WAN can support each other.

My original email wasn't asking for big Politics or Activism or changes in practice. It was more a call for kindness, thoughtfulness and respect for the needs of different bodies. Specifically I called for honesty and the inclusion of access information in project design and publicity. This really isn't a huge task but would have a very positive impact. I suggest adding something like "This performance takes place on pavements and in public spaces throughout the town. There are no steps and we will cross roads only where there are dropped kerbs. The route is 1.5 miles and will take approximately 2 hours without a break. There are toilets and refreshment facilities at the beginning and end of the performance. If you have any particular access needs please contact us at XXXXX and we will do our best to help" or "the gallery is on the second floor and is accessible by lift. There is limited seating available, please let us know if you would like us to reserve you a seat or if you have any questions about access".

The most important thing is to be honest, open, and to listen. Ask people what their access needs are because they know much better than you do. There is no one size fits all. If you want a detailed assessment of your work / venue I strongly suggest contacting local disabled people's organisations, access groups, and experts in your area (if you are in or near North West England I will gladly pass on my contacts). There is a wealth of knowledge built up over many years. Please also think about what you are asking and be prepared to pay for / reward expertise especially if it is benefiting your own enterprise. Sara Ahmed is typically brilliant and insightful on the nature of complaint, and how the person raising an issue can be constructed as a problem and responsible for the solution. For the record I am a disabled person and of course my lived experience and my academic research both give me insight, but I am not an expert on all aspects of disability and access and I am not able to take on lots more labour. However I am really happy to carry on this conversation and to facilitate positive change as far as I can.

I would like to propose collating freely available resources on access and amplifying / celebrating the work of disabled walking artists. I am willing to coordinate this. If people send stuff to me off list I will add to those I have collected and then share on-list for all. I hope this will enrich existing work on intersectionality and diversity in Walking Art; this is only one aspect of a much bigger challenge.

At the time of writing, this compilation of resources is still under development. I hope by the time this essay is published it will be online and evolving. The aim is to celebrate, promote and share work made by disabled walking artists. It aims to be as inclusive as possible and welcomes contributions from anyone who identifies as physically disabled, has sensory impairment, chronic illness, mental health issues and / or is neurodiverse. There is also a section which compiles existing good practice guidelines on accessible events and writing about disabled walking artists. Providing access information, toilets and lifts is a minimum and there is so much more that can be done such as free tickets to PAs, having quiet spaces and a variety of seating, to improving the format and accessibility of texts we share.

If you struggle to find this resource, or have questions, comments or work to add please do not hesitate to contact me by email mlrose@thelrm.org or twitter @thelrm. I will continue to work with others to make Walking Art as accessible, diverse, challenging and creative as possible. The social model of disability teaches us that the environment is disabling and we face massive structural issues. This does not give us an excuse to not be caring, kind and self-reflexive. There are many wonderful walking artists and projects to be inspired by, here are just three I especially love but there are so many more.

Sue Porter and Dee Heddon's work as part of 'Walking Interconnections: performing conversations on sustainability' project (2017) challenged the lack of disabled people's voices in debates around environmental sustainability and included Heddon's (2013) excellent verbatim audioplay *Going For a Walk*.

Carmen Papalia states his "socially engaged practice is an effort to unlearn visual primacy and resist support options that promote ablest concepts of normalcy" (Papalia: online). Amongst a splendid portfolio I particularly enjoy 'Mobility Device' (2013) where he replaces his white cane with a marching band.

Alec Finlay is an artist and poet whose work often focuses on rewilding, connecting people with the landscape and his 'Day of Access' campaign (Travelling Gallery 2019) is particularly engaging. He believes that *everyone* should have the opportunity to experience wild nature and calls on estates to open their lands for all.

We are all walking in a world that can be hostile to many and where disabled people are too often marginalised, ignored or discriminated against. I urge everyone reading this to pause and think about how we can challenge ourselves to make things better. Samuels (2019) conceptualises walking together as a way to take and hold space, building connections and creating communities as we do so. The question I am asking is who are *you* willing to make space for? Please do not leave any walker behind.

My walking is a kaleidoscope: personal, political, angry, loving, creative, meandering, direct, painful, joy filled, clumsy, beautiful, accident prone, poetic, stubborn, furious, curious, mischievous, contradictory, and confusing, meaningless depending on the day, time, mood, any, all, and and and miscellaneous other. One thing it will no longer be is apologetic.

Acknowledgements

Thanks to Blake Morris, Bethan Evans, Steve Graby, John Hawes, Joan Rutherford, Jane Samuels and the editors for inspiring and generous conversations which helped inform this work. Heartfelt thanks also to all who walk with The LRM.

References

Ahmed, S. (2010). 'Killing Joy: Feminism and the history of happiness'. *Signs: Journal of Women in Culture and Society, 35*(3), 571–594. doi: 10.1086/648513

Crenshaw, K. (1989). 'Demarginalizing the intersection of race and sex: A black feminist critique of antidiscrimination doctrine, feminist theory and antiracist politics.' *U. Chi. Legal F.,* 139

Elkin, L. (2016). *Flaneuse,* Chatto & Windus

Finlay, A. (online) www.alecfinlay.com (accessed 21.2.20)

Heddon, D. (2013) Going For A Walk (verbatim audioplay)

Heddon, D. and Porter, S. (2017) 'Walking Interconnections', *CSPA Quarterly,* no. 18 pp. 18-21

Morris, B. (2019) 'British Summer Time: American Extension', bit.ly/wnm125 (accessed 21 Feb 2020)

Papalia, C. (online) https://carmenpapalia.com/ (accessed 01 Jan 2020)

______ (2013) *Mobility Device,* performance walk, Grand Central Art Center, online at: bit.ly/wnm111 (accessed 21 Feb 2020)

Qualmann, C. and Sharrocks, A. (curators) (2016) 'Walking Women, Somerset House London and Forest Fringe Edinburgh Information' online bit.ly/wnm130 (accessed 01 Jan 2020)

Rose, M. (2015) 'Confessions of an anarcho-flâneuse or psychogeography the Mancunian way' in T. Richardson (ed.), *Walking Inside Out: contemporary British psychogeography* (pp. 147-162). Rowan and Littlefield International

Samuels, J. (2019) 'Taking Space' in C. Rose (ed) *Psychogeography and Psychotherapy Connecting Pathways* (pp. 31-50) PCCS Books

Smith, P. (2014) *On Walking… and Stalking Sebald,* Triarchy Press

______ (2015) *Walking's New Movement,* Triarchy Press

The LRM – Loiterers Resistance Movement (2007) postcard (personal collection). Available at: bit.ly/wnm97 (accessed 21 Feb 2020)

Travelling Gallery (2019) Alec Finlay 'Day of Access'. Available at: bit.ly/wnm96 (accessed 01 Mar 2020)

Mind the Gap

Philippe Guillaume

August 14, 2019, Toronto, Canada. Corner of Dundas West and McCall, 7:00 AM, 'Walker at Work' undertook a walking performance to create spontaneous bubbles of communication with strangers. The performance ended at 7:00 PM at the north-east corner of Dundas East and Jarvis.

This ephemeral relational work was Walker at Work's intervention to momentarily divert the automatic and utilitarian practice characteristic of pedestrian mobility. Those encountered were asked to indicate an object or a place they would like to see in a picture, which Walker at Work then meandered the city to find and photograph. In exchange for these directives the random walkers were offered a numbered picture depicting a place from *Walker at Work's* home in Montreal, Canada.

November 1, 2019, Plymouth, UK. In a public provocation, Walker at Work presented each photo with five words noted during a post-performance thirteen-minute meditation for every picture. The names of the strangers encountered, the time of the meeting, the objects or places for each directive, and the rational given by these random pedestrians for their choices follow the listing.

This is *Walker at Work's* recitation:

The seat of conscious, awareness, thoughts, volition, and feeling.

Attention, concentration.

The intellect, intellectual power.

Remembrance, memory.

One's opinion.

A way of thinking or feeling:

MIND

Denoting one or more people or things under discussion, implied, or familiar.

Serving to describe, to be unique.

Unit of time:

THE

An unfilled space or interval.

A break in continuity.

A wide diversion of views:

GAP

MIND THE GAP!

Hub, Pivot, Focus, Contact, Maze

John. 7:10 — School, because it looks nice

Mind the Gap!

Circle, Ring, Compass, Perimeter, Periphery

Valery. 7:25 — Bicycle because, it's universal

Mind the Gap!

Edge, Boundary, Margin, Corner, Fence

Julia. 8:07 — Church, because of time

Mind the Gap!

Step, Trace, Measure, Stage, Process

Nancy. 8:45 — Kensington Market, because it's a funky area

Mind the Gap!

Imagination, Resource, Illusion, Inspire, Recycle

Magnus. 9:21 — Graffiti Alley, because of the nice walls

Mind the Gap!

Rhizome, Vine, Earth, Growth, Ramp

Alberto. 10:19 — Jimmy's Coffee, because he just arrived in town from Italy and it is where he took his first picture in Toronto

Mind the Gap!

Earth, Shadow, Windmill, Rust, Uncountable

Marishka. 10:40 — The sculpture garden on Augusta, because it's weird

Mind the Gap!

Window, Line, Unknown, Anonymous, Number

David. 11:19 — The phone booth at Fun House, because of the colour and it's whacky

Mind the Gap!

Power, Top, Acanthus, Invasion, Storm

Phineas. 11:58 — Campbell House, because it sparks inspiration

Mind the Gap!

Foundation, Ground, Blood, Elephant, Place

Sarah. 12:16 — Osgood Building, because of Canadian history

Mind the Gap!

System, Balance, Open, Space, Form

Oona. 12:29 — Osgood Hall Pillars of Justice, because of
what's missing

Mind the Gap!

Emblem, Market, Water, Moving, Commodity

Lily. 12: 57 — Toronto at City Hall, because it represents life
and culture

Mind the Gap!

Pot, Corner, Feet, Addiction, Junk

Jake. 13:20 — Eaton Center Screens, because they're busy

Mind the Gap!

Water, Island, Edge, Map, Appropriation

Coslyn. 14:12 — Sugar Beach, because it reminds her of
sugar at her home in Granada

Mind the Gap!

Preserve, Garden, Path, Lost, Heat

Jason & John-Elicia. 16:40 — Allan Gardens, because it's
inspiring

Mind the Gap!

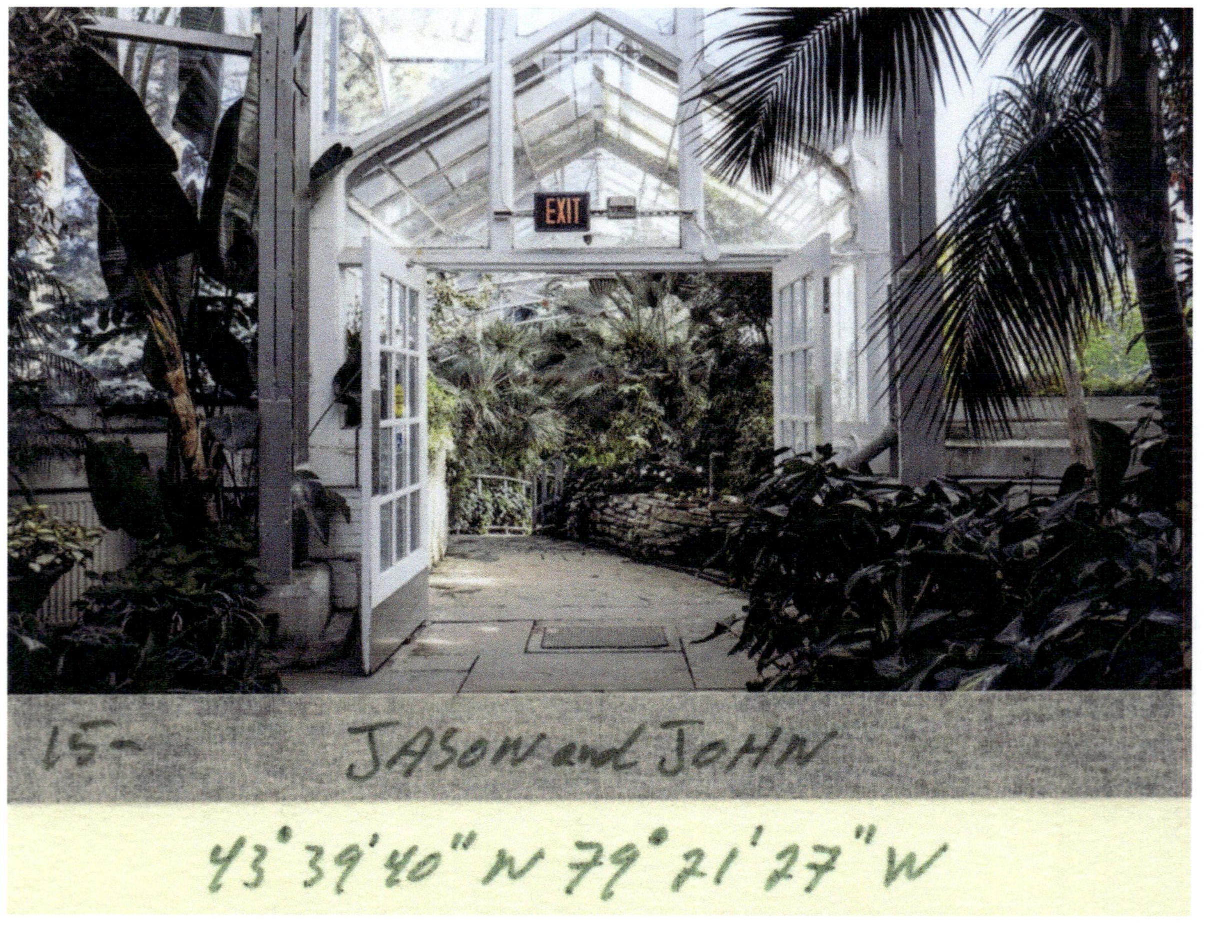
EXIT
15-
JASon and JoHN
43°39'40"N 79°21'27"W

Pain, Hear, Heritage, Walk, Stand

Strawberry. 17:40 — Indigenous art, for her murdered sisters

Mind the Gap!

Home, Lines, Meet, No, Connection

Jim. 18:24 — New building at the corner of Jarvis and
Dundas, because the neighbourhood has changed

MIND THE GAP!

The Documentary Drift: Lutyens, Cockington and Poetry

Sam Kemp

I did not set out to write a poetry collection about the architect Sir Edwin Lutyens (1869-1944). Influenced by Cecile Oak's (2017) mytho-geographical journey across South Devon in *Anywhere*, I set out to write a poetry collection exploring the pastoral contradictions of Cockington, a heritage village in the south west of England. But after an encounter with a collection of letters by Lutyens, who designed the village's Drum Inn, the village soon became a fantastical theatre where his questions of language, craft and beauty could unravel. In this essay I'll highlight the role that walking played in a bleeding together of a documentary and geographical landscape.

I began by walking through and around the village. I took different routes, visited at different times and generally sought out different conditions. My notes and photos from this time reflect just this: a place seen through the ever-shifting lenses of sunshine, tourism, rain, nostalgia and more sunshine. The tricky part was writing about it. I began the early poems with the date as a title and attempted to weave my notes into something more coherent:

> I sucked the Domesday Book dry
>
> leaves like cremated hearts.
>
> And here and there
>
> a dog barks
>
> a wedding party

I was interested in multiplicities, how the village could be both a pastoral retreat and a complicated mash up of commodified rural tropes. Cockington is in a deep valley around a mile from Torquay sea front in South Devon, meaning that the village centre gives an impression of both undisturbed seclusion and claustrophobia. Approaching the village from different paths is key to understanding its appeal. From the south you pass through the wealthy suburbs and busy roads of sprawling Torquay. From the west you leave the hectic dual carriageway to amble along country lanes for a few miles, and the path from the north east crosses that same dual carriageway and patches of suburbs. These are only the major routes, and most people approach from the south, but the transition from urban to rural is an integral part of the tourist's Cockington experience. Its deep valley has seemingly cut it off from the world of progress and commercialism. This is a place that you descend into. Here was one of the last pockets of innocence and charm, set within a picturesque village and immaculate country park. When the whole village was up for sale in 1946 the auctioneers' brochure implored potential buyers to preserve Cockington's "deep and fundamental beauty", claiming that "A more perfect gem of rural beauty would be hard to imagine".[1] The village is sold along similar lines today. One recent TripAdvisor review mentions what a "hidden treasure" it is and another is titled "A walk through Cockington to see Old World ways" (Nov 2019). Of course, this is just one side of the village, but it was the side that, up until this project, I knew best.

To me, the village had always meant boredom. My family have run The Forge giftshop for nearly twenty years and when I was young I spent many long and slow days there waiting for something, anything, to happen. From the Forge's open window, the scene rarely changed. The horse and carts touted for business and trotted up to the court as visitors wandered around gathering family members for photos. Opposite us, on the other side of the village centre, were two other gift shops and two cafés, all, like us, disguised as something else. The Old Forge. The Schoolhouse. The Weaver's Cottage. The Granary. Nothing is quite what it seems.

Simply walking the village as a visitor was a new experience. Up until then, it had always been a place of tension. Despite the picturesque cottages and trimmed lawns of the village centre, The Forge could be a place of isolation. Over the years I have given up feeling any sense of

---

[1] Item 4694Z/8 held at the South West Heritage Trust

ownership of the place. As legal owners we are custodians at best, and capitalists at worse. For a surprisingly large part, The Forge belongs to people's memories. 'Why isn't it a working forge' is a persistent question with a fairly straightforward answer. It was the blacksmith himself who after years of dwindling trade, converted it into a gift shop in the 1970s. But a stalwart few refuse to accept it. I can understand why. The pastoral retreat that Cockington sells can only go so far.

Given these complications, it's no surprise that the village is a mythogeographical hub, and it was Phil Smith's numerous writings on Cockington that first gave me a new perspective on the place. Cecile Oak, the narrator of Smith's *Anywhere,* describes the confused role modern day Cockington plays. The village is something of a hangover from feudalism, a place in which "the contract with things is broken". The rise of international shipping (or looting) in the sixteenth century led to a sense of things "melting into air". Produce is no longer grown in nearby fields

> nor are they ground in local mills, nor burnt down to lime in nearby kilns, nor woven in the cottage down the lane, nor are they the fruits of the trade with equivalent produces elsewhere; instead they are driven by a surplus riven from its source, an alienation born of thousands of miles of splitting and rending (Smith, 2017: Kindle Loc. 1063).

Cockington is a complicated place, seemingly still stumbling for a precise role. It boasts numerous craft studios and the shops specialise in locally produced gifts. In short, the village sells itself on loose ideas of old world charm and retreat, yet relies on a system of national tourism and digital marketing in order to upkeep any sense of the local and traditional. Perhaps this contradiction stems from the surplus being 'riven from its source'? Perhaps the commercial village underneath the façade was far more authentic than the façade? I had these questions in my mind as I explored the village, and free from my role at the forge, I realised I knew next to nothing about this place. Smith's Cecile also taught me to look for Cockington's future, a challenge when it feels so swamped with the past.

> The pictorial sweep of the front lawn is suggestive of the so called 'empty-space' of theatre, theatre's universalising fantasy that there is a neutral, virgin, non-space, a launch pad, a mere airport lounge in which great performers do greatness, unhindered.
>
> Such is a place like this, but without greatness; just the ache for something special. (ibid: 1179)

But it took me a while to fully realise the potential of that ache. I was looking backwards. So far I had been walking with the lens of a commodified pastoral, seeking evidence that punctures Cockington's film of a serene land. I found plenty. The rough sleepers. The struggling businesses. Death in every corner of the parkland. The stifled utopia under the car park. Then there's just the simply bizarre finds that don't fit anywhere. Abandoned fridges. Half of a fish dropped in a quarry. A Victorian cast iron drainpipe in the middle of the forest. The archives tell the story of the residents' increasing desire for commercialisation as far back as the early twentieth century, and the local council's crackdown on anything remotely progressive. At one point they stipulated what goods could be sold and how they should be displayed. So far, I had what I was looking for.

Yet the more I delved in Smith's practice and writings, the more I realised I was refusing to allow myself to drift. It was all going too well. Smith states that mythogeography, as opposed to psychogeography, aims to engage people with "theatre rather than politics" (2012). This style of walking poses more questions than answers, and I had only been searching for answers. After a year or so of walking the village I had amassed piles of poems, most of them reports of my walks that I had attempted to tie together into a narrative. But the poems were predictable, more critiques than personal accounts.

There wasn't enough theatre. I wasn't fully drifting around the village, and so I couldn't fully drift on the page. I have struggled with this relationship between walking and writing. The poetry needed to be something more than just a narrative report of my drifts, yet I wanted the loose ethos of the drift to influence the page. My attempts at writing up my walking felt too calculated, almost too easy. My approach to the village, and the page, needed less of an agenda. Again, Cecile Oak's reflection on her journey gave me some guidance:

> I wonder if I have ever properly understood what research is. That only if I put myself at the mercy of my subject, only when I am caught up and becoming part of my subject and only when that subject is caught up and disrupted and diffracted by me – leaving a footprint, climbing a fence to trespass – am I really researching (Smith, 2017: Kindle Loc. 1718).

I wondered if I was trying too hard. I started to take different people to the village and resisted the urge to slip into tour-guide mode. Now the place began to open up rather than be closed down with critique. I stopped searching and theorising and began to see the beauty in the place, even the beauty in its contradictions. A group of mostly South American researchers highlighted the abundant colours in The Rose Garden and Lakes, linking this quintessentially English locale to more tropical climes. Some colleagues were charmed by a particularly sunny day spent lounging around on Yonder Lawn in front of the Court. One person highlighted the boggling bureaucratic speak on a planning permission notice, a bizarrely wordy juxtaposition to the picture postcard scene around us. An adventurous friend led me through the undergrowth up and over unmapped trenches from where we could see the valley haze into horizon. Another took me on a night-time raid of the Quarry where we stumbled across a seemingly ritualistic arrangement of animal skulls. My supervisor and I stood helpless as a resident lectured us about the correct length of the trees overhanging Cockington Lane, and for the first time I noticed an incredibly bulbous and proud horse chestnut crowning the lane. Most of these places I had seen before, but I was now seeing it through their eyes. I was beginning to let myself enjoy the village, sink into, as Cecile puts it, its own "hallucination" (ibid: 1074). I began to simply walk. Crucially, I abandoned any idea of writing up each walk as a defined poem, but rather allowed these experiences to simmer together into what became the finished collection. Cockington was no longer just The Forge and a nostalgic pastoral. It was a haunted yet progressive landscape, a place of genuine beauty disguised by a façade of itself. In short, it unravelled into a place I no longer recognised or understood. Smith's advice of mythogeography as a collaboration was beginning to make sense:

> No one makes a mythogeography until they learn how to walk in
> more than one body; until they can walk in a place where they are
> at home as if they were a stranger, and in a place where they are
> a stranger as if they were at home (ibid: 50).

And then in came Lutyens, my deceased co-conspirator. I had read a collection of his letters hoping to spot any mentions of Cockington's Drum Inn which he designed in the early 1930s. This began a journey down a rabbit hole of his archives that spawned a new Cockington on the page, a village existing in, and only in, that 'ache for something special' that Cecile finds on the village's Yonder Lawn.

Lutyens' constant striving towards a perfect sense of beauty became a catalyst for questions of craft and led to my experiments with a visual and sonic page-based drift that were influenced by, but free from, the wonders and limitations of Cockington Village. He believed that architecture could achieve a level of beauty that language could not. Partly this reflected a frustration at what he felt to be his own inadequacy over articulating his feelings towards his wife, Lady Emily. In his letters, words are "impotent" (Hussey, 1953: 216), slippery animals that frequently eluded him, wielded by those who duped the public into a "government by phrases" (Percy & Ridley, 1985: 277). He saw the early twentieth century as a time in which "words, words, words" (295) seemed to be the only way to attain respect and fame, a society slipping away from the tangible into a world of ideas. In his modestly counter-cultural style, Lutyens even reflected mythogeography. As Smith remarks, The Spectacle that plagues modern society was fuelled by "... the advent of mass media in the twentieth century" and

> manifested itself first as the dominance of images over things ...the dominance of representatives over what they represent.... the dominance of the ideas of freedom, democracy, happiness over people actually being free, happy and democratically active (Smith, 2014: Kindle Loc. 175).

It's a short leap (with more creative rather than critical intentions) to replace Smith's "pictures" with Lutyens' "words". The link is one I built on when reconfiguring his character through the poems. A historical Lutyens was not enough. His Drum Inn was the pivotal point for a grandiose village extension consisting of shops and tearooms and a new green. It would have dwarfed the existing village. It was utopian in its scale and ambition, and its ghost began to accompany all of my walks. The fact that it never moved beyond paper is my greatest asset, and now me and Lut set out to re-envision the village with the only tools we had – language. As Gillian Darley in *Villages of Vision, a study of strange Utopias*, explains: "The picturesque village is surely the architectural expression of all the myths of rural life" (2007: 231). We aimed to take this to the extreme.

This new village, a palimpsest of past and future Cockingtons, can exist only in language, only on the open horizon of the page. For an architect, it's an artistic fantasy: an unlimited budget, an absentee client and a boundless site. For a poet, the concept allows me to explore the limitations of visual and linguistic forms of beauty, holding up the word as a building in constant relation to its surroundings. We would build in language, and Cockington would be our launchpad.

bone, says the rain
the moon breaking bone held, hips
into fifths   in the rain, moon's error
                            in looking forward
feigning error, moon's back
turned up against the rain
our hold on each other
                each moon-streak
back up, rain   holds chalk
held above water
breaking our hold your back
                down
moon phases out   for just a second
all form is error
you say
rain holding itself

the hour here
is really a repitition of   our
an abscence of stillness

as in, an our moving across the fields
or an our spent in building the village
measure this by grams   between us
one here   one here
and tell us, village
which one holds more?

A bird in the hand = 5g

A bird in a word = 5g

Two in the bush = 13g

where is the weight
of England
its capital and catchy
                land
                land
                land?

E E E -ded valley our tongues
    in your name, Lut, Amen

between us buildings
I held the word   ribbon
as my future,
as an undoing of bulk

now that it's happening
ribbon   ribbon   ribbon

all I feel are the edgelands of type
my home in the printer's offcuts

In the poems, Lut is a complex construction, both hopeful and defeated, reborn and weighted, witty and inarticulate, contradictions spurned from glimpses of his historical character. My aim for 'Lut Lut Lut' is to open up these contradictions of his relationship with language, pairing them with the beauty and disappointments of Cockington's pastoralism. He spent most of his time away from home and his wife, and although he was ever distrustful of words, they were, at times, all he had to maintain his marriage. The Royal Institute of British Architecture hold the nearly five thousand letters between him and his wife, detailing the moments of tenderness, frustration and misery that span a life. Crucially, I do not propose any new understanding of his history or artistic ethos, and any 'original' insights into his character should not be taken as historical suppositions. Instead I propose a future for the man and his texts, with a new Cockington as the perfect playground.

Lutyens died in the early hours of New Year's Day 1944, surrounded by designs for buildings never to be realised, and this collection of pages laid out in 2020 have formed from a splinter of his life among the scattered archival and published texts I have forced together. A young and idealistic lover speaks to his future failings as a husband and the heartbreak of a world abounding in ugliness. The pre-articulate urge for beauty is bogged down in the limitations of language as the stubborn designer in Lutyens ages into the rambling president of the RA softened into saying "we must be our own poets". [2]

My drifts took on a documentary landscape. His life, sketched out in biographies and scraps of book introductions, newspaper articles and personal letters, is riddled with complications and confusions. He was an imperialist and a humanist, a patriarchal Edwardian and a radical designer. The more I researched, the less I knew about him, but the more I realised the fragility involved in curating a life. The truth was that there was no singular Lutyens. The archives store a life glimpsed in haste, in postscripts, marginalia and the textual off-cuts never intended for posterity. I was reminded of Smith's idea of an *Anywhere*:

> In place of Utopia arose the idea of 'anywheres'... the very unevenness of what has been explored, the bittiness, the unsatisfying half-interwoven, the tangle, the dissipation, these all began to seem hopeful, even utopian in an unutopian way, when subjected to wandering (Smith, 2017: Loc. 2267).

My wandering around the village influenced my wander around the RIBA archives. I requested boxes almost at random, noting down striking

---

[2] Quoted in Hussey (1953: 560). From a letter to fellow architect Sir Herbert Baker.

language from Lutyens, his wife, friends, and colleagues. I took time to feel the aged documents, sift through his typos and doodles, noting contradictions and disparities. On the back of the designs for Cockington's utopian extension is a floating eastern dome. In his correspondence regarding Liverpool Cathedral is the extraordinary and unexplained line "The Devil Comes Lutyens" (more on this later). Between the boxes detailing the geometric sophistry of the sombre and iconic WW1 Thiepval Memorial and Cenotaph are the pages of P&O Cruise logos morphed into colourful tigers and comic designs. Among his intimate love letters are doodles of googly eyes and figures peeking above the text. These details of his life can only be encountered through wandering through the RIBA catalogue. I had read through the numerous biographies and studies of his life and work, all attempting some kind of coherent narrative of the man himself. But here in the archives I could feel a sense of closeness to Lutyens' life precisely because of its fragmentation. I was struck by the parallels of my walks through Cockington. The disparate nature of the archives forces you to drift across time, leaping through papers that may bear little relation to one another. There is no singular narrative, just as Cockington was a weave of competing places layering and re-laying a sense of place, the archives were the scattered odds and ends of stories. Returning to the quote above, the collection started resembling an 'anywhere', valuing a juxtaposing and awkward weaving together of Cockington's pastoral dreams and excepts from Lutyens letters and Cockington's archival documents[3]:

Expanding on the approach of "layering" a landscape, Smith encourages us to seek out the structures of place by disassembling the "already fragmenting evidence, seeking meaning in texture, grain, minutiae, details, marginalia and etiquette" (2017: Loc. 7993). A "layering" approach to landscape values a hypersensitivity to the everyday, in my case, a zooming in of the language of disparate archival materials. In 'Lut Lut Lut's' case this becomes a questioning of the accuracy of words. I became obsessed with the sound and feel of certain pastoral words. Meadow. Green. Brook. In the poems, we would hold these words up as words, neither condemning but nor fully believing them.

---

[3] In the case of 'As Coloured Yellow', text is lifted from document 4694Z/8, the 1946 sales brochure for the village, and a letter from Lutyens to his wife printed in Percy and Ridley's 1985 collection, p. 247. The extract refers to his time in India.

The question of craft remains. Why turn a man who distrusted words into a poet? For me, the answer was in the question. It was exactly this acute awareness of the slippery, ambiguous, even menacing nature of language that makes him already poet. He just didn't use words. Christopher Hussey, Lutyens' first major biographer describes him as a "poet in practice", his buildings being...

> such a union of visual harmonies, structural intricacies, overtones, fantasy and technical skill, that the result stirs in the beholder a spontaneous delight akin to that produced by a good poet by similar means (1953: 93)

43

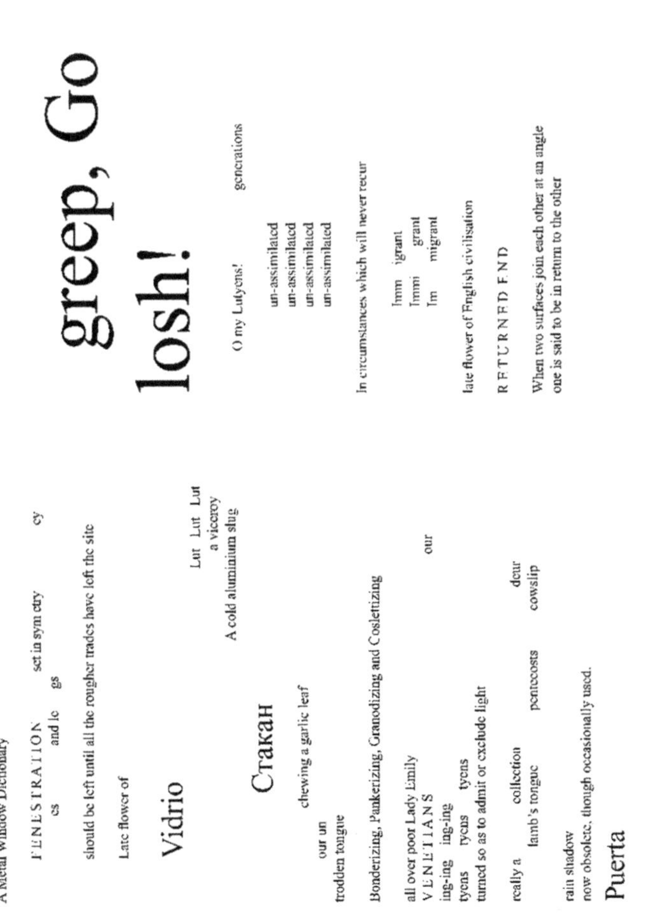

I began to realise that it was my own increasingly obsessive interest in Lutyens that was at the core of the project. I shifted even further from viewing him as a historical figure and positioned myself as part of his story, my poetic voice challenging and intermingling with his own. Unexpectedly, the man who "distrusted words and those who wielded them" (Brown: X) became a poet-mentor, questioning my own sense of poetics and art. Rather than just noting his bewildering personality mix of playfulness and anxiety, I needed to embed it into the form and tone of the writing. There needed to be more visual and sonic play, accepting that play can be a serious act. As his most recent biographer Jane Ridley commented, "There was something slightly desperate about Ned's clowning. Being a balding forty-two-year-old who refused to grow up wasn't easy" (2002: 200).

His archives and literature became more textual playgrounds than scholarly wisdom and I was drawn deeper into questioning my own sense of language, visual play and movement, culminating in the concept of the text as an ever-shifting landscape:

My drift extended to other texts and my search for language became a feature in the poetry. I plundered phrases from a number of craft books, the poem above taking phrases from *A Metal Window Dictionary*.

The poems are experiments of varying degrees, striking found text against found text in a way that further fragments their archival origins. The tension of the archives was in how it attempted to curate his life, and my experiences sifting through boxes and letters were a confusing mix of humour and minute human tragedy. In a box of letters (LuE/33/3/1-17) sent by Lutyens to the Canon Alexander regarding St Paul's Cathedral were phrases that reached across to my experiences of Cockington. There are no replies. Each letter features a nugget of questioning advice in the top left. One reads:

> it is at least a gain that
> we are beginning to perceive
> how small we are
>
> (12th December 1938)

The comment is without context and cast adrift from any details that may begin to explain it. I let this sense of a Lut character build or re-build from these fragments. The other letters follow this form, a nugget of wisdom tucked away in the top right. The lines are typed, with an inky heaviness on the 't's. My photos of them are zoomed in, the words presented as an island of text surrounded by white. One reads "Christianity, like art, is the apotheosis of the commonplace". Another: "parents will neither correct their children nor let them alone" and "it is the congregation that preaches the sermon quite as much as the preacher". And finally, "In times we ought to be listening to a still, small voice, we are deafened by the babble of the market-place." All these unwarranted gems of advice from a man who avoided language. In the early 1940s a typed line reading "From the Exor. Of the late", slips above the "From Sir Edwin L. Lutyens, O.M., P.R.A.".

There is also an unsettling distance. Lutyens was not really in the archives, but nor was he entirely in his buildings, his biographies or his grave, but somewhere between them, or simply nowhere at all. Lut was borne from this distance, the human tragedy that a life, a works, and a death have no solidity.

The Lutyens' letters became a lens by which to re-construct Cockington Valley, its topography and cultural histories, but also its future. Each poem is a gathering of splinters, curated to form a landscape around Lut, a figurehead for the hopes, dreams and disappointments invested in the land. I wanted a sense of a drift through place and space, the latter being that of the documentary fragments of the archives. Walking and stumbling across multiplicities began the project and eventually extended to the page, with the process of researching and writing the village being a narrative that runs alongside the more tangible written and experienced histories. It was important to engage with that multiplicity, to sneak in, but, at the same time, confuse my presence as author. The poems would not just be showing up different sides of this village, but they would form a village of themselves, a new Cockington made up of fragments of sources.

It was only by letting go of the village in the first place and allowing myself to be led, both by the living and the dead, that I was able to experience its multiplicities. The act of walking, moving forward with no definite destination, both through a geography and an archive, reminded me that the fragments of time and place are in constant motion. The past is unsettled by our traipsing through it, splintering off into that all-important future. This is the greatest lesson of my wanderings, recognising and following that 'ache for something special'.

References

Brown, J. (1997) *Lutyens and the Edwardians,* Penguin Books

Crittall, W. F. (1953) *A Metal Window Dictionary,* Curwen Press

Darley, G. ([1975] 2007) *Villages of Vision.* Revised Ed., Five Leaves Publications

Hussey, C. (1953) *The Life of Sir Edwin Lutyens,* Country Life

Percy, C. and Ridley, J. (1985) *The Letters of Edwin Lutyens,* Collins

Read, B. (2015) *Cockington Bygones,* Portcullis Publishing

Ridley, J. (2003) *Edwin Lutyens: His life, His Wife, His Work,* Pimlico

Smith, P. (2010) *Mythogeography: A Guide to Walking Sideways,* Triarchy Press

______ (2014) *On Walking,* Triarchy Press

______ (2017*) Anywhere, A Mythogeography of South Devon and how to walk it,* Triarchy Press

Venturi, R. ([1966) 1990) *Complexity and Contradiction in Architecture.* 2nd ed. Butterworth Architecture

'It started with a film and ended with a walk':

Walking as a creative emergency exit

Sam Christie

36°11'36.5"N 44°04'11.0"E Havalan, Erbil

At about 17:00 hrs on the 1st October 2016 I hung up the phone to the administrator of the language school I was working for and recognised that in two weeks, at the end of the Eid holiday, I would quite possibly be the second NGO worker from Britain who would hold the dubious honour of being homeless in Erbil, Kurdistan. The first was a colleague from Hull (who had actually been homeless in Hull), who ended his contract sleeping in the airport waiting for his plane home. In Kurdistan, business was pragmatic and sometimes brutal, in this semi-autonomous region people had no time to mess about. Once your contract ended you were expected to leave the country. If you weren't practically engaged in the business of conflict, resolution or otherwise, you were an anomaly; here tourism simply didn't happen and *hanging about* was an oddity.

It is odd, however, that I did not particularly mind this flipped state of affairs, more pressing for me was the epic documentary I hadn't made in my three months living in Kurdistan, where surely a story existed. It was this I needed to return to the UK brandishing but unfortunately, after several months promising this filmic document that might at least contribute a little to peace in the Middle East, I had nothing much to speak of in the can.

Pacing around my recently emptied shared house in the mostly Kurdish district of Havalan in Erbil, I pondered how I could use my last two weeks (I had enough money for that) to filmically save the day. I had snippets of work: interviews, cutaways, half started documentaries, but nothing that cohered, nothing that would stand up to the rigorous dissection of my film scholar colleagues. Nothing I had tried had a narrative sufficient to develop into a recognisable, structured documentary. I was in the middle of what might be termed an *'art crisis'*. It was in light of this that I decided I would walk, and not just walk, but film my walk around the boundary of the city of Erbil. I could clearly see how I might disseminate this film. I knew there existed conferences and exhibitions that featured art through the optic of walking. I finally, and gratefully, screened the resulting footage at the Plymouth University 'Walking's New Movements' conference in 2019. In some way my decision had been the right one, but I want to reflect in this essay on why it was, or rather why did I walk? Was it so I could use my tendency as a documentary filmmaker, as described by Stella Bruzzi as "that dangerously unstructured instinct" (2000: 101) to propel me into the world to encounter what might be there, much as Jean Paul Sartre suggests when he says, "It is not in some hiding place that we will discover ourselves (or anything); it is on the road, in the town, in the midst of the crowd, a thing among things, a human among humans". (1947: 3) Or did I walk in order to cash in cynically on walking/art as practice and package my film as 'Middle Eastern psychogeography' or something along those lines?

It could be argued that I originally travelled to the semi-autonomous region of Kurdistan because of a certain compassion fatigue generated by Facebook. Social media in 2016 (the middle of the ISIS crisis in Iraq and Syria) seemed alive with rhetoric about refugees and I decided rather impulsively to actually contribute by using my language teaching qualification to lend a hand in person. In honour of my self-deprecating subtext in this essay, however, I must confess that having recently completed a PhD around documentary and climate change, indeed in this context I had created a documentary about climate change that relied on encounter to uncover some sort of truth, I felt driven to show myself as a genuine documentary filmmaker by making a film in a conflict zone. The difference here was that at the time of making my PhD film, no one on the coast of Wales was being killed. It was easier than expected to find myself a mere 40 or so miles from ISIS lines, living in a place that elicited considerable interest from my connections on social media. My day job out here was teaching IDPs, a rather clinical acronym standing for 'Internally Displaced People', who came from all over the Middle East; I taught Iraqis, Syrians and Kurds. I taught people from all socio-economic backgrounds, all affected, mostly brutally, by the nearby conflict.

36°11'28.2"N 44°00'33.1"E Citadel, Erbil

The fear of zapping is becoming universal (Virilio, 2000: 126)

The decision to walk meant I had to walk something. At least for me this signified a "twin impulse… to push random events into a narrative, a structure, a logical form" (Bruzzi, 2000: 101). In truth perhaps I could have taken a map of Mosul and walked Erbil according to that, perhaps one of my hometown of Southampton? I could create a palimpsest of multiple geographies, hoping that within this a narrative might emerge on the screen. In the end, rejecting more radical psychogeographical tactics, I decided to walk the circular road known as 100 Metre Street. Erbil is constructed from the centre outwards in concentric circles of roads. The centre of Erbil (said to be the longest inhabited city in the world, at around 6,000 years) is known as the Citadel, claimed by the Kurds as a great embodiment of their own endless struggle, but more likely of Assyrian origin. From the Citadel the roads that circle it open outwards towards the penultimate road known as 100 Metre Street. My theory, albeit sacrilegious, was that by following my infrastructural filmic structure (a road), whatever I filmed along the way would stand some chance of cohering in the cutting room. From my room in Havalan I decided this. I rationalised the thesis of my documentary, hoping that the empirical evidence captured by the lens would in the end agree.

No one in Erbil seemed to know the length of 100 Metre Street, also known as Qasi Muhammad. The 100 metres, of course, refer to its width. Those from whom I managed to elicit estimates gave wildly differing numbers. These varied from 4 to 40 kilometres, but after some research I narrowed it down to 25. In reality the length didn't matter to most people as they recognised this workaday route as a place of transit requiring little attention. The only people who might need to know its length were engineers or town planners, or those like me who wanted to walk it over the Eid holiday. My decisions already bothered me and I recognised that I wasn't so much interested in what I might discover, but much more concerned with completing the mission. The danger here was that the mission itself would become the film. In the Middle East many western filmmakers, journalists and NGO workers (who were often young ambitious western European gap year students) had certainly been using the place and its tragedy as a rung on the ladder. Dromology was breathing down necks. Instagrammed wars and hastily blogged, vlogged and logged copy had become the new race and some, like James Foley and John Cantlie had suffered as a result of it. As Paul Virilio summarises,

The new 'theatrical representation', characteristic of the perspective of the time of the acceleration of the real and its *relief,* attempts uneasily to react to the *hurried presentation* of events by the media of mass communication, all of which favour the 'scoop' and the 'sound-bite' over the narrative and its unbearable '*longueurs*'. The aim is to avoid at all costs the remote-control handset coming into play. That sudden *symmetry-breaking* between transmitter and receiver' (Virilio, 2000: 126)

Of primary concern to me, in moments of lucidity up on the roof of my house, was that I had firmly joined the scramble for attention in the conflict zone, laying aside the stark reality that it is precisely this '*longueurs*' that was required to decode the complexity laid before me in the city of Erbil and that, in a modern media landscape, would never do.

36°11'07.8"N 44°02'50.7"E Havalan, Erbil

Havalan, where I had lived for longest while in Iraqi Kurdistan, was in the eastern area of Erbil. Not many Westerners lived here, indeed our teachers' house sheltered the only four Westerners here, I'm certain. Havalan is dominated by two things: the most dominant was the white monolithic Majidi Mall, which, springing from the sandy scrub and lit from all sides, dominated the landscape, perhaps mainly due to its totally incongruous marble-esque-ness. As with anything special in Kurdistan, and doubtlessly Iraq in general, it was gated – hived off from the workaday realities of this residential district. The second Havalan landmark was the then President of the western Kurdistan region Marsoud Barzani's failed Mega Mall. All that existed of this huge attempt at shopping paradise were foundation columns. These columns, recalling the 'Memorial to the Murdered Jews of Europe' in Berlin, jutted out of the ground ready to balance the car parks, escalators and retail spaces above. It was possible to decipher the final look of the building with judicious use of the squint and the block plan of the columns. This failed space, stalled after the 2009 financial crash and resulting increase in sectarian conflict nearby, could arguably be considered Barzani's Tower of Babel, as one unifying language in Erbil appeared to be the *joy of buying things.* As the monstrous mall began reaching into the heavens, as if to declare the establishment of a unification of Kurdistan through financial ostentation, so the global financial crash followed, the God of Lehmann brothers tapped Barzani on the shoulder, and shortly after that the Arab Spring, mobilised IS/ISIL/ISIS.

Havalan had reached as far as Majidi Mall and got no further, but this in itself was surprising and exemplified contradictions which became all too obvious to the observer. Kurdistan, a profoundly Islamic place, hinted at Western disapproval, a place where Imams warned vigorously in the noisy Mosques, however, the most popular activity here seemed to be spending money. The popularity of the mall was not entirely down to the air conditioning (which was both extremely welcome and efficient) but it exemplified the well-rehearsed idea of the universal motive in people the world over which appears to be the desire to consume. Here, however, the mall did not conceal its purpose. In juxtaposition to the mosque it existed pragmatically to perform the function of pleasure, as much as the mosque existed to perform the function of repentance. In truth, however, the malls across Erbil stood out because, as yet, the city had not yet embraced the 360° spectacle of the modern Western city, where we expect our respective landscapes to sell us something.

36°11'38.3"N 44°02'37.8"E Koya Road, Erbil

> In societies where modern conditions of production prevail, all of life presents itself as an immense accumulation of *spectacles*. Everything that was directly lived has moved away into a representation (Debord, 1967: 1)

Leaving Havalan after passing by the Majidi 'box', I passed other half-constructed buildings, abandoned as if frozen like bank accounts. Some of these had been taken over by displaced families. It was easy to spot the ones that had been hastily repurposed as temporary homes by the UNHCR tarpaulins that covered the gaping openings where doors and windows should be. These precarious coverings hid bare light bulbs and huddled people. It was possible, without being too intrusive, to notice the movements familiar in front rooms the world over. I pause, of course, and switch on my camera and consider my options. I want to film them, but know they would never agree. There could be many reasons for this, many that I may not understand or know. I do, however, know that somehow, especially given the fact that I have not *even one* formulated reason to film them, that it wouldn't be right. What am I likely to learn anyway, what would be the point of this meaningless invasion other than capturing something that I was simply *supposed* to film? Here it occurs to me that I wonder if them filming me in their scenario may actually be more interesting as I recalled John Berger speaking of the poor and storytelling,

> The secret of storytelling amongst the poor is the conviction that
> stories are told so that they may be listened to elsewhere, where
> somebody, or perhaps a legion of people, knows better than the
> storyteller or the story's protagonists what life means. The
> powerful can't tell stories: boasts are the opposite of stories, and
> any story, however mild, has to be fearless; the powerful today
> live nervously. (Berger, 2007: 95)

Documentary production is haunted by the pre-formed thesis. The commissioning editor asks to know what a documentary 'will look like' before the camera is out of the bag. In Erbil this pre-formed thesis is on endless repeat among endless journalists and filmmakers. Outbound the bandwidth is stuffed with **war** and **migration**. Journalists who attempt Iraq lifestyle pieces, do this in theatrical juxtaposition with war. #everydayIraq is defeated as a concept in its misunderstanding that Iraq, especially in 2014, simply couldn't be considered *everyday*. Clearly in such a complex place as Erbil, there is more than war and migration to be revealed, so could walking reveal it? How, for example, do these Internally Displaced People relate to the nearby Majidi Mall, or Barzani's folly? What do they think of Havalan, of Erbil, of Iraq or perhaps the world? Surely an encounter through walking should give back more? Surely walking, as he'd always argued, might make sense of Guy Debord's spectacle and neutralise it through its unearthing? At any rate, these IDPs, crammed into makeshift shelters, should not be spectacles. "The images detached from every aspect of life fuse in a common stream in which the unity of life can no longer be re-established. Reality considered *partially* unfolds, in its own general unity, as a pseudo-world *apart*, an object of mere contemplation." (Debord, 2010: 1) As I walk past these makeshift places of sanctuary, I not only wonder how long they will serve their purpose, but also how my encounters with them might serve to dissolve the gaze they elicit.

36°11'42.7"N 44°02'32.7"E Peshawa Qasi, Erbil

However misguided it might be to attempt to promote an everyday Iraq, or an everyday Kurdistan, the fact remains that there are many everyday things about the city. Inflatable toys seem popular in Kurdistan. Paddling pools and plastic dinosaurs are on sale on many of the streets. These peculiar improvised stalls (basically scattered blown up swans or dolphins) seem entirely out of place in a city so far from the sea. Here in Erbil water is scarce and owning it a matter of staying alive. In an area so troubled by conflict, these inflatables act as a reassurance that everyday life is still here; they have the ability to allow many of the harrowing tales that abound to remain buried for a while. Walking in Erbil reveals a tension between normality, for certain this place is normal, but also, often due to the presence of a gun or military vehicle, is extremely abnormal. American Blackhawk helicopters often, and all too suddenly, loomed low into sight, scatter these inflatables around, forcing the vendors to chase after them in the Blackhawk's wake.

Erbil is alive with white taxis. A record 55° Celsius heat meant that occasionally these cars would burst into flames as they sat in the direct and unprecedented sunlight. These soaring temperatures had never before been seen here and many blamed climate change. Erbil, which was after all a place of some trauma, seemed entitled to be exempt from climate change, but these exploding cars highlighted the fact that even though it be unfair, even though people here had been through quite enough, climate change, as universal as it is, would wreak havoc long after ISIS had gone. What appeared 'everyday' in Erbil actually served to highlight the extraordinariness of the place and the situation it had become pivotal in.

36°11'46.0"N 44°02'33.3"E 100 Metre Street, Erbil

Leaving Havalan and joining 100 Metre Street in the direction of Family Mall, I pass by the military shop in Gulan district. Here the Peshmerga (the Kurdish army – Peshmerga meaning 'towards death') stock up on supplies before heading out to the frontlines. This is no curiosity shop, unlike the army surplus places in the UK which have a tendency to *fetishise*. Here they sell real military hardware required to survive on a very active frontline. Peshmerga soldiers often go home after a day at the front, back to their families and, like they're going to work, drift back for another stint. Seeing soldiers commuting to the frontline, stuck in hooting traffic, never quite added up. Here in the West we are shielded from these things through screens of varying sorts (until, outraged, we witness terrorism entering through a crack under our door). 'Our boys' *go off* to war returning with exotic, dislocated and impossible tales, but war in Erbil was as interwoven into everyday life as buying bread. You often saw openly carried pistols and quickly became familiar with the weight of an AK47 whether you liked it or not, because someone would hand you one at some point. Often it was possible to hear a burst of gunfire somewhere in the city, strange for a place so apparently secure and likely some practice fire or over enthusiastic celebration.

36°12'34.5"N 44°02'41.3"E Family Mall, Erbil

Family Mall is an enormous, temple-like building on 100 Metre Street. The Erbil experience revolves around malls. In these places you can more or less have anything you want, from a night at the cinema to a new designer outfit. For the homesick Westerner, the air-conditioned vaulted halls and familiar high street outlets provided relief, but for one thing, booze. My colleague was temporarily barred from entry once as he had drunk an excess of whisky – trapped at the metal detectors, the security staff banned him and his heavy scent as drinking here, of course, is Haram; guns can be left at the entrance to be picked up later.

36°13'08.1"N 44°02'21.4"E Berkot, Erbil

Generally it is illegal to film indiscriminately in Erbil. This walking film was probably the most dangerous thing I had done during my stay. President Barzani's palace at Berkot district was certainly one place not to film. The crossroads opposite the palace, where refugees gathered – to catch the attention of the president perhaps – was, however, photogenic. There was a mixture of filmic factors: soldiers, refugees, occasional armoured vehicles and Arabic sign. These intoxicating trinkets of trouble should not be filmed; indeed, there were signs. The story here could only be filmed in snippets, where permission could be found, and this was why I was walking and was perhaps why the outgoing reports from Western journalists seemed stalled on a feedback loop.

36°13'15.0"N 44°02'04.7"E Salhaddin Park, Erbil

There were open spaces in Erbil. Salhaddin Park apparently boasted a climbing wall, however, for some reason there was no access to the public. In the park old Kurdish hands – possibly one-time Peshmerga fighters – walked together in traditional dress. These parks, of which there were a generous amount across the city, gave a chance for respite and sometimes a break from the dust and heat. The existence of parks showed something beyond conflict, a promise of sorts; a level of care.

I was often confused by this subtext of kindness and peace. What was Erbil really about? Its identity was entirely skewed by the nearby war and, possibly more importantly, the concomitant migration. When Derrida states, "If we look at the city, rather than the state, it is because we have given up hope that the state might create a new image for the city". (2001: 6) it is as if here the reality is reversed. The state in Erbil had created this temporary image and the international community, globalised political decision making had created the conditions here.

While the idea of London is different to the idea of the UK, in Erbil it was tough to pick up the distinction. In a sense, Erbil was different to the idea of Iraq as much as it was Iran or even the USA. In my search for the city, additionally in contradiction to Derrida, I wanted to find the art galleries or museums of Kurdish culture but there were none. Erbil appeared to agree with Robins' definition of cities: "The nation, we may say, is a space of identification and identity, whilst the city is an existential and experimental place". (2001: 87) A city so full of diversity through adversity had not yet been given the opportunity to settle in order to express what was truly within it.

There are plans for a museum in Erbil, placed near the historic Citadel and designed by the US/Israeli architecture firm Studio Libeskind. They are waiting for stability to return to the region and for funding to be located before the project might begin, but it is easy to argue that the museum is exactly what the semi-autonomous Kurdish Regional Governorate needs for this stability. Unfortunately for Erbil and its residents, allies and 'outside' money are not guaranteed. Erbil is part of the precariat class of the twenty-first century, its future built on the contingency of conflict and expedience. Towards the end of my stay Trump was announced president; I watched his mouth moving on my hotel TV on Shoresh Street, recognising that this was not good news for the Kurds or the city.

36°13'26.6"N 43°59'58.6"E Ainkawa, Erbil

Ainkawa is the oasis of Western influence. It's the Christian part of the city. Next to the airport and jutting out onto the surrounding desert, this is where scores of foreign visitors live. The gated communities of Italian Village or English Village house anyone from diplomats, journalists, NGO workers or mercenaries. Nights out here can be interesting.

One evening I overheard a raging argument between an office-based NGO worker and a former US Marine turned logistician (who was often on local TV rescuing people in one suspiciously filmic event after another). They were arguing about who had been in Erbil the longest, but in fact I suspect they were arguing about who 'was the most real'. Observing from the side lines I had to conclude that in truth neither of them were.

36°11'24.8"N 43°57'46.7"E 100 Metre Street West, Erbil

The approach to the Mosul Road is a seemingly darker, more barren section of 100 Metre Street. Somewhat before the infamous road lies the University of Cihan, the main Kurdish university in the city. After Mosul University was partially destroyed by the Joint Task Force in a bombing raid to oust a supposed ISIS chemical weapons lab, Cihan remains one of the last higher education establishments in the region that teach through an Islamic optic. American Universities specialising in oil extraction, engineering and the English language are springing up all over Kurdistan. It is not a huge assumption to suggest that they are probably run by the CIA.

36°10'48.6"N 43°57'47.6"E Mosul Road, Erbil

It is odd to stand at the start of the Mosul Road going out of the city. It's even more odd that any cars turn down there. Only a matter of 50 or so miles down this road, the horrors of the ISIS-occupied Mosul unfolded. It is down this road that you'll find the frontline. Interestingly the streetlights at the start of the Mosul Road are unlit and cars disappear into darkness. They appear to be sucked into a void. In truth, standing at the start of the Mosul Road is horrifying.

Walking on from the start of the Mosul Road – which I barely filmed – I wondered how I could convey this horror in a film. Maybe this was the road to walk? Obviously to walk it entirely would result in certain death, but this road was *a* story. There was a narrative between Erbil and Mosul, from Kurdistan into Iraq. The Mosul Road was a straight line into the empirical. The Mosul Road was the documentary – for certain, the migrants' story (at least those migrants fleeing Mosul), was one about a precise distance from conflict and all that lay in between. 100 Metre Street was a circle and to walk it was to circumnavigate the story in a sense, to repeat the contradictions over and over again.

36°09'21.3"N 44°00'06.3"E 100 Metre Street South, Erbil

The final leg in the circle back to my home in Havalan went through the most Kurdish districts – Newroz, Majidawa, Mahabat and Badawa. All I could think here, away from the Western enclaves, the sharp suited mirror shade-wearing ghosts, the US embassy with broad shoulders of blast walls, the horrifying Mosul Road and the exposed airport, was how a sense of safety had returned to my mind. This comfort made me wish I could return to Iraq and the KRG to offer a simple thanks. I want to express my admiration for a people who took it upon themselves to protect all-comers and despite playing host to manipulators, magnanimously provided sanctuary in the city of Erbil. Perhaps the film I didn't find was the one that asked the Kurdish why they had done this? From my objective position in the UK upon my return, I couldn't shake the realisation that it may not be enough to simply be there and it's probably not enough to simply film *something*. There is an intention somewhere in the creative/professional process that might change everything and maybe what I should have done, maybe the best practice was, to simply *ask* what it is your subjects want you to say.

On one level I can take comfort that my plans, whatever they really were, meant I had at least something to say – or at worst recount – and that I had managed a film of some sort, but it troubles me that for the first time the conditions on the ground did not easily offer up anything. I can take the view of documentary filmmaker Richard Leacock when he states, "My obsession has been – and still is – the feeling of being there. Not of finding out this and analysing this or performing some virtuous social act or something. Just what's it like to be there." (cited in 'Documentary Is Never Neutral', 2008) I can claim to have achieved this on a walk which was like many others in many ways, but was an extraordinary walk none-the-less.

Full essay film 100 Metre Street available below with password: Erbil
https://vimeo.com/374959809

References

Berger, John (2007) *Hold Everything Dear: Dispatches on Survival and Resistance,* Verso

Bruzzi, Stella (2000) *New Documentary: A Critical Introduction,* Routledge

Debord, Guy (2010) *Society of the Spectacle,* Black and Red

Derrida, Jacques (2001) *On Cosmopolitanism and Forgiveness,* Routledge

'Documentary Is Never Neutral' (2008) Available at bit.ly/wnm133 (Accessed 20 Dec 2019)

Robins, Kevin (2001) 'Becoming Anybody: Thinking Against the Nation and Through the City', *City,* 5 (1), p.87

Sartre, Jean Paul (1947) 'Une idée fondamentale de la phénoménologie de Husserl: l'intentionnalité' in *Situations I* (Gallimard), trans. J.P. Fell

Virilio, Paul (2000) *The Information Bomb,* Verso

Chip Walks

Hilary Ramsden & Clare Qualmann

Art and food have a long history of intersections; from Alison Knowles 'Make a Salad' Fluxus score (1962) to Gordon Matta Clark's 'Food' (1972), Rikrit Tirivanija's 'Pad Thai' (1992) to Jorge and Lucy Orta's 'Hortirecycling' (1997), Ceri Buck's 'Invisible Food' (2008), to Company Drink's 'Going Picking' (2014). Food connects people; sharing in its gathering, production and eating enables the building of new knowledge and new understandings of place. These works also have in common the way in which they engage with people – beyond the role of audience – as participants who are central to the creation and realisation of the work; human relations and their social context (Bourriaud, 1998).

In this paper we give some background to the ongoing artwork 'Chip Walk' that operates through walking for, and with, food. We begin with the history of the work and chart its development from roots in East London where Clare is based, to a global spread, with a focus on Lesvos, Greece, where Hilary spends time. In each of these locations we consider what the Chip Walk does; how it connects with people, politics and place in a site-specific and political-timing-specific way. We conclude with a discussion around the potentials of walking art to connect people, place and politics as artivism.

The Chip Walk is an artwork that has developed over a number of years. It began in 2005, when, as part of a wider project entitled 'walkwalkwalk an archaeology of the familiar and forgotten' the artists Gail Burton, Serena Korda and myself, Clare Qualmann, found a chip fork. This was one of a number of found objects that formed the 'archaeology of the familiar and forgotten' of our subtitle. These things were gathered from the streets of Bethnal Green, Whitechapel and Shoreditch – the area of East London where we were living and working. The objects played a core role in our on-foot exploration of a part of the city that we felt was familiar – exploring and re-exploring to see afresh what we had thought that we knew.

In 2007 this one particular find, the chip fork, became the basis for a new branch of the artwork – an exploration of the postcode district of E8, just to the north of our core territory. We were invited by Transition Gallery, who had just moved to E8, to create a walk for their exhibition 'E8: The Heart of Hackney'. Although E8 bounded one side of our existing walk area, none of us knew the district well – the key point that we could think of was the chip shop on Broadway Market, and another on Kingsland Road.

From the late nineteenth century, fish and chips became a popular dish in the UK – with numerous shops serving the fried combination. Widely understood as a 'national' dish, fish and chips still hold an important place as a ubiquitous British foodstuff – available in pretty much every community that is sizeable enough to sustain a fast food business. Although the fish element of the food – usually taken away to eat in a paper wrapper – is now relatively expensive, a bag, or 'poke', of chips is still a very cheap, quick and easily available food stuff.

Our exploration of E8 mapped every chip shop. We specified that these should be 'traditional' chip shops, those making thick cut chips from potatoes – rather than the 'chicken shop style' skinny chip or French fry, often made from reconstituted potato (for example those served in Burger King or McDonalds). We mapped them by walking, starting out at a known chip shop and buying a bag of chips, then walking and eating until we found another, or until the chips ran out. Over a number of weeks we used this method to locate every chip shop in the area, walking and eating and walking. We created a chip shop map, and two custom chip paper wrappers – one with chip stories, and one with chip facts – and we persuaded the chip shops to wrap their chips in these for the duration of the month-long exhibition at Transition.

As we walked and ate and mapped the chip shops – talking to the owners and the people who worked in them along the way – we began to consider the shifting food map of the area as an indicator of the gentrification that was then in its early stages. One chip shop on our route closed down during the period between the mapping and the public tour that we led. As a London borough Hackney in 2005 was experiencing rapid change, with the introduction of new transport routes opening up previously difficult to reach areas, and dramatic improvements in the state education system. The resulting gentrification was pushing out low-rent businesses, like chip shops, as craft brewers, sourdough bakers, vegan cafes and cocktail bars began to appear.

The Chip Shop Tour of E8 took a group of around 30 people on a walk, stopping at each chip shop to buy and eat chips. The tour involved participants in discussions about food, what we want to eat, where and when. We talked (informally and conversationally) about our memories of food - our favourite regional variations in chip shops – and the chips of our childhoods. We discussed the combinations of chips with other national cuisines – for example Chinese restaurants like Ming Hai and The Golden Star on our route that serve Chinese dishes alongside fish and chips. What quickly became apparent is that chips are a lens through which to explore a place – a lens that brings into focus food cultures, changing demographics, regeneration, and the interconnecting threads that spread out from those factors.

In 2014, when developing the content for the book *Ways to Wander* (Qualmann and Hind, 2015), I (Clare) revisited the chip shop walk, restructuring the concept as an instruction for anyone to use. It instigated a revisiting of the project through multiple locations, using the bag of chips as a tool to explore the places that walkers were in – and it was this translation that has led to my collaboration with Hilary.

Hilary's walking and theatrical practice of clowning both involve interruptions – of assumptions and expectations, of logic and habit, of seriousness and play and of everyday movement and all these elements are linked. For her the Chip Walk is a further interruption in an intentional everyday kind of walk and one that brings together people around a common purpose, buying and eating food; and noticing and perhaps discussing in some depth the surrounding environment might happen almost as an aside, in a deceptively easy and simple way. In this way the chips might be considered almost a playful misdirection, in magician's terms, where other issues emerge almost by chance, through incidental conversations, imaginings, local knowledge, the re-surfacing of memories and the periodic attention to surroundings as the Chip Walk moves on.

A bag of chips happens to be one of my (Hilary's) favourite foods: my mother used to make fantastic chips and I make sure I get to know the best (a personal opinion, of course) chip shops wherever I live. The story of my connection to Lesvos is too long to go into here but it is enough to say that on Lesvos and in the village of Skala Eresos, almost every restaurant makes their own homemade chips. This was a most delicious revelation to me and one of many reasons when early in January 2018 when Blake Morris asked for people to accompany him during his year of working and walking through the artworks in the book *Ways to Wander*, I naturally chose the Chip Walk; he happened to be walking it on my birthday, in August, and I would be on Lesvos – what better way to celebrate than to go from restaurant to restaurant in Skala Eresos eating chips.

During that spring and summer questions to do with resilience and sustainability also started to emerge as I worked with Cookie Arnone, an artist-activist who was coordinating different kinds of projects, from building a women's centre to organising paper and paint for arts workshops at One Happy Family (OHF), a resource day centre for refugees in Mytilini (capital of Lesvos). OHF is a long but walkable distance from Moria Camp and is organised largely by refugees themselves with support from European NGOs. Resources include support from medical doctors and lawyers as well as a café, shop, play area, and large space with tables for eating a free lunch made by the refugees themselves, room for sitting and talking, sockets for charging mobile phones, a school room, workshop space and a developing garden area where food for the kitchen is grown. All these have been organised and built from scratch by refugees and volunteers. The theatre work and puppetry I was making with adults and children at OHF was a tiny part of this network of creating sustainable activities and projects that would build resilience in an arguably hostile and inhospitable situation. Resilience in a sense of creating the "capacity to retain a degree of integrity, self organization and self awareness by engaging a process of finding value in the constant flux of everyday life." (Douglas, Fremantle, Delday: 2004). Situations where people can regain or find this resilience become crucial in these life and death circumstances and creating and participating in artworks offer such opportunities. Felski suggests we might begin to do this by "addressing the practical and experiential logic of everyday modes of orientation rather than seeking to transform or transcend them" (2002: 617). Thus a familiar walk with additional elements took root as an idea.

So what, then, was my birthday Chip Walk with Blake? It felt frivolous and strangely irresponsible: I became increasingly uncomfortable with the idea that I would be walking small distances between eating places in Skala Eresos, getting food easily, celebrating with friends whilst not that far away in Mytilini people would be walking eight kilometres from the Moria refugee camp to the not-for-profit taverna, Home for All, for a free evening meal. It might be the only meal of the day for them in a camp filled to more than four times its capacity and where a two-hour wait for sub-standard and sometimes inedible food was the norm. Moreover, it is still the norm that many people all over the world walk miles to get food and water each day.

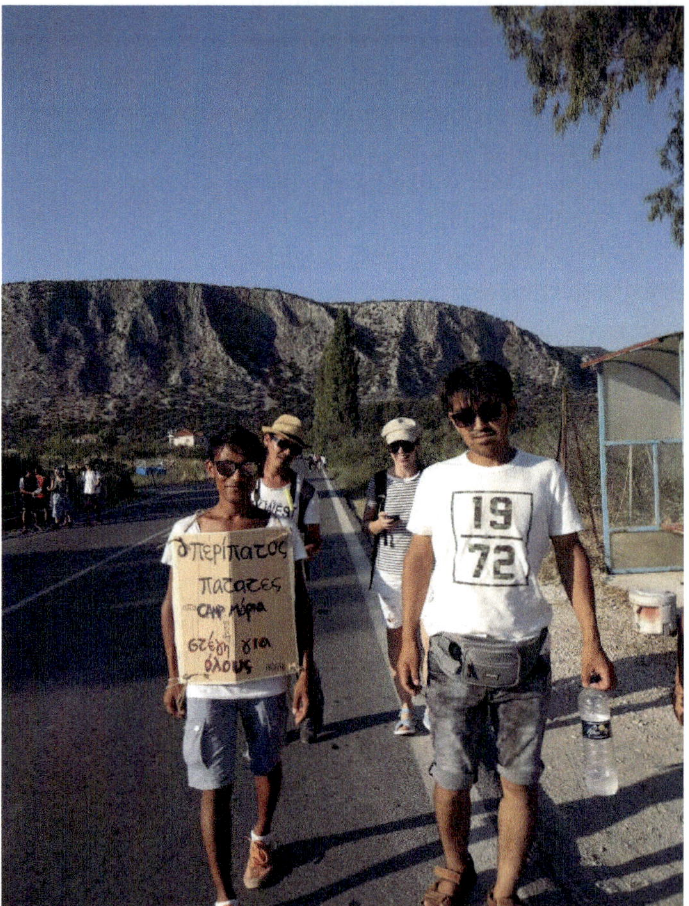

Chip walkers with sign 'Chip Walk from Moria Camp to Taverna Home for All', August 2018, photo: Hilary Ramsden

To highlight this fact and to continue to raise awareness of the desperate situation for refugees in Moria camp, I decided I had to walk a different kind of Chip Walk. I collaborated with Cookie to organise a Lesvos Chip Walk to start at Moria camp and end with a free meal at Home for All. There was a chip van just outside the gates at Moria camp where I could buy us chips at the start of the walk then there would be food at the end of the eight kilometres at Home for All. We advertised the walk and asked people to join us; it would be hot and dry, but we received enthusiastic responses and started out with 62 walkers, refugees, asylum seekers and NGO workers and volunteers from all over the world: from Afghanistan, Syria, Iran, Tibet, Greece, UK, France, The Republic of Congo, the Netherlands, Germany, many of whom had crossed the sea in tiny plastic rafts to Lesvos from Turkey.

People were so enthusiastic to start the walk that they left before the chips were cooked. Three of us waited to get four large portions of chips, more as a token to symbolise the essence of the walk than anything else, because even when we caught up with everyone people did not attack the chips with the gusto that I have come to expect from UK chip eaters. By contrast, the chip brooches I had made from cutting up yellow car sponges were much more enthusiastically received and worn. These were my attempt to document and add a further aesthetic aspect to the walk, where "Metaphor can shine light on particular aspects of an issue, make unexpected depth visible, or bring into focus what is yet unclear or previously unexplored" (Korza, Assaf & Bacon, 2003:7). For it was important to me that the walk was still an artwork as well as an activist intervention and making sponge chips was just as important a part of the process as buying the hot chips from the van outside the camp gates.

The walk gave each of us a chance to walk and talk with different people, at different paces and at different levels of engagement. Some people were already friends, some worked together, had become friends in the camp or had crossed the sea together. All wanted to engage in conversations and discussions – many about family, about their situation in the camp, about their desires and dreams for the future – where they wanted to be and what they wanted to be doing: not living in the camp and not being sent back to where they had fled from. We were creating what Grant Kester (2004: 3) calls dialogic art where we take "the traditional art materials of marble, canvas or pigment" and replace them with "socio-political relationships."

Along the way we talked, introducing ourselves to each other, hopefully creating what Kester (2004: 6) suggests is "an open space where individuals can break free from pre-existing roles and obligations, reacting and interacting in new and unforeseeable ways."

We continue to conduct further iterations of this convivial and participatory artwork: In July 2019 there was a simultaneous Chip Walk in East London and in Prespes, Greece as part of the 'Walking Encounters

/ Walking Bodies / Walking Practices' conference. For 'Walking's New Movements' conference in Plymouth 2019 we conducted a shorter chip walk sampling chips around the Barbican area of the city, having discussions with chip shop workers and taking note of the regeneration of buildings and structures that has resulted in a particular mix of architectural transformations of the area. The chip walks forefront food as a lens through which to connect walking, urban regeneration, conviviality, migration and research methodologies for social change.

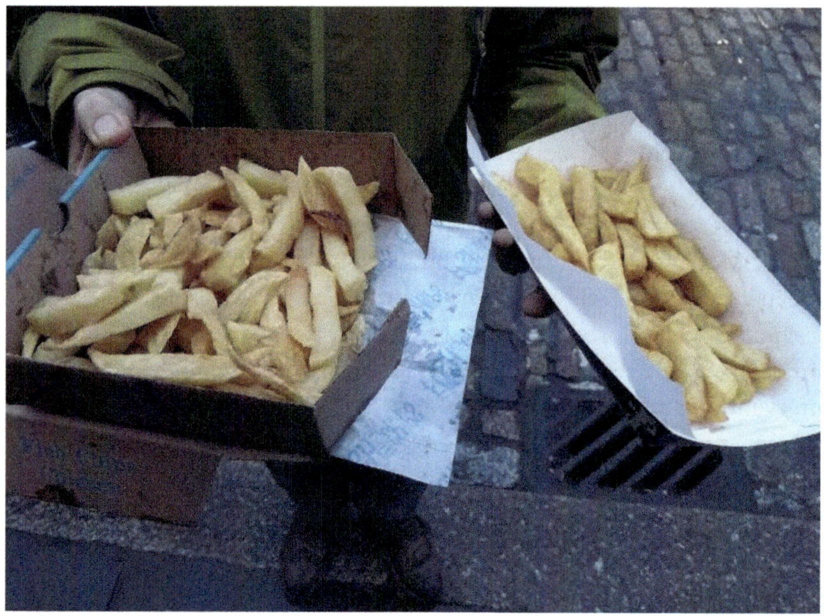

'Comparing chips in Plymouth', November 2019, photo: Clare Qualmann

These subsequent Chip Walks and the recounting of the Lesvos Chip Walk have enabled me (Hilary) to raise money (by selling sponge chips for €1 each) which I have been able to give to Home for All, contributing to the purchase of a pizza oven which now provides more free dinners for more refugees.

What further Chip Walks on Lesvos point to is the creation of a longer, continued story – not only of personal stories from the people in the camps but the creation of dialogue with others – in other places on Lesvos, beyond, to mainland Greece, to other countries and peoples in Europe where there is the potential to raise awareness and money, as well as to fight for justice through the legal systems for people seeking asylum and fleeing oppression.

"The challenge is to facilitate movement from 'my personal story' to a deeper understanding of collective implications, to a capacity for communication in a diverse public realm, to *civic dialogue*. From expressing to *being heard*, and in hearing in return. From sharing to *contributing*." (Americans for the Arts, 2003: 9)

Those of us who are lucky enough to be able to walk to the local chip shop to get food with money that we are privileged to earn easily must be able and willing to contribute time, money and energy to fight bureaucracy, to resist complacency and to go beyond our fear of the other in order to assist in making it easier for people to flee oppression and injustice and to live with respect and hope.

In this way the value of walking and talking (and in this case, eating) is a "kind of orchestration of voices, interests and exchanges that can illuminate issues, advance understanding and have a lasting, cumulative impact over time."(ibid: 10)

In London the rewalking of the chip shop tour of E8 revealed many shifts and changes in the food landscape of the East End. The first shop on the route – Broadway Fish Bar had a sign in the window saying closed for refurbishment – but the date given for reopening was April 2019, and we were walking in July. The Star Fish bar on Wilton Way has become Pidgin – voted the UK's best restaurant in 2017. Ming Hai, the Chinese restaurant and chip shop was still intact, though closed for the afternoon. The Golden Star has been turned into residential space, the glass shop front removed and built over. Faulkners, the long standing 'posh chippy' on Kingsland road looked like it was closed in the gap between lunch and dinner but on closer inspection the dusty counter and littered floor suggest that the closure might be longer term. Slightly brighter news is that despite the closures of all but one of the shops on the 2007 route Sutton and Sons – a new 'posh chippy' has opened on Graham Rd – catering to new demands for vegan food options alongside the more traditional offer of cod and chips – and upscale menu items like lobster as well.

In London the gentrification that was in its infancy in 2007 is now full blown. Hackney house prices have risen by a staggering 568% in the last twenty years. Alongside this influx of wealth is a huge disparity in income, and many neighbourhoods within the borough score highly on the Indices of Multiple Deprivation. Food is not at the vanguard of this wave of change, but it:

offers a particularly visceral entry point into the politics and processes of gentrification. It is not just that humans must eat to survive. Food is an economic anchor for community development. Food is also culture. Food is therefore a proxy for social divisions and social cohesion. (Sbicca, 2018: 3)

The Chip Walk enables us to interrogate the commonalities of circumstances (people gathering together for simple, everyday activities of walking, eating and talking) and of disparities that exist in these worlds apart - between incomes, accessibility to work and housing, in addition to issues of gentrification, sustainable building and urban planning. The two main contexts that we have practised this work in; Lesvos and Hackney, are worlds apart, yet the action of walking and eating and talking, following a score for an artwork, creates in each location a temporary community with 'rich opportunities to engage people in the examination of issues of societal concern.' (Romney, 2005: 3).

There is also the element of repetition, the reiteration of previous walks, that also enables us as walk artivists to consider the similarities and and differences between walks. Repetition not being a means to subordinate individuality or uniqueness but rather a way of making sense of patterns of culture (Felski, 2002). Additionally, it enables us to look askance at our processes and methods, refining, re-interrogating our practices, in exchange with others.

References

Bourriaud, N. (1998) (2004) *Relational Aesthetics*, Les Presses du Réel

Douglas, A., Fremantle, C. and Delday, H. (2004) *The Dynamic of the Edge: practice led research into the value of the arts in marginal spaces* 'Sensuous Knowledges 1' international conference proceedings. National Academy of the Arts

Felski, R. (2009) 'Everyday Aesthetics', *The Minnesota Review*, Winter/Spring 2009 ns 71-72, bit.ly/wnm197 (Accessed 04 Apr 2010)

Korza, P., Assaf, A. & Schaffer Bacon, B. (2003) 'INROADS: The Intersection of Art & Civic Dialogue', in (Korza, P. & Schaffer Bacon, B. (eds), 2003) Available at: bit.ly/wnm195

Korza, P. & Schaffer Bacon, B. (2003) *Animating Democracy, Resource Guide for Community Arts Network*. Americans for the Arts

Qualmann, C. & Hind, C. (2015) *Ways to Wander*, Triarchy Press

Sbicca, J. (2018). *Food, Gentrification, and the Changing City*. 43. Available at: bit.ly/wnm196

Noble & King, Walking with Correspondence

Simon King and Corinne Noble

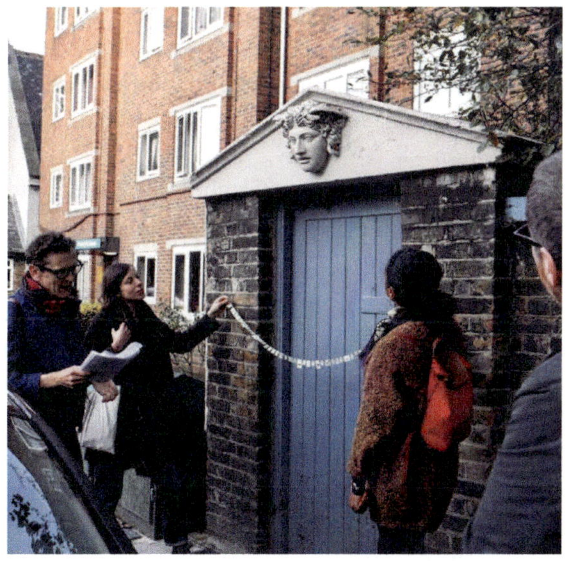

Medusa, Camberwell Correspondence

THE INTRODUCTION

I am a writer and researcher who since 2017, alongside my own practice, has worked collaboratively (as 'Noble & King') with the artist Corinne Noble.[1] The following is an account of how we incorporate literal and

---

[1] Unless otherwise indicated as the voice of Corinne Noble or the comments of participant walkers (both italicised), in what follows the 'I' refers to me and the 'we' / 'our' refers to Noble & King.

metaphorical correspondences in our walking – fragments of text including literary quotation, old photographs, reportage and, particularly in the last year, through the device of antique postcards – that have some connection to the urban locations we are walking through. It situates this too, within the broader context of the methodology that informs my own psychogeography-inflected and Walter Benjamin-influenced walking and writing practice; one in which returning to the same route over time allows each walk to act as a mechanism for excavating new knowledge.[2]

THE SNAPSHOT

> We can think about today's walk being not only just with ourselves, gathered here at our final stop, but also with others who we've met via some historical correspondences on the way. As these others join us and move with us, their words become part of a bigger conversation and our walking with them is like a form of inscription.
>
> (Our concluding remarks at 'Camberwell Correspondence')

The Medusa's gaze stalls history in the sphere of speculation. It short-circuits, and thereby suspends, the temporal continuity between a past and a present. This break from the present enables the rereading and rewriting of history, the performance of another mode of historical understanding, one that would be the suspension of both "history" and "understanding" (Cadava, 1997: 59-61).

In Benhill Road we walkers have paused in front of the walled garden Medusa centrepiece, handsomely mounted on its neo-classical pediment, the final stopping point of Noble & King's October 2019 'Camberwell Correspondence' walk for the London Art Licks Festival weekend. By serendipity, during one of our preparatory walks ahead of it, we had happened upon this somewhat incongruously located mythic figure in an otherwise nondescript side street in Camberwell, south east London. Such chance encounters – this, for me, a visual echo of Benjamin's 'Medusan' historiography (or historical materialism) – typically provide the materials for our group walks; materials which serve as literal and/or

---

[2] In 'Elephant Memory' (King, 2018: 249-266) for example, this returning revolved around questions relating to urban change and what happens to communities through migration, gentrification and city planning.

metaphoric devices and which allow us to reinforce a central conceit, the creation of an overarching narrative comprised of subjective thought processes and experiences with historical research; using quotes from published sources and private correspondence relating to pertinent social, historical and local histories which lead to a playful and convivial juxtaposition of thoughts, images and historical narratives.

THE 'STANDARD'

In respect of these elements, I seek to distinguish the walkers' possible experience of our form of tour-guided walking from more commercial and templated variants. I'm thinking particularly, for example, of the seeming boom in recent years of historical walks in Whitechapel.

From my field notes:

> A weekend late afternoon on Brick Lane, East London and I use my phone's camera to capture an image of a crocodile of tourists moving slowly in front of me in the direction of Bethnal Green Road. The pedestrians are clearly part of a guided tour as, in the foreground their leader, wearing what looks like a stove pipe hat and a Victorian-style cape, is shepherding them towards the next stopping point. Perhaps this will be to nearby Fournier Street, the site of a notorious murder in 1888, and, given his stagey apparel and the location, I assume this is just one of the many Jack the Ripper-themed walks you can pay to go on every day of the week.

Urban walking tours like this usually have certain key elements in common; you pay to go on them and they are led by someone in the role of an expert following a loosely scripted narrative and, in some way, performing it. Another presumption about such walks is that they are dependent on some additional knowledge held by the tourist-walker, whether this be about the Ripper and his victims, Virginia Woolf or Harry Potter. There is an implicit contract too, that in the main, the leader will talk and the walkers – save perhaps for questions drawing on the tour leader's knowledge and expertise – will listen.

Phil Smith is critical of this tendency for "standard" guided walks like this to be top down, non-participatory and performative, asserting that:

> They tend to be segmented and episodic, made up of static episodes punctuated by short walks, fragmented in narrative structure (one thing after another rather than interwoven) and

often without the kind of fully explanatory framing that might assist enquiring spectators in making independent critical judgements. [...] At their worst, they court and reproduce (sometimes by mirroring) their audiences' general preconceptions, sustaining (and sustaining itself with) ideologically inscribed binaries: us-now/them-then, heroes/villains, quotidian/historical, political-agency/ commercial-determinism. (2013: 104)

Smith's critique of the limitations of such guided walks – which I would summarise as their overly historicist and empirical framing – was a useful starting point for the reflections on a guided tour that Corinne and I went on in 2018.[3] We recorded our thoughts as part of a settling of what distinguishes our practice from walks like these. We were certainly attracted to the premise of the walk – that its leader, a professional actor, would lead us on a tour of London EC1, taking in its social and architectural history, through the device of speaking as if these events were unfolding around us. However, though not without interest, we found the overall experience missing something:

> SK: What I really like is this idea of the tour leader using the present tense to talk about the past – what grammarians of English call the 'historic present' tense – however, my feeling about the walk was that though it was the device that governed every stop, there wasn't a focus. It reminded me of those online images of London streets where you move the mouse left to right, right to left, and you see a street changing over time. It struck me as a bit of a gimmick.

> CN: *There's something in those time-travel images that excites me, but when I see the 'now', I'm thinking, 'so what?' In the same way on the walk, the message of 'then' being 'now' fell short. It strikes me there's more to be said, because I find myself wanting some speculation, some insight, some better device to spark the sensation of being transported, not just 'that' is 'this'.*

We agreed that while the tour leader was on top of the detail and was charismatic and entertaining, it felt as if he was performing a dramatic

---

[3] This was organised as part of the Royal College of Art's Walkative Society programme of walks and was free to join.

mystery (*"If you listen hard, you can hear the clatter of hooves on cobbles!"*) and what was really lacking was an element of dialogue and convivial participation from the walkers. I would concede that we (amongst the other walkers) did nothing to challenge this state of affairs, to perhaps open the walk up to speculation and what Smith (2013) calls the "significance of accidental and spontaneous encounters". It would have been interesting to see if the tour leader would have been receptive to this sort of unscripted intervention.

THE 'RADICAL'

> The city absorbs history, reflecting and deflecting the markers of power. (Benjamin, 1999: 518)

> What we try to do is find out what the story is, why is this ... here? What is the significance of ... that? In other words, we connect to material aspects of history in terms of the way people lived, the social conditions, and the politics of the time. (My reflections on the walk described on p.269)

A few weeks after the Plymouth conference Corinne and I meet to clarify what constitutes the 'radical' in our collaboration, particularly, as our proposal outlined, in respect of how our "walking with hand-held 'correspondence' including postcards, ... has prompted alternative histories to surface in familiar places and given rise to new talking points along the way." For both of us, the incorporation of 'alternative histories', particularly in the form of our speculations on the lives hinted at within the boxed confines of these antique postcards gives our walking arts practice a radical dimension in two key respects: firstly, our speculation about them is unique to us. Secondly, the discussions they generate on the group walks represent a radical shift from the hierarchical and literal mode characteristic of certain standard urban walks to a more democratic and lateral mode.

Walking with correspondence like this is also 'radical' because it lends itself to a historical materialist approach to viewing the past; one that, hopefully, avoids the historicist pitfalls of the standard tour Phil Smith skewers so acutely above. In connection to this, the Basque curator and writer Peio Aguirre provides an elegant summation of Benjamin's way of working which I think is also present in the way we like to work and walk, particularly that which characterises his method in the unfinished 'Arcades Project'. For Benjamin, to quote Aguirre, "nothing was ever attained as the result of a ritual of established steps that led towards a set goal, but rather through a procedure comprised of shortcuts, deviations, unconscious associations, labyrinths, turns i.e. anything that involved indirect thought processes." (Aguirre, 2000)

Corinne, when I ask her, causes me to think about 'radical' beyond its more usual political denotations and connotations. She makes a ready connection between the analogy of genealogical 'roots' and the botanical 'root' which provides 'radical' with one of its meanings. We talk about this idea of the radical in connection to her interest in antique postcards and her use of them in her artwork and our subsequent collaboration:

> CN: *The appeal for me was primarily the nostalgic element, and a certain printing quality (colour, scene) and furthermore in connection to ancestors who had once lived locally – as if these cards were a tangible link to their dwelling in a place in that era. In the first place my interest was in the pictorial view, but gradually the by-product of this would be gaining a puzzling postal address or personal message on the reverse. These incidental lines to other places and people took on a significance and triggered further questions.*

Corinne also identifies a radical (or innovative) dimension to our method in relation to the privileging of text over image and vice versa which occurs in some online transactions for antique postcards. That is, some sellers advertise cards on the basis of the address only (as a matter of 'genealogical interest'), others on the basis of the pictorial view. As she observes, this makes sourcing 'correspondence' not only on the basis of the image, but also, or separately, on the basis of the postal address alone, an innovative possibility for our research methodology.

THE METHODOLOGY

Whether through an initial drift (approximating to a way of walking the city suggested by Benjamin's (2003) gnomic "method as detour" or something more planned, we accrue research material in the form of personal, public and commercial artefacts including photographs, press reports, letters and antique postcards – the latter purchased by Corinne.

To unpack this a little more, Corinne and I brainstormed a list of methods or 'articles of faith', key components of the overall methodology, one that owes something too, to Benjamin's notion of literary montage[4] that have emerged over the last few years of our walking together. In no particular order of importance:

- We construct the narrative through iterative walking and gathering of historical fragments or annotations.

- We are like detectives when we walk and sometimes more like clairvoyants or mediums contacting past voices.

- We seek out palimpsestic traces.

- We draw upon literal and metaphorical connections – from semiotics we think in terms of 'address' 'anchor' and 'relay'.

- We arrive at this via a dialogic and accretional process i.e. through our joint mapping over time of an emerging and then mutually agreed final route.

- We consider ourselves researchers when we walk together like this e.g. documenting *before, during* and *after* the walking through image capture, notetaking, and online searches via smart phone, or, through the researching of published sources.[5]

- We use postcard correspondence collected by Corinne to somehow connect sender/receiver, word/image in time and space.

- We construct personal histories from the evidence available which become interdependent in our minds linking this to Rebecca Fortnum's evocative phrase "knowing without knowing" (Fisher & Fortnum, 2013) and what Phil Smith, in respect of mythogeography, calls "the bigger picture".

- We talk about these histories being in totality like constellations.

---

[4] "The method for this work: literary montage. I have nothing to say. Only things to show. I am not going to uncover anything precious or attribute to myself spiritual formulae. But rags and castoffs: I do not want to make their inventory, but allow them to obtain justice in the only possible way: by using them." (Benjamin, 1999: 460)

[5] For example, we have made particular use of the 1890s Charles Booth London poverty maps, the London County Council Bomb Maps, and Iain Nairn's *London* (1966).

- Our values include 'walker participation' and 'conviviality'–connecting these to what the artist Richard Wentworth (2016) calls 'mutual agency'.

- We believe that words depend on their past – etymologically stamped with what precedes them and their meanings interdependent.

- We like to be 'led' by our titles.

THE ADDRESS

'Commons & Corrections, SW2', was early arrived at following an initial 'drift' in Brixton in which our conversation, via the visible remnants of common land as we walked up Brixton Hill, turned to a discussion of land enclosure in the late eighteenth century and with it the forcing out of local land workers; a form of 'outlawing' that, by a series of lateral associations, linked to nearby Brixton Prison and remembering that this had originally been called the Surrey House of Corrections. As well as providing us with an elliptical and alliterative title and two key loci punctuating the eventual group walk, it provided a springboard too, for other lines of thinking including the inconsistent punctuation on Brixton street signs (a matter of 'correction' when noticing).

THE LABYRINTHINE

Our focus will be on how our participatory walks accompanied by handwritten antique postcards (c.1900-1920) evolve and take place. We will reflect upon how 'correspondence' is employed to prompt informal and critical exchange between ourselves and walk attendees; used to provoke chance discoveries and unexpected 'lines of enquiry', and how we study overt and covert relationships between sender and addressee, printer and illustration, origin and destination, intention and interpretation, language and thought to achieve these ends.

(Noble & King, Plymouth Conference proposal)

The lack of walker participation that Corinne and I felt was such a feature of the 'walking in the present' ambulation of EC1 is, then, something we are conscious of avoiding in our own group walks. We are, of course, aware of the tension between the commitment to the participatory experience of group walking and doing this within a tour format which might presume a form of leading. In our practice this leading – particularly at the key stopping points – has a number of performative elements: it is (to a degree) scripted, it is (to a degree) acted and it is (to a degree) stage managed. There is too, for me, a theatrical sense of *mise-en-scène* which includes props e.g. the antique postcards, and costume (usually an agreement about what we will both wear that in some way points to the theme of the walk). Thus, to ensure that this is opened up to spontaneity and conviviality, to the participant walkers' own 'chance discoveries and lines of inquiry', we share a number of tools and tactics with the participant walkers that draw from psychogeography, which in part serve as critical incidents or reflection *in* and *on* the walking. Two key examples: Federico Careri's list of actions – "a useful aesthetic tool with which to explore and transform the nomadic spaces of the contemporary city" – (2002: 19) and, particularly for this discussion, Tim Ingold's schema for experiencing the city as a labyrinth (2013: 8).

Careri:

To construct   relations   to wonder

(Walkers choose from a series of verbs and noun phrases set out in three vertical columns and comment on how these signify in the experience of their walk).

Ingold:

Labyrinth   Maze

(Intentional) Navigation   (Attentional) Wayfaring

'Tactical manoeuvring'   <De Certeau>   'Strategic navigation'

(Walkers sort between phrases that are ordered according to whether they reflect walking in a labyrinth or walking in a maze. They are invited to comment on to what degree the experience of the walk has been maze-like or labyrinthine).

Reading the feedback comments below from 'Camberwell Correspondence' I am struck by the flashes of observational insight mixed with the more personal and affective experiences of the participant walkers reminding me of what Tim Edensor calls a "suffusion while walking". They put me in mind too, of a phenomenological way of thinking – what one walker (K.L.) called, "a different way of being in the world", and to something I later jotted down in my notebook at the conference that reminded me of this, "walking is always shifting and in a state of becoming" (Bean & Lounder, 2019):

> AV-F: *This is the first walk I've been on, in which there felt a sense of the interconnectedness of us all, immersed in the landscape, which took us beyond the confines of Camberwell. The use of text combined with the physical activity of walking, linked to the stories within those texts evoked a palpable sense of the lives of ordinary everyday people through this shared experience of walking. As the texts were read aloud, the physicality of being in a particular place, the visual representation of the postcard, and the regional and/or informal language used in writing the card created a layering of meaning, which felt dynamic and active.* (Feedback from participant walker)

…

> KL: *Slowing down to an amble gave me another perspective – I noticed things usually overlooked, I listened actively, I became more aware of my body in space; a kind of mindfulness emerged that also allowed for more thoughtful conversations to arise – conversations not hell bent on arriving at a resolved end point, but that instead privileged an open speculation and playful enquiry and that collapsed a sense of time and space into interconnected layers. I considered how to think and observe like a tree or a brick or an architectural mould and how to sense through the eyes of a figure in a postcard – which produced moments of feeling outside of myself, of looking back from a non-human perspective at myself, at all of us … the postcards were haunting and the discrete leaving of a trace of acknowledgement at the bread shop to mark our attending, and playfulness of the bunting that connected you and Simon brought a light touch of ritual to the whole experience that left an impression.* (Feedback from participant walker)

…

This last comment about 'wormholes in time' causes me to think about how Noble & King consciously employ antique correspondence to act as portals into the past. How we do this requires a further mining.

THE EXCAVATION

"The private space within the postcard is brought into the public space of the street and the group." (Corinne Noble)

We think about how these postcards operate semiotically, we approach them forensically, we excavate them in each re-reading for further clues. I see this as a form of parsing in which we speculate on all the evidence about the lives of sender and receiver. As an exercise, we look through a selection of postcards we have used on the walks. All are handwritten, in some, for example, the appeal might be in the idiosyncrasy or Edwardian copper-plate elegance of the handwriting, in others the orthographic variation such as in spellings (*"Perhaps a matter of being written in haste or degree of education"*). We conclude that what is common to these affective and homely communications is their human connection and a palpable kind heartedness. They, as Corinne observes, *"have been passed from one hand to another."*

Employing a kind of discourse analysis, we list the common elements in this correspondence and notice the following. There is:

- (Nearly) always an address (*'Dear ...'*).

- (Nearly) always a farewell salutation.

- Often an enquiry after health.

- Often a summing up (*'should like a line from you ... leaving Sunday week'*).

- Usually an assessment of place (this more common to holiday postcards).

- Usually an account of activities e.g. the lonely mulberry postcard.

- Sometimes the image as integral to the message (*'On the other side are the ducks and swans you used to feed'* – the lake in Brockwell Park from daddy and mother to Rene).

- Sometimes a characterisation of someone the sender is staying with.

- Occasionally a coding (or our interpretation of it) e.g. physical – mirror writing in Brixton Road postcard – making it more difficult to read

- Occasionally an assurance – about not forgetting somebody or something.

- Occasionally a request or instruction (*'Dear S ... light the fire for me.'*).

We might also think of these hastily written messages as place holders or perhaps time holders for a more significant communication to come, we might too, feel a hierarchy of correspondence or an interdependence here.

We apply this analysis to our Plymouth postcard from 'loving Aunt A.S. to Master Harrold Bromidge'; it was purchased by Corinne on the basis of its view and destination. Relay-like,[6] the postcard also references our 'Commons and Corrections' walk in Brixton in early 2018.

THE PLYMOUTH POSTCARD

...street names must speak to the urban wanderer like the snapping of dry twigs, and little streets in the heart of the city must reflect the times of day ... as clearly as a mountain valley. (Benjamin, 1900/2006: 54)

On the front right-hand side, perpendicular to the image:

I expect you think the Hoe
better than the balcony at St Thomas's Hey? A.S.

---

[6] Informing our thinking about the content of a communication like this is Ingold's writing on the idea of correspondence as being "rather like a relay in which each participant takes it in turns to pick up the baton and carry it forward ..." (2013b: 105)

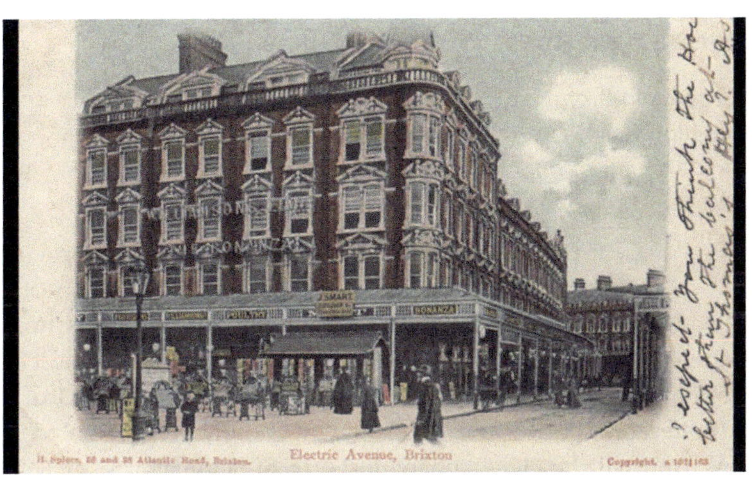

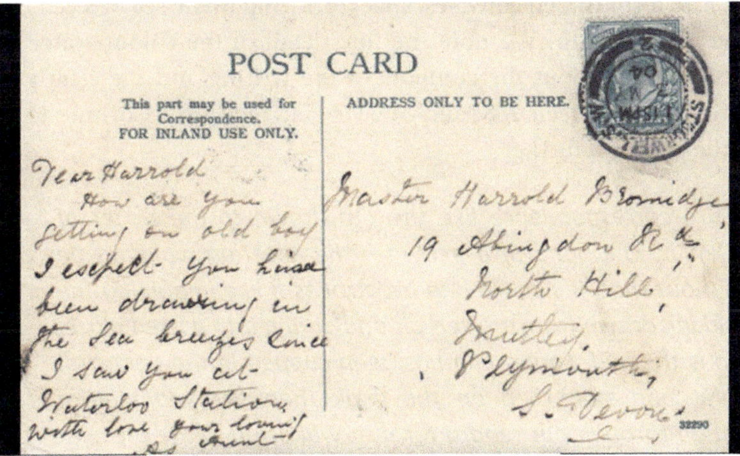

On the reverse left ('This part may be used for Correspondence'):

Dear Harrold
How are you
getting on old boy
I expect you have
been drawing in
the sea breezes since
I saw you at Waterloo Station
With love your loving
Aunt
AS

On the reverse right (the Address):

> Master Harrold Bromidge,
> 19 Abingdon Road,
> North Hill,
> Mutley,
> Plymouth,
> S. Devon

The postcard depicts what was then the Bonanza Provision Market in Electric Avenue, Brixton circa 1900. Further examination yields that it was sent from nearby Stockwell to Mutley, a district of Plymouth on 3rd May 1904. It references both a recovery from illness (not explicitly stated but we think from all the clues, tuberculosis) in St Thomas' Hospital, Westminster to a continued convalescence ('drawing in the sea breezes') on the Hoe in Plymouth. We note the fine detail of the colour-tinted image and speculate about the contents of the writing and the clearly warm relationship between A.S. and Master Harrold. I ask Corinne to scrutinise the postcard further:

> *In postcard correspondence like this I'm drawn to the traces of energy left by the hand of a person – the lettering wouldn't be there without that, it's charted in ink strokes. I like imagining the once fluid ink drawn from a reservoir and drying into a fixed place. The card is the bed. Something has been cupped in the postcard, held quiet and still, then on the walk there's a moment of reactivation through our regard for it, it wakes up in the present. Characters revive as their messages are read, repeated and shared – they're passed on again, relayed and regenerated. They have a real hand in where we take our walks and what's said.*

THE FUTURE WALK

Finally, we loop back to the Benhill Road Medusa and "what was frozen until we touched it again"; a "sphere of speculation" to do with how we phenomenologically experience the words and images in these affecting correspondences and why we use them to animate and reanimate those that walk with us. With this in mind, the walk will be a recuperation in two senses; the physical recuperation of 'Master Harrold Bromidge' and the temporal and spatial recuperation of the postcard from its temporary lodging in the stock of a philatelist. We propose a walk that could take

place in 2020 that connects London and Plymouth (between St Thomas'
Hospital, Westminster and the Hoe, Plymouth) over time – 1903, 1940
and the present day. An early foray has been made, a line of thinking
pursued and a modest proposal will follow.

References

Aguirre, Peio (2000) *Methodologies.* Available at: bit.ly/wnm198 (Accessed:
13 Nov 2019)

Bean, Robert & Lounder, Barbara, (2019) 'Breathing-in-the-Unbreathable',
paper for Walking's New Movements, Univ. of Plymouth

Benjamin, Walter (1900/2006) *Berlin Childhood Account* (trans. Howard
Elland), Belknap Press of Harvard Univ. Press

______ (1999) *The Arcades Project,* trans. Howard Eiland and Kevin
McLaughlin, Harvard Univ. Press

______ (2003) 'Epistemo-Critical Prologue' in *The Origin of German Tragic
Drama,* trans John Osborne, Verso

Cadava, Eduardo (1997) *Words of Light: Theses on the Photography of
History.* Princeton Univ. Press

Careri, Francesco (2002) *Walkscapes,* Editorial Gustavo Gili

Fisher, Elisabeth & Fortnum, Rebecca eds. (2013) *On Not Knowing: How
Artists Think,* Black Dog Publishing

Ingold, Tim (2013a) 'Foreword' in *Walk On – From Richard Long to Janet
Cardiff: 40 Years of Art Walking,* eds. Cynthia Morrison-Bell and Mike
Collier, Art Editions North

______ (2013b) *Making: Anthropology, Archaeology, Art and Architecture,*
Routledge

King Simon, 'Elephant Memory', *The Journal of Writing in Creative Practice*
(2018) 10.02: Parallel Urbanisms. Intellect

Nairn, Iain (1966) *London,* Penguin

Smith, Phil, (2013) 'Walking-Based Arts: A Resource for the Guided Tour?'
Scandinavian Journal of Hospitality and Tourism, Vol. 13, No. 2, 103-
114, http://dx.doi.org/10.1080/15022250.2013.796223

Wentworth, Richard (2016) *Making Do and Getting By,* Koenig Books

Chasing Mists: walking to scent and sense the atmosphere of the Hoo Peninsula

Anna Sanders-Falcini

Do places have atmospheres and if so, how do they manifest themselves? Atmospheres by their very nature are hard to pin down. As the philosopher Gernot Böhme has suggested, atmospheres are by their nature, diffuse, not always easy to locate and "seem to fill the space with a certain tone of feeling like a haze". (1993: 11).

I have been chasing the atmosphere of the Hoo Peninsula for many years. The area is a strange and peculiar place, an estuarine landscape on the edge of the Thames and Medway rivers in North Kent. It has been identified because it offers a particularly dense, rich and variable source of information from which to explore the question of whether and how a distinct atmosphere exists and can be defined in a specific location. The variability of the landscape, of large open agricultural spaces, ruins, industry, redundant nuclear bunkers and its shoreline amongst other features, presents a range of atmospheric conditions. In any one of these places, the phenomenon is present fluctuating between degrees of a subtle or more overt nature.

These separate incidents of atmosphere are relatively insignificant as isolated episodes yet, when experienced cumulatively, these variables result in an overall, singular phenomenon that is powerful and potent. This nebulous force of atmosphere is complex in its geographical context alone, and the problem of making manifest any research findings led me to the act of walking through a psychogeographic methodology.

In order to experience the atmosphere and to be receptive to it, I have immersed myself in the landscape. Walking therefore, has been at the core of this investigation, and as a female psychogeographic explorer, walking has articulated (as my body speaking to me) of how the atmosphere can be evidenced: through its geography, archaeological matter, botany and, more abstractly, through its mapping, as well as elusive and ephemeral materials such as mists and memories. In particular, the distinctive smells and scents of the place, what Böhme (1993) describes as tinctures and as "determinations" of a thing, are triggered through my walking.

A material outcome of this research is Louisa Cornford's 'Archive of Atmosphere', a collection of found objects from the landscape. Cornford, a fictitious character of my own invention, is an Edwardian amateur archaeologist, an alter ego of myself, who drifts in the peninsula, accumulating items for the archive; things that have the potency of the place's atmosphere. Akin to how Charles Fort's *Book of the Damned* (1919) sought to deal with phenomena that science at that time excluded, Cornford is interested in the forgotten and disregarded matter of the peninsula.

It is through walking in the landscape where Cornford has gathered the artefacts that are described by her as 'curiosities' (Sanders-Falcini, 2014: 54). Frequently these items are derivations of consumerist production, from both manufactured and re-processed sources. For example, post-industrial functional objects produced in factories, objects that have often fallen out of use and have either been cast out or may briefly have been given a second/third life and subsequently thrown away. There are also the hand-crafted and re-purposed objects fabricated for specific uses (maritime activities, for example) from existing materials/objects; actions of resourcefulness and economic necessity on the peninsula.

These objects may have come to rest on the peninsula through a number of possibilities; they have been discarded, washed up, abandoned, lost, forgotten, become function-less and useless. Largely they have no economic value and as Tim Edensor (2005) states, have been replaced with up-to-date models or more fashionable items. These curiosities are unpredictable and are adrift from their 'ordered settings' and in a limbiotic state, 'a threat to good order' and 'objectionable' in their original setting/s. As they come to rest in the peninsula, they are impure things that have lost their danger and cease to threaten the 'intensively policed' material worlds of home and work (Edensor 2005: Douglas 1966). It is often the settings of the objects such as the shoreline, or the objects themselves that are identified as encapsulating the atmosphere.

In order to explore each object, Cornford has adopted her own unique methodology, the 'Cornford Analytics'. Typically, the model for museum artefacts is to scrutinise the materials, histories, environments, and significance of items, but in the 'Archive of Atmosphere', found objects are subject to an alternative set of criteria and catalogued under the 'Cornford Analytics'. These analytics are a series of techniques and a distinctive methodology described in the following terms:

> a process of labelling and documenting objects that resists an archaeological dating and origin of items but instead attributes other data to the object itself and the scene of a found object such as sensory attributes (sound and scent of object/location), the atmospherics of the location (weather, type of place, textures & surfaces etc), the situation of Cornford at the time of discovery (clothing worn, food consumed) (Sanders-Falcini, 54: 2019).

In the 'Archive of Atmosphere', the focus is concerned with atmospheres and the material bodies in which they are present. The preservation of these atmospheres in their pristine states is, however, potentially exhaustive and counterproductive. In her capacity as an archaeologist she is wholly unsuitable; untrained, flouting museum protocols and bringing dubious looking objects into the archive. Cornford's approach is far from the standard of museum methodologies outlined by the work of academics such as Susan Pearce and is instead concerned with the experiential in connection to the specificities of the Hoo Peninsula and the agency of the object to the landscape (Pearce, 2005). As Charles Fort (1919) noted, "We are not realists. We are not idealists. We are 'intermediatists'" and Cornford is tapping at this seam of between-ness where the atmosphere is often most prevalent.

These objects have become the focus of a series of performances, where, as Louisa Cornford, I have performed the archive. Selected artefacts from the archive are exhibited upon a series of plinths and tables covered with black cloth. Through a series of actions, Cornford interacts with particular artefacts during a performance, as a way of activating them and triggering their latent atmospheres. Cornford also interweaves and re-enacts the experience of recovering those artefacts.

Parts of the archive were performed during the 'Walking's New Movements' Conference. At this particular performance, three items from the archive were selected: rosehips, an iron bolt and cockleshells and they were performed alongside the more formal presentation of the research materials. The source of each artefact introduced a range of sites in the Hoo Peninsula where atmosphere was identified. These included: High Halstow Marshes, Egypt Bay and The Isle of Grain.

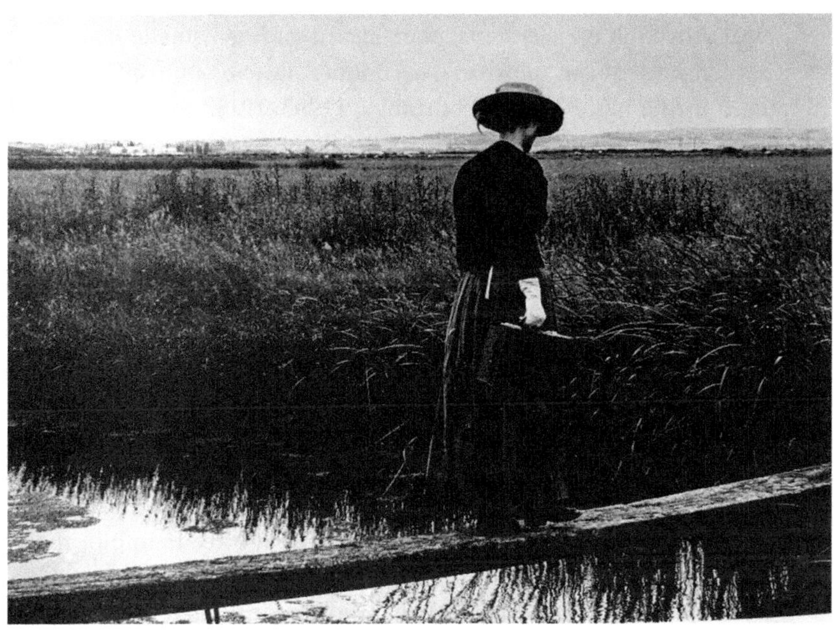

Image from the Marsh Project (2001)

Rosehips from Halstow Marshes

Performance 1: A handful of rosehips are on a length of black fabric. Louisa lays prone on the floor, directly over the rosehips. She picks up a handful, smells their faded musty scents, takes one and bites into its dehydrated skin, releasing its sour taste and a mouthful of husk and seeds. She spits out the rosehip seeds.

Walking entails staying at ground level and because of the flatness of the land in the peninsula, this results in a constant perspective with few degrees of variants. In one sense this encumbers the walker and the flatness literally flattens the experience. This is not to imply that the experience is unrewarding but that the figure is perpendicular to the ground and in being so, she feels the atmosphere at this axis. A spiritual counsellor, Sharon Elliot, implored me to put my bare feet on the soil of the peninsula, in order to "connect with the land, with the spirits and ancestors" (Elliot, 2018).

At this level, I am in close contact with elements that might trigger any of my receptors: smell, hearing, taste, sight and touch. Smell, for example, locates and records a range of scents including salt, seaweed, mud, apple blossom, stagnant water and marine diesel. Smell is invisible yet present through the elements, plant-based and man-made materials, so it is grounded but elusive. As Böhme notes, atmospheres are "tinctured through the presence of things" (1993: 121).

On a walk in the late summer of 2018, in a quest to source medicinal plants of the peninsula, I harvested bags of rosehips that were in abundance all along the track that led out to the marshes at High Halstow. The estuary is reputed to have had many medicinal plants, its unique climatic conditions sustaining an unusual range of species including marshmallow, sea lavender, St John's wort, bugleweed, common yarrow, agrimony, tansy, willow and mullein. In late summer, most of these plants had gone to seed but the rosehips were in their prime. They shone like intense beacons all along the pathway (Ackroyd, 2008: 293-4).

These plants, once treasured for their healing properties, appeared to self-seed in abundance and reproduce in the most inhospitable places. As well as experiencing their olfactory qualities I also wanted to imbibe them to see if I could ingest the atmosphere.

I produced rosehip syrup and, in an experiment, I consumed a teaspoon of syrup every day to take the atmosphere as Victorians might have once taken the waters at a spa. Some rosehips left over were dried and ,when I bit into them, they released a strong taste of rosehip and their seeds scattered.

An Iron Bolt from Egypt Bay

Performance 2: Louisa puts on a pair of white cotton gloves. She walks towards a large iron bolt and bends to carefully pick up the heavy object. It is held in the crook of her elbow as she walks nowhere but repetitively up and down or around in circular patterns. It is a re-telling of the journey on foot to Egypt Bay where the bolt had come to rest, embedded in the salt marsh grass. She bends down and lets the bolt gently roll down her arms, delivering it to the floor like a birthing procedure.

In the early days of my relationship with the peninsula, the unfamiliar landscape activated the psychogeographic approach. The open, flat plains of the peninsula invited a drift and, significantly, its seawall and coastal edge was like a hidden decoy in the distance, luring its victim who would get snagged on covert ditches and creeks. It was a fuzzy form of psychogeography, rooted in a series of intuitive actions that became a methodology to study the atmosphere in the Hoo Peninsula.

Walking from the pathway of rosehips, the land opens out into the typically wide expanse of reclaimed marshland beyond Swigshole Farm and past Decoy Fleet and on towards the seawall where I dropped down into Egypt Bay. Amidst the rugged grass, concrete seawall and mud is a tiny golden beach with a view to the cranes of London Gateway Port where shipping containers enter the UK.

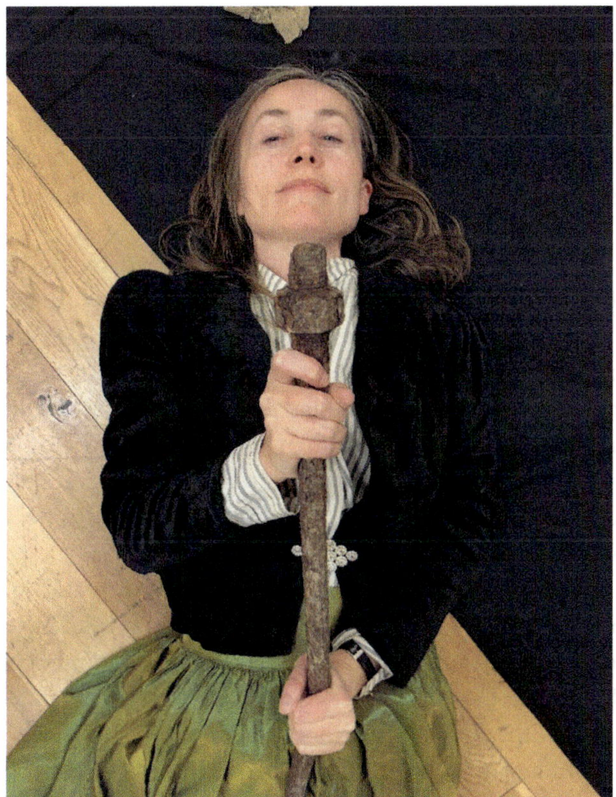

Louisa Cornford Performing the Archive (2019)

I walked along the fringe of the beach, the tideline where things had washed up or disintegrated. The lower links of this consumer chain, the estuary is an odd watery conveyor between production and decay.

As Louisa, I scoured the beach, 'clustering' for materials that might offer up an atmosphere. Here is a place of spectres, the anchor points for 18th-century prison hulks, the heart of the smuggling trade that was rife in the area in the 18th and 19th centuries (Sanders-Falcini, 2019: 55).

As I scanned the shoreline, I came across a heavy iron bolt, corroded and shedding its epidermal skin at every disturbance. It was dense and weighted, both materially and historically. Its skin-shedding persisted from retrieval through the rhythmical journey on foot, the 200-mile drive home and the boxing up in the archive. The archived atmosphere was being contaminated by particles of rust and the bolt continually flaked, leaking its atmosphere into other atmospheres of my vehicle and studio.

Cockleshells from the shoreline of The Isle of Grain

Performance 3: A pile of cockleshells on the black cloth. Louisa picks up a handful, dropping them over her bent head in an act of self-baptism in atmosphere. Stray shells on the floor are crushed under foot where she walks evoking the memories of walking over cockleshells on the beaches of Allhallows and The Isle of Grain.

To 'lay the cultch' refers to the laying of crushed cockleshells on the estuary floor as a hard bed upon which mother oysters are put to spawn new oysters (ZSL, 2019). Oysters are so depleted in the Thames estuary that human intervention is necessary and a recent project by the Zoological Society of London has led to the first Mother Oyster Sanctuary. I walk upon the cultch, on the beaches of Grain and Allhallows at the very edges of the estuary. Here there were empty oyster shells along with mussels and cockles. In this intertidal zone, the estuary birds take advantage of the rich diet.

It is not the oysters though that most fascinate me but the cockleshells, which are abundant in this area. Grain even has a shoreline called Cockleshell Beach, a place that is white and shimmering in the hot sun of July with the multitude of cockles. The beach is close to the London Stone, the official line where the river and sea meet. The stone, an obelisk underpinned by a gnarled wooden base, rises from the mud on each swell of tide.

In the late 1990s, I drifted into the Hoo Peninsula and settled into a rhythm of wanderings that continued over a period of years. Entangled were the shadows of an embodied position, vulnerability and female mobility. It was imperative that I walk alone, for to walk with others, though useful, was an unnecessary distraction. However, I was also aware of the connotations of walking in a remote place as a solo woman. As Rebecca Solnit notes, for women, "Access to public space, urban and rural is one limited by fear of violence and harassment." The narrative to this fear is the real suppression of women walking alone and particularly at night that had historically been enforced by the policing of spaces in the Victorian period and earlier. As Solnit reasons, "Women have routinely been punished and intimidated for… taking a walk because their walking… ha(d) been construed as inevitably, continually sexual in those societies concerned with controlling women's sexuality" (2002: 233). Solnit identifies the example of an innocent Victorian woman, Caroline Wyburgh of Chatham, who is arrested under suspicion of prostitution, for merely "walking out" at night with a sailor in 1870. Wyburgh was forced to undergo a humiliating medical examination against her wishes. The sailor was never identified or pursued for his part in this act (ibid: 232-3). In a strange coincidence, Chatham exists at the very fringes of the Hoo Peninsula; the historic naval dockyard of Wyburgh's sailor was closed in the 1980s.

What I began to understand and experience was that the atmosphere in the Hoo Peninsula was activated by my encounters with it through my solitary position as a female in the landscape. Atmosphere "is experienced and felt by being in the landscape… revealed through an acclimatization of the body to the space" and by adopting a psycho-geographic position, 'interesting matter' was revealed, such as the intangible (strong feeling of something in the air) or the tangible (an

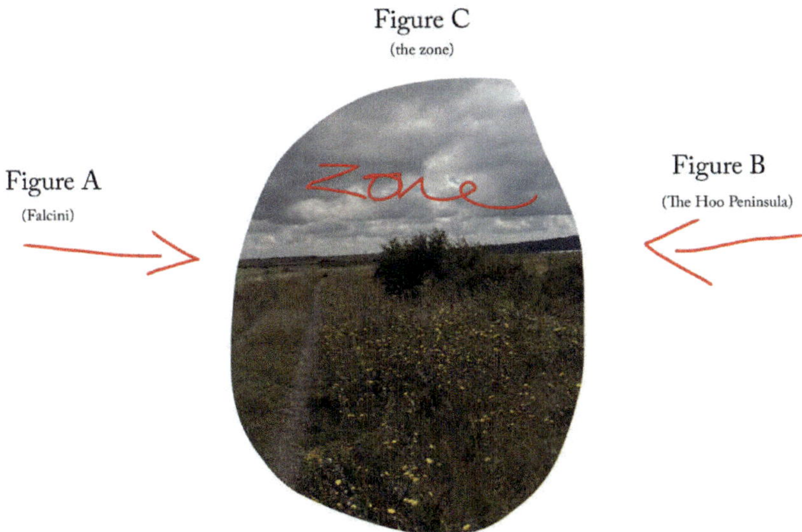

Illustration of the 'Zone' of research

object on the ground that is curious and totemic that contributes to an atmosphere) (Sanders-Falcini, 2019: 70). In the latter part of the research

I developed a diagram from a theory I devised about my relationship to the peninsula. On entering the landscape, I concluded that I encountered a zone identified as Figure C and that this was a unique intersection between myself (Figure A) and The Hoo Peninsula (Figure B). The zone was the confluence between me and it: of stepping onto/into the peninsula and its very unique geography. The moment I physically entered the peninsula alone, it activated the zone; a seam that I understood as a place where I experienced its unique atmosphere.

Becoming Louisa was a further creative strategy to burrow into the atmosphere, providing a covert infiltration of the landscape. The wider problem in psychogeography of "masculine and heterosexist assumptions" both in the collection of this material and its consumption developed the necessity of Louisa's archaeological investigation of the land (Bridger, 2013: 289). It further provoked the narrative of women being confined to safe spaces; often interior, domestic or commercial areas. It would perhaps have been unthinkable for an Edwardian woman in the early 1900s to march out alone, into the North Kent marshes. In this same period, Paris for example, was predominantly a male privileged space, yet women were an important part of the city, visible on the streets and in cafés in the early 1900s as Elisabeth Wilson notes (Tamboukou, 2010). Single women were, however, chaperoned and vulnerable to male attention as the Welsh artist, Gwen John, living in the city from 1904 till her death in 1939, commented: " I am obliged to walk very quickly, so that men will not talk to me." (ibid: 116). Walking without regard for their safety, was not an option for women at this time.

> Have you ever had the urge to disappear, to escape from your own life for just a little while – like walking out of one room, then into a different one? (Cardiff, 2005: 18)

The sound artist Janet Cardiff's voice falls into the listener's ear on her work 'The Missing Voice, Case Study B' and contemplates the imaginary drift out of the deep grooves we may find ourselves in. I had discovered this strange and melancholic landscape when we lived on a Dutch barge in the area. Despite the hot summer's day when I first encountered it during an arbitrary walk, this remote unpopulated marshland area had a distinctly eerie feeling. Walking in this landscape was, initially, about disappearing momentarily from my own deep groove and finding solace and connection there. I knew nothing then of its dark histories (prison hulks and disease, for example) but instinctively I sensed an underlying feeling that drew me back and eventually developed into a body of research.

The research drew me towards the more inhospitable areas of the peninsula. At The Isle of Grain, a strange polarity of beauty and disfigurement emerged from its distinctive marshes, coastline and scarred areas of industrial activity. At this edge of the estuary, the atmosphere was dense; its areas, often out of bounds, meant trespass and crawling through holes in wire fences. I explored dangerous buildings like the eighteenth-century Grain Tower that could only be reached at low tide via a causeway and precarious makeshift ladder up to its entrance. Once inside these buildings, the ghosts of past histories and lives appeared to leak out.

The Isle of Grain was a place plundered from the inside out, in particular, by the energy industries to supply oil, gas and electricity. BP had swallowed a large section of marsh to construct an oil refinery in the 1950s and subsequent energy industries had expanded around its fringes, occupying a zone that one had to pass through in order to reach the village and coastal area of Grain. It was a hostile place where I had experienced interrogation and near arrest by the police, as I stood on a public highway in 2016, for example, and photographed the remains of an old orchard, at the edge of the E.ON site.

The image of a few remaining apple trees hemmed in by concrete and steel encapsulates in microcosm not only the rapid changes to the Isle but also the resistance to change the landscape held. These tensions of time where the past refuses to be buried and is ready to rupture the surface, are repeated continuously over the Isle. For example, we can witness the hole at the bottom of a steep wooded hill that is the hidden entrance to Grain Fort or the tank traps that protrude from Cockleshell beach. Shallow graves of atmosphere exist all around this space.

It was on Cockleshell beach that I began walking at night, making a series of drawings in the pitch black. Navigating the remains of World War Two defences, the tank traps and iron bars beneath my feet, was hazardous, but here were also the delicate materials of the cockleshells underfoot and the choral notes of estuary birds feeding on the shoreline at the intertidal zone. The water was a dark liquid swell. Ships silently moved on the water; speculative beings out at sea.

Conclusion

This article is a glimpse of a larger body of research where I have sought to identify the phenomenon of atmosphere present in the Hoo Peninsula. In this research, I have investigated atmosphere as a phenomenon of 'feelings in the air', that one senses in connection to a specific place, in this case, the North Kent marshes in the peninsula (Böhme et.al., 2014). The atmosphere I argue, is present and like a figure lingering in the background appearing to haunt the place. It is palpable. The atmosphere appears both as an all-enveloping phenomenon and as a more intimate, series of phenomena that are localised (ibid: 91; Böhme, 2017: 14). The research has led to the finding that the Hoo Peninsula's atmosphere is uniquely characteristic, attributable to its location and is experienced only in this location.

To identify and understand the atmosphere, an interdisciplinary methodology articulating the ephemeral qualities of atmosphere was adopted, a key element of which was a psychogeographic approach through the mode of walking. Practically, I have been on foot, drifting (but always with a map in my bag), sensing the sites of particular atmosphere through intuition, building an atlas of those locations which I can then return to. Thus, I was not always making fresh 'travelogues' but marking out places like a fox or dog, scenting the site, not with bodily fluids but notes, markers, photographs and memories of place I wished to return to.

Walking led to a cognitive mapping of the atmosphere and through a wayfaring rhizomatic movement I wandered over the marshland through a series of routes that revealed the portals of atmosphere. Here I often came to experience what I identified earlier as Figure C in the 'Zone of Research'. This was a seam and the point where not only were the qualities of atmosphere to be found through the objective nature of the landscape but also where, phenomenologically, my body sensed the acute atmosphere. In order to be receptive to it, the feelings of displacement and immobilisation were triggered when I first encountered the Hoo Peninsula as a young woman and these continued to be provoked on subsequent visits to the landscape. The body had to be in a position to absorb these sources of atmosphere and it was only when I repeatedly entered this situation that it began to operate in this intermediary space, becoming inextricably intertwined.

I have felt the atmosphere through taste, smell and sound; through the weather, the tides, the ground. I have walked in redundant power station car parks, in marshes, along the seawall and on Cockleshell beach. I have been a part time botanist, cartographer, writer, scavenger and historian. I have been Louisa Cornford, the amateur Edwardian archaeologist archiving the atmosphere.

References

Ackroyd, P. (2008) *Thames: Sacred River.* Vintage

Binns, P. (2016) Interviewed by the Author, 20th July

Böhme, G. (1993) 'Atmosphere as the Fundamental Concept of a New Aesthetics', *Thesis Eleven,* 36, pp. 113-126 Available at: http://www.thesagepub.com (Accessed: 26 Jun 2016)

______ (2017) *Atmospheric Architectures: The Aesthetics of Felt Spaces.* Bloomsbury Visual Arts

Böhme, G., *et.al.* (2014) 'Atmospheres, Art, Architecture: A Conversation Between Gernot Böhme, Christian Borch, Olafur Eliasson & Juhani Pallasmaa' in Borch, C. (ed) (2014) *Architectural Atmospheres: On the Experience and Politics of Architecture.* Walter de Gruyter.

Bridger, A.J. (2013) 'Psychogeography and Feminist Methodology', *Feminism and Psychology.* Available at: bit.ly/wnm140 (Accessed: 17 May 2019)

Cardiff, J. (2005) *Janet Cardiff: The Walk Book.* Thyssen-Bornemisza Art Contemporary

Douglas, P.M. & Douglas, M. (2002) 'Purity and Danger: An Analysis of Concepts of Pollution and Taboo'. Available at: bit.ly/wnm139 (Accessed: 12 Feb 2019)

Edensor, T. (2005) 'Waste Matter: The Debris of Industrial Ruins and the Disordering of the Material World'. *Journal of Material Culture* 01.11.05 Available at: bit.ly/wnm135 (Accessed: 01 May 2019)

Elliot, S. (2018) Spiritual Therapy Session, 2nd May 2018

Fort, C. (1919) *The Book of the Damned,* Project Gutenberg Literary Archive Foundation. Available at bit.ly/wnm141 (Accessed: 15 Jan 2020)

Pearce, S. (2005) 'Thinking About Things' in Pearce, S. ed. *Interpreting Objects and Collections,* Routledge, pp. 125-132

Sanders-Falcini, A. (2019) *Stalking the Atmosphere: Journeys into the Hoo Peninsula Through a Multi-disciplinary Fine Art Practice* (Doctoral Thesis) University for the Creative Arts

Solnit, R. (2001) *Wanderlust: A History of Walking.* Verso

Tamboukou, M. (2010) *Nomadic Narratives, Visual Forces: Gwen John's Letters and Paintings.* Peter Lang Publishing

The Zoological Society of London (ZSL) (24th June 2019) *Essex Estuary to be Sanctuary for 'Mother Oysters'.* Available at bit.ly/wnm134 (Accessed 20 Oct 2019)

On Mythogeosonics

John Bowers & Tim Shaw

Introduction

Since 2015, Bowers and Shaw have developed a creative practice we call mythogeosonics. We study the many, layered significances which can be attached to places and investigate their traces by working with sound. Adapting the concept of mythogeography, we acknowledge the multiple and contested characters of place and the value there is in creatively juxtaposing them, making this friction audible. Walking is key to our practice as a means for researching the places we work within, for gathering materials through field recording, photography, geophysical data gathering, paranormal investigation, concurrent writing, and as on-site performance. This is our first extended published reflection on mythogeosonics and we will discuss its conceptual and practical development, the works we have made in its name, the techniques and technologies we have formulated and made, and how our practices critically engage with a variety of topics, from debates over site and artistic agency to how we extend conventional techniques of field recording. We close with some speculations about how mythogeosonics might relate to fashionable concerns artists have with the archive.

Mythogeosonics: The Very Idea

In terms of its scholarly and artistic lineage, mythogeosonics can be regarded as lying at the remeeting of two drifts, both of which take psychogeography as a starting point, one taking us via mythogeography, one via psychogeophysics. Let us take a moment to introduce and stroll around these waymarks.

As Guy Debord (1955: 23) outlined it, psychogeography is "the study of the precise laws and specific effects of the geographical environment, consciously organized or not, on the emotions and behaviour of individuals". This compact presentation of the concept has the advantage that it is easy to identify points of departure from it.

Debord's emphasis on precise laws and specific effects could come from any manifesto for a new scientific discipline. It has a rationalism about it which runs in tension with lawlessness, playfulness, the speculative, the slapdash and the sketchy. This is, of course, somewhat curious given the practices of many who work in the name of psychogeography, and we grant that it has been the subject of many corrections and adjustments before us. Psychogeography as a portmanteau word combining psychology and geography, together with Debord's emphasis on the emotions and behaviour of individuals, creates a primary focus on the individual and ways of understanding them which borrow from psychology. The psychology Debord had in mind would be a détournement on psychoanalysis, one that is "envision[ed] for situationist ends" and is concerned "not with the individual structure of our minds, nor the explanation of their formation, but their possible application in constructed situations" (Internationale Situationiste #1, 1958: 49). While this is a heterodox psychology, there is still ontological and epistemological work going on here which restricts room for scholarly and creative manoeuvre. In addition, the individual is seen as experiencing the emotional effects of the geographical in a way that seems to set the two apart as cause and effect and makes it harder to see more entangled relationships of place-making – or at least harder to see them outside constructed situations of revolutionary potential.

We do not wish to deny the continued relevance of a Debordian psychogeography, nor do we wish to downgrade the value of the methods of exploration its practitioners engage in, nor even do we wish to rule out the possibility of a hijacked psychoanalysis for counter-spectacles. But we would like to explore a more open ontology, one which sees many existents, and, accordingly, brings more varied understandings to the epistemological party. In this, we have been influenced by Phil Smith's (writing sometimes as Mytho or Crabman) formulation of mythogeography (Smith, 2010). By substituting psycho with mytho, a more diverse field is opened up.

Mythogeography "describes a way of thinking about and visiting places where multiple meanings have been squeezed into a single and restricted meaning (for example, heritage, tourist or leisure sites tend to be presented as just that, when they may also have been homes, jam factories, battlegrounds, lovers' lanes, farms, cemeteries and madhouses).

Mythogeography emphasises the multiple nature of places and suggests multiple ways of celebrating, expressing and weaving those places and their multiple meanings" (Mythogeography website). This is a very different picture from Debord. The single and restricted meaning of a site (or, for that matter, of a Debordian spectacle) is seen as a contingent accomplishment, something which can be undone through recovering other identities and initiating new celebrations. This is a rather different framing from how the individual is an effect of geography in the Debordian scheme, or elsewhere in his thought, from how the subject of capitalism encounters the spectacle. It allows more strategies for participation in the remaking of places and, through that perhaps, more scope for political optimism.

Our second drift takes us via psychogeophysics, formulated as an expansion of psychogeography by Jonathan Kemp, Martin Howse and colleagues (see Psychogeophysics website). "Psychogeophysics expands this artistic research [psychogeography] to embrace geophysics, defined as the quantitative observation of the earth's physical properties, and its interaction with local signal ecologies." Over the last 10 years, numerous public workshops, performances and related events have taken place under this banner, including two extended Psychogeophysics Summits (one in London in 2010, one in Suffolk the following year), an extended handbook and reader has been published online, and schematics for building DIY sensing technologies have been made available. One of us has participated in several psychogeophysical events. For example, at the Piksel Festival in Bergen, Norway, 2012, as part of a workshop leading to a participatory performance, Ryan Jordan, Jonathan Kemp and John Bowers explored the claim that electromagnetic anomalies around particular rock formations can have a subtle influence on people's perception – perhaps giving rise to an uncanny sense of the presence of otherwise imperceptible beings. As part of the summative performance from the workshop, the electromagnetic fields around various locally scavenged rocks were amplified and made audible to the audience as well as relayed to 'God Helmets' worn by two of the performers who reported on their experience.

Our work exemplifies several features of psychogeophysics as a form of artistic research. There is a concern for making sensing technologies and using them to extend our everyday perception of a site. In particular, signals which are otherwise imperceptible are often amplified or processed to make them audible. Our work is typically conducted onsite with members of the public being able to participate or intervene. A performance or installation summates the work. And interestingly, there is an openness to the kinds of phenomena and theories that might be broadly called Forteana – the forms of marginal epistemology that Charles Fort (1919) referred to as "the procession of damned data". In this, psychogeophysics has a relation with Smith's practice where "occulted and anomalous narratives are among those available to mythogeography, not as ends in themselves, but as means and metaphors to explain, engage and disrupt" (see Mythogeography website).

This last proviso sets the mythogeographic interest in Forteana apart from, say, professional paranormal investigation as much as it does from the scientific sceptic or debunker. The occult, the anomalous and other damned data are not of a special character requiring the conspiracy theorist, red pill taker, debunker or other ontological warrior to pull back the curtain of ideology or deception. What hides the occult is the monolithic understanding of a site as a Roman Fort rather than also a jam factory. In this way, damned data can strategically open up monological understandings of place to the mythic.

Investigations

Over the course of the last five years, we have conducted 11 different mythogeosonic 'investigations' at varied sites nationally and internationally. Let us present an account of three of these to give a flavour of our workings.

Bergen Invocation, Piksel Festival, Bergen, Norway, 2015

In Bergen, we aimed to create a performable installation that offered an imaginative remapping of the city. The materials for the installation were gathered through soundwalks undertaken with other attendees at the festival. We explored the place of execution of Anne Pedersdotter, tried as a witch in 1590, making recordings of the ferries which pass the point today and placing electrodes in the soil, amplifying the current flow between them and recording this as sound. We made underwater hydrophone recordings at the site of the sinking of the German cruiser Königsberg in 1940. We rode and recorded the Fløen funicular railway and at the top recorded ice on a lake creaking as we stepped upon it. We walked out of the city around Svartediket lake, retracing the steps of the mysterious and tragic Isdal Woman. Amongst other walks. We collected artefacts along the way, rubbish that seemed poignant, rock and earth samples, and took many photographs. We made recordings in the busy shopping centre and at tourist locations. Over the course of the three days we worked in Bergen we incrementally created an installation which layered our collected materials, sounds, images and scavenged objects, together intended as a layered mapping of the city. On the final night of the festival, we moved our installation into the main concert space and performed a duo improvisation with all the materials collected.

Walk Write Repeat, Algomech Festival, Sheffield, UK, 2016

Algomech in Sheffield was a cross-arts festival which, broadly, explored the intersection of the algorithmic (the computational, the digital) and mechanical movement. Our contribution took as its conceit the idea of the city as being a massive, distributed repository of symbolic data which we access by walking, writing (to our own recording devices), and repeating the procedure. We imagined the movements of the head of a Turing Machine, reading and writing to tape and moving over it, as in Alan Turing's classic 1936 thought experiment in the history of computing, as if they were instructions as to how to walk the city. We traced the line of the River Don, making above and below surface recordings, and encountering the city's trams. We recorded the electromagnetic fields around malfunctioning lights set into pedestrian walkways. We recorded the resonances of the chapel in City Road Cemetery and the sounds of a broken parking meter nearby. We walked through T J Hughes store recording the store announcements, escalators, laughing toys, and other noisy merchandise as a continual soundscape. Amongst many other activities over the course of two days. We brought our materials together in a 25-minute improvised performance which also featured animated collages based on photographs we had taken.

Berlin Sensor, Transmediale/CTM Vorspiel, Berlin, Germany, 2018

In Berlin Sensor we worked with the conceit that the city itself was a giant sensor device which could report on various features of its history, geography, politics and ecology, and which our devices could tap into. We walked to the site of Spandau Prison where Rudolf Hess, Albert Speer and five other Nazis convicted at Nuremberg were imprisoned from 1947, with Hess's suicide in 1987 leading to its swift demolition. While some older buildings still stand, a supermarket that is part of the

Kaufman chain occupies the prison site. We made recordings of the shopping trolleys and filmed a security screen which was showing CCTV images until we were asked to leave. We noted that some of the trees from the prison garden remain around the supermarket car park and collected fragments of tree bark that had fallen from them. We walked on to Teufelsberg, the Devil's Mountain, constructed with debris from the bombing of Berlin as the city was cleared for rebuilding. On the top of the hill, a US listening station was active between 1963 and German reunification. The buildings that remain are privately occupied and in varying states of disrepair. As we passed we recorded a soprano singing in one of the giant radomes that once hid the station's antennas. From Teufelsberg, we walked to Langenscheidtbrücke, the iron bridge where the angel Damiel comforts the dying motorcyclist in Wim Wenders' 1987 film 'Wings of Desire'. We recorded the resonances of the bridge as traffic crosses it and the suburban trains pass underneath. Amongst many other recordings in these sites and between. The following evening as part of the Vorspiel of the Transmediale/CTM Festival we performed our recordings and showed photography from the sites we had visited prefaced with a performative lecture concerning mythogeosonics and the concept of the city as a sensor.

Techniques

For our mythogeosonic investigations we have developed a number of technologies which accompany us on our walks. These include artist-made technologies, some repurposed mass-market devices, and our own DIY 'makes' of varying sophistication and scientific soundness, some developed in our studios, some in the field. In this section, we informally discuss some of our many devices and how they are put to use in our work.

• Extended Field Recording

Field recording is a foundational technique for our investigations, and on walks we take a selection of different devices for environmental listening. These include air-pressure microphones for acoustic sense data, contact microphones for surface vibration, hydrophones for underwater listening, inductive coils for electromagnetic interferences and accelerometers to record movement. Not only do we use these devices to record these data but we also respond to live microphone feeds in our on-site performances.

• I Am Sitting In An X, Impulse Responses and Feedback

Adapting Alvin Lucier's technique in 'I Am Sitting In A Room' (1969) of recording from one device to another until the original signal is smoothed by the accumulated reverberation of a room, we have conducted a number of similar experiments in both indoor and outdoor environments. As another strategy for making the reverberant quality of an environment an active feature of our work, we have collected many Impulse Responses (IRs) using both of the common techniques of recording the response to a noise burst or a sine wave glissando. We also commonly create feedback arrangements using small portable amplifiers and microphones.

• Earth Synthesizer

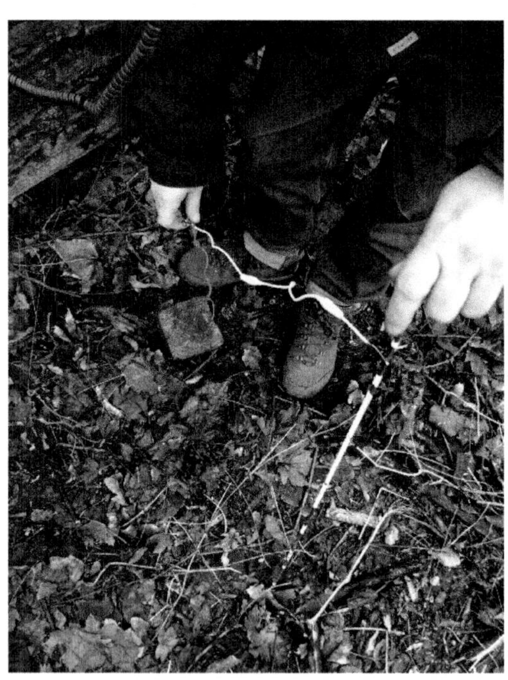

We place electrodes of dissimilar metals in the earth and amplify the signal. This technique can sometimes pick up telluric currents running through the earth's surface or act as a natural battery as earth salts interact with the electrodes electrolytically to power attached circuitry. Sometimes a current source is also added in to the circuit so that a sample of earth can be used in a voltage divider design to send varying control voltages to, say, an attached portable synthesizer.

• Rock Harmonium, Sonifying Geological Textures

Drawing on the work of UK artist Ryan Jordan, we place rock samples in a circuit to function as a transistor and amplify the result to create interesting sonic effects which are sensitive to the kind of sample and its internal structure. We have also experimented with sonifying geological textures by scanning images of geological formations using a digital camera or microscope.

• Radio

We have developed a number of ways to use radio in our investigations. These include listening to radio signals with an 'All Band Receiver' which receives a broad bandwidth of signals at the same time. We have made very low frequency (VLF) receivers which pick up natural radio from lighting strikes and other atmospheric phenomena. We also experiment with receiving signals using non-conventional aerials including trees, large metal objects (such as bridges or lampposts) and aerials constructed onsite using found materials.

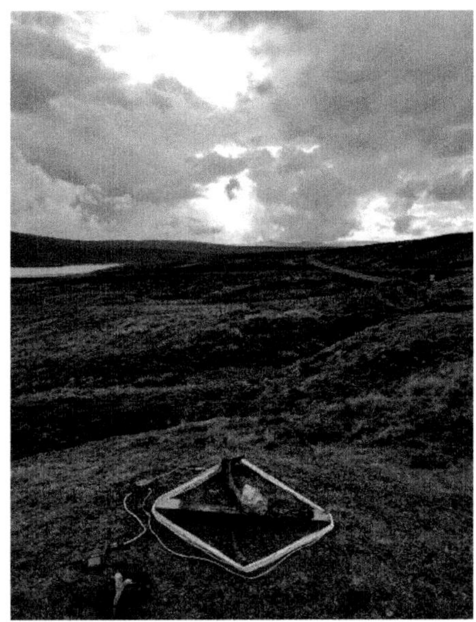

• Scavenged Materials

We commonly collect materials and objects from the sites we visit taking care not to remove anything that might be someone's property or anything that is ecologically important. Indeed, most of what we scavenge would be deemed by many to be rubbish but, even so, we do not always permanently remove objects or materials from where they were found, often preferring to work with them in situ. We often explore this material using various microphones, such as a contact microphone, or by reverberating them by direct contact with a transducer following David Tudor's technique from his various Rainforest performances and installations (1968 onwards).

• Esoteric Devices

Some of the devices we take for a walk in our investigations have been influenced by the use of the technologies used by paranormal researchers. For example, we have developed and made a spirit box, a Raudiver receiver, an electromagnetic Field Recorder and an Electromagnetic Pump.

• Environmental Data Catching and Tracking

As well as listening to and recording acoustic data we use a variety of sensors to record environmental data. These sensors include those that can record light, temperature, humidity, air pressure, wind speed and direction. These sensors are wired through a small microcontroller (usually an Arduino) and data can be sent to other devices or written to an SD card for later use. Similarly, we sometimes record the trajectory of our walks using mobile phone apps which track and plot our wanderings through GPS data. We have also used apps which record the phone's movement. Tucked into a sock, this can serve as a pedometer which gives some insight into the shape of our strides over the course of a walk.

• Journalling and Photography

We typically document our walks as we do them by writing a concurrent journal. While there is no rule to this, the journals often have the character of a series of essayistic impressions and responses to the unexpected contingencies we encounter while walking and sounding, to the way heritage or other authoritative historical discourses are present or disrupted as we investigate a site, to the presence of anomaly or anachrony, and, in particular, to any procession of damned data that we pick up on. We take many photographs too. As well as illustrations for our journalling, we are also drawn to textures which perhaps suggest a mythogeographic complexity to a site or otherwise catch our eye. We sometimes scan textures in digital audio software we have made to create audible waveforms. Layerings of our photographs and extracts from our journals are often present in our performances and installations.

• Interfacing to Synthesizers

We often carry with us small, portable, low-priced synthesizers, made by us or other artists and musicians. When conducting a mythogeosonic investigation we often accompany our activities with some environmentally responsive sound synthesis, in which we take one of our data streams, e.g. from the environmental sensors, and attach it to one of the inputs of our synthesizers. This gives us another sound to accompany the feeds coming from the listening devices and to record for later use.

Upshots, Reflections and Emerging Concerns

Mythogeosonics is an open, developing practice for sound walking, performance and installation, drawing on traditions of psychogeography, mythogeography, psychogeophysics and other byways which encourage us to extend and rethink our relation to place and movement.

Mythogeosonics is a multifaceted way of working that incorporates many different creative practices including field recording, data collection, electronics, software and hardware development, instrument building, writing and photography. We like to keep our investigations open and experimental. With each investigation we research and build new devices and techniques but also draw upon old ones from previous walks. Our walks can be done with just the two of us or can be opened to collective participation. The making of our devices can be the basis of accompanying workshops for public participation. We can present our work in various formats from gig-like appearances on a bill of musical acts to installations which themselves can be made performable. While out walking we often stop and play to whoever or whatever might be listening. Let us close with a few of the topics that mythogeosonics has encouraged us to think about.

Extending Field Recording Practices

Sometimes field recording is understood as the act of moving sound material from one place to another. A recording is made in one place, taken back to the recordist's studio to edit and process and then at a later date presented in a gallery, cinema, music venue, warehouse or squat, or as part of a published release, a CD or whatever. Mythogeosonics approaches the act of field recording (and data collection in general) as a live and embodied process, rather than just the transportation of audio material from one site to another. Within media theory, some writers consider the act of sound recording to be a disembodying process, removing sound from its source (e.g. Kittler, 1986). We see (and hear) mythogeosonics as a practical, embodied engagement with sonic phenomena. To this end we attempt to reorient field recording, or more generally field work, as an activity which flattens process and presentation and where the artist leaves an inevitable agential trace. Often mythogeosonic investigation involve us playing back field recordings within the site itself. It also involves extended field recording practices, such as using experimental aerials for picking up radio broadcasts or inductive coils for hearing hidden electromagnetism. From time to time, these devices may be themselves built onsite. We are concerned with real-time listening, data collection and phenomenological experience. Our investigations work with the immediate environment as a source of data and we often perform with this within the site itself. If we finish a mythogeosonic investigation with a public performance, these are more like reports on the activity of investigation and, indeed, we often read from our journals or otherwise introduce our performances to emphasise that framing. Furthermore, since we inaugurated mythogeosonics, towards the end of the calendar year, we have performed an Annual Report (2017 in Newcastle, 2018 in New York, 2019 in Plymouth) drawing on all our materials gathered in the year. In this way, field recording is an activity we extend and embed within our overarching practice.

Site, Technology and Significance

'Site-specific' (or one of its variable permutations) is a term used by many artists who engage with walking as an artistic methodology. As mythogeosonics responds to various sites it would be naive of us to ignore reference to this artistic concern. With mythogeosonics we choose to participate within a site, rather than just respond to it. In a similar vein to our approach to field recording, rather than move material from one place to another, we prefer to, whenever possible, work directly with features of the site in our creative work. In practical terms this could include performing from within the site using portable equipment and battery-powered sound systems or working with the characteristics of the performance venue as productive and responsive elements in the creative work. We do not use technology here to recreate a virtual 'realistic' space, rather we allow the site and our chosen devices to intersect, using technology as a way of revealing aspects of the site not normally within perceptual reach.

In our work here we have approached the technologies we make as intrinsic to artistic processes, rather than as mere means to an aesthetic end or presentation tools or products. We have resisted solutionist approaches to technology, whereby technology is rendered invisible or used to solve problems, create products, market services or be encapsulated as an 'application'. The devices we use are in constant development, evolving with each mythogeosonic investigation. Indeed, we see the technologies we use as creative material in their turn – material that is continuously revisited and reshaped.

Our techniques and devices each give their own account of the character of the sites we visit and the walks we undertake. A Raudive receiver will pick up a lot of stray electromagnetism and, if we are very lucky, something that can be heard as a voice from the other side. An arrangement of devices to create acoustic feedback will be sensitive to the resonances of the site and to our activity within it. A synthesizer based around electrodes plunged into the earth will respond to its saltiness and the movement of the particles which compose it and of ourselves as we stomp around. We have many such devices, all with their own sensitivities and 'voice'. As such our approach is suited to the mythogeographic sensibility to open out sites to multiple significances and to have fun at the expense of monological readings of geographical and historical identity.

This is further reinforced by our adoption of what we have called 'conceits', ways of framing an investigation by taking a sideways glance at the sites we walk between and around, and what we might be doing. Regarding a city as a giant sensor or as a program that gives us instructions as to how to walk, read and write, or as a contradictory layering in need of equally enigmatic remapping and invocation are all framing devices that give organisation to our activities and suggest the development of technologies for the investigation while redistributing received understandings.

Archiving Walking

As we continue to present mythogeosonics in different contexts and in response to different invitations we have built up an archive of sounds, images, salvaged and scavenged objects, listening devices, and other paraphernalia. All of these materials have formed an archive for our walks and we keep personal collections of these things. It is now over 15 years since Hal Foster (2004) wrote about artists' 'archival' tendencies. It seems to us that it is time for us to reflect on what archival tendencies mythogeosonics should have. In a recent performance during a day examining the work of artist John Akomfrah in relation to archival sources, as well as mixing in our various recordings along with some live synthesizer improvisation, we presented our scavenged objects underneath a rostrum camera, creating live assemblages of the things we had collected. In addition, across two screens we presented images of these objects photographed in a tongue-in-cheek archivist's style, flat against a white background. One of these screens layered up multiple photographs slowly transitioning from one layering to another to create an animated collage effect. In this way, we were mixing and juxtaposing the objects collected in a manner that was similar to the combination and layering of recordings while counterposing this to the separated neutral backgrounded photography in the archivist's style. This seemed to us to be a strategy in which we can connect mythogeosonics to the archive in ways which are self-consistent and begin to juxtapose institutional practices to our personal artistic ones. How one might walk up to, through and around archives of walking's own making is one of our current concerns.

Mythogeosonics: The Manifesto

With mythogeosonics we study the many, layered significances which can be attached to places and investigate their traces by working with sound. Adapting the concept of mythogeography, we acknowledge the multiple and contested characters of place and the value there is in creatively juxtaposing them, making this friction audible.

We work with multiple and extended timescales.
Think of the simultaneity of cosmology, geology, landscape, history, biography, fiction.

We resist fixed uniform ideologies of the sort that can be found in heritage discourse. Rather than 'responding' to a space, we prefer to participate within it, unfixing and reformulating its many meanings.
Think of this place as a noisy transmission that can be tuned in to and played with/in.

Mythogeosonics works with an extended conception of field recording to incorporate such diverse practices as geophysical data sonification and paranormal investigation.
Think of all the fields: radio, magnetic, electric, esoteric.

We cross between on-site investigation, installation-making, soundwalks, and an improvisatory performance practice combining soundscapes, documentary recordings, film, text, and process material using modular synthesizers, resonant found objects, DIY software and self-made instruments.
Think of all the ways that the mythogeosonic can be heard, witnessed, appreciated and transformed.

References

Debord, G. (1955) 'Introduction to a critique of urban geography'. Reprinted in Bauder, H. & Engel-Di Mauro, S. (2008) *Critical Geographies*. Praxis (e)Press

Fort, C. (1919) *The Book of the Damned.* Boni and Liveright

Foster, H. (2004) *The Archival Impulse.* MIT Press

Internationale Situationiste #1 (1958) 'Preliminary problems in constructing a situation'. Reprinted in *Situationist International anthology* (2006) Bureau of Public Secrets

Kittler, F. (1986) *Grammophon film typewriter.* Brinkmann & Bose

Mythogeography website. www.mythogeography.com (Accessed 05 Mar 2020)

Psychogeophysics website. bit.ly/wnm200 (Accessed 05 Mar 2020)

Smith. P. (2010) *Mythogeography: A guide to walking sideways.* Triarchy Press

Contributors

Iain Biggs

Iain works as a writer, artist and researcher and is Visiting Research Fellow at the Environmental Humanities Research Centre at Bath Spa University and Honorary Research Fellow at the University of Dundee. Building on twenty years of 'deep mapping' work, he is currently contributing to various ecosophically oriented projects in the UK and Ireland. His chapter 'Ensemble Practices' appears in the ecology section of *The Routledge Companion to Art in the Public Domain* (2020).

Helen Billinghurst

Helen is a multidisciplinary artist, educator, researcher and writer, working within the expanded fields of painting and drawing. A lecturer at Plymouth College of Arts, her research interests include the performance of making, site-specificity and embodied process. Recent solo exhibitions include 'English Diagrams' (Royal William Yard, Plymouth, 2018). Collaborating with Phil Smith as Crab & Bee, Helen makes walks, performances, poetry and exhibitions, including 'Plymouth Labyrinth' (2019); their next book, *The Pattern,* is based on walks across Southern England and Wales.

John Bowers and Tim Shaw

John works with modular synthesisers, home-brew electronics, reconstructions of antique image and sound-making devices, self-made software, field recordings and esoteric sensor systems. Amongst many collaborations, he works with Sten-Olof Hellström, Tim Shaw, Kerry Hagan, Paul Stapleton and the noise drone band Tonesucker. He helps coordinate the label Onoma Research and works in Culture Lab and Fine Art, Newcastle University, UK. He is a Director of Allenheads Contemporary Arts and a Trustee of Monkfish Productions.

Tim is an artist working with sound, light and communication media. Presenting work through musical performances, installations and sound walks, Tim is interested in how listening environments can be constructed or explored using a diverse range of techniques and technologies. He works with field recordings, electronics, video, modular synthesis, sound objects, self-made hardware and DIY software. He has worked with Chris Watson, Phill Niblock, John Bowers, Dirty Electronics, Tetsuya Umeda, Jacek Smolicki and Sébastien Piquemal.

Emma Bush

Emma works in the field of art and ecology through performance, site-specific walks, writing and workshops. Her practice maps processes of sensory exchange between ourselves and others, including places, species, systems and elements. Fields, Village Walk, and City Walk emphasised careful placement of attention, listening, co-species interdependence and playful reverence. Emma is currently making PhD research into memory shared across bodies, times and places and is a Lecturer in Fine Art at Plymouth University.

Carly Butler

Carly is an interdisciplinary artist who lives and works on Vancouver Island in Ucluelet on the traditional territory of the Yuułuʔiłʔatḥ First Nation. Her practice reinterprets nautical knowledge around navigation and survival to reflect on longing, regret and nostalgia. **http://carlybutler.com/**

Megan Calver and Gabrielle Hoad

Frequent collaborators since 2015, Megan Calver and Gabrielle Hoad share an interest in generating site-responsive work through oblique approaches to field study. Their approach often draws on the input of human and nonhuman participants.

Gabrielle's work is ecologically oriented and includes live, ephemeral elements as well as more lasting traces such as photographs, moving image, sound, text and objects. Commissions include *SERGE/ SURGE* (2019) made with Preston Street Union for Exeter's Royal Albert Memorial Museum and *Turn (the) leaves* (2018) with Megan Calver for Thelma Hulbert Gallery and East Devon AONB.

Megan makes sculptural interventions and live actions in a process of teamwork with people, places and things. A recurrent theme is her speculative relation to the other-than-human lives with which she co-exists. Work includes *SERGE/SURGE* (2019) made with Preston Street Union for Exeter's Royal Albert Memorial Museum and *Materiality: Provisional States* (2018) for Hestercombe House, Taunton.

Sam Christie

Sam is a filmmaker and academic who made his way to film through his work as a sound designer and radio producer. He has produced two feature documentaries and many shorter works. Sam wishes to pose a simple question, 'what is good about human influence?' In 2016 Sam spent three months in Iraqi Kurdistan trying to make a feature documentary in response to the humanitarian crisis around the occupation of Mosul.

Ami Skånberg Dahlstedt

Ami is a Swedish performer, choreographer, filmmaker and writer who creates award-winning stage work – solo, and collaborative – on the basis of life stories and Noh dramas in particular themes. The Japanese dance practice is essential in Ami's artistic practice, which she has studied since 2000 with Nishikawa Senrei in Kyoto, Japan. Since 2014, Ami walks in suriashi in urban and rural spaces. She is a lecturer at University of Gothenburg.
studiobuji.com/kalendarium/ ~ ami.skanberg.dahlstedt@hsm.gu.se

Gudrun Filipska

Gudrun is an artist and researcher of Welsh and Polish descent who lives in the Fens, UK. Her work considers the cultural and literary associations of journeying often aiming to re-configure these narratives to include feminist and 'other' itinerant practices – and offering counter positions to colonial and male-centric travel and walking cultures.
http://www.gudrunfilipska.com/

Matt Fletcher and Kevin Butler

Out There Actions are based in Southampton, UK, and specialise in outdoor performance of a psychogeographical and/or archaeological bent, designed to be resolutely accessible to the widest diversity of curious spectators and participants. Matt is Senior Lecturer in Acting and Performance at Solent University. Kevin is a seasoned performer and home-schooling father.

James Frost and Sonia Overall

James is a puppeteer and puppet maker with extensive experience in street, folk and other rough theatre practices. He is an independent researcher and versatile educator.

Sonia's work includes writing and abridging text for street theatre, published fiction and poetry, academic papers and journal articles. She is an avid psychogeographer and founder of Women Who Walk, a network for creatives and academics.
www.jamesedwardfrost.com ~ jf129@icloud.com
www.soniaoverall.net ~ sonia.overall@canterbury.ac.uk

Hamish Fulton

Walking Artist Hamish Fulton was born in 1946 and grew up in Newcastle Upon Tyne. Fulton made his first 'artwalk' with other students in February 1967 and, since October 1973, has specialised exclusively in the restrained materialisation of his walking experiences. Fulton entirely rejects all and any association with Land Art; he has exhibited internationally since 1969.

Rachel Gomme

Rachel is an artist and researcher working in performance and installation. Her practice in durational, site-specific and one-to-one performance explores the overlooked detail of bodily being and spaces and phenomena perceived in terms of absence or lack (silence, stillness, waiting). *Undergrowth* is part of a body of work reflecting on how organic being negotiates, adapts to and subverts urban space. Rachel has presented work, taught and performed throughout the UK and internationally since 1998. **www.rachelgomme.webeden.co.uk**

Philippe Guillaume

Philippe is a walking artist, photographer and art historian based in Montreal, Canada. His frequently relational artistic production features walking, making photographs, and performances that continue to exist through pictures, installations and artist books. His projects prioritise banal and everyday contexts that provide an ever-changing but recurring backdrop. His process also includes walks that are the basis for relational ventures where, what he terms, "ephemeral spontaneous moments of communication" are provoked.

Sarah Harper

Sarah is an artist, theatre-maker, teacher and scholar, creating work with urban arts company Friches Théâtre Urbain for 30 years. Based in Paris, her work now centres on long-term socially engaged relational, participatory arts and community theatre in response to critical social contexts within multi-cultural suburbs. Her current PhD research, at Queen Mary University London, focuses on the reasons people do not or *cannot* participate in such projects, and what refusal might mean in the French *banlieues*.
www.friches.fr ~ www.lagrandetraversee.org
sarah.harper@wanadoo.fr

Duncan Hay, Leah Lovett, Martin de Jode and Andrew Hudson-Smith

Duncan holds Research Fellowships at UCL and Lancaster University. Combining critical and digital humanities approaches; his research investigates the relationship between place, culture, and technology.

Leah is an artist and Research Fellow at the Bartlett Centre of Advanced Spatial Analysis, UCL, employing digital technologies to address questions of social and environmental justice in arts practices and urbanism.

Martin is a lecturer in Connected Environments at the Bartlett Centre for Advanced Spatial Analysis, UCL. His current interests include ubiquitous computing and the Internet of Things.

Andrew is Chair of Digital Urban Systems at the Bartlett Centre for Advanced Spatial Analysis, UCL. With a focus on data in places and spaces, his core interest is in the 'things' part of the Internet of Things, allowing retrofitting of everyday objects with new types of connectivity.

Vicky Hunter

Vicky is a Practitioner-Researcher and Reader in Site Dance and Choreography, University of Chichester. Her research explores site dance and corporeal engagements with space, place and lived environments. She is co-author of *(Re) Positioning Site Dance: Local Acts, Global Themes* (2019) with Melanie Kloetzel and Karen Barbour, and editor of *Moving Sites: Investigating Site-Specific Dance Performance* (Routledge, 2015). Her latest monograph is *Site, Dance and Body: Movement, Materials and Corporeal Engagement* (Palgrave, 2021, in press).

Ishita Jain

Ishita developed a performative research methodology to investigate non-canonical and alternative historical accounts during her post-graduation in Architectural History at Bartlett School of Art and Architecture, UCL, London. She pursues films, cinétracts, performative lectures, exhibitions, critical writing and transmedia installations as her chosen mediums of dissemination. Along with being a member of the Out of India Collective, she co-founded Living Midnight Narrative Outfit, is Research Director and Founder at Scan the World – India, and Assistant Professor of Architectural History and Theory at Jindal School of Art and Architecture, JGU, India.

Sam Kemp

Sam is a poet and practice-based researcher at the University of Plymouth. He has published in numerous international journals and presented his work at conferences across the UK. He has been walking through and around the village of Cockington for a number of years and currently lives with four whippets in Mountbatten, Plymouth.

Chloë Lund

Chloë is a curator and producer on Land in Curiosity's 'Yearlong' walking project in the UK. Previous work includes delivering social and community arts projects in the West Midlands.
www.landincuriosity.co.uk ~ chloe.c.lund@gmail.com

Corinne Noble and Simon King

Corinne and Simon are an artist and a writer who walk and work collaboratively. Founded in 2017, Noble & King create and lead convivial walking tours that employ and explore the use of ephemera (antique postcards, maps, fragments of text) personal recollection and speculation to prompt engagement and interaction with walk participants in the context of urban space. Walks include: October 2019 'Camberwell Correspondence', July 2019 'Camden Relay', February 2019 'Commons & Corrections', July 2018 '(Or)landscape(s)'.
www.thearmsofcorinne.co.uk/nobleandking

Elspeth (Billie) Penfold

Billie is a textile artist who brings her experience of teaching and research into performative works. In 2012 she formed a group called 'Thread and Word'. Through call-outs she works collaboratively to develop work with a focus on materials and process, using walking to explore creativity.
www.facebook.com/ThreadandWord ~ twitter.com/elspethpenfold
www.instagram.com/elspethpenfold
www.elspeth-billie-penfold.com

Clare Qualmann and Hilary Ramsden

Clare is an artist/researcher whose work focuses on participatory, site specific, and experimental modes of contemporary creative practice. She was a founding member of the Walking Artists Network and led an AHRC-funded project (2012-2015) to develop international inter-disciplinary connections with others using walking. Her teaching, research and art practice explore the interconnections between art, activism and the radical potentials of participation.

Hilary is a researcher and artivist whose practice involves a particular interweaving of walking, clowning, theatre and street arts to create opportunities for encounters and conversations in public space. She is a faculty member in the School of Creative and Cultural Industries at University of South Wales, Cardiff. She uses humour, play and improvisation to interrogate assumptions about the ways we inhabit and engage with our neighbourhoods and local environments. She is co-artistic director of Walk & Squawk and a co-founder of the Clandestine Insurgent Rebel Clown Army (C.I.R.C.A.).

Morag Rose

Morag Rose is an artist, activist, academic and anarchoflaneuse. She worked in the voluntary sector for 15 years before completing her PhD "Women Walking Manchester: Desire Lines Through The Original Modern City" (University of Sheffield, 2018). In 2006 Morag founded psychogeographical collective The LRM (Loiterers Resistance Movement) and they have performed, presented and exhibited widely. Morag is a part-time lecturer in Human Geography at The University of Liverpool and remains committed to a walking praxis that is communal, accessible, awkward and thought-provoking.
www.thelrm.org ~ @thelrm ~ mlrose@thelrm.org

Anna Sanders-Falcini

Anna is an artist, researcher and writer who investigates elusive and ephemeral subject matter through an interdisciplinary art practice. Her research publications include 'Re-illuminating the Hoo Peninsula Through the Media of Film' for the *British Art Studies Journal*, Issue 10 (2019). As her alter ego, Louisa Cornford, she performs the *Archive of Atmosphere* re-enacting journeys and archaeological investigations in the North Kent marshes.

Sarah Scaife

Sarah is a practice-based doctoral research student in the University of Exeter Department of Drama, exploring Magical Aesthetics and the body. She started out as a field archaeologist. This relationship to buried places left a deep mark. Her subsequent museums career centred on widening access to collections and protected landscapes. Sarah joined Encounters Arts as a creative producer in 2010. In 2019, she gained an MA in Drawing at Plymouth College of Art. **www.berrybrowngown.uk**

William Sharpe

William is professor of English at Barnard College, Columbia University, New York, where he teaches a course on ambulatory culture called 'Walk This Way'. Author of *Grasping Shadows* (2016) and *New York Nocturne* (2008), he is currently working on a visual history of walking.
https://barnard.edu/profiles/william-sharpe ~ wsharpe@barnard.edu

Phil Smith

Phil is a writer, artist and researcher, specialising in walking, site-specificity and mythogeographies. With Helen Billinghurst he is one half of 'Crab & Bee' who created the art project 'Plymouth Labyrinth' (plymouthlabyrinth. wordpress.com). They are currently preparing a new book: *The Pattern*. Phil's publications include *Guidebook for an Armchair Pilgrimage* (2019), *Making*

Site-Specific Theatre and Performance (2018), *Walking's New Movement* (2015), and *Mythogeography* (2010). He is company dramaturg of TNT Theatre (Munich) and Associate Professor (Reader), University of Plymouth. **www.triarchypress.net/smithereens**

Cathy Turner

Cathy is Professor of Drama at the University of Exeter. She co-founded 'Wrights & Sites' with Stephen Hodge, Phil Smith and Simon Persighetti and has written about walking in a range of contexts, including in her book, *Dramaturgy and Architecture: Theatre, Utopia and the Built Environment* (Palgrave 2015). She led the UK-India research network 'The Politics of Performance on the Urban Periphery in South India', funded by AHRC, 2018-19.

Richard S. White

Richard is a freelance walking and multimedia artist/researcher and Senior Lecturer in Media Practice at Bath Spa University. Current projects include: 'Walking the Names', a cycle of walks on poverty, privilege and response-ability attending to the unmarked burial ground of Bath's former Workhouse. 'Sanctuary and Exile', a commission from the Lake District Holocaust Project in collaboration with artist Lorna Brunstein, to explore the experience and contemporary resonances of sanctuary and exile walking with the story of child Holocaust survivors and their hosts in Windermere. **www.walknowtracks.co.uk ~ r.white2@bathspa.ac.uk**

Ken Wilson

Ken teaches English and Film Studies at the University of Regina in Saskatchewan, Canada, where he is a PhD student in Interdisciplinary Studies. Part of his MFA work included a solo walk through the Haldimand Tract in southwestern Ontario which addressed ongoing histories of colonialism and land theft. His PhD work will include a series of walks in Treaty 4 territory in southern Saskatchewan as a form of embodied territorial acknowledgement.

Gary Winters and Claire Hind

Gary has over 20 years' experience of creating and presenting cross-artform projects nationally and internationally. Predominantly working in live art and public engagement he is Co-Artistic Director of the celebrated company Lone Twin.

Claire is an Associate Professor in Theatre and Performance at York St John University, UK. Her collaborative practice with artist Gary Winters tours locally and internationally under the name *Gary and Claire* offering a range of diverse performance and audience experiences including walking performance. **www.garyandclaire.com**

Acknowledgements

Claire, Helen & Phil would like to thank all at University of Plymouth for their support and assistance in organising the conference; particularly Libby Chapman-Lane and Sally Smerdon. We would like to thank all those who volunteered to usher, guide, perform and assist with the tech: Natalie Raven, Dagmar Schwitzgebel, Dylan Jones, Tina Kutter, Josh Wilton, Cristina Varga, Sue Langford and Andrea Vassallo. We would like to thank *everyone* who offered papers, provocations, walks, performances and artworks (not just those who are represented in this selection). Also we acknowledge the generous assistance of all who chaired sessions: Roberta Mock, Morag Rose, Anthony Caleshu, Cathy Turner, Blake Morris, Sonia Overall, Jonathan Pitches and Hilary Ramsden. Thank you to the National Lottery through Arts Council England for funding 'Dream Yards'. Finally, we would like to thank all who contributed to the conference in submitting abstracts, making walks, sharing time, support, ideas and conviviality, showing artworks, offering publications, and presenting papers, provocations and performances, only a proportion of all of which are we able to represent here.

About the Publisher

Triarchy Press is a small, independent publisher of books that bring a wider, systemic or contextual approach to many different areas of life, including:

Government, Education, Health and other public services

Ecology, Sustainability and Regenerative Cultures

Leading and Managing Organizations

Psychotherapy and Arts and other Expressive Therapies

Walking, Psychogeography and Mythogeography

Movement and Somatics

Innovation

The Money System

The Future and Future Studies

For books by Nora Bateson, Daniel Wahl, Russ Ackoff, Barry Oshry, John Seddon, Phil Smith, Bill Tate, Patricia Lustig, Sandra Reeve, Graham Leicester, Nelisha Wickremasinghe, Bill Sharpe, Alyson Hallett and other remarkable writers, please visit:

www.triarchypress.net